WORKS ISSUED BY

The Hakluyt Society

THE VOYAGE OF CAPTAIN BELLINGSHAUSEN
TO THE ANTARCTIC SEAS 1819–1821

VOL. I

SECOND SERIES

No XCI

ISSUED FOR 1945

COUNCIL
OF
THE HAKLUYT SOCIETY
1945

EDWARD LYNAM, ESQ., D.LITT., M.R.I.A., F.S.A., *President.*
THE RIGHT HON. THE EARL BALDWIN OF BEWDLEY, K.G., *Vice-President.*
JAMES A. WILLIAMSON, ESQ., D.LIT., *Vice-President.*
PROFESSOR E. G. R. TAYLOR, D.SC., *Vice-President.*
J. N. L. BAKER, ESQ., M.A., B.LITT.
SIR RICHARD BURN, C.S.I.
A. HUGH CARRINGTON, ESQ.
PROFESSOR F. DEBENHAM, O.B.E., M.A.
SIR WILLIAM FOSTER, C.I.E.
GUILDHALL LIBRARY (RAYMOND SMITH, ESQ.)
SIR GILBERT LAITHWAITE, K.C.I.E., C.S.I.
EVANS LEWIN, ESQ., M.B.E.
PROFESSOR KENNETH MASON, M.C., R.E.
WALTER OAKESHOTT, ESQ., M.A.
PROFESSOR E. PRESTAGE, D.LITT.
S. T. SHEPPARD, ESQ.
J. A. STEERS, ESQ., M.A.
R. A. WILSON, ESQ.
EDWARD HEAWOOD, ESQ., M.A., *Treasurer.*
G. R. CRONE, ESQ., M.A., *Hon. Secretary* (Royal Geographical Society, Kensington Gore, S.W. 7).
SIR WILLIAM FOSTER, C.I.E. ⎫
EDWARD HEAWOOD, ESQ., M.A. ⎬ *Trustees.*
MALCOLM LETTS, ESQ., F.S.A. ⎭

THADDEUS BELLINGSHAUSEN

(From a portrait painted about the time of the Expedition)

THE VOYAGE
of
CAPTAIN BELLINGSHAUSEN
to the
ANTARCTIC SEAS
1819–1821

Translated from the Russian

Edited by

FRANK DEBENHAM, O.B.E., M.A.
Director of the Scott Polar Research Institute, Cambridge

VOLUME I

LONDON
PRINTED FOR THE HAKLUYT SOCIETY
MCMXLV

PRINTED IN GREAT BRITAIN
BY W. LEWIS, M.A.
UNIVERSITY PRESS, CAMBRIDGE

PREFACE

THIS TRANSLATION of Captain T. Bellingshausen's account of his remarkable voyage into the Antarctic Ocean in 1819–21 has been so long heralded that a brief notice of the vicissitudes through which it has passed should accompany its appearance in print.

The idea of its publication in English first occurred to the present editor in 1920, when, by the kindness of the Hydrographer to the Admiralty, Sir John Parry, he was permitted to see a translation which had been made during the last war at the instance of Mr W. S. Bruce, leader of the *Scotia* expedition to the Antarctic (1902–1904). This translation was accordingly submitted to a Russian scholar, Mr (afterwards Professor) Edward Bullough, of Gonville and Caius College, Cambridge. He found that it contained many technical faults, and very kindly undertook a fresh translation of the original, which, with the aid of grants from the Scott Mansion House Fund, he completed in 1924. This was, with Mr Bullough's consent, examined and revised by other experts, of whom the chief was a Russian student of the editor, N. Volkov, a descendant of Lazarev, who rendered valuable service. The present editor then set about harmonizing the work of the various translators, in order to produce a text which would be uniform in style. In this he was greatly helped by his assistant at the Scott Polar Research Institute, Miss W. M. Drake (now Mrs Hayes).

Some of the officers who accompanied Bellingshausen wrote independent accounts of the voyage, and these were deposited in the archives of the Russian Admiralty. The present writer thought that extracts from these, added as footnotes or appendices, would increase the interest and value of Bellingshausen's narrative, and accordingly applied to the Russian Admiralty for permission to use them. The Russian authorities replied in the most courteous spirit, but unfortunately were not able to locate the journals—if they still existed—before the invasion of Russia by Germany in 1941.

The fact that Bellingshausen's voyage was practically unknown to the general public made it no easy task to find for this translation a publisher who would bring it out in the style which it merited. One was found, however, in 1938, and the book was going through the press when the war broke out. Unfortunately the restrictions and difficulties caused by the war seriously hampered the work of this firm, which in 1940 was forced to ask to be released from its contract. In 1942 the Council of the Hakluyt Society was approached, and almost at once accepted the proposal that this translation should be published as one of their famous series of first-hand narratives of exploration and travel.

The preparation of the book for press in the midst of manifold war obligations has only been made possible by the willing co-operation of many people, to some of whom particular acknowledgment is due. General assistance of a secretarial kind has always been available from Miss Christina Wanklyn and also from other voluntary helpers at the Scott Polar Research Institute. Thanks are also due to Dr Lynam, the Hon. Secretary, now President, of the Hakluyt Society, and to the Cambridge University Press for their advice and assistance at all stages of publication.

FRANK DEBENHAM

Scott Polar Research Institute
    Cambridge

CONTENTS

VOL. I

	PAGES
PREFACE	vii–viii
INTRODUCTION	xi–xxx
PRELIMINARY MEMOIR . . .	1–29
THE NARRATIVE	30

ILLUSTRATIONS

VOL. I

THADDEUS BELLINGSHAUSEN . . . FRONTISPIECE

		BETWEEN PAGES
1	Seaweed and Plankton	64 & 65
2	View of the town of San Sebastian, Rio de Janeiro	
3	Lyeskov, Visokoi, and Zavodovski Islands	96 & 97
4	Candlemas, Saunders, and Montagu Islands	
5	Bristol, Thule, and Cook Islands	112 & 113
6	Macaroni and Ringed Penguins	
7	View of Ice Islands	120 & 121
8	Ice Islands	
9	Wandering and Sooty Albatrosses	128 & 129
10	Petrels	
11	Blue and Antarctic Petrels	144 & 145
12	Crab-eater and Leopard Seals	
13	View of the town of Sydney at Port Jackson	160 & 161
14	Natives of New Holland	
15	Chief of the Broken Bay tribe and his wife	184 & 185
16	Prince Regent and Abbott Birds	

CONTENTS

BETWEEN PAGES

17 *Banksia*, Blue Tit, Honeyeater and Waratah
18 View of Mount Egmont; Entrance to Queen Charlotte Sound; Oparo, Henry's coral and Moller's coral islands } 192 & 193

19 Principal settlement of Queen Charlotte Sound
20 War Dance, Queen Charlotte Sound } 208 & 209

21 Wife of New Zealand chief, New Zealand chief, and Natives of Arakcheev and Oparo Islands
22 View of the coral island of Moller } 216 & 217

23 Natives of the coral island of Nihera
24 Natives of the Palliser Islands } 240 & 241

MAPS

South Georgia   FACING PAGE 88

Mercator's Chart of the South Sandwich Islands and the newly discovered Marquis of Traversey Group   BETWEEN PAGES 104 & 105

Oparo Island   FACING PAGE 224

Moller and Bow Islands   BETWEEN PAGES 232 & 233

Volkhonski, Barclay de Tolly, Arakcheev, Yermolov, Nihiru, Witgenstein, Second Palliser, Third Palliser, Greig, Saken, Prince Kutusov, Raevski, Miloradovich, and Chichagov Islands   BETWEEN PAGES 250 & 251

Map *in pocket at end*

INTRODUCTION

THE HIGHEST AUTHORITY on the history of Antarctic exploration, Dr Hugh Robert Mill, says in his *Siege of the South Pole*, that the voyage of Captain Bellingshausen was "one of the greatest Antarctic expeditions on record, well worthy of being placed beside that of Cook".

The reader of these volumes will probably agree with that verdict, but he will also be curious to know how it was that so remarkable a voyage came about and why the Russian nation should enter so briefly and so honourably into the Southern Seas, a sphere which they have neglected ever since. The explanation lies chiefly in the history of Russia in the previous half century, which amounts to the same thing as ascribing it chiefly to the influence of the great Empress Catherine II.

Continuing and expanding the general policy of Peter the Great she sought the sea to the south of Russia just as he had sought it to the west, and she added the shores of the Black Sea to her dominion just as Peter had striven for and attained a seaboard on the Baltic.

When Bellingshausen was born (1779) the Russians had only just taken from the Turks the outlets to those great Russian rivers, the Don, the Dnieper and the Bug. The sea which was to be the scene of much of his service life was not thoroughly Russian until he was a midshipman. Throughout his narrative constant references to scenes and phenomena of the Black Sea betray his abiding interest, and several of the names he selects for the new islands which he discovered in the Pacific commemorate the commanders of the Black Sea Fleet. Just as Peter the Great had laboured to make his subjects navy-conscious and Baltic-wise, the age of Catherine turned their attention to the Black Sea and to the infant navy which wrested the local sea power from the Turks. In fostering that attention the Empress and her advisers, and her grandson Alexander I, steadfastly pointed to the British Navy as a pattern for their own, a fact which produced two direct consequences, and these form a continuous background, implicit or explicit, to the narrative of this voyage. One is a great respect held by the Russians for the British Navy, its technique and its tradition, and the other is an admiration, amounting almost to worship, of Captain James Cook.

So much for Russia's new interest in the sea and in her navy; her interest in the Pacific was due to another set of circumstances, also set in train by Peter the Great, namely, the discovery and settlement of the easternmost parts of Siberia, Okhotsk and Kamchatka.

In the eighty years between the expedition of Bering and that of Bellingshausen the progress of these distant settlements had been slow, mainly on account of the great time it took to cover the distance either by land or by sea, but also, according to the Russians themselves, because of lack of support from St Petersburg. Desperately long as the journey was from the capital to Kamchatka, the voyage by sea was still more objectionable as viewed by the Russians, and though the trade in fish and furs was entirely based on the sea, all the Russian ships involved were built at Okhotsk, and the commerce was in the hands of local people with little capital.

The building of these ships was not so difficult in a land of good timber, but their outfitting was a tremendous problem since everything which could not be made locally had to be brought all the way across Siberia. Cables, for instance, made in Europe, were cut into pieces of about 50 feet in length, transported by waggon and packhorse and then spliced together again at Okhotsk; anchors too had to be carried in pieces. Upwards of 4000 horses were employed on this transport alone, and naturally the price of such goods was multiplied to a prohibitive extent.

In 1785, however, the Russo-American Company was founded with "factories" on Kamchatka and the Aleutian Islands, and the value of these distant colonies began to attract more attention in Russia itself, and alternative routes began to be considered.

There are adequate explanations of this delay in establishing a connection by sea. The Portuguese, the Dutch, the English and even the French, all had possessions along the route from Europe to the Far East and were accustomed to long sea voyages for trade, but the Russians had no such possessions, and therefore no body of seamen with experience of such ventures.

It was not uncommon at this period for young Russian nobles to take service with the British Navy, and it fell to one such, A. J. von Kruzenstern, to be the means of breaking this vicious circle of no attempts to make the long voyage because no Russian had made it. After serving in the English Navy from 1793 to 1797 Kruzenstern went out to India in an English frigate and on to China in a merchantman with the set purpose of becoming acquainted with those seas, and with the technique of the trade to the East. He returned in 1799 to Russia and set about trying to convince the Russian authorities that it would be far better to send their own ships to Kamchatka from Europe than to build them locally and entrust the valuable furs either to land transport or to carriage by the ships of other nations.

At first he failed, but when Alexander I came to the throne he gained the ear and the confidence of the new ministers and in 1802 found himself appointed to the command of an expedition of two ships to make the voyage and incidentally make the first Russian circumnavigation of the world.

Kruzenstern was a remarkable man, an excellent seaman, far sighted and firm of purpose, well fitted to become the spiritual mentor and doyen of the group of Russian explorers who date from his voyage. He sailed in the *Nadezhda*, with the *Neva* as consort, and he had with him as fifth officer Baron Bellingshausen, and as a 15-year-old cadet Otto von Kotzebue, both destined to become famous for their own voyages.

The voyage lasted for three years, from 1803, and was quite unique in Russian annals. The route taken was by way of Cape Horn, the Marquesas and Sandwich Islands to Kamchatka and thence to Japan, where the Russians attempted without success to establish friendly relations with the Japanese, having carried an ambassador and his suite especially for that purpose.

The return via the Cape of Good Hope was as full of incident but barren of accident as the outward passage, and the expedition returned to Russia without the loss of a single member of the crew, a result which was astounding in an age when losses by scurvy were accounted as inevitable as was the ordinary wear and tear of the rigging. To gain his experience under such a leader was of the greatest value to the 25-year-old Bellingshausen, and it is most interesting to see how closely he followed, in his own voyage, the precepts learned under Kruzenstern, including, unfortunately, a certain turgidity of style in his narrative, a defect which was avoided by young Kotzebue.

Bellingshausen, in his care of his ships, his passion for accuracy in his navigation and his constant preoccupation with the health of his crew, was a mirror reflection of Kruzenstern, and he obtained similar successful results. Both, it may be added, patterned themselves quite openly on Captain Cook, uniting in an admiration for their English predecessor which was almost extravagant. Kruzenstern, for instance, was never so happy as when his position for an island or cape approached that of Captain Cook, which he invariably took to be final and accurate though made thirty years earlier.

Such was the nature of the training of our author, born of noble family and with the spirit to serve his Emperor in any capacity. Unfortunately we can give no picture of the young fifth lieutenant from the pages of Kruzenstern's narrative, for his book was characterized by its translator as having "an uncouth stile and a cold precision of expression" and no word of either praise or blame of his junior officers is ever allowed to enlighten its somewhat heavy array of incidents.

The sole reference to his future successor is in the following cautious yet commendatory terms: "The choice of Baron Bellingshausen, my fifth lieutenant, I made without being personally acquainted with him. His reputation as a skilful and well-informed officer in the different branches of navigation, which I found to be perfectly just, induced me to propose to him to sail with me."

The expedition returned in 1806 to find Europe once more ablaze with war, Russia playing an increasingly important part in the balance of power and Alexander I beginning to feel his way towards the great rôle he was to assume a few years later.

Bellingshausen returned to his naval duties, in the Black Sea for the most part, and into an obscurity which was perhaps inevitable for a young officer gradually climbing to higher rank throughout a prolonged series of great national events. At least we can trace no details of interest in his life beyond those which can be inferred from his own narrative. He was obviously devoted to his profession and especially to his navigational duties, while his genuine admiration of his senior officers and his loyalty to his Emperor grew until he became the very efficient but somewhat restrained and unemotional captain of the "second rank" who was selected, as a second choice, for the Antarctic expedition, thirteen years after his return from the Pacific.

In that period the prestige of Russia and the stature of its Emperor had increased enormously. The campaign of 1812 had awakened the national feelings of Russia's people, the prominence of Alexander in the concert of Europe had given him new reins to hold, so that in spite of the infelicities of his Holy Alliance and the uncertainty whither his growing mysticism would lead him he was the grand figure of Europe, governing his vast dominion "from the seat of a post chaise" with vigour and restless travel. Yet her navy, still somewhat pent up in the Baltic and the Black Sea, was clearly an instrument which needed wider fields for expansion and training and there were still no overseas possessions which required voyages, except the small trading settlements on the Alaskan coast.

There had been some more official voyages to the Pacific, the most notable being that of Kotzebue from 1815 to 1818, and more exploration of those dusky seas between Siberia and America, all of which had the development of Russian trade as its partial if not its main object. This did not fully satisfy the far-seeing Russian ministers in charge of her marine affairs, in particular the Marquis de Traversey, and including Bellingshausen's own senior officer, Admiral Greig, the son of a Scotsman who had himself taken service in the Russian Navy.

These officers recognized, as did those of the British Admiralty at the same period, that for training in navigation and seamanship in time of peace there could be no better sphere than the arduous and often perilous one of the polar regions.

The detailed instructions to the commander from various branches of the Admiralty, printed in full in the Preliminary Memoir, are most enlightening in this respect and indeed follow closely the pattern set by British official expeditions, and in some respects improve on it.

It would be possible to demonstrate this training aspect of the voyage in many ways, but perhaps the most obvious example is in the methods of navigation so assiduously practised by all the officers. The impressive array of observing instruments taken, the seizure of every opportunity for determining position, the constant use of the exacting and somewhat abstruse method of finding longitude by "lunar distances" and the high order of accuracy attained, all furnish clear proof that in the commander's view training in navigation was a prime function of his responsibility as well as an abiding interest to himself.

In the comprehensive instructions from the Imperial Admiralty Department navigation is particularly emphasized, and the only civilian scientist on the expedition was the astronomer Simanov. The results of such application are to be seen in the charts published with the "Atlas", and reproduced, greatly reduced in scale and redrawn, in these volumes. This method of reproduction was necessary since the names had to be in English, but it does less than justice to the originals, which can hold their own with any of the contemporary work of that kind. The survey of the South Shetland group of islands indeed set a new standard for polar charts, and the field work from which the chart was produced was never surpassed until steam took the place of sail and revolutionized the methods of mapping coast lines from the sea.

This very high standard in technical matters was not confined to navigation but is evident also in the drawings reproduced in the Atlas. It is clear, therefore, that the Russian Admiralty were determined to do as good a piece of work as any other nation had done, and they succeeded in every respect except that of natural history, a shortcoming for which they were not entirely responsible.

To aid in a proper appreciation of this voyage it is necessary to sketch the background of the picture, especially the less known Antarctic part of the scene on which these two Russian ships were to cast such unexpected illumination.

When Captain James Cook set out on his second voyage in 1772 his avowed purpose was to establish the existence or otherwise of a large Antarctic continent in latitudes which had never yet been reached.

By an unkind fate neither Cook nor Bellingshausen, in spite of all their gallantry and persistence, was to prove that what had been guessed at on the slenderest grounds did in fact exist, a very large and indeed the highest of all the continents, hidden behind the barriers of ice which turned them back from their repeated assaults.

Perhaps Bellingshausen's was the unkinder cut of the two since, as we shall see, he did view the continent but did not recognize it as such; but both returned with a small bag of islands only and evidence of the "not proven" type as to whether there was a large mass of land farther south than they could push their ships.

Cook did at least explode the theory that there was a vast continent filling most of the southerly latitudes of the Pacific, a suggestion so firmly held by fairly competent persons that Alexander Dalrymple, rival to Cook for command of an earlier expedition and later Hydrographer to the Navy, could assert that it was probably larger than Asia and must contain fifty million inhabitants whose trade "would be sufficient to maintain the power, dominion and sovereignty of Britain".

Whether it was owing to the thoroughness of Cook's examination or the sober doubts he expressed as to the presence of land beyond his route, it is a fact that no attempt to settle the question was made between his voyage and that of the Russians nearly fifty years later. Quite apart from doubts as to its existence, Cook's own summary of the matter was trenchant enough to discourage any idea of profit from discovery in those seas when he wrote: "Should anyone possess the resolution and the fortitude to elucidate this point by pushing yet further south than I have done, I shall not envy him the fame of his discovery, but I make bold to declare that the world will derive no benefit from it."

Cook's "bold" pronouncement remains true to this day as far as the land of the Antarctic is concerned, though he himself sowed the seeds of commercial development in the seas which surround it when his reports of the animal life led to the sealing ventures which were in time to provide discoveries of a piecemeal kind of many sub-Antarctic islands and one or two promontories of the mainland. Except for the region to the south of Cape Horn Bellingshausen began his voyage with the map of the Antarctic exactly as Cook had left it fifty years earlier, almost completely blank, and the Antarctic Circle as yet crossed only in three places.

Where Cook had been able to sail over 24° of longitude within that Circle Bellingshausen was able to sail over 42°, and the latter was very careful to choose sectors not visited by Cook, despairing, as he says, of improving on his predecessor's record. As Dr Mill most aptly remarks, "the voyage was a masterly continuation of that of Cook, supplementing it in every particular, competing with it in none". Between them the two great navigators therefore covered about 60° of longitude within the Circle, one-sixth of its circumference, yet were unlucky enough to miss the mainland entirely, though one-quarter to one-third of its coast is very close to the Circle. Moreover Cook's Sandwich Land turned out to be a group of small islands, while Bellingshausen's Alexander Land, believed for a long time to be part of the mainland, has quite recently been proved to be a large island, not that there need be any real distinction between mainland and large islands hardly separated by narrow channels from the continent proper.

It would, nevertheless, be very unjust to allow such remarks as these to give the impression that these expeditions were unfruitful, and it will be as well to discuss at this point the positive gains of the Russian voyage in a more comprehensive way than is possible in the footnotes.

It will be best to consider the discoveries in their chronological order.

As will be seen from the end map, Bellingshausen sailed from the South Atlantic easterly round the world. His first valuable piece of work was his survey of the south side of South Georgia which he did because Cook had done the north side, and until at least the end of last century the Russian survey was the only one available for parts of this very inhospitable coast and was therefore incorporated into official charts.

Strictly speaking, this is a sub-Antarctic island, having a latitude about 2° more northerly than Cape Horn, and thence he steered for the capes to the east and some 4° to the south which had been discovered in misty weather by Cook and grouped hopefully by him as Sandwich Land, though he fully expected them to turn out ultimately to be islands. The Russians discovered the whole group and did a running survey of them with sketches. The highest praise which can be given for the topographic sketches made by the artist Mikhailov is the fact that they are still used in the British Admiralty publication, *The Antarctic Pilot*, published in 1930.

It is unfortunate that the Hydrographic Office in transliterating the Russian has called the northern group the "Traverse" Islands from which one would deduce quite a different origin to the true one, for the leader hastened to name his first new discovery after the real promoter of his expedition, the Marquis de Traversey, Minister of Naval Affairs at St Petersburg.

Having completed this task in a manner which was to defy competition for over a century, the ships sailed to the south-east towards a region hitherto unvisited. The commander made his first crossing of the Antarctic Circle on January 15th, 1820 (O.S.), without even mentioning the event in his narrative.

On the 16th and again on the 21st of January he was so close to the land that had the weather been clear he must have recognized it as such, but the journal of the 5th and 6th of the next month is still more tantalizing in that he describes very clearly an appearance of land without claiming it as such.

As suggested in the footnote for that date, there can be no reasonable doubt that the commander was looking at the continent, covered with ice and rising in low folds one behind the other to a great distance, yet was failing to realize that ice alone could not take that shape or attain that thickness while afloat. No better description than his can be applied to literally hundreds of miles of this stretch of the Antarctic continent as we now know it.

Why then did he miss what in many respects must be looked upon as the greatest chance of his voyage, the recognition of the continent which he, like Cook before him, had been sent to prove or disprove? We can hardly dismiss it as due to his characteristic caution and reluctance to give rein to any suspicion that it might indeed be ice-covered land, for if that had been the case he would surely have lingered in the vicinity longer or at least have voiced some doubts as to its being ice alone.

The explanation seems to be that the great size of the Antarctic icebergs had convinced him that there was no limit to their height and area. He was much interested in the icebergs, and in places in his narrative he pauses to wonder at their origin. In each case he appears to have satisfied himself that they were the fragments of still larger and higher masses which were either afloat or resting on a bottom well below sea-level, and therefore not to be recorded as a land mass supporting ice.

The editor, having seen for himself such massive ice hiding the continent, to be described in precisely the same terms as "a surface sloping upwards...to a distance so far that its end was out of sight...," was far from satisfied that some of the many keen pairs of eyes had not interpreted the discovery more correctly. He therefore instituted an inquiry for the journals of the other officers of the expedition which, as recorded in the narrative, were all handed in on their return and deposited in the archives of the Russian Admiralty. To his infinite regret he was unable to trace them and the hope of finding that Captain Lazarev or Commander Zavodovski had at least expressed polite doubts as to their commanding officer's verdict must continue to be unsatisfied.

The polar historian can divert himself with postulates as to what the effect would have been had the Russians returned with news of continental land in that quarter. We dare not follow such interesting but fruitless imaginings beyond stating that almost certainly Dumont D'Urville, Wilkes and Ross would, some twenty years later, have made that their first area of search, instead of the Australian sector.

It is interesting to note here two of the reasons why Bellingshausen and others after him had such difficulty in recognizing the coast when they were near it. One is the effect of the winds and their weather, particularly upon sailing ships. When the wind comes from the north in those latitudes, while helping the ship to sail south it invariably brings thick and snowy weather so that the land cannot be seen. When, on the other hand, the south and east winds bring clear weather they hinder the sailing ship in getting south, and bring out the loose ice from the coast, fending the ships off from a close approach. The other reason for failure to recognize the proximity of land comes from the peculiar soundings. Off nearly every continental coast in temperate and tropical regions there is a fairly well-defined change of slope, the soundings increasing gradually to the "continental shelf" at about 100 fathoms, beyond which the gradient is much steeper. Round the Antarctic continent, however, the depth of the continental shelf is nearer 200 fathoms than 100. On the two occasions now under review, for instance, Bellingshausen failed to get soundings at 100 fathoms in the first case and 200 in the second. Had he let out a little more line he might have found bottom and been more hopeful of land but still would not have considered he was definitely over the shelf, a term which in point of fact was not then in use.

Lest it be taken as mysterious that the Antarctic should be unique in this way it should be added that there is a perfectly adequate explanation. A continental shelf has a natural termination or edge at 100 fathoms because it is made up of debris which is distributed down to that depth and not beyond it by waves and currents. In the Antarctic Ocean, however, there is another disturbing agency in the form of countless icebergs whose bases are rarely less than 100 fathoms deep and often up to 200 fathoms or over, so that the shelf is literally "scraped" to a greater depth than elsewhere.

We may end this comment on Bellingshausen's failure to recognize a new continent by inviting readers to consider whether such a remarkable voyage did not deserve a better fate, all the more so since later explorers by exercising too much imagination have recorded continents which were afterwards sailed over.

The long voyage from this region to Port Jackson was full of minor incidents of the type inseparable from polar exploration in a sailing ship, but it was barren of result as far as discovery is concerned. Bellingshausen himself was a conscientious observer of all that was seen, but the expedition was sadly handicapped throughout by having no naturalists with it, a lack which calls for almost the only bitter criticism he permits himself to make of his organizing committee.

The two visits to Sydney occupied altogether some months, and the narrative devotes a good deal of space to them. Bellingshausen himself had no English and though Lazarev, having served in the British Navy, could make up for this in the ceremonial visits, it meant that the captain's impressions, as far as verbal contact was concerned, were coloured by the constant need for an interpreter. While we miss the personal element in his description of the people he meets we gain from the fact that his observations of the infant colony were his own.

He was there at the end of the long reign of Governor Macquarie, who, for all his faults and pomposities, was chiefly responsible for pulling the settlement out of a state of misrule. The Russians were clearly impressed by what they saw, if only in contrast with what they had expected from a penal settlement.

Contemporary reports of what the British thought of the Russians are rather meagre, but here too surprise was evident at the efficiency and equipment of the Russian ships. The contacts were in fact not very close, partly because the crews were kept very busy at refitting the ships, partly because they were somewhat isolated both by the language difficulty and by their land headquarters being on the northern, uninhabited shore of the harbour. Nevertheless, the long account of what they saw and heard in New Holland is a useful addition to the historical record of the early days there and will be welcomed by those who have laboured to collect such evidence.

In the true spirit of Captain Cook, Bellingshausen grudged every day spent at anchor in known waters and his pleasure at departing for fresh exploration is obvious enough.

The cruise of the ships in New Zealand waters was very much after the pattern of Cook's, and to the same locality. While it added nothing important to the charts it gives a clear account of the natives, who were still little influenced by occasional contact with whites since the earliest visits.

Sailing out into the southern Pacific the Russian ships set about their second self-imposed task, the thorough examination of the most dangerous archipelago of low islands, now known as the Paumotu or Tuamotu group. From the point of view of the hydrographic surveyor this was a highly technical and difficult piece of work from sailing ships; to the ordinary reader it has less appeal, not least because there were no mishaps. Nevertheless the account, from a more facile pen than that of Bellingshausen, would be very readable, as was the narrative of Otto von Kotzebue's voyages in the same seas both before and after this time. Our author, however, rarely feels at home with his pen except when detailing his surveys or his details of welfare for his ships and crew.

At Tahiti, however, that lotus isle of the late eighteenth-century Pacific explorer, he is stirred out of his log-book style and sets out his feelings in a way which for him is almost lyrical. His attitude to the natives is as correct as ever but he does permit himself reflections on their character with some freedom. He has little of the abandon of Kotzebue yet he improves considerably on the laconic manner of Kruzenstern. One feels that here too his lack of English hampered him, for his interpreters spoke English, and it is clear that some of this information, particularly that concerning the natural products, was written up afterwards from other sources. In the return voyage to Port Jackson he finds more new islands, for he assiduously avoids following the tracks of former ships and is thereby rewarded. Like Captain Cook he is particularly attracted by the Friendly Islanders, but his stay is so short that he is able to add little beyond local surveys to our knowledge of the group at that early period.

His journal of their second stay in Port Jackson is most disappointingly brief, but it is clear that the Russians felt much more at home with their hosts, and it is even possible that the social events and entertainments were the cause of the slender entries in his journal. As far as space is concerned he makes amends to some extent by including a long account of "the colonies of New South Wales". In places this is not much more than a gazetteer, but interspersed amongst the statistics are observations and opinions, always rather guarded but betraying real interest in this great experiment of a community removed twelve thousand miles from its homeland, and gradually working out its own salvation.

Soon after setting out on the second half of his circumnavigation of the Antarctic regions certain rather serious defects in his own ship became apparent, notably a persistent leak which was a constant cause of anxiety. Yet never in the course of the narrative do these anxieties cause the commander to abandon his purpose of sailing as far south as he can at every opportunity. We need not review in advance the tedium and danger of the first two months of this voyage, but pass on to his first real reward in the discovery of new land, the island which he named after Peter the Great. It may seem a small reward for so much toil and hardship, yet it may be pointed out that it was the first time that land had ever been seen within the Antarctic Circle. More precisely, it was 250 nautical miles farther south than any other land yet discovered. Such sentiments carried but little weight with Bellingshausen, who was probably still worried because he had not by 100 miles got as far south as Captain Cook had reached.

It was to be ninety years before this small high ice-covered island was seen again, or indeed his next and larger discovery, but it may be taken as the world's tribute to the Russians that both appeared on every reputable map without question until they were confirmed, and this in spite of the fact that no translation of the narrative in any language appeared until the end of the century. The same tribute in more belated form is now perpetuated by naming the sea to the north of these discoveries and west of the Graham Land peninsula after the Russian captain.

Sailing eastward again and as far south as the pack ice would permit, he at last found land extensive enough to allow his cautious temperament to name it as a "Land", after his reigning emperor.

He saw it clearly on a beautiful day and his artist's drawing is innocent of the cloud and haze which are the too frequent concomitants of Antarctic views. This is the one occasion on which the editor can find any fault with Bellingshausen's leadership, for the following reasons.

It was the last chance he had of making good southing and he had made his largest and most nearly continental discovery, yet he spent only one day in that vicinity, and then sailed north again.

On the other hand, his next objective was a more definite mission, to visit the islands discovered two years before and reported to him by the ambassador in Brazil in a letter sent to Port Jackson. He had made his last new discovery and was about to merely confirm and survey those of others. Normally it would be sufficient to allow the narrative to tell its own story, but it so happens that of recent years a fierce controversy has raged round these very discoveries, and Bellingshausen has, in a minor sense, been called in as witness on one side or the other. Without actually entering the lists it is therefore necessary to be especially careful over the translation of this part of the voyage and state the facts as dispassionately as possible. At the same time the unbiased historian of polar history may be permitted to deplore the fact that far more ink and paper has been spent on this controversy over priority of discovery than would have been needed to print Bellingshausen's voyage in English five times over.

To the not too biased mind the undoubted facts about the discoveries in this sector are as follows. In February 1819 the South Shetlands were first discovered by William Smith in the brig *Williams*, and he revisited them again in October of the same year. The brig was then chartered by the British Admiralty to survey the new discovery, and under a naval master, Edward Bransfield, and with Smith aboard as pilot, a survey was made of the islands during which more continuous land was sighted on January 30, 1820, and plotted on the chart to the south of the South Shetland group itself, the land being named Trinity Land "in compliment to the Trinity Board". It is interesting to recall that on the day that Bransfield saw this land Bellingshausen was 60° of longitude to the east and 5° (300 nautical miles) of latitude farther south, and two days before had been within 30 miles of the main continent, hidden from him by foggy weather. It is strange to reflect that but for that fog there might have been a difference of opinion over a century later as to who first, by an hour or so, saw the mainland of the continent, though one side of the current dispute alleges that Bransfield did not in fact sight it at all.

The protagonist for this side is in fact none other than the American sealing captain who came on board the *Vostok* on January 25th, 1821, from his 44-ton sloop, the *Hero*. Rather more than two months earlier than the date of this meeting and ten months later than Bransfield, this captain, Nathaniel Palmer, had re-discovered the Trinity Land of Bransfield. More accurately, he had been sent to look at land which had already been seen from Deception Island (Teille Island of Bellingshausen). There can be no doubt that Palmer made this short voyage of 60 miles or so to verify the land, and what took place in the interview between Bellingshausen and Palmer would, at first sight, appear to have nothing to do with Bransfield's voyage a year earlier.

The argument on one side has, however, taken the form of an attempt to prove that Bransfield never saw his Trinity Land, that Palmer was the first to sail close to it and that therefore the latter's name should have priority of all others. To this end two other accounts of the interview between the Russian and the American which have appeared in print are used as evidence.

INTRODUCTION

The Russian account is brief enough and one gathers that Palmer was aboard for less than an hour and gave (almost certainly through an interpreter) an interesting account of the sealing, the ships engaged, the anchorages and so on. He may have described his discovery of land 1° farther south, but if so it is strange that Bellingshausen does not mention it, especially as he had not heard of Bransfield's discovery of Trinity Land but only of Smith's earlier discovery of the group of islands.

The two other accounts go far beyond this, however, and in justice to history some mention must be made of their embroidery. The first and more accurate is one given by Edmund Fanning in a book called *Voyages round the World* published in New York in 1833, twelve years after the event itself. The meeting is described in some detail, including an offer by Palmer to pilot the Russian ships into Yankee Harbour (Deception Island), almost certainly true though it is not in Bellingshausen's account. Bellingshausen's alleged reply, however, cannot be true as given in Fanning: "The commodore thanked him kindly, 'but previous to our being enveloped in the fog', said he, 'we had sight of those islands, and concluded we had made a discovery, but behold, when the fog lifts, to my great surprise, here is an American vessel....'"

Either the interpreter bungled his translation very badly or else Bellingshausen was being flattering to the extent of sheer falsehood, since he had come expressly to that place to see the islands which he had heard of six months before. The account goes on: "His astonishment was yet more increased, when Captain Palmer informed him of the existence of an immense extent of land to the south...the commodore was so forcibly struck with the circumstances of the case, that he named the coast then to the south, Palmer's Land." We are left with the alternatives that either this conversation did take place but that Bellingshausen did not believe Palmer and therefore avoided all mention of it either in text or map, or that the conversation did not follow that course.

Perhaps the most charitable conclusion is that with the difficulty of language neither had a very clear idea of what the other had been saying.

No such treatment can be applied to the later account, which might be ignored altogether were it not that it conveys an entirely false impression of Captain Bellingshausen. If it were true, indeed, it would convict our author of a very serious act of *suppressio veri*. It is in a paper by a niece of Captain Palmer, presented in 1907, that is, eighty-six years after the event, but said to be based on a journal of Captain Palmer himself. The niece, Mrs Loper, gives a graphic account of the meeting and the conversation, of which the relevant part runs as follows:

"On hearing that Palmer had been so far as 63° 45′ S., Bellingshausen 'rose much agitated', asked to see the log and chart, and while it was being fetched had luncheon served; asked many questions about the sealing; examined the papers without comment, then rose and said: 'What do I see and what do I hear from a boy in his teens—that he... has pushed his way to the pole through storm and ice and sought the point I... have for three weary anxious years searched day and night for.... What shall I say to my master? What will he think of me? Be that as it may, my grief is your joy; wear your laurels with my sincere prayers; I name the land you have discovered in honor of yourself, noble boy, Palmer Land.'"

Setting aside the fact that this long speech would have to be through an interpreter, and ignoring the curious envy attributed to a man who had just come from discovering land nearly 400 miles farther south, the unpleasant deduction remains that if this conversation were true Captain Bellingshausen has pointedly omitted all mention of it, an accusation which his editor will in no circumstances allow to pass unnoticed.

In the first place so ornamental a speech by a man of Bellingshausen's seniority and gravity hardly rings true. Allowing for the embellishments of copiers, whether nieces or others, one might conclude that the Russian captain had indeed made some diplomatic and complimentary speech to the cheerful young American which had grown with passage of time to such an extravagance, were it not that his complete suppression of every mention of its subject would be entirely out of character for such a man. Throughout the book he is always intensely interested in and studiously appreciative of all discoveries by other men. Nor, if he had indeed been shown a log and charts of the new discovery, would he have disbelieved the story entirely, the only other explanation for his neglect to mention it.

There is a more significant sentence of Bellingshausen's two days later when he had discovered and named the "Three Brothers" group of islands. He says, "Farther south, it appeared to me that land was visible in the heavy clouds, but the thick weather hindered our observing it properly. I therefore left it to some future navigator to determine if there really is an island in this direction."

That would be the strangest language to use if indeed Bellingshausen had understood from Palmer that in that very direction there was extensive land, making his suppression even more palpable, and one by which he could not possibly profit.

With that we must take leave of this unhappy and distasteful sequel to the undoubted fine work of three men, Bransfield, Palmer and Bellingshausen, which has been distorted or disparaged in order to press the question of priorities and the extent of map to be covered by a name. The editor would be rightly criticized if he boldly proposed to replace the alternatives of Palmer Land or Graham Land for the 400-mile long peninsula with the name Alexander Land, yet in truth he would have a better case, since it is by far the most difficult end of the peninsula to discover and fortunately has never been questioned as to date or accuracy.[1]

After their careful survey of the South Shetlands and part of the South Orkneys the Russian ships turned northwards for a comparatively uneventful voyage homeward.

As they sailed into the Gulf of Finland back to Kronstadt, their port of departure, they did, in fact, all but vanish from the pages of exploration which they had so worthily laboured to enrich.

It is not clear whether the enthusiasm with which the Russian Admiralty had sent out the ships had cooled or whether the Court, prime mover in publicity, was otherwise engaged, but it is clear from the Russian Preliminary Narrative that even when the narrative had been written it required special pleading to have it published and even then it attracted but passing attention.

It is difficult to believe that this was wholly due to its being in Russian, and one is led to seek further explanation.

One contributory cause of the apparent indifference of foreign readers is no doubt that the book is comparatively heavy reading, and

---

[1] Readers may well ask for the sources of the argument which has taken up so much space. The essential pros and cons are to be found in the following: (1) *The Discoveries of Antarctica within the American Sector, as Revealed by Maps and Documents*. By William Herbert Hobbs, University of Michigan. Philadelphia, 1939. (2) "On some misrepresentations of Antarctic history." Article by A. R. H. in the *Geographical Journal*, vol. xciv, October, 1939. (3) "The Charting of the South Shetlands, 1819–28." By Lieut.-Commander R. T. Gould, R.N., ret., in *The Mariner's Mirror*, vol. xxii, No. 3, July, 1941.

a second is that the voyage is not eventful in the sense that many others were. There was no tragedy and no outstanding discovery. History shows that it is the expedition which has either great good fortune or great disaster which finds a large reading public.

Further, it appeared at a time when polar interest was directed chiefly to the North-West Passage and the far more eventful expeditions of Parry, of Franklin, and of Rae, in all of which land travel with its more vivid adventures captured attention.

Whatever the reasons, it is a fact that little but a bare outline of the voyage found its way to the nations most busy with exploration, and it was not until 1837 that any English chart showed the track of the expedition. The Hydrographic Section of the British Admiralty duly noted the discoveries and in due course used extracts from the narrative in its publications.

It is therefore to be confessed that this very remarkable voyage had but small effect on subsequent Antarctic exploration for a very long time.

Bellingshausen's immediate successor bent on discovery in the South Atlantic was James Weddell, who must have known of the Russian voyage as he was at the South Shetlands immediately before and soon after, but his own remarkable voyage was made long before the Bellingshausen narrative appeared.

The contrast between the expeditions of the Russian naval captain and the British ex-naval master was mainly one of facilities, both men being of that calibre which pursues a purpose to the utmost. Weddell with his 160-ton brig, the *Jane*, and his 65-ton cutter, the *Beaufoy*, and his total crews of but 35 men, had even less luck than the Russians as far as discovery of new land was concerned. He had the good fortune to have an extraordinarily ice-free season and reached a point nearly 3° farther south than Cook, but as his deep thrust into that open sea produced no landfall his voyage was on the whole of negative value.

When in the late thirties there was a revival of official interest in the Antarctic culminating in the despatch of French, American and British expeditions under Dumont D'Urville, Wilkes and Ross, the work of Bellingshausen became better known, but only Biscoe visited the same areas of the Antarctic.

In the brig, the *Tula*, and the small cutter, the *Lively* of but 50 tons, Biscoe made a circumnavigation somewhat similar to that of Bellingshausen, some ten years after him. He had similar difficulties with the pack ice, but partly on account of his greater mobility in the small vessels he was able to get farther south at several points. He thus discovered Enderby Land in February 1831, the first discovery of truly continental land in the Antarctic, as we now know. Later, on the same voyage, he discovered Adelaide Island and the Biscoe Archipelago, both north of the Russian discovery of Alexander Land.

As already noted, the great revival of official Antarctic exploration in the late thirties and early forties was directed towards the sector south of Australia and New Zealand, a part which Bellingshausen had not visited. It was not till the beginning of the twentieth century therefore that a renewal of exploration led to further assaults on the regions to which the Russians had paid most attention.

These, then, are some of the reasons why the Russian text has remained untranslated into English for more than a century. Now that it is available in full the historian of exploration of the Antarctic will be able to assess its value in more detail than can be given in a short introduction.

It is less easy to draw a clear picture of Bellingshausen himself than of his expedition and it would remain so even were biographical details more readily available. He was clearly of that breed of naval men who are prone to sink their private affairs and opinions beneath the calls of their duty and who have earned the cognomen of the silent service for the navy. Born in the province of Estonia, on the island of Oesel, he was within the influence both of German culture and that of the intelligentsia of St Petersburg. All internal evidence, however, points to his having difficulty in expressing himself, as being a man of action rather than of words. Not that he was barren of ideas in any way; indeed his excursions into scientific hypothesis in the book are almost brilliant for a man of strictly naval training.

In the social sphere he appears to have been on the whole friendly but punctilious, and probably acted more formally than he really felt. His relations with his officers, too, seem to have been good but official and correct, and even when he betrays great satisfaction with them he does so in terms exhibiting the restraint proper to a report.

There is no doubt that he was a firm disciplinarian and there are rumours of an incredible number of lashes awarded as punishments to his crew on the voyage. Yet he treated his men with a consideration as to their health and welfare which was unusual in his day and was obviously not based solely on his desire for efficiency. A similar solicitude for the natives he met is explicit in the narrative and could not have been due entirely to the orders of his Emperor on the subject. He was in fact probably as kindly as his office would permit him to be, and as friendly as his seniority allowed.

It is clear both in this narrative and from other sidelights upon his character that his passion was the Russian Navy and that, together with a sense of loyalty to his sovereign, ruled his conduct and his career. His later service was cast in less stirring times than that of his youth and he went up the ladder of seniority in a normal way and with little opportunity to distinguish himself beyond his fellows. Becoming an Admiral in 1831, his last appointment was that of Governor of Kronstadt, where he died in 1852.

The best known portrait of him is one which used to be in the Library of the Imperial Naval Department in St Petersburg. Painted in late life, it is not entirely flattering to him. The firm chin and the keen eye are there but they are rather at odds with a somewhat dyspeptic cast of expression as well as the stoop of advancing years.

The portrait as frontispiece to the first volume, which we owe to the kindness of the Russian Admiralty, does him better justice and we can read into it some of the attributes we have mentioned.

No less famous in his way was his second in command, Mikhail Lazarev. His four years in the British Navy and his greater social capacities made him more popular with the people he met than was his taciturn and less linguistic commander. There can be no doubt of his splendid seamanship and his readiness to take risks from the fact that he followed his leader round the world in a slower and less handy ship and never lost touch for more than a day or so at a time.

He too rose to be an Admiral, and his bluff and hearty countenance as shown in the frontispiece to the second volume is probably a very true index of his character.

To the two commanders, together with the able second-in-command of the *Vostok*, Lieutenant Zavodovski, must be largely ascribed the success of an expedition which followed, and in places excelled, the very best traditions of Captain Cook. It was unfortunate that their very success, and lack of tragic incident, robbed them of praise due at the time, for then, as now, it is the model expedition which has least of adventure to tell.

PRELIMINARY MEMOIR

EMPEROR ALEXANDER PAVLOVICH (ALEXANDER I) of glorious memory, desiring to help in extending the fields of knowledge, ordered the despatch of two expeditions, each consisting of two vessels, for the exploration of the higher latitudes of the Arctic and Antarctic Oceans. Following His Majesty's commands, announced on the 25th of March 1819, two vessels were selected for exploration in the Antarctic Sea, viz. the sloops *Vostok* (*East*) and *Mirnyi* (*Peaceful*), under the command of Captain (2nd rank—now Vice-Admiral) Bellingshausen. The corvette *Otkryitie* (*Discovery*) and the transport *Blagonamyerenny* (*Well-intentioned*), under the command of Commander (now Rear-Admiral) Vasilev, were selected for the expedition to the northern Polar Region.

Both squadrons started on July 4th, 1819. The former returned in 1821, the latter in 1822.

In 1824, Captain Bellingshausen presented to the Admiralty a report of his voyage with all charts and sketches belonging thereto. The Admiralty, on March 17th, 1825, made representations to the then Chief of His Imperial Majesty's Naval Staff to obtain the Imperial sanction for printing 1200 copies of the work, with all appendices, and for a grant of the necessary sum of money for this purpose; but no decision was taken upon these representations.

On the establishment of the Scientific Committee of the Imperial Naval Staff in October 1827, Vice-Admiral Bellingshausen requested the Committee to recommend the printing of at least 600 copies of his report, adding that neither had he previously asked, nor did he now ask, for any personal advantage from the publication, but only wished that the work might be more generally known.

The President of the Committee expressed his own opinion as follows:

1. "The voyage of Captain Bellingshausen, which was undertaken, by order of His Imperial Majesty Alexander Pavlovich of glorious memory, especially for exploration in higher southern latitudes, and with the object of proceeding as far as possible towards the South Pole, is, by reason of this alone, worthy of special attention and remark.

2. "The expedition was carried out by Captain Bellingshausen with complete success, wherefore both he and those under his command were duly rewarded by His Majesty.
3. "The publication of the account of his voyage will do honour to our sailors, while its non-publication would afford grounds for the assumption that the object of their task had not been fulfilled.
4. "Navigators of various nationalities continue every year to visit all seas as yet imperfectly explored and it may happen, if indeed it has not already happened, that the scientific discoveries of Captain Bellingshausen, if not now made known, may be claimed by others as their own, and that the honour of them will go to foreign, and not to Russian navigators.
5. "The appointment of two expeditions for the Survey of the Earth in its most inaccessible regions in the north and south, resulting from the personal initiative of His Imperial Majesty, the Emperor Alexander Pavlovich, showed his wide interest in the extension of knowledge. Accounts of these travels will, therefore, help to make known His late Majesty's ever remembered care for the general progress of exploration.

"For all these reasons, I propose that the Committee should report to the Chief of the Naval Staff requesting him to procure His Majesty's authority for the publication of Captain Bellingshausen's Voyage, according to his wish, in an edition of 600 copies."

This proposal was agreed to by the Committee and was laid before the late Chief of the Naval Staff.

His Imperial Majesty was pleased to grant from the Privy Purse the sum of 38,052 roubles[1] necessary for the publication, the proceeds of which were to benefit Captain Bellingshausen.

In the following work, which consists of two parts with an atlas of nineteen charts and forty-four lithographed sketches, the readers will learn for themselves the remarkable naval feats performed by Vice-Admiral Bellingshausen and by Rear-Admiral Lazarev, commanding the other vessel of this squadron, aided by their ships' companies.

At the time when Vice-Admiral Kruzenstern was carrying out the first Russian circumnavigation of the world, many other vessels were also sent out; some carrying food to Kamchatka and to American colonies, others for purposes of exploration and discovery. All these expeditions carried out their tasks successfully, but all followed, so to speak, the track of Vice-Admiral Kruzenstern, who had set an example for such voyages.

---

[1] About £4000. A rouble was worth about 2s. 1½d.

PRELIMINARY MEMOIR

Vice-Admiral Bellingshausen's work was carried out in regions which had never been touched by Russian ships. He prosecuted his discoveries within the Antarctic Circle, in the midst of ice, in a struggle with strong winds, in fog, snow and frost. He only turned back when he encountered immense tracts of impenetrable ice, along the edge of which he continued his work for three months. In the winter he proceeded to lower latitudes but returned as soon as practicable to his laborious explorations and continued them amidst the same difficulties of ice and weather for another three months. He did not return until he recognized the impossibility of continuing his voyage farther, and then, in obedience to the orders given to him, having completed the second voyage, he was obliged to return home.

By reason of these remarkable achievements, the name of Vice-Admiral Bellingshausen as commander of the squadron, no less than that of his second-in-command, Rear-Admiral Mikhail Lazarev,* will remain for ever renowned in the annals of Russian navigation.

GOLENITSCHEV-KUTUZOV
President of the Committee

* The name of Mr Lazarev is given here in full because two of his brothers are now serving in the Fleet and, on account of their rank and good service, may soon also be Rear-Admirals.

TWO VOYAGES OF DISCOVERY IN THE ANTARCTIC & A VOYAGE ROUND THE WORLD

CHAPTER I

Appointment of the two Squadrons for the Voyages of Discovery. Preparation of the *Vostok* and the *Mirnyi*. His Majesty's visit to the ships. Voyage from Kronstadt to England.

ON MARCH 25th, 1819, the Minister of Naval Affairs, the Marquis de Traversey, announced to Lieutenant Lazarev that His Imperial Majesty had been pleased to order the despatch of two expeditions on voyages of discovery, one to the Antarctic, and the other to the Arctic Regions.

The first was destined to explore those parts of the Antarctic Sea into which, as yet, navigators had not penetrated, and to survey, in regions which were already known, such islands as had not previously been visited. This expedition was called the First Squadron.

The second expedition was to proceed to Behring Strait to seek the North-West Passage along the coasts of North America and, after passing through it, to return to Russia via the Atlantic. This expedition was called the Second Squadron.

To the latter, the corvette *Otkryitie* (*Discovery*) and the transport *Blagonamyerenny* (*Well-intentioned*) were assigned, under the command of Lieutenant-Commander Vasilev and Lieutenant Glyeb Shishmarev. The First Squadron was to consist of the sloop *Vostok* (*East*) and the transport *Ladoga*. The well-known Captain Ratmanov was called to St Petersburg to take command of these ships. He was at that time in Copenhagen, having suffered shipwreck off The Skaw, and was awaiting the summer to return to Russia, and his uncertain health, which had suffered during his service, did not permit of his accepting the command of so arduous an undertaking. Captain Ratmanov, with whom I served on the *Nadezhda* under the command of Captain Kruzenstern at the time of his voyage round the world, proposed to His Majesty's Minister that the command of the First Squadron should be entrusted to me, in his place.

In consequence I received a letter from the Minister of Naval Affairs dated 24th of April, 1819, as follows:

> His Majesty the Emperor having instructed Vice-Admiral Greig[1] immediately to despatch you to St Petersburg, I send the same information also to you, convinced, as I am, that you will hasten your arrival here to receive His Majesty's commission and instructions.

Under these circumstances I left Sevastopol, where, at the time, I had the pleasure of serving as Commander of the 44-gun frigate *Flora*, and had just received orders from the Commander of the Black Sea Fleet, Vice-Admiral Greig, to make a survey of the Black Sea in the above-mentioned frigate during the summer, and to fix the geographical positions of all the principal places and capes. I should have been delighted and honoured to have carried out the orders of my beloved chief, but I had of necessity to proceed to St Petersburg.

On my arrival in the capital on the 23rd of May, I received the following information from the Minister of Marine: "It has pleased His Majesty the Emperor to entrust you with the command of the two ships, the *Vostok* and the *Mirnyi*, which have been selected to carry out a voyage of discovery in the higher southern latitudes, and to circumnavigate the ice-belt of the southern Polar Circle."

I promptly proceeded to Kronstadt to take over the command of the vessels, which were almost ready for the expedition.

Preparation of the Vessels

Until the appointment of the actual commander of the sloop *Vostok*, First Lieutenant Ignatiev had been appointed by the Chief Commander of Kronstadt, Vice-Admiral Moller, to superintend the pre-

---

[1] Vice-Admiral Sir Alexis Samuilovich Greig was of Scots descent. His father, Sir Samuel Greig, was born at Inverkeithing (Fifeshire) and enlisted in the Russian Navy in 1763. In that capacity he quickly rose to fame and was eventually made Governor of Kronstadt. He did much to reform the Russian Navy and was joined in the service by quite a number of his fellow-countrymen. This, no doubt, accounts for the presence of Roman Adams as midshipman on the *Vostok*. Alexis was born in 1775 at Kronstadt. He was made, at birth, a midshipman in the Russian Navy. He distinguished himself in the Russo-Turkish Wars of 1807 and 1829, when he was made a full Admiral.

paration and refitting of the ship. The *Vostok*, whose dimensions were as follows: length 129 feet 10 inches, beam 32 feet 8 inches, draught 9 feet 7 inches, had been built at St Petersburg in the Okhta dockyard by the shipbuilders, Stoke, in 1818. She was considered by the Minister of Marine as suitable for this voyage, all the more as Captain Golovnin, in 1817, had sailed round the world in the sloop *Kamchatka* of the same build and dimensions. The *Vostok* was built of unseasoned pinewood and had only the usual strengthening; the under-water part had been reinforced and on the outside it was protected by copper sheathing. This work was carried out at Kronstadt by the shipbuilder Amosov, under whose direction the structural alterations, etc., were effected.

On my arrival at Kronstadt, I was struck, as soon as I saw the ship, by the unusual length of her masts and spars. As I was expected to sail in all weathers and in all seas, in bad climates and far from a base or other ports, I proposed to reduce the masts and to make a few other alterations. However, owing to the lateness of the season, there was no time to do this and I had to be content with finishing the work already in hand. At my request the shipbuilders ordered the spare spars $3\frac{1}{2}$ feet shorter than those already in position and I proposed to substitute these on the way out. I intended then to have the existing spars cut down by my own carpenters.

Second Lieutenant Lazarev, who had done four years' voluntary service in the English Navy and had then, while serving in our own Fleet as Commander of the *Suvorov*, owned by the Russo-American Company, successfully completed a voyage round the world during 1813, 1814, 1815 and 1816, was appointed to the command of the transport *Ladoga* which was then re-named the naval sloop *Mirnyi*. Notwithstanding this change of name, however, any naval officer could at once perceive the difference in speed between this slower vessel and the *Vostok*, and could appreciate the difficulty of keeping the ships together and the consequent delay on the voyage. The *Mirnyi* was a ship of 230 tons, 120 feet in length, 30 feet beam and 15 feet draught. She had been constructed by the shipbuilder Kolodkin, of good pinewood, and provided with iron reinforcements for navigation in the Baltic. To make the ship more suitable for the difficult voyage before her, and capable of resisting without danger the stormy seas of the southern Ocean, the Admiralty proposed to add further reinforcements. Fine weather permitted this sheathing of the vessels to be completed in twelve days. The rafts on which the carpenters and caulkers worked were continually visited by naval officers, who took the greatest interest in the despatch of the expedition and, as we noted with satisfaction, would not pass a single nail untested. When this had been finished, the copper sheathing was begun. The iron rudder hinges were changed for copper ones, the rudder of pinewood replaced by one of oak. The bitts, catheads and camels were all constructed of oak, and in short the ship was equipped for her intended voyage in every possible way. After several discussions between the shipbuilders as to the method of strengthening the ship, it was decided to fit iron stanchions running across the crossbeams on the lower deck and also on the beams of the orlop deck;[1] to fit supporting knees under the beams on the lower deck; to double the riders, and to add at the bows two breast-hooks of solid wood as well as those made of several pieces of wood bolted up together. At the stern the transoms were to be strengthened by wooden knees above and below.

The Minister of Marine announced the order of His Imperial Majesty to change the name of the transport *Ladoga* to that of the naval sloop *Mirnyi* as being more suitable for her destined voyage and, by minor additions, to give her the appearance of a warship.

Lieutenant Lazarev, with the permission of the Minister, changed the masts of his ship; and the alterations of her sails and rigging and of all her internal fittings were carried out according to his wishes. Her guns consisted of 14 three-pounders and 6 carronades. The boats of both ships were built to designs selected by Lieutenant Lazarev.

Commissioning. Selection of Officers and Crews

When the ships were almost ready, we proceeded, by special permission, to select the officers and crews. The number of officers who volunteered, in spite of the difficulties and dangers to be expected during our proposed voyage, was so great that we were caused no little embarrassment in making our choice. In the *Vostok* we only required three lieutenants, and two sub-lieutenants, and in the *Mirnyi* two lieutenants and two sub-lieutenants. We were, therefore, to our great regret, unable to satisfy all who were anxious to accompany us.

[1] This was situated below the lower gun deck. On it cables were coiled and sails stowed.

THE OFFICERS OF THE *VOSTOK*

COMMANDER
Thaddeus Bellinghausen
  Chief of the Expedition and Captain of the *Vostok*.

LIEUTENANT-COMMANDER
Ivan Zavodovski
  Served under me for seven years in the Black Sea in the frigates *Minerva* and *Flora*. I knew the worth of this officer.

LIEUTENANTS
Ivan Ignatiev
  Appointed by the Commander of Kronstadt Port, Vice-Admiral Moller, for the outfit of the vessel and subsequently appointed to her by the wish of Vice-Admiral Moller.

Constantine Torson
Arcady Lyeskov
  Appointed on account of excellent reports from their Captains.

SUB-LIEUTENANT
Dimitri Demidov
  At the request of Rear-Admiral Korobka.

ASTRONOMER
Ivan Simanov
  Professor Extraordinary, graduate of Kazan University.

ARTIST
Paul Mikhailov
  Academician of the Imperial Academy of Fine Arts.

STAFF-SURGEON
Jacob Bergh
  Chosen from the Fleet by General Staff-Surgeon Leiton.

NAVIGATING OFFICER
Jacob Paryadin

PAYMASTER WITH RANK OF OFFICER
Ivan Rezanov

MIDSHIPMAN
Roman Adams
  Appointed by the Minister of Marine on my recommendation.

Second Mates with rank of Petty Officers	2
Assistant Mate with rank of Petty Officer	1
Quartermasters	4
Bugler	1
Drummer	1
Seamen	71
Assistant Surgeon	1
Carpenter's Apprentice (2nd Class)	1
Blacksmith	1
Carpenter (2nd Class)	1
Caulker	1
Sailmaker	1
Cooper	1
Gunnery Petty Officers	2
Bombardier	1
Gunners (1st Grade)	11
Stewards	4
Total	117

THE OFFICERS OF THE *MIRNYI*

LIEUTENANTS
Mikhail Lazarev (in Command)   Nikolai Obernibessov
Mikhail Annenkov

SUB-LIEUTENANTS
Ivan Kupriyanov   Paul Novosilski

NAVIGATING OFFICER: Nikolai Ilin

SURGEON: Nikolai Galkin

Second Mate with rank of Petty Officer	1	Carpenters	2
Assistant Mate	1	Locksmith	1
Boatswain	1	Caulker	1
Quartermasters	2	Sailmaker	1
Seamen (1st Class)	44	Cooper	1
Drummer	1	Gunnery Petty Officer	1
Steward	1	Gunners (1st Grade)	6
Assistant Surgeon	1	Total[1]	72

STORES

Provisions and equipment for the expedition were prepared in St Petersburg under the supervision of Major-General Minitzki and later, in his absence, by order of the Imperial Admiralty, under the direction of Lieutenant-Commander Bogdanovich, to whose activity and judicious arrangements we were very much indebted.

I consider it my duty to place here on record the names of all those whose integrity contributed to the success of the expedition; badly prepared provisions may produce many unforeseen maladies.

The merchants who provided the salted beef were: in St Petersburg, Peter Shpanski; in Narva, Peter Pechatkin and Akinh Oblomkof, the latter a citizen of St Petersburg and known as having already supplied stores to the first Russian expedition round the world, under the command of Captain Kruzenstern. He furnished on that occasion salted beef which remained unspoilt by all the variations of climate in the course of a three years' voyage. It was stowed in good oak barrels, about 6 poods (216 lb.) in each. Gerrat, Master Baker, made excellent wheat and rye biscuits for us. Although a small part of them went bad,

---

[1] A chaplain must be added to this list. He is mentioned several times during the narrative, though he may have been serving in some other capacity as well.

it was the result of damp in the vessel and not for want of care on the baker's part. Sauerkraut (pickled cabbage), which had been a little over-salted for its better preservation, was packed in small barrels, and was supplied in sufficient quantity; it remained perfectly good throughout the whole of the voyage. Beef tea in tablets, which had been prepared for our use, had not sufficiently dried in time and we consequently only took an eighth part of the quantity ordered—$2\frac{1}{2}$ poods (90 lb.) to each ship. I believe, if such prepared beef tea, before it sets, is poured into sound tins soldered all round and the tins then closed with tin covers and also soldered down, the beef tea, having no contact with the outer air, will never go bad, or at least not for a long time.

Clothing

Since clean clothing and fresh linen, refreshing the body, produces a feeling of health in man, and in some manner prevents him from falling into bad habits, it was decided to provide the crews with the following necessary articles of clothing. To each man:

Sailor's uniforms with cloth jacket	4	Warm boots lined with cloth	1 pair
Trousers of cloth	2	Shoes	4 pairs
Summer trousers of Flemish linen	6	Blanket	1
		Bed	1
Working coats of dimity[1]	4	Pillow	1
Working trousers of dimity	4	Sheets	4
Overcoat of grey cloth	1	Woollen stockings	8 pairs
Fur cap (for warmth)	1	Linen shirts	11
Hat	1	Flannel shirts	7

Scale of Pay and Allowances

In order to guarantee in some way the prospects of each man, and to provide thereby an incentive in their difficult undertaking, it was decided to pay the ship's company at eight times the normal rate, and to give the officers and scientists, besides their pay, a mess-allowance. In addition, before our departure, His Imperial Majesty ordered me to be given, as reward, a gratuity of five thousand roubles and, for the journey from the Black Sea to the Baltic, besides the posting expenses, a thousand roubles. Three thousand roubles were granted to Lieutenant Lazarev, and a year's pay extra to all the officers and men. We

---

[1] A kind of coarse cotton.

fully appreciated the Emperor's graciousness and the interest which His Majesty deigned to take in our welfare, by thus anticipating any hardships which might arise in a voyage of such duration and such manifold difficulties.

Selection of Scientists

His Imperial Majesty, in sending out this expedition, hoped to increase man's knowledge about the earth and about the contact between native races and Europeans and at the same time to add to the existing knowledge of natural history. For this purpose the Minister of Public Instruction, on His Majesty's orders, selected the following scientists, and appointed them to the position of naturalists of the expedition: Mertens of Halle and Doctor Kuntze of Leipzig, who were to proceed to Copenhagen by June 12th.[1] Professor Simanov, a member of Kazan University, was appointed as astronomer, and Paul Mikhailov, of the Imperial Academy of Fine Arts, was chosen as the artist to accompany us.

Presents for the Natives

We were ordered to distribute medals at any islands or shores which we might discover, and also during our stay in other places during the long voyage—silver medals for important personages, and bronze ones for those of lesser importance. These medals were specially struck at the St Petersburg Mint, bearing on the obverse the image of His Imperial Majesty Alexander I, and on the reverse the inscription, "The sloops '*Vostok*' and '*Mirnyi*', 1819", i.e. the year of our departure.

In order to induce the natives to friendly behaviour towards us, and also as a means of barter for fresh provisions and specimens of native work, various articles were issued to us at St Petersburg which might prove attractive to such natives as were in a primitive stage of culture.

Here follows a list of the articles:

Knives, assorted	400	Handsaws	10
Cobbler's knives	100	Cross-cut saws	10
Pruning knives	20	Planes	15
Knives ¾ arsheen in length		Pincers, large and small	10
(21 in.)	2	Chisels	30

[1] These men failed to join the expedition at the rendezvous, which was therefore without naturalists for the whole period of the voyage.

PRESENTS FOR THE NATIVES

Vices	10	Night lamps	24
Gimlets	125	Combs, horn	250
Rasps and files	100	Combs, wooden	50
Graters	50	Knitting needles, assorted	5000
Axes	100	Studs	100
Choppers	50	Lead in 2½ pood portions, 4 pieces	10 pood (360 lb.)
Shipbuilder's augers	50		
Scissors, assorted	50	Rings	250
Lamps	300	Earrings	125 pairs
Small bells and trumpets	185	Beads	20 bunches
Red and blue linen, striped	500 arsheen (389 yd.)	Garnets	5 bunches
		Glass beads (large and small)	20 bunches
Old buttons	12 dozen		
Linen printed handkerchiefs	100	Threading needles	40 packets
Fringes of different colours	60 arsheen (47 yd.)	Cotton wick	80 lb.
		Wax candles	1000
Ticking and tent cloth, striped	100 arsheen (78 yd.)	Fishing lines	12 pood (430 lb.)
		Various wrought-iron vessels	27½ pood (1000 lb.)
Unbleached linen	250 arsheen (195 yd.)	Various kinds of mirrors	1000
Tinder	10 lb.	Flower and vegetable seeds	100 lb.
Dyed thread	10 lb.	Kaleidoscopes	24
Flints	1000	Burning glasses	18
Hussar jackets	10	Large iron fish hooks	6
Glasses	120	Wire fish hooks, coarse and fine	1800
Decanters	12		
Copper wire	100 lb.	Red baize	218 arsheen (169 yd.)
Iron wire	80 lb.	Blue and green flannel	62 arsheen (48 yd.)
Drums	1		
Tambourines	2	Frieze blankets	70
Huntsmen's horns	5	Tobacco twist	26 pood (900 lb.)

Before my departure I received the four following sets of Instructions:

1. FROM THE MINISTER OF THE NAVY

His Imperial Majesty, in entrusting the First Division, sent out on a voyage of discovery, to Bellingshausen, Captain (2nd Grade), has been pleased to issue the following instructions on the general plan of the work:

Between the time of departure from Kronstadt and arrival in Brazil, the expedition will touch at an English port and at Teneriffe.

As soon as the suitable season for exploration in high southern latitudes sets in this year, Captain Bellingshausen will proceed to survey South Georgia, which lies in latitude 55° S., and thence to Sandwich Island,[1] passing along its eastern shores. He will then steer south, continuing his explorations in as high a latitude as he can reach. Every effort will be made to approach as closely as possible to the South Pole, searching for as yet unknown land, and only abandoning the undertaking in the face of insurmountable obstacles.

If his efforts to advance southward along the meridian first selected should prove unavailing, fresh efforts must be made on another meridian, never for a moment losing sight of the main and important object of the expedition and hourly renewing his efforts in the direction both of discovering new lands and of approaching as closely as possible to the South Pole.

For this purpose he must make use of the whole of the navigable season; at the approach of the winter season, he must return to lower latitudes, endeavouring to follow routes not hitherto traversed by other explorers, proceeding to the Auckland Islands and passing through the Queen Charlotte Straits. Thereafter he will continue the voyage to Port Jackson to lay in a store of provisions and allow the expedition to rest and refit. This will probably be in the early part of April 1820.[2]

After a rest and when all necessary stores have been taken aboard and all repairs completed, the Commander of the First Squadron will sail from Port Jackson and proceed on an eastward course in the latitude of New Zealand and the northern portion of New Holland. He should then turn towards the Society and the Marquis (de Mendoza) Islands[3] and proceed by the least frequented routes of the equatorial regions, visiting the inhabited islands which were touched at by Kotzebue and exploring others in the vicinity, of which he may obtain information from the inhabitants of the former. He will survey the Solomon Islands, and, if time permits, New Caledonia, returning either to Port Jackson or to the southern port of Van Diemen's Land to refit. He may only go to the latter if, according to

---

[1] Captain Cook had reported the group now known under that name as either a long island or possibly an extensive projection of a continent.

[2] These instructions betray either ignorance or lack of care at the Russian Admiralty. Thus a route to Port Jackson via Auckland Island and Queen Charlotte Sound would be very roundabout, nor is the latitude of New Zealand anywhere near that of the north of New Holland.

[3] The Marquesas.

previous information, he can obtain all necessary stores there. He will supply the ships' companies with fresh food and prepare for a further attempt on the Polar region.

On the approach of the navigable season, towards the close of 1820, the first expedition will again sail for high southern latitudes. The Commander will renew and continue exploration on the lines of the previous year with the same resolution and tenacity and will cross the remaining meridians for a circumnavigation of the earth, keeping at or beyond the same latitude in which he started on the longitude of the Sandwich Islands. At the end of the time required for the successful completion of the expedition, he will start on the return journey to Russia.

His Imperial Majesty relies implicitly on the zeal, knowledge and talents of Captain Bellingshausen, and, not wishing to restrict his activities he is content to indicate the main objects for which Captain Bellingshausen is despatched. He authorizes him to act according to circumstances, as seems to him best for the welfare of all on board and for the advancement of the great object of the expedition: exploration in the closest possible vicinity to the South Pole.

He is especially recommended to devote tireless care to the health of the members of the expedition, which should at all times and in all circumstances be the object of his most sedulous efforts.

Whenever and wherever the expedition may make a stay in inhabited lands, His Majesty commands that the inhabitants shall be treated with the greatest kindness and humanity, avoiding as far as possible any occasion for giving offence or displeasure, and, on the contrary, invariably attracting them by gentleness; the Commander shall never resort to severe measures, except in cases where the lives of those entrusted to his care would otherwise be imperilled.

His Imperial Majesty has made known his wishes to the Minister of the Navy concerning special instructions to be given as to further details of the voyage and the supply of all necessary information, charts, publications and instruments, suitable to this work, together with stores of such objects as are necessary for barter with any natives with whom the expedition may come into contact.

His Imperial Majesty desires that those officially appointed for the scientific and artistic sections of the expedition should also be furnished with all equipment necessary for their respective activities and work.

His Imperial Majesty is also pleased to command that, in the event of very important discoveries being made, Captain Bellingshausen shall promptly despatch one of the ships under his command to Russia to report them: but this must only be resorted to if the discovery is of sufficient importance to warrant it; the other vessel is meanwhile to carry out the instructions received.

His Imperial Majesty has confirmed the above Instructions to the First Squadron, consisting of the *Vostok* and the *Mirnyi* under your command, and these Instructions I now forward to you, together with a copy of those given to the Commander of the Second Squadron, Lieutenant-Commander Vasilev.

Apart from these Instructions and those which you will receive from the Imperial Admiralty Council and the Admiralty Department, I consider it necessary to communicate to you the following orders:

At all places which you may touch, you must endeavour to get all available information as to the habits of the people, their customs and religion, their weapons, the types of boats which they use, and the products of the country. Furthermore, you should obtain information as to the nationality of the other travellers who visit these savage races, which nation is preferred by the natives, besides other details concerning trade and barter and the benefits accruing therefrom.

You must always, both when at sea and whilst lying at anchor, be prepared against attack either by pirates or natives.

You must endeavour to collect all available information on the military strength of the foreign countries and ports at which you may touch, as to their war strength, their forts, guns and munitions, etc., noting all in detail, and making charts and plans of all ports, bays, and coast outlines.

At the conclusion of the voyage, the scientific and artistic members of the staff must hand over to you, as Chief of the expedition, all their journals, taking care to sign their names to them, so that, whenever it may please His Majesty so to direct, they may be returned to their authors.

When you happen to be amongst savage tribes, you should secure their friendship by kindness. Yet, never forgetting the possibility of danger, you must always be ready to forestall any hostile attempt and to prevent the idea of attack from entering their minds. Savages, noticing your vigilance, will probably not attempt to do you any injury.

You must never send any boat ashore without seeing that she is well armed with guns, muskets, sabres, pikes, etc.

In addition, the officers in command of boats must take all necessary precautions not to get separated nor to go far from their boats without leaving with them a sufficient number of the crew for purposes of defence.

If it be necessary to land, either to make observations, to trade or to recruit the health of the crews, you must choose a position which seems suitable and fortify it in such a way that you will be safe from attack by the natives. In short, such a place should resemble a fortress and must be kept well stocked with arms.

You must not let slip any opportunity of sending information of your voyages, and for this purpose it is necessary to have despatches always ready, so that on meeting vessels at sea, on their way to Europe, you may request them to forward such despatches from their European port to the Russian Minister of the Navy.

If you should find it necessary and advantageous to separate from the other vessel under your command, in order to pursue different objectives, you are not forbidden to separate for a short or even a long period and to arrange a rendezvous.

If, during the voyage, it is found necessary, in view of any important consideration, for one vessel to return to Russia, care must be taken that only the provisions and materials necessary for the period of the voyage are retained on board her, the remainder being left with the other vessel.

Before starting on any voyage, you should, against the event of your ships becoming separated, make a complete chart of your course and agree upon a rendezvous.

In order that you, as Commander of the division, should have complete authority for preserving the necessary order, obedience and respect due from the lower grades to the higher ones on the vessels under your command, you are hereby authorized to punish all subordinates, whether officers or lower grades, of the executive who may prove negligent, lazy, disobedient, rude, or who commit any other offence, according to the measure of their guilt with all the severity of the law, by imposing a suitable punishment. You have also the right to court-martial them on occasion, dealing with them in the ordinary way, and informing me of all particulars at a convenient opportunity, for report to His Imperial Majesty.

In dealing with the lower ratings, those below executive rank, and the crew, you have the right to punish them for minor offences according to your own judgment. For serious offences, you must call together a court, competent to inflict legal punishment (with your confirmation as Chief of the expedition), except such heavy punishments as are provided by law in lieu of capital punishment. In such cases the matter is to be reported in the usual manner together with your opinion on it, when a suitable occasion presents itself.

Foreign scientists have been appointed, with His Imperial Majesty's approval, with the title "Naturalists", to both expeditions, namely, Herr Mertens and Dr Kuntze, who are to join the expedition at Copenhagen. You will, by agreement with the Commander of the second expedition, pick them up there and assign one to each ship.

Your division is supplied with silver and bronze medals, with the object of having them distributed as souvenirs to any important persons whom you may meet on the voyages. You may also distribute them on any of the islands you visit, at your discretion, but more especially on any previously undiscovered.

A "carte blanche" (power to act at your own discretion in any matter placed under your charge) from the Ministry of Foreign Affairs, written in Russian, French and German, is herewith enclosed. In addition, the Foreign Affairs Committee have sent particulars to all our accredited representatives in different foreign countries, for their information, regarding this expedition. There are also forwarded to you herewith, under separate register, cartes blanches received from all those foreign representatives of Maritime Countries who are accredited to the Ministry of Foreign Affairs at the present time.

2. INSTRUCTIONS FROM THE IMPERIAL ADMIRALTY COUNCIL

By His Imperial Majesty's orders, you are appointed Commander of the First Squadron, which consists of the two sloops, the *Vostok* and the *Mirnyi*. With these ships you will carry out an extended voyage of discovery. You are hereby instructed to start the voyage immediately on the completion of the equipment and commissioning of the two vessels, according to the special Instructions which will be given you by His Imperial Majesty's orders. On the part of the Admiralty Council certain regulations affecting the material conditions of the expedition are enjoined upon you. These rules are, for the greater part, embodied in the Code of Naval Regulations, Orders and in other Ordinances, and are therefore familiar to all ranks of the Fleet. As, however, thanks to the extension of human knowledge derived from just such voyages as the one you are about to undertake, we know that occasions will arise of which no mention is made in these standing orders, such points are set out in the following paragraphs:

1

The preservation of the health of the crew is one of the first duties of all navigators. Past experience has proved that the best way to attain this is to devote special care to the cleanliness of the vessel and of the crew; keeping the air in the lower deck and the hold as pure as possible; seeing that the ship's company has a sufficient but not excessive amount of exercise; noting carefully that the men do not remain in wet clothes for any length of time, and still more particularly, that they do not sleep in them; and lastly, to supply them with the best provisions and drink. The Admiralty Council expects you to attend to all these matters, and to see that these, and all other "personal" rules drawn up by medical advice for the preservation of general health, are thoroughly carried out.

2

You are in particular to attend to all cases of sickness, and to see that every endeavour is made to ameliorate their condition and expedite their convalescence, encouraging the medical staff appointed to your ships to work for that end. It will be your duty to report to your Chiefs on either the zeal or the negligence of the medical staff.

3

You are further to take all possible steps to obtain fresh provisions for the crews, and not to let slip any opportunity for so doing. Whilst in port, you must see that the crew are provided with the best fresh stores procurable, whilst at sea the men should fish wherever local conditions permit. Rum and wine should be issued, according to climate and circumstances. The following places are to be called at for the purchase of fresh stores and beverages: Copenhagen, England, Madeira or Teneriffe; wood, if necessary may be obtained at Sant'

Iago, observing however that it is not wise to stay at the latter as the climate is unhealthy. Salt beef should first be steamed in sea water, for the removal of all dirt and grease, which might otherwise give rise to scurvy.[1] Salt beef treated in this manner, and served with cooked cereals, becomes fresher and quite pleasant to the taste. In warm parts butter should be used in very moderate quantities, and should it seem to be on the point of going bad, do not use it at all but serve beef tea instead of butter with peas. Whenever the ovens are rigged on board, you must order freshly baked bread to be issued to the crew from time to time, since this, as is well known, is much more wholesome than biscuits. Water barrels must be burnt out very frequently, in order that the water may keep fresh and untainted, taking care that they are always kept clean; when need arises they should be filled with salt water and used as water-ballast. When they are again needed for fresh water they must first be thoroughly cleaned out. There is nothing more prejudicial to health or more conducive to the development of scurvy than tainted water. You will be provided with clear soups, tea, molasses, sugar, cocoa, spruce essence, cider, vinegar and mustard, all necessary for the preservation of health. A sufficient quantity of quinine for cases of sickness is essential. It will be useful to obtain a few barrels of strong beer at the last European port. As a barrel is emptied, pour hot water and spruce essence over the lees, mixed with molasses; this mixture will, in 23 hours, or in hot weather after 10 hours, begin to ferment. It may be used after three days. In this way it is possible to decoct, from the lees of two barrels, about 200 litres of good new beer. On former voyages between St Helena and Copenhagen, the proportion of ingredients required to one barrel of 200 litres was three jars of spruce essence and 54 lb. of molasses, the daily ration issued being half a tankard. As beer is the healthiest drink at sea, it would seem beneficial to give it frequently to the men. This suggestion is laid before you for adoption on your further consideration.

[1] It is generally known that this disease is contracted from a diet which is devoid of fruit and green vegetables. No complaint is more amenable to treatment both as regards prevention and cure than scurvy—the simple remedy of fresh fruit and vegetables or lime juice being almost immediately effective. The regular issue of lemon or lime juice in the British Navy introduced in 1795 had the effect of practically extinguishing scurvy in the service. Admiral Bellingshausen seems to have taken special care with regard to the feeding of his crew and to their personal cleanliness. He was apparently rewarded for this by a very clean bill of health.

4

The ship's company should not be exposed needlessly in bad or wet weather and must not sleep in the open air. In bright sunshine the head should always be covered. All beds should be aired as often as possible, and fires should be lighted in the lower decks in properly tended stoves, this being the safest means of purifying the air.

5

During your voyage, navigating officers, paymasters and other grades should not be relieved from drill, conforming in this matter to the Imperial Instructions, of which you will receive a copy.

6

The saving of powder, though not unimportant on your journey, should not, however, prevent your carrying out firing practice on your ships, at your discretion. In this matter act according to the Regulations of Peter the Great, as well as in the matter of salutes; for the cleaning of guns, etc., use charges according to the Regulations confirmed by His Imperial Majesty on April 13th, 1804. You must honour all foreign official visitors on board according to their rank as directed in the Code of Peter the Great.

7

On entering a friendly foreign port, either for the purchase of fresh provisions, or for repairs to your vessels, you must promptly notify the local Government there, or the accredited representative of the Russian Court, of your arrival, and inform the Admiralty Council of the well-being of your ships and crews.

8

When you are in foreign countries or amongst natives, deal kindly with all and observe every courtesy and politeness, instilling the same into the minds of your subordinates. No deserters may be received on the vessels under your command, this being contrary to the Law of Nations. Even Russian subjects must not be received on board until after communication with the local Government or the accredited representative of the Russian Court, resident there.

9

In saluting vessels and forts of states with which treaties have not been concluded, proceed according to the Code of His Imperial Majesty Peter the Great, saluting always at such a distance that the discharge may be both seen and heard. Moreover, all treaties and conventions so far concluded, will be sent to you for your information by the Chancellory of the Foreign Office. You must also obtain at Kronstadt, for your information, a copy of the instructions which were issued in 1805 for the use of cruising ships, for stopping vessels coming from ports infected with yellow fever.

10

As your office obliges you to safeguard the honour of the Russian Navy, the Admiralty Council hopes that you will not lose sight of anything calculated to ensure the safety of the vessels entrusted to you; and to prevent any insult; you must maintain your ships constantly in readiness, that no one meeting you may insult the flag or cause injury to the vessels. In case of hostile attack endeavour to defend them as is the duty of a brave and skilful officer. When meeting merchant vessels or sailing with them, take care not to cause them any injury, but on the contrary to lend them every assistance possible.

11

A sum of money will be placed at your disposal for all the needs arising on your voyage. To keep the accounts you should obtain from Kronstadt the necessary account books.

12

As a mark of the confidence which the Chiefs of Administration place in you, you are given the right of distributing, on occasion, yearly, half-yearly and quarterly allowances to all lower grades as rewards (as was formerly done in the case of the sloop *Diana*). To fill any vacancies caused by death, others of the lower grades are to be raised in rank, according to merit. It is permissible to provide the crews, when in any foreign climates, with sea stores and provisions not laid down in the Regulations but warranted by the example of the best navigators, at your discretion. It is also permissible, for the preservation of the general health, to issue, according to circumstances and climate, special clothing, both of linen and other cloths (of which each vessel should have a sufficient quantity), from the ship stores, and to purchase, in case of necessity, further stores and materials for the vessels.

13

In awarding emoluments and allowances, you must be guided by the scale confirmed by His Imperial Majesty on the 10th of June of the current year, of which a copy is attached.

14

Inasmuch as navigation in the seas of both hemispheres must depend on the peculiarities of the climate and seasons of the year, you must be guided by the accounts of voyages round the world of other celebrated explorers; these will serve as examples for the improvement and maintenance of the vessels and crews. Copies of these will be provided by special orders.

15

As regards the aim of your voyages until the time of your return to your European port, you will receive special orders and instructions. The Admiralty Council has therefore only to add that, as a skilful and distinguished officer, you will doubtless perform with exactitude the commission entrusted to you, and follow without hesitation all instructions given in both the Naval Code and the Orders of the Admiralty Council, as also all other ordinances laid down with regard to the command of vessels. By so doing, you cannot fail to justify the confidence reposed in your ability and capacity as leader of the expedition.

3. INSTRUCTIONS FROM THE IMPERIAL ADMIRALTY DEPARTMENT

Since by order of His Majesty you have been appointed to the command of two ships about to depart from Kronstadt for distant seas, and as you have received from the Minister of Naval Affairs all necessary written instructions concerning the arrangements for your voyage and also for all the principal commissions entrusted to you, the Admiralty desires only to give you a few absolutely necessary rules to be followed during your voyage.

(1) The astronomical, mathematical and physical instruments necessary for the purposes of this voyage will in part—as far as they can be provided here—be supplied to you. The others, which cannot be obtained here, you will receive on arrival in England. A letter has been sent to the Russian Ambassador from the Minister of Naval Affairs to arrange for their readiness. All these instruments must be tested by you, and, if any errors are found in them, they must be corrected.

(2) During the expedition, at the expiration of each 24 hours, the dead reckoning and observed position should be determined by bearing and by the distance from some known point, wherever possible one whose latitude and longitude have been accurately determined.

(3) In the event of any great difference between the dead reckoning and observed positions, you should determine its amount, in bearing and distance, and endeavour to discover the source of such discrepancy.

(4) It will be necessary for this purpose to have various charts on which to plot the reckonings, noting at the time both the discrepancies and also which of the charts you consider the most accurate. For this purpose astronomical observations must be made as frequently as possible. You will require charts of all the seas over which you will have travelled before completing your voyages. Many have been supplied to you from the Admiralty, and those which are lacking you can obtain in England from among those published by the British Admiralty.[1]

(5) For the observation of latitude, you must not be content with one observation of the altitude of the sun at noon. The meridian altitude of twilight stars and ex-meridian altitudes of the sun should also be observed, if it should have been impossible to observe at noon owing to clouds.

(6) For the longitude lunar distances should be taken whenever circumstances permit, and the results of these observations should be compared with those given by the chronometers, which latter should

---

[1] At this date the Hydrographic Office of the Admiralty was only just beginning to earn the reputation it has since maintained. Though established in 1795 it was ruled by the masterful and eccentric Alexander Dalrymple, who produced excellent charts but withheld them from issue for many years. His successors were more reasonable, but charts were still produced by semi-official firms such as Cary and Arrowsmith and used by navigators.

be carefully checked before your departure by observations of the altitude of the sun. Even in the course of your voyage, whenever you come near shore or approach within sight of land whose position has been accurately determined, the opportunity of re-rating the chronometers should not be missed.

(7) For the correct rating of chronometers, note the temperature at sunrise as well as at noon, so that, in case of irregularity or disparity in the rate of the chronometers, you can form an opinion whether they may have been due to heat or cold.

(8) All observations for the determination of latitudes and longitudes of places and for the correcting of compasses and chronometers should appear in the log in full detail, so that later, if necessary, it will be possible to verify reckonings by them.

(9) Wherever circumstances and time permit, you should endeavour to take observations yourself of the height of the flood tide and to determine the time of high tide; but where it is impossible for you to do this, on account of the shortness of your stay, then at least obtain information on these points from the pilots. Further, if you happen to observe the structure of any vessels different in any respect from our construction; any special measures used to preserve the timber; vessels constructed in a special manner for special purposes; nautical rules observed in the command or the crew; any new instrument or methods such as may be used with better results than with us; leave nothing undescribed. In addition, you should not only describe, but make drawings of all conspicuous types of vessel observed in different countries and also of the boats used amongst savage races. Endeavour also to collect and bring back to Russia any interesting natural products in duplicate, for the Academy and for the Admiralty. You should also endeavour to bring home any curiosities in the way of native weapons, clothes or adornments.

(10) When you happen to be in parts seldom frequented by navigators, and which have not been fixed as yet by astronomical observations, and of which no hydrographic survey has been made, or if you happen to discover either mainland or islands not indicated on charts, endeavour, as accurately as possible, to describe them, giving the chief points by observing the longitude and latitude, and draw a chart with a view of the coast and details of measurement, especially of such parts as may be useful for shelter. For making such surveys, follow the rules set out in *Marine Surveying* by Vice-Admiral Sarvitchev.

(11) Endeavour particularly to make use of your stay both in foreign possessions and in lands yet to be discovered, for the advantage of future Russian navigators. You will have occasion to discover for yourself the lie of the sea-coast in many places, to make known or even to discover the most advantageous harbours; endeavour to make use of all your leisure moments to describe these and to mark their position on the chart with the necessary measurements, especially with regard to harbours. By detailed information regarding these countries you may discover possibilities of establishing future permanent sea communications or places for the repair of ships. With a view to this, pay special attention to climatic conditions and other details of life there and endeavour to get correct information as to the nature of the soil and its capacity for various products, and the species, peculiarities and quantities of local vegetation, especially the quantity and quality of woods, etc.

(12) Finally, in order that on your return you may be able to compile an interesting and useful account from your notes, do not leave anything without remark that you may happen to observe anywhere as new, useful or interesting, not only with regard to navigation, but as being of general service in the spread of human knowledge in all parts. You will traverse wide oceans and pass many islands and various lands. The diversity of Nature in different places will naturally arouse your interest. Endeavour to describe all this in order to communicate it to future readers of your travels. For this, it is indispensable that you should have the accounts of any noteworthy travels in those places which you will be visiting. By reading them and comparing them with your own personal observations you will be able to note how far they are correct or inaccurate.

(13) Having kept the journal of your voyage in this manner to the end of the expedition, you will finally present it signed to the Admiralty.

(14) In the same way, if any amongst the officers make personal observations and desire to communicate them, these must be placed at the end of the log, with the signature of the officer. For such observations, if they prove useful, the author will receive honour and due thanks.

(15) An astronomer, a naturalist and an artist are to accompany you and will receive special instructions from the Academy of Science. You, on your side, must give them all possible assistance in their work.

The artist must make sketches of any notable places in which the vessels may happen to be and must also make drawings of the natives, of their dress and amusements. Every sort of material collected, its description, all sketches, etc., must on your return to Russia, be handed over by the artist to the Commander of the Squadron, who will submit everything without exception to His Imperial Majesty, through the Minister of Naval Affairs.

(16) As a few of the pupils of the Navigation School go with you, you have, besides keeping constant watch over their conduct, to see that they occupy themselves in the pursuit of studies suited to their profession, so that, through their long absence from the School, they should not forget what they have already acquired, but that rather they should make themselves useful in the Service by the practical experience gained. A copy of these instructions is to be given to the Commander of the other sloop for his guidance.

4. SECOND SERIES OF INSTRUCTIONS FROM THE MINISTER OF NAVAL AFFAIRS

The Imperial Academy of Science, owing to lack of time, has not prepared instructions for the scientific staff in your division about to start on the voyage. Consequently, I am now forwarding herewith, for their guidance, the outlines of a few matters of scientific and artistic interest, trusting to you to inform them that the Minister of Naval Affairs expects from them practical information and the exact fulfilment of all that appertains to their own special branch of the work.

Below are given the outlines referred to:

As you are starting out on this expedition by order of His Imperial Majesty with the aim of acquiring the fullest knowledge of our globe, you are to furnish the scientific staff who are accompanying you with means and frequent opportunities for observations for scientific purposes.

As regards geodetic, astronomical and physical work, no opportunity must be lost of investigating all interesting phenomena pertaining to these sciences. Notes should be taken, and records are to be kept of the conclusions to be drawn from them.

Experiments should be carried out to determine the length of the seconds pendulum in different latitudes in order to ascertain the changes in gravity; to ensure that the results obtained are reliable, the observations should be made with the same instruments and by the same persons and should be repeated with all possible precision in all places where the vessels make a stay.

To fix the longitude is one of the daily tasks of the sailor; the astronomers should also specially and assiduously note it. They are enjoined to preserve their original calculations of the observations obtained by lunar distances from fixed stars. Knowing the predicted time of eclipses occurring in the course of the voyage, and also the places where they will be visible, the astronomers are not to confine themselves only to the determination of the moment of the beginning and of the end of an eclipse, but are also to note the other phenomena of eclipses with all possible detail. Flood and ebb tides deserve special observation; it is necessary to note carefully the time and height of two flood tides in the course of every 24 hours. As regards physics, observations should be made of everything appertaining to the subject, including the variation of the compass. It would be of interest to measure the magnetic force in such places where the greatest or smallest variations of the magnetic needle occur. This section must also keep an accurate record of the height of the barometer at different hours of the day.

The atmospheric conditions and their constant changes are to be carefully noted, as also the direction of the winds at different altitudes in comparison with that near the surface of the sea. The difference in the force of high-level and low-level winds in cloudless weather can be observed by means of small air-balloons which will be provided. Currents in the sea must be observed wherever it can possibly be done, and records must be kept of any such observations. Phenomena such as Meteors, the Aurora Borealis, and the Southern Aurora will be carefully noted, and it is also desirable that their altitude and intensity be noted. It is desirable to make observations of waterspouts, and, as hitherto there has been no agreement as to their cause, endeavours should be made to investigate these phenomena in order to arrive, if possible, at some explanation. Measurements of the temperature of the sea should be made, and of its salinity in different parts and depths, in order to discover the differences in the specific gravity of the water and the degrees of its salinity. The changes in temperature at known depths should also be compared with that noted on the surface of the sea.

Observations should be made on different ice formations, e.g. flat ice, or ice rising up out of the sea, like mountains, in order to throw light on any theories of such formations. In the same way phosphorescence of the sea is to be observed. It would be very interesting and instructive to elucidate the reasons for this with greater detail than has been done hitherto. As regards chemistry, it is necessary to keep in mind throughout the expedition all matters related to this science, to note the colours used by the natives for dyeing their products, the substances from which the colours are obtained, and the methods of their use devised by the natives.

The anatomical section should carry out investigations into everything related to differences in the human race, such as: colour, stature, constitution of peoples, etc., and should attempt to extend research to the inner anatomy should it be possible to obtain bodies for dissection. Enquiry should also be made as to average length of life, and the age at which puberty is attained in both sexes. In zoology all relevant observation should be made and, where possible, specimens should be collected.

In the same way for mineralogy collections should be made. In particular the soil should be studied and its relation to the soils of other lands and in respect of the different layers; in short, nothing in this field of observation should be omitted. Similar efforts should be made by the botanical section so as to gather a collection of plants together with their description, and a collection of samples of every species of tree. It would be useful to know something of the strengths and quality of such species as are so far little known.

The artists have the means of presenting to view in their art all that may be seen in Nature, and an accurate delineation of any rare and curious things worthy of note will be expected from their efforts.

Finally the navigators must not neglect any opportunities for making investigations, notes and observations of anything which may help in the advancement of science in general, or in any one of these branches in particular.[1]

---

[1] One may be permitted to imagine the feelings of the naval captain after reading this comprehensive list of scientific observations to be supervised by him. It was not, however, the first or the last time that such an exhaustive programme was set out by a scientific body and thrust upon an expedition.

[The Narrative]

23rd. The ships were in readiness, except for some carpentering and painting work. By order of the Minister of Naval Affairs, we were towed out to the smaller Kronstadt Road, where we anchored in mid-channel in $5\frac{1}{2}$ sazhen (7 fathoms). The *Otkryitie* and the *Blagonamyerenny*, commissioned for the expedition to the North, accompanied us to the smaller roadstead. The Minister of Naval Affairs was anxious that we should start at an early date and, together with the Commander-in-Chief of the Port of Kronstadt, inspected the vessels, on which work was still proceeding.

24th. On the 24th of June we had the pleasure of seeing His Imperial Majesty at Kronstadt, who had come to see the vessels, which, by his orders, were to carry the Russian flag into the most distant regions of the North and South. His Majesty deigned to honour the *Vostok* and the *Otkryitie* with a personal visit, examining everything and wishing us a most happy voyage. His Majesty then returned to Peterhof via Oranienbaum. Throughout the day the work of the men from the Royal Dockyard was suspended, but on the following day they began again and continued until we weighed anchor.

25th. The Commander of the Second Division, M. N. Vasilev, and I were invited to Peterhof and presented to His Imperial Majesty. On this occasion His Majesty expressed the desire "that during our sojourn amongst both civilized and savage races we should endeavour to gain their affection and esteem; that we should deal as kindly as possible with savage races, and never, except in extreme need, use firearms". We were then presented to the Imperial family and had the honour of being invited to the Imperial table. After dinner we returned on board. The kindness thus shown to us will ever remain in our hearts. Prince Lobanov-Rostovski, who arrived at Kronstadt on his own yacht from St Petersburg, sent me, as a present, a copy of the Voyages of C. Baudin[1] and the Atlas annexed to it. This present was useful at a later date and was all the more welcome to me in that it came as a proof of good wishes for our success in the difficult task before us.

---

[1] *Voyage aux Terres Australes*, 1800–4, by Nicholas Baudin. His ships were the *Naturaliste* and the *Géographe*; most of his survey work was on the southern coast of Australia and Tasmania, where French names are still on the map.

26th. By order of the Imperial Admiralty Council I went to St Petersburg to receive the money assigned to us for pay and other needs. Lieutenant-Commander Zavodovski was ordered meanwhile to do all in his power to complete the work as soon as possible, to take on board powder, gun-charges and fireworks, the latter being for uncivilized peoples we might meet in order to give them an idea of European pyrotechnic displays, especially in places where a hospitable reception might call for recognition on our part. In a word, everything needful to win the esteem and favour of savage races had been foreseen, everything selected of the best quality, and placed on board.

3rd. Having finished my business in St Petersburg, I returned on board and found to my great pleasure that all my orders had been carried out in full and that the vessels were quite ready. The Minister of Naval Affairs arrived very soon. He wished to accompany us for some distance in his yacht. July 4th was fixed for our departure.[1]

4th. At 6 p.m. with a fresh east-north-east wind we passed the bastions of the Central and Commercial Port, where the Commander of the Port of Kronstadt and the Governor, Vice-Admiral Moller, the Officer Commanding the Fleet, Rear-Admiral Korobka, and a large crowd of the inhabitants were all gathered to wish us success and a happy voyage. The spectators waved their caps and cheered us heartily. We replied with five "hurrahs" with a deep feeling of gratitude, and, having saluted the fortress, made more sail. The *Mirnyi* had also weighed and took station astern of the *Vostok*. Our speed and the darkness of the night soon hid from us the spot which seemed to us on that day to be an enchanted one. The second division, the *Otkryitie* and the *Blagonamyerenny*, weighed and passed out astern of us.

5th. On the 5th of July, we had a favourable wind and a clear sky. The ship's company were employed stowing and making everything ship-shape for the voyage. Our speed was so good that at 8 a.m. we were abeam of the Hochland Lighthouse at a distance of 1 mile from the shore, and at 7 p.m. we passed Kokschanky Lighthouse. At 9 p.m. we met the Squadron under the command of Vice-Admiral Kron, which had put out to sea for manœuvres. It consisted of six ships of the line, two frigates and one brig. While mentioning the

---

[1] As explained in the Preface, the Russians did not adopt the Gregorian Calendar until 1923. In the early part of the nineteenth century the English date was twelve days *in advance of* the Russian. Throughout the narrative the date as originally printed is given, so twelve days must be *added* if the corresponding English date is required.

lighthouses, I must add that the accurate lighthouse service in the Gulf of Finland and the careful attention given to the lights, thanks to the efforts of the Director of Lighthouses, Major-General Spafarev, have greatly facilitated navigation in the Gulf of Finland. By day there is no need to worry about the exact reckoning of the ships' course, because the lighthouses are as conspicuous in daylight as they are reliable points at night.

6*th*. At noon by observation we were in Lat. 59° 8′ N. With the lighthouse of Dagerort to southward, we proceeded with a favourable wind at 6½ and 7 knots. At 4.30 we lost sight of the lighthouse, distant about 24 miles. Towards evening the wind fell and we experienced a calm. We were then in sight of Öster-Garnholm.[1] During the three following days we proceeded on our course as well as we could with light variable winds. The *Otkryitie* and the *Blagonamyerenny* were still visible on the horizon. The *Mirnyi* had dropped considerably astern of us. Instead of shortening sail, I ordered the officer of the watch to teach the sailors how to reef and shake out the topsails.

10*th*. In the morning the weather was beautiful. We passed very near the Danish fortress of Christiansö.[2] I saluted with seven guns. They replied with a like number from the fortress. Towards midday, we passed the northern extremity of Bornholm Island at a distance of 1½ miles. However much we tried to distinguish objects on the island, it was impossible to make out anything in the mist and, as the ships were going at a good speed, the island was quickly lost to view. With a fresh cold wind we made 7 knots and at 8 o'clock we passed Falsterbo.[3] From this time we altered course more to the northward, in order to pass into the Sound. At 11 o'clock the wind fell. I made a signal to anchor if possible. The depth was 9 sazhen (11 fathoms), bottom ooze, with sand. The *Mirnyi* came to anchor close to the *Vostok*.

11*th*. At 6 a.m. on the following day, we weighed and tacked up to the first buoy; then a favourable light wind sprang up. Although two hours earlier we had hoisted the pilot jack[4] on the fore topgallant mast, and had fired a gun to show that we required pilots, no pilots came and I decided to proceed without them. Just after passing the

[1] A small island off Gotland. [2] A small islet near Bornholm.
[3] The extreme south-west point of Sweden.
[4] The Union Jack with a white border, which, when hoisted at the fore, denoted that a pilot was required.

first buoy on a shoal to the south of the pilot's village of Dragör, the *Vostok* ran on to the shoal. The buoy may have been displaced by the waves, but more probably the pilots had, for their own benefit, not placed it correctly so as to have the work of and the payment for hauling off any vessels which might run on to the shoal, or for rendering other assistance. I refused their help because I had already lowered the long boat, and I told them I should lodge a complaint with the authorities. Meanwhile other pilots arrived whom we took on board. We laid out the stream-anchor from the stern and very easily got clear. We then proceeded into the fairway and as there was a head wind we anchored.

12th, 13th. On the 12th and 13th, as we had thick weather and a head wind, we remained at anchor.

14th. In the morning we weighed and tacked about with a favourable stream and a light wind. At 5 p.m., passing the buoy off the northern extremity of Mittelgrund, we proceeded into the little roadstead, saluting the fort with seven guns and receiving in return a similar salute. The *Otkryitie* and the *Blagonamyerenny* were already anchored there, their pilots being better than ours. We lay at anchor in the vicinity of the fort.

15th. In the morning, hearing that the Minister Plenipotentiary and Ambassador Extraordinary of our Court, Baron Nikolai, had returned from his country residence, I went with Mr Lazarev to call on him, to enquire about the naturalists, Mertens and Kuntze, and also to request his advice on the best way to obtain as quickly and inexpensively as possible some quantities of rum, wine and vinegar. We were delighted with the kind reception we had on the part of Baron Nikolai. He informed us that he had received letters from Mertens and Kuntze in which they declined to accompany our expedition, giving as a reason the very short time available for the necessary preparations for the voyage and for the journey to Copenhagen. This news was very annoying at this late hour and I immediately begged Baron Nikolai to try to find some volunteer in Copenhagen to take the place of these naturalists. He promised to assist us as we desired, but later he explained that, although he had found a young naturalist who had agreed to the proposals made to him, his parents could not be persuaded to let him go and had sent him out of town. In this way our hopes of making discoveries in the field of natural history were dashed to the ground and we had to console ourselves with the intention of doing our best to collect all we could find and, on our return, to submit it to specialists to distinguish between the known and the unknown. As the voyage continued we deeply regretted, and still regret, that two students of natural history were not allowed to go with us from Russia. They had wished to do so, but had been rejected in favour of unknown foreigners.[1]

During our seven days' stay in Copenhagen we had the pleasure of making the acquaintance of Rear-Admiral Löwenörn, who is the curator of the Royal Archives of Sea Charts, and is indeed a most enthusiastic worker. He provided us with a few indispensable charts, and pointed out to us details of different voyages. He also explained to us the best method of using sextants, and advised us to have a short telescope fitted to ours in Copenhagen instead of a long one. I had this done, merely as a matter of courtesy, as the short telescope was of no real utility. Rear-Admiral Löwenörn also advised us to purchase a machine for purifying water, and took the trouble to find out for us where one was to be obtained. This machine was of great use to us later. Rear-Admiral Löwenörn has no love for the English. With considerable heat he expressed his dissatisfaction with them, on account of the inaccuracies in the charts and almanacs issued by them. Probably the charts obtained by Rear-Admiral Löwenörn were not amongst the best, but the nautical almanacs published in 1816, 1817, 1818, 1819 and 1820 were certainly no credit to the English Board of Longitude,[2] and it is possible that they were the cause of disaster to some vessels. As late as November 1818, errors to the number of no less than 108 were discovered in the 1819 nautical almanac by the Board. It seems that with the death of the astronomer, Maskelyne, who was practically the originator of these useful publications of nautical almanacs, the accuracy which had marked the work at first also ceased.[3] Many, wishing to justify Mr J. Pond, the Chief Astro-

---

[1] It is very rarely that the author permits himself any criticism of his superior officers, but in this particular case events proved the grounds were valid, and the credit of the expedition has suffered in consequence of the lack of scientific results.

[2] The primary purpose of the Board of Longitude, which was in existence from 1713 to 1828, was to encourage and reward the search for a method of determining longitude. In 1767 it was saddled with the responsibility of the Nautical Almanac.

[3] The Rev. Nevil Maskelyne, 1732-1811, the father of lunar observations, was Astronomer Royal for forty-six years, from 1765. His passion for accuracy led him into many controversies, especially with regard to the performance of the early chronometers. As a very active member of the Board of Longitude he was the sternest critic of these instruments, but was open to the accusation of bias since he was the champion of the lunar method of finding longitude.

nomer at the Greenwich Observatory, declare that he had no part whatever in these errors and that the mistakes were due entirely to the Board of Longitude themselves. It is difficult to believe, however, that the Senior Astronomer of the Greenwich Observatory, on whom it seems the selection of the members of the staff for the verification of these publications necessarily depended, should not share the responsibility for these inaccuracies.[1]

We visited the Copenhagen Observatory, which is erected on a tower. The ascent to it is by an internal inclined plane, leading up to the top, like the interior of a snail shell. From the top it is possible to overlook the town of Copenhagen with its beautiful environs and the Sound beyond. The instruments seemed to us not very well kept. Possibly their value far exceeded their external appearance.

Although the Admiralty Council had given me complete discretion in the issue of the daily rations to the crew, according to climatic conditions and the experience of previous explorers, during the voyage between Kronstadt and Copenhagen I followed the Naval Standing Orders of Peter the Great, i.e. "On Sunday a pound and on four other days of the week 60 zolotnik of beef,[2] boiled in a sort of water gruel. On Wednesday and Friday for dinner boiled peas and, for supper, thick gruel with butter." On arriving in Copenhagen, I ordered the daily ration on both ships to be raised to one pound of meat, and on Sunday one and one-half pounds of meat which was to be prepared with soup made from fresh vegetables and, in addition, a tankard of beer per man. Good and nourishing food is very necessary, especially at the beginning of the voyage. The men are thereby brought into a good condition to withstand all the hardships before them, and it is well to try at the beginning to stimulate the crew a little with luxuries. We filled the empty water barrels and, having washed the crew's linen, we were ready for our long voyage.

19*th*. In the evening we hoisted the pilot jack and, firing a gun, we signalled for a pilot, who arrived at once, and on the following morning at 10 a.m. with an east-south-east wind, we weighed, saluting

---

[1] John Pond, 1767–1836, succeeded Maskelyne in 1811 as Astronomer Royal. He went to Trinity College, Cambridge, where Maskelyne had been 7th Wrangler, but delicate health prevented him from taking a degree. He was known as a very skilful observer and was certainly less interested than his predecessor in the production of the Nautical Almanac.

[2] About 11 ounces.

the fortress with seven guns and being saluted in return with a like number. In the distance we observed that the squadron under the command of Commander Vasilev was also weighing and following us out.

Passing Hveen Island, we noticed a great number of the inhabitants close to a small building which resembled a church in appearance. A steamer and some sailing vessels from Copenhagen with a number of people on board on their way to the island attracted our attention. Our pilot satisfied our curiosity by telling us that the first observatory of the astronomer Tycho Brahe[1] had been erected there, and, in order that this should not be forgotten by future ages, grateful Danes had erected the above-mentioned house, to which an annual pilgrimage takes place on July 19th. It is thus that the great astronomer, who died in 1601, is commemorated not only by scientists but by the people at large. It was a pleasure to us to see this proof of the tribute paid by the Danes to learning.

21st. I have had to pass through the Sound several times in the course of my years of service and I have always looked with the greatest pleasure on its green shores, its gardens, its cultivated fields, the houses of the villagers and the two fortresses, one on the Danish and the other on the Swedish coast. It cannot, however, rival the scenery of the Bosphorus, the like of which can hardly be found anywhere. At Elsinore we changed our pilots, set all sail and, saluting the fort, received salutes in reply, gun for gun. Nowhere is the etiquette of saluting more punctiliously carried out than in Denmark. Passing Kol Lighthouse and having no further need of the pilots, we sent them ashore. At 10 p.m. we passed Anholt Lighthouse at a distance of 10 miles and, having on the following day rounded the Skaw, we passed out into the North Sea.

I had much to arrange for our voyage during our stay in England and therefore considered it necessary to avail myself of the superior speed of the *Vostok* over the *Mirnyi* in order to arrive in Portsmouth ahead of the latter. I had arranged with Mr Lazarev that this should

---

[1] Tycho Brahe, 1546–1601, was responsible for much of the observational work which was so brilliantly used later by the German astronomer Kepler. He was of a vivid personality, somewhat inclined to arrogance and insubordination. Whilst a young man he lost his nose in a duel and therefore wore an artificial one made of copper. He disappointed his family by marrying a peasant girl, but his great qualities attracted the patronage of princes. The King of Denmark gave him the island of Hveen for life.

be our rendezvous and, making more sail, went ahead. A fair wind and beautiful weather favoured us and we stood on under almost full sail until we reached the English shores.

26th. At 8 a.m. we sighted the Galloper Lighthouse to westward at a distance of 11 miles. At noon we met the boat on which the pilot usually comes out to sea and heaves-to, awaiting the opportunity of piloting vessels amongst the shoals. I ran up the jack on the fore top-gallant mast and fired a gun to indicate that I required a pilot, and he arrived immediately, as the pilots are always standing by for a call. There was a very light wind and I wished to enter Deal Roadstead, so as to lie there during the continuance of the contrary stream.

At 10 p.m. with a light wind and a contrary current, we anchored in Deal Roadstead in a depth of $8\frac{1}{2}$ sazhen (10 fathoms), gravel bottom. The North Foreland lay $10\frac{1}{4}$ miles distant from us, bearing N.E. 25°. An officer from an English frigate on guard came on board and, congratulating us on our arrival, asked us the usual questions, whence we came, our destination, etc.

27th. At daybreak, with a favourable current and a head wind, we weighed and set sail. At 12.30 p.m. a contrary current again forced us to anchor in a depth of 17 sazhen (20 fathoms), bottom fine yellow sand and shells. Dungeness Lighthouse was 7 miles distant from us, bearing N.W. 79°. At 6 p.m. we had a favourable wind and current and again set sail. At 8.30 we passed Dungeness Lighthouse at a distance of 2 miles.

28th. In the morning I took another pilot and arranged with him that he should not demand more than the legal English rate of payment from me for bringing us into Portsmouth Road. This pilot was very useful to us during our stay there. On arriving in the Road, all the officers with their telescopes, as usual, began to examine the ships and frigates anchored there, commenting on their beauty and good qualities. We were very glad to see, amongst those lying in Spithead Road, one flying the Russian flag. We could easily guess what vessel it was. We expected the return of Captain Golovnin[1] in the *Kamchatka* on his homeward trip from North-West America. Our pleasure was

---

[1] Golovnin was a famous Russian sailor and admiral. He explored the coasts of Kamchatka and Alaska. He was taken prisoner by the Japanese in 1810 and held captive till 1813. He commanded an expedition round the world during the years 1817–19.

all the greater as this unexpected meeting took place in these foreign waters, where a Russian loves even more, and feels more bound to, a compatriot than at home. As soon as we approached our anchorage, several of the officers of the *Kamchatka* came on board. Our delight at this meeting with our countrymen can easily be imagined.

29*th*. At 7 p.m. we anchored off Portsmouth, in Spithead Road, in a depth of 7 sazhen (8 fathoms), bottom mud with yellow sand and shells. The Officer Commanding the Port, Admiral Campbell, sent a lieutenant to welcome us on our arrival and to enquire whether he could in any way be of service to us. I thanked him for his courtesy and said that the only things we required were provisions of fresh water and fresh food, and that we would be supplied with these through our Consul, Mr March.

At midnight the *Mirnyi* anchored beside the *Vostok*. Mr Lazarev had passed on the other side of Goodwin Sands and, profiting by an unexpected change in the wind, he had not been delayed in Deal Road. The other division under Mr Vasilev also arrived and lay off the Isle of Wight.

30*th*. On the following morning I went with Mr Lazarev on board the *Kamchatka* to visit the officers. I noticed the most remarkable order all over the ship, and that the health of the crew was excellent after their difficult voyage. I was heartily delighted to find colleagues in a handful of enterprising Russians returning from distant lands to the fatherland, well and happy, having acquired fresh knowledge and a great deal of experience. We called on Admiral Campbell to thank him personally for having so kindly offered his assistance on the previous day. The Prince Regent had arrived on his yacht a few days before us at Portsmouth. The yacht was richly gilded and accompanied by warships and a great number of spectators in gaily decorated boats of all sorts. Only in England is it possible to see such a picture of animation. Every time that the yacht passed our ships we manned yards. The crews gave seven hearty cheers and we fired a salute of twenty-one guns.

1*st*. This morning the captains of the ships left by coach for London.

We were anxious to make all preparations for the provisioning of our ships and to proceed on our voyage with all speed, but quite unexpectedly we remained in London for almost nine days. The chronometers[1] and other astronomical instruments kept in readiness for us did not quite meet with our wishes and some alterations, therefore, had to be made. We experienced much difficulty in obtaining sextants ready for use and certain other instruments, as well as the books and charts necessary for the voyage. Mr Troughton, the well-known instrument-maker, satisfied us completely on his part by providing us with the best sextants, transit instruments and very ingenious artificial horizons. Our chronometers came from two makers: Arnold and Barraud. Planimeters and also a few sextants and achromatic telescopes, 4 and 3 feet long, we obtained from Mr Dollond.[2] We obtained our charts for the voyage from Mr Arrowsmith and books from various booksellers. A ready-made pendulum was not to be found, and the makers declined to make a new one as time was too short. I begged Count Lieven to help us to find a naturalist who would be prepared to go with us. Although the celebrated Sir Joseph Banks,[3] President of the Royal Society, at the request of the Count, endeavoured to find someone, in the end, other

[1] At the date of this expedition chronometers, chiefly owing to the industry of British makers, had become fairly well standardized, but they were still far from forming part of the regular equipment of a ship. It was not until 1825, for instance, that they were officially issued to H.M. ships. The care which the commanders of the Russian vessels took over the selection of their chronometers is in pleasing contrast to the story of a British admiral about this time, told by R. T. Gould in his excellent book on *The Marine Chronometer*. On seeing an officer bringing aboard an instrument in a box, he asked what it was. On being told it was a chronometer, he ordered it to be put ashore at once, saying that he would have no necromancy aboard his flagship.

Although individual chronometers by the same maker might vary in performance, it is significant of Captain Bellingshausen's care in selection that Barraud won the prize of £300 in 1822 for the best chronometer of the year's trials, while the firm of Arnold had been the first to produce high-class instruments in numbers during the closing years of the last century.

[2] The firm of Troughton was at this period famous for its accurately divided instruments. Edward Troughton, 1753–1835, with his brother John, paid great attention to the mechanical parts of instruments, but, being totally colour blind, did not attempt to advance the optical side. They designed and made the first modern transit instruments, and they also produced a pocket or box sextant with an arc of only one inch radius. The firm was joined by Simms in 1826 and, under the double name, is still in business. The Dollond firm was more famous for its optical work and were specialists in achromatic lenses.

[3] Sir Joseph Banks was now at the close of his long and distinguished career and he died a year later. He was probably the only one of Captain Cook's officers alive at the time and had he been a little younger he would almost certainly have found some naturalist to accompany the Russians. He himself was on Captain Cook's first voyage only, not the one which explored Antarctic waters, but although he had grown somewhat domineering with age he was still interested in all attempts at scientific exploration.

necessary preparations having been completed, we had to start without a naturalist. Mr Donkin supplied us sufficiently with specially prepared fresh soups with vegetables and beef tea in tins, and also with pinol essence.[1] It seems to me that nothing could have been better than these provisions for the health of the men, setting out for distant lands, and especially for the sick for whom fresh food is undoubtedly the best medicine. Having bought in London everything necessary for our vessels, we returned on the 10th to Portsmouth, arriving there the same evening.

Although we had a great deal to do in London and not a few difficulties to overcome in doing it, we nevertheless had some leisure to see some of the sights of that city, such as St Paul's Cathedral, the Gothic building of Westminster Abbey, with all its objects of interest, the Tower, the ancient fortress of London, Vauxhall and the theatres. We had expected that on our return to Portsmouth we should find there the instruments, charts and books, which we were expecting from London, instead of which we received them through the Russian Consul-General Dubachevski only on the 20th August. During our stay in London work had been proceeding on the ships with great activity and everything had been completed, except certain carpentry work.

On the *Vostok* the alterations in the portholes, which were unsatisfactory, had proceeded very slowly, because Mr March had hired workmen by the day without making any arrangements as to payment for the whole work. The workmen certainly did not lose sight of their personal advantage, and delayed the work in order to receive more pay.

20th. On the 20th August we had the pleasure of seeing the arrival of the Russo-American Company's[2] ship *Kutuzov* which, under the command of Lieutenant-Commander Hagenmeister, had completed a voyage round the world. One could hardly call this a fortunate

[1] A similar assortment of stores was supplied to Parry, who sailed to the Arctic in the spring of that year. Amongst others is mentioned essence of spruce, probably the same as the essence of pinol taken by Bellingshausen. The firm of Donkin and Hall was the first to use tinned iron containers for food products, and they had supplied the Russian explorer Kotzebue for his expedition in 1815.
[2] The Russo-American Trading Company was founded in 1798 at the initiative of a Russian in Kamchatka named Baranov, with fish and fur as its chief interests. It had a large settlement at Sitka on Baranov Island but its activities extended as far south as San Francisco Bay. The Company was wound up in 1867 when Alaska was sold to the United States.

voyage as, in the course of it, they had lost nine of the crew. During the last war between France and England (Napoleonic Wars), the Spithead Road had presented at times a splendid picture of activity. But now the English Fleet "in its white dress" is resting on its laurels. When the ships lie in harbour they are painted white in order that the sun shall not warp the wood. One ship of the line, two frigates and two sloops were anchored near us in Spithead.

25th. On August 25th all work on the vessels was completed, and accounts settled with the Consul. I received no information from London about our naturalist and, as the season did not permit of further delay, I decided to start on our voyage.

I arranged with Mr Lazarev that in the event of our being separated either through storm or fog, we should arrange to await each other in Santa Cruz Road, Teneriffe, where we had to lay in a store of wine for the crew as well as for the officers. In consequence of the hot weather at the time of our departure from Portsmouth, we found it impossible to lay in a store of fresh meat for the crew for more than three days, and only sufficient fresh cabbage for a week, with enough onions to last us until we reached Teneriffe.

26th. At 5 p.m. on August 26th all the boats were hoisted in and on our signal the pilot arrived; we weighed and set out with a light, rather variable, wind from the north-west. At 10 o'clock we were becalmed and this continued until morning, which compelled us to anchor all night in St Helen's Roads. On the following day, early in the morning with a light north-west wind, we weighed and beat up. But the wind held only until noon, when we again had a calm, and the tide forced us to heave to. At 2 p.m. a west wind rose and we again beat up, but to our great delight it soon shifted.

CHAPTER II

VOYAGE FROM ENGLAND TO TENERIFFE AND THENCE TO RIO JANEIRO—STAY IN RIO JANEIRO

1819 AUGUST

29*th*. On the following morning the wind shifted to the east and gradually increased, then eventually settled in the north-east quarter. The *Mirnyi* set all sail, but on the *Vostok* we carried only sufficient canvas to keep just ahead of her.

30*th*. At noon we were in Lat. 49° 46′ 20″ N. by observation; the North Lizard Lighthouse was bearing N.W. 27°, i.e. $13\frac{1}{2}$ miles distant. We proceeded west-north-west in order to get clear of the Channel. In the English Channel close in to the English shore the water is in some places a whitish colour, due probably to the bottom. Passing into the Atlantic Ocean, I ordered the ship's company to be organized in three watches, so as to keep them in good health, and in addition, made the following arrangements:

In the event of any heavy work for any one watch, I ordered that the preceding watch should turn out to their assistance, to give the third watch, which would follow, a period of rest, and that this part of the crew should be employed only in cases of necessity. The officer of the watch was instructed, in case of rain, to see that the crew were, as far as possible, protected against it, so that their clothing should not be soaked. Should they be drenched, they should, on their watch being relieved, change their clothes and not leave them on deck but deposit them in the appointed place. In fine weather the men of the watch on deck should bring up all their shipmates' damp clothing and spread it out to dry. As cleanliness and neatness are necessary for health, I ordered that all linen should be changed twice a week, and strictly insisted upon this, for there is always some lazy member who, wishing to avoid much washing, after putting on a white shirt on Sunday, tries to change again into the soiled one, in order to put on the same white shirt on the following Wednesday evening. This attempt, however, did not often go without its punishment. Wednesday and Friday were set apart as washing days as far as practicable, for on these days only one copper was in use to boil peas for dinner and in the evening a thick soup with beef; to protect the other copper against the action of the fire, it was used for heating the water for the washing. It was ordered that the hammocks were to be washed twice a month, i.e. on the 1st and 15th of the month. The ships themselves and the decks were washed down twice a week when under sail, and every day when at anchor. The officer of the watch had to see that all the crew who were doing the washing took off their boots and rolled their trousers up to the knee. At the end of the washing, all washed their feet in clean water, dried them thoroughly and then put on their boots. Instead of smoking the 'tween decks,[1] I preferred to have stoves lit more frequently which, rarefying the air, changes and dries it and leaves no smuts. In the process of smoking, the smuts stick to the damp deck, walls and everything and provide a greasy surface which attracts and holds the damp. Frequent smoking is consequently harmful to health rather than the reverse. The crew had dinner, as is usual at sea, a little before 12.0 and supper before 6.0, because at 12.0 and at 6.0 the watches were changed, and in this way the coming watch had time to finish their dinner or supper. In fine weather I made it a practice on my ships to have dinner and supper on the quarter-deck and forecastle, in order that the lower deck should remain free of the steam of the cooked food and of all untidiness. The plates and spoons were kept on the upper deck in a special place for them.

No one was allowed to remain below in fine weather from 6.0 p.m. until 8.0 p.m., when the hammocks were triced. During these two hours, as a rule, various of our numerous popular games and amusements were resorted to, such as singing, story-telling, leap-frog, heaters, jumping over each other, dancing, etc., and meanwhile the lower deck was aired. At 8.0 p.m. "Pipe down" was given, and strict watch was kept that each man triced his own hammock in his appointed place and slept neither on deck nor elsewhere. The crew on deck were ordered to keep their heads carefully covered whilst in hot climates and not to sleep or stand about without some sort of head covering when exposed to the sun, which certainly has very ill effects. Below

---

[1] The practice of "smoking the 'tween decks" was a common one in the days of wooden ships for the double purpose of drying and fumigating. When carried out with indifferent fuel it had its disadvantages as above.

decks, on the other hand, they were told to wear neither hat nor cap, so as to prevent their getting into the habit of muffling up the head, and to keep the crew in touch with the ordinary courtesies of the service.

When passing out of the English Channel, I ordered Staff-Surgeon Bergh to examine the crew so as to be quite sure there were no signs of venereal diseases. I was very glad to hear from him that there was not the slightest sign of any infection at all on the *Vostok*. This may be regarded as very unusual, as there are more prostitutes in England than anywhere else, particularly in the chief ports.[1] Mr Lazarev informed me that three of his best men were suffering from venereal infection, but that Dr Galkin had given him hopes that they would be very quickly cured, and this was all the more urgent as the remedies are likely to produce scurvy. Admiral Kruzenstern, at the time of his voyage round the world, did not touch at Portsmouth, but at Falmouth instead, so as to avoid infection. Only a few vessels touch at Falmouth, and therefore there are fewer prostitutes in that town.

There was a fair wind, and we altered course so as to pass Cape Finisterre at a distance of about 60 miles.

1st. At 8 a.m. I ordered course south-south-west. The *Mirnyi* was a long distance astern of the *Vostok*. I signalled to her by gun-fire to alter course as above, but she was unable to make out the signal owing to the distance, and I therefore had the *Vostok* put on a west-south-west course to get nearer to the *Mirnyi*. As soon as she had got closer, I repeated the signal, and both vessels proceeded on a south-south-west course. At noon we were in Lat. 45° 56′ N., Long. 10° 9′ W. From then until 7.0 p.m. the wind fell and finally we were becalmed.

2nd. At noon the wind shifted to the west. We went on another tack and steered southward. Towards 6.0 p.m. the wind shifted to north-east and blew fresher. We altered course to south by west-half-west. We carried little sail on the *Vostok* so that the two ships might proceed at the same speed. This difference in the speed of the two vessels was so marked that they should not have been used together, especially for the very difficult voyage before us.

[1] The Editor finds himself unable to refute this charge as far as the ports are concerned, such references as he can find to the subject tending on the whole to support rather than to rebut the confident assertion of the Russian captain.

3rd. At 7.0 a.m. I ordered two reefs in the topsails in order to wait for the *Mirnyi*. Whilst we were waiting we met two merchant ships beating up, a French brig and a Dutch galleon. At noon we were in Lat. 43° 18′ N., Long. 11° 52′ W., with a fair wind. At 9.0 p.m. and at midnight we sent up blue lights to indicate our positions to each other. The wind brought a heavy sea with it, and the *Vostok* rolled considerably; we were going at 8 knots. We were obliged to double-reef the topsails so as to remain near the *Mirnyi*. From nightfall the wind increased steadily. Although the *Mirnyi* was carrying as much sail as she could throughout the night, still at daybreak, to my regret, she was not in sight, and I had to close-reef the main and fore topsails. At 4.0 a.m. the *Vostok* turned into the wind and the *Mirnyi* was then showing on the horizon for the first time; but a favourable squall quickly brought her up to join the *Vostok* and both ships then turned on their former course, making all possible use of the fair wind.

7th. The fair north-west wind continued until 9.0 a.m. of the 7th, when it began to fail, and at 6.0 p.m. we were becalmed.

In order to soak out the salt from the salt beef and to improve it as food, I ordered the crew to take the quantity required for the daily allowance, place it in a net bag made for the purpose, and hang it from the cap of the bowsprit, so that the salt beef should be constantly washed by fresh waves with the movement of the vessel. By this process the beef is very quickly soaked and more effectively than by the usual soaking in a tub, which generally leaves it fairly salt in the middle and tends to increase the chances of scurvy. Admiral Kruzenstern adopted the same plan on his voyage round the world. The mariner travelling over the open seas has nothing before his eyes but the sea, the sky and the horizon; therefore, every new object, no matter how unimportant, is of great interest to him. So when a rapacious shark (about 9 feet long) appeared, trying to get at the crew's salt beef which was hanging from the bowsprit, as described, every member of the crew crowded to the fore end of the ship and on to the bowsprit to watch. However, his failure to secure the beef and a blow on the back from a harpoon drove him off.

8th. Towards midnight we had a light head wind from the south, and the two vessels were at a considerable distance from each other. We tried to approach one another by tacking, and at noon we were in

Lat. 35° 4′ N., Long. 13° 56′ W. The stream had set us S. 56° E. 14 miles in 24 hours. The mean variation of the compass obtained from six observations was 22° 28′ W. As we proceeded southward, we experienced a great increase in temperature; at noon the thermometer stood at 68° F. and at midnight at 66° F. For this reason I ordered all hands to give up their woollen clothing and to change into summer clothing. During my first voyage round the world, I observed that several of the scientists did not change their frieze suits even under the equator, and that they showed a tendency to develop scurvy. It is true that those who prefer to dress warmly quote as a justification for it, that in hot climates in Asia the natives, amongst whom scurvy is unknown, wear furs. These natives, however, have been accustomed to it from childhood and spend their whole lives on *terra firma* and they are not like the sailor afloat on long voyages, when dress, salt provisions, not quite fresh water, and an atmosphere vitiated by many being crowded together, the smell of the bilgewater, the continual monotony and the consequent depression of spirits, little movement and exercise or too much rolling of the vessel, combine to produce scurvy and tend to spread it.

10*th*. A heavy swell, which set in a few days previously from the north-west, had foretold the strong wind which now began. By noon we were in Lat. 33° 10′ N., Long. 12° 30′ W.; the stream set us S. 80° E. 16 miles in 24 hours. Taking advantage of the north-west wind, we directed our course to Teneriffe. For some days I had noticed in my cabin and all over the ship a smell of putrefaction, and after much searching we discovered that it arose from decaying flour amongst the stores for the officers' mess. This flour had been kept in the gun-room and had become soaked with water which had leaked through the cornice owing to weakness of the stern piece and bad caulking. To prevent this bad air from spreading over the orlop deck and to keep the air in the gun-room and in the bread-room fresh in future, we constructed a ventilating pipe of sheet copper leading from the gun-room through the deck and the Captain's cabin to the quarter-deck. By this means the air below could easily communicate with the air outside.

11*th*. A favourable wind and fine dry weather during the two following days gave us an opportunity to bring on deck for drying all our biscuits and the presents intended for the natives.

13*th*. At noon we were in Lat. 29° 45′ N., Long. 15° 10′ W. After midday, by four computations each taken on five lunar distances,[1] I fixed the mean longitude at 15° 16′ 20″ from Greenwich; the difference between this and the mean based on the three chronometers was 4′ 53″ W. Mr Lazarev, from thirty-five lunar distances taken by him, found the longitude 9′ 6″ more to the east than that given by his three chronometers.

At sunset we sighted the Peak of Teneriffe at a distance of 94 miles. Its height above the visible horizon was 31′ 05″ from an elevation of 16 feet. We estimated the effect of the refraction to be a 13th part of the whole height and from that calculated the height to be 1797 French toises.[2] I do not give this as accurate, and I would add that it is not always possible to rely on such calculations in the case of long distances, as it is impossible to trust the eye, the instrument, or the allowance for refraction.

Humboldt* says that the true height of the Peak of Teneriffe was fixed by M. Borda. This distinguished mathematician made three measurements, two trigonometrical and one barometrical. According to the first measurement, in 1771, the height of the Peak was fixed at 1742 toises; later on MM. Borda and Pingre, observing it from the sea, calculated its height to be 1701 toises; lastly, when M. Borda was on the Canary Island in 1776 with M. Chastene de Puysegur, they undertook new trigonometrical measurements by which the height of

* *Humboldt's Voyages*, Part I, p. 424, "Reise in die aequinoctial Gegenden des neuen Continents", von Humboldt.

[1] The method of finding the longitude by lunar distances came into use in the latter half of the eighteenth century, and was in general use about the time of this voyage.

The angular distance of the moon from certain fixed stars on the Greenwich meridian was calculated and printed in the Nautical Almanac. The distance was observed with a sextant on board the ship and by interpolation from the tables the Greenwich time at that instant could be calculated. The local time would be found by the ordinary means and the difference between the two would give the difference of longitude. The observations had to be very accurately made, an error of as little as one minute of arc in the distance producing an error of as much as thirty minutes in longitude. The computations were also rather laborious. To reduce the error as far as possible it was customary to take a large number of lunar distances and take the mean. For these reasons the method was only open to really competent observers and computers, and it speaks well for the navigators of the Russian ships that so many of the officers were taught the method, and that such reasonable results were attained.

The value of the method in this expedition was not so much to check the chronometers, which were good, as to ascertain which, if any of them, was changing its rate.

[2] A French toise = 6 feet $4\frac{1}{2}$ inches.

the Peak was fixed at 1905 toises, which until now has been regarded as correct. According to barometric measurements made by M. Lamanon at the time of the La Pérouse Expedition in 1785, and according to his calculations, based on the Laplace formula, the height came out at 1902 toises.[1]

14th. We proceeded with a light wind in the direction of Cape Nago (Punta Anaga) and at 6.0 a.m. set a direct course for Santa Cruz Road. The coast between Cape Nago and the town of Santa Cruz consists of heaps of huge rocks, scattered in various positions, in stratifications probably caused by volcanic action like the island itself. We passed the small village of Sant' André lying in a gorge not far from the town of Santa Cruz. We gazed at it through our telescopes with the greatest curiosity, everybody wondering if it could be really true that human beings actually lived there. And indeed, seeing these precipitous, inaccessible cliffs, with here and there narrow gorges and streamlets flowing from the hills, the external view gave no idea of the beauty and abundance of the interior of this island, with its population of 80,000 human beings. At 1.0 p.m. we were within 2 miles of Santa Cruz town; even at this distance all objects were clearly distinguishable. The beautiful town which lay before us was built on the side of the mountain like an amphitheatre, adorned by two high towers, one of which stands at the western side of the town with a colonnade leading up to it. The other stands in the middle of the town, and has a similar colonnade and is surmounted by a cupola. The former marks the Dominican and the latter the Franciscan monastery. Along the shore are four small forts for the defence of the town. The principal one is called San Cristoval, over which the Spanish flag was flying. At one time there had been a small battery on the northern height of the mountain, but it was levelled to the ground by the Governor, the Marquis Cascagigal, because an enemy taking possession of it would have the town at his mercy. The land on the slopes behind the town appeared to be divided into allotments; farther off loomed the purple mountains. When the island is not covered by clouds, which happens now and then in the evening, the silvery summit of the Peak gleams like some huge giant placed on a vast table-land. It receives the first and the last rays of the rising and the setting sun.

At 2.0 p.m. we lay at anchor in a depth of 25 sazhen (29 fathoms),

[1] The accepted height from recent trigonometrical determinations is 12,200 feet or about 1930 toises.

bottom mud and sand, on the same spot where, sixteen years before, the Captains Kruzenstern of the sloop *Nadezhda* and Disyanskoy of the *Neva* lay at anchor.[1] The north-east corner of the island bore N.E. 62° from us, the south-west extremity S.W. 34° and the tower of the former Inquisition, in the town, S.W. 71°.

A small boat flying the Spanish flag came out from the shore to the *Vostok*, with the Captain of the Port, Fleet Lieutenant Don Diego de Meza, on board. He asked the usual questions, whence we came, our destination, health on board, etc. Lieutenant Meza informed us that in Cadiz infectious diseases were rampant and warned us that there were two brigantines tacking about near Santa Cruz Road which had arrived from Cadiz, but the Government would not permit them to enter the Port. To my question, "Would we be allowed to communicate with the shore?" Lieutenant Meza replied that there was nothing to hinder our doing so. Thereupon, I at once ordered a boat to be lowered, and sent Mr Demidov to visit the Governor, Lieutenant-General Chevalier de Laburia, to inform him of the reason of our arrival and to settle the question of salutes with him. Mr Demidov returned from the shore with the report that the Governor had received him very courteously and, concerning salutes, had said that the fort would reply, gun for gun, to our salute. The *Vostok* therefore fired a salute of seven guns, and the fort on which the flag was hoisted replied with the same number. In the evening an officer in the Spanish service arrived from the Governor to congratulate us on our safe arrival. He brought with him, as interpreter in French and English, a certain Don Pedro Rodrigua, a native of Santa Cruz and an agent of the firm Little & Co. This house had done business on the island for the last seventy years uninterruptedly. I asked Don Rodrigua about procuring Teneriffe wine. He readily undertook to do so, and soon obtained wine of the best quality for us at 135 Spanish dollars the pipe,[2] and newer wine at 90 dollars. He also provided both ships with water by his own boats. That cost us in all £11. 2s. 0d.

15*th*. On the following morning I went ashore with Mr Lazarev to the Governor, who received us with the greatest courtesy, declared

---

[1] Bellingshausen was a junior officer on the *Nadezhda* at the time, and of his selection Kruzenstern wrote as follows: "The choice of Baron Billingshausen, my fifth lieutenant, I made without being personally acquainted with him. His reputation as a skilful and well-informed officer in the different branches of navigation induced me to propose to him to sail with me."

[2] A measure equivalent to a "butt" of ale or beer, containing about 120 gallons.

his readiness to render any assistance and said he had received instructions from his Government to this effect. Thanking him, I asked if he would have a place appointed where it would be possible to have our chronometers corrected. I also sought permission for some of the officers to go sight-seeing in the interior of the island. The Governor granted these requests, and added: "I well know the unrivalled hospitality of Russians and I am very glad that now, in my old age, I have an opportunity of being of service to them." We were astonished to see among the orders he wore the Russian military Order of St George, fourth class. This estimable old gentleman informed us that he had been in the Russian service under the Empress Catherine II, took part in the battle against the Swedes, under the command of the Prince of Nassau, and shared the victories of Field-Marshal Rumyantzov, of whom he spoke a good deal. He seemed delighted to remember that the cross for gallantry and merit was given him personally by the great Empress. On my return on board the *Vostok* I ordered the officers and crews of both vessels to attend a service of thanksgiving on the anniversary of the coronation of His Imperial Majesty, Alexander Pavlovich I. To the sound of "Ad multos annos" we dressed ships and fired salutes from all the guns. The officers and crews of both vessels were entertained to dinner on the *Vostok*. Over and above the ordinary allowance, a glass of hot punch was served out to each man after dinner.

Permission was granted to some of the inhabitants of the island to come out on boats with fruit for sale provided they did not, at the same time, bring alcoholic liquors. I permitted the purchase of fresh fruit at all the ports, knowing from experience that it is more useful for purifying the blood and hence is also a preventive against the tendency to scurvy. To test our chronometers, the house of Naval Captain Don Antonio Rodrigo Ruiz was assigned to us. The flat roof of his house seemed to be fairly suitable for taking observations, but on account of the great vibrations produced by the slightest movement and even by the sea breeze which is always fresh at noon, I only set up the clinometer in order to obtain the magnetic variation; the instrument, however, gave impossible readings. After several experiments, we found that in the stucco of the walls and roof there were quantities of fine iron particles. Whilst walking through the town I had carried a pocket compass which dipped towards the ground at various points in the streets; at all these places there were great quantities of iron particles which affected the magnet. I gave orders for sand to be brought on board from the seashore and found that that too was full of iron. A quantity of this sand, which I brought back with me to St Petersburg, is deposited, one portion in the Museum of the Imperial Admiralty Department, another in the Mineralogical Cabinet belonging to M. Rozenberg, and a third in the Collection of the St Petersburg Mineralogical Society. Very probably the whole of the volcanic island of Teneriffe abounds in this sand, and for that reason I believe all observations of the magnetic needle taken on the shores of the town of Santa Cruz to be worthless.[1]

Upon request, we were allowed to take observations from the fort of San Cristoval to correct the chronometers, but as the sun was frequently hidden by clouds at the time, the correction of the chronometers was not of the best.

The Commander of this fort, Don Jose de Monteverde, received us in a very friendly way. He was married to a relation of the Russian Lieutenant-General Bethencourt.

Santa Cruz is now one of the nicest small towns. The streets are well paved; the principal square is almost completely paved with large flagstones like the foot pavement, and the people saunter about here in the evening. The large numbers of monks as well as of prostitutes which have always been noted here by other travellers no longer exist. The former are no longer seen as the Archbishop and the Inquisition have now moved to the island of Grand Canary, and many of the monks died of plague in 1810. Probably the same epidemic also reduced the number of prostitutes, and the severe measures taken by the Government have prevented a recrudescence.

The town market-place is embellished by a marble cross and a marble figure of the Blessed Virgin with cross in hand, who, according to tradition, appeared in the sea town of Candelaria.[2] On the pedestal the Guanches, the original inhabitants of the island, are represented receiving the Christian Faith and turning their gaze on the Holy Mother. It is all made of the finest white marble brought at great

---

[1] The magnetic quality of the soil was first noted by La Pérouse and is referred to by Kruzenstern on his voyage sixteen years earlier than this date.

[2] This is a reference to the story that in about A.D. 1400, and at least 100 years before Christianity reached Teneriffe, a wooden image of the Virgin and Child was found on the seashore. It was handsomely clothed and the figure bore a candle in one hand. It was venerated by the natives and subsequently became associated with miracles, under the name of Our Lady of the Candle. The image is still in existence.

expense from Genoa, and dedicated to the town by a native of Santa Cruz, Montaniego.

There are two monasteries here, a Franciscan and a Dominican. In the former there are only four friars and in the latter six. They appeared to us to be in poor circumstances. Their numbers do not increase, because they receive practically no offerings from the inhabitants, who show themselves much more independent of the clergy than in other Spanish colonies. The houses in Santa Cruz are all built of stone, the lower part of hard stone and the upper of a soft kind. The best houses have flat roofs surrounded by low walls, 3 feet high, so that the roof takes the place of a balcony in fine weather, which is almost continuous in Santa Cruz. During the rainy season, the water which collects on the roof is led down through conduit pipes into cisterns, which are attached to almost every house, so that in the event of a drought in the summer, or if the pipes bringing water from the mountain should happen to be damaged, they should not suffer from lack of water. The inhabitants of the island of Teneriffe are said to number about 80,000. In the town of Santa Cruz there are 9000,[1] almost all of Spanish extraction, as the greater part of the original race of the Guanches have died out and the remainder have intermarried with the Spaniards. The military forces on the island number some 4000. The men and women of the better class dress as Europeans; amongst the common people the men all wear a short jacket, and the women a thick white woollen shawl, over which they put on a man's round hat; in this attire with their swarthy faces they certainly are not prepossessing. We made the acquaintance of the Mayor of the town, Don Juan Megliorina, during our stay at Santa Cruz. He is of Italian extraction. He invited us to see his natural history collection, and we greatly enjoyed examining the many specimens from all parts of the world which he had been at great pains to collect. He is very expert at stuffing specimens, and all the animals and birds in his collection were stuffed by himself. Amongst all the curios he showed us, the most curious was a Guanche mummy, with a few skulls and other parts of human bodies found by chance in caves; their pottery and the grindstones they used were also interesting. Judging from the mummy and the other various parts, as also from the description of Humboldt, it is to be concluded that they were not a people of large stature.

[1] The present population of Santa Cruz is 58,200 and of the whole island of Teneriffe, 93,709.

A number of baked objects and some lava from the Peak, together with a few migratory birds from Africa, were all that Mr Megliorina had been able to collect on the island of Teneriffe. Poisonous snakes and other reptiles do not exist on the island according to his statement.

Horses, camels, donkeys, horned cattle of every species, pigs, rabbits and other animals have been introduced to the island by the Spaniards. Donkeys and camels are chiefly used for driving and carrying heavy loads, as the roads leading to Santa Cruz are very mountainous. The view from Santa Cruz Road does not present the island of Teneriffe to the best advantage. Bare heights surround the town; a few of those to the east are precipitous, completely sterile and scarred with deep ravines. All this affords, it would seem, no convenience to the inhabitants of the island. Many of our officers, viz. the astronomer Simanov, Lieutenants Obernibessov, Lyeskov, Annenkov and Demidov, made use of the three days' leave granted to them to go to the town of Orotava and see the view from the opposite side. On their return they stated that the Orotava Valley was extremely beautiful and abounded in all the gifts of Nature. They had had the pleasure of seeing the place which had once belonged to the conqueror of the island of Teneriffe, Jean de Bethencourt,[1] and which now belongs to his descendants. The very remarkable dragon tree[2] growing not far from Señor de Bethencourt's estate had attracted the attention of the officers; the trunk was 36 feet in circumference at a height of 10 feet above the ground. In the Crimea, on Major-General Govorov's Albat estate, there is an oak, fully grown and of certainly not less astonishing proportions than this tree; this also, at 5 feet from the ground, is 36 feet in circumference. This oak is of especial interest, in that the Empress Catherine II and the Austrian Emperor Joseph II lunched in its shade when travelling through the Crimea. During our five days' stay in Santa Cruz there was always a land breeze at night, and at about 6.0 a.m. there was a fresh north-east wind from the sea, continuing all day. In the evening the wind fell.

[1] In 1404 the King of Spain granted the conquest of the Fortunate Isles to a French knight named Jean de Bethencourt, with the title of King of Canaria. He duly subdued the islands though his descendants lost the title.

[2] A tree which grows to a large size though the wood is light and spongy. It exudes the gum known as dragon's blood. This particular tree at Orotava was for many years the meeting-place of the national assembly, before the conquest by the Spaniards. It was injured by a severe storm in 1827 and destroyed by another storm in 1851.

From observations made in the roadstead on the *Vostok*, we found the latitude of our anchorage to be 28° 28′ 30″ N.; mean longitude from the three chronometers 16° 11′ 57″; by lunar distances on six calculations, each on five distances, 16° 17′ 29″ W. From observations on the *Mirnyi* the latitude of the anchorage was found to be 28° 28′ 25″ N. The longitude by Barraud's chronometer 16° 23′ 45″ W. From four reckonings, each on six lunar distances, 16° 14′ 30″ W. Compass variation 20° to the west.

The badly built quay is insufficient to accommodate in-coming rowing boats. The fresh sea breeze blowing in all day causes a heavy sea. The quay of the town is consequently always swept by surf and is very inconvenient for landing. I record here observations of atmospheric temperature and of variations in the course of the day, made at intervals of six hours during our stay of four days; the following average values were obtained: Thermometer: At midnight 71° F.; at 6.0 a.m. 72° F.; at noon 78° F.; at 6.0 p.m. 73° F. The least variation of the thermometer from the mean readings was at night. The difference from the average in the course of the 24 hours was half a degree. The greatest variation was at noon, the difference from the average being three degrees. Barometer: At midnight 30·18; at 6.0 a.m. 30·16; at noon 30·21; at 6.0 p.m. 30·15. It stood highest at noon and fell lowest at 6.0 p.m.

19*th*. Having procured a store of such provisions as the island abounds in, filled up all the barrels with water, and having completed all other necessary arrangements, we weighed anchor at 9.0 a.m. on the 19th and with a light land breeze set our course to give a wide berth to the island of Grand Canary so as to avoid being becalmed in its vicinity. At 1.0 p.m. the wind shifted to north-east with sufficient strength to enable us to proceed at 5 knots. In the evening in Lat. 28° 1′ N., Long. 16° 16′ W., on a south by west course we had a magnetic variation of 20° 12′ W.

20*th*, 21*st*, 22*nd*. During the 20th, 21st and 22nd the strong swell from the north continued; with this and the north-east trade wind our rate was from 5½ to 7 knots. We took our course direct for the western side of the Cape Verde Islands. On the 22nd at 3.0 p.m. we crossed the line of the northern tropic in Long. 21° W., and thus entered the so-called torrid zone. The thermometer at midday indicated 77° F. and at midnight 72° F.; the wind fell somewhat and we lost the satisfaction of making speed.

24th. This morning at daybreak for the first time we observed some bonito fish (*Scomber pelamis*), which seemed to try to stop the progress of the ships; one was struck by a harpoon but, to our general regret, it wriggled off the harpoon, and we had to do without excellent fish soup. Together with the wounded fish, all the other bonitos retired to a distance from the ship. The continuous fine weather had dried the cables, and as there would be no need to use them until we reached Brazil, I ordered them to be detached and removed so that the ends should not become worn needlessly and to make more room on deck.

25th. At noon we were in Lat. 21° 29' N., Long. 23° 15' W., and observed flying fish for the first time. It was my intention whilst passing through the region of the trade winds to replace all the topmasts by the spare ones, which had been made at my request in Kronstadt and which were $3\frac{1}{2}$ feet shorter than the original ones. It was now a convenient time to have this done, and, as the *Vostok* had considerable advantage in speed over the *Mirnyi*, I hoped that the work might not delay the voyage. In order that the crew should suffer less from the great heat whilst carrying this out, I decided to spread the work over three days. On the first day the mizzen topmast was changed, on the second, the fore topmast, and on the third, the main topmast. The sails were likewise removed and replaced. I preferred to have all this work done at sea, as there are always things to be done when lying in port.

26th. On the 26th in Lat. 16° 09' N., Long. 26° 37' W., we observed the variation to be 14° 51' W. Before noon by lunar distances from the sun on the average of three calculations, we found our longitude to be more to the eastward than that shown by the chronometers; the difference with chronometer No. 722 was 10' 16"; with No. 518, 18' 22"; and with No. 2110, 15' 44". From similar observations, Mr Lazarev found the longitude to be 10' 22" more to the eastward than that indicated by chronometer No. 920.

27th. Continuing our route to westward of the Cape Verde Islands, we passed the southern extremity of the island of San Antonio on the 27th at a distance of 100 miles. Following the example of other navigators, I took a course south-south-east-half-east. We observed a duck which flew several times round the ship, from which it may be concluded that these birds find their way out to sea a distance of 100 miles and probably even farther. Bonito fish in great numbers followed us; we tried to catch some with hooks, but were unsuccessful. The strength of the bonito is quite surprising. They leap out of the water, chasing the flying fish, which seem destined to be a prey in both elements. In the water the bonitos devour them, and if they save themselves by jumping out of the water, the Tropic bird[1] (*Phaethon aethereus*) and other birds catch them in flight. Many flew on to the chain-plates at night and were found there in the morning.

29*th*. From our departure from Teneriffe to the 29th September, the stream had set us continually towards the south-western quarter, i.e. parallel to the African coast which lay to the east. During this time, in each 24 hours, the stream flows 10 miles to the east. The stream, setting south parallel with the shore, is connected with that known as the Florida Stream (Gulf Stream). The trade winds between the two tropics drive the waters of the Atlantic Ocean continually from east to west, which finally reach the shores of the continent of America where the Gulf of Mexico lies. This water, passing along to Cape San Roque, sets the stream running in a north-westerly direction parallel to the shores of South America; by passing between the islands of the Caribbean Sea, San Domingo and Jamaica, between Capes Catoche and San Antonio, it enters the Gulf of Mexico and, filling it, continues in a direction parallel to the curve of this gulf. It then passes round the Florida Peninsula, out through the Bahama Channel (Straits of Florida), and, when parallel with the eastern shore of Florida, turns north-east following the line of the eastern shores of North America. When approaching the Newfoundland Shoal, it is reinforced by the current or stream of the St Lawrence River and thus receives an easterly direction and, as it leaves the coastline, spreads out like the top of a palm tree. The northern branch of this stream reaches the western shores of the British Isles, the middle one goes direct east and the southern one spreads out between the Azores to the south-east and then runs along the western shores of Africa, replacing the waters of the ocean as they are driven to the west, in the northern hemisphere by the north-easterly trade winds and in the southern hemisphere by the south-easterly trade winds.

30*th*. At noon we caught a glutton fish[2] on a hook and brought it

---

[1] *Phaethon*, of which there are three species, owe their name to the fact that they are rarely found outside the tropics. They have two of the tail quills longer than the rest which gives them a characteristic appearance.

[2] A shark.

on deck along with a sucking fish (*Echeneis remora*). The latter is always found near the former, feeds on the remainder of its prey, attaches itself to it with its sucker, and keeps near it as a protection from other fish which are always afraid to approach the glutton fish. The latter, in spite of its greediness, does not appear to harm the sucking fish. Knowing that the glutton fish can be eaten, I advised the sailors not to despise this food. Mr Mikhailov sketched both fish, and Staff-Surgeon Bergh removed the skins and prepared them for preserving. On the same day we saw another slippery sea creature called a "Portuguese Man o' War" or nettle fish (*Physalia*). The rate at which the ship was going did not permit us to observe this beautifully coloured creature in detail.

1*st*. The trade wind from east-north-east continued light. During the night the sky was bright, but there were heavy clouds to southward lit up by flashes of heat lightning. At 9.0 a.m. the wind freshened and a heavy downpour of rain began. In order to catch as much rain water as possible, the order was given to stretch the quarter-deck awning which had been kept ready, and to let down sleeve-pipes, sewn on to it and held in position by cannon-balls. Orders were given for all the linen to be washed on deck by the crew. We gathered enough rain water to fill two barrels and ten ankers [small casks of 10 gallons each], and it was used later on for the animals and birds.

2*nd*. At 3.0 a.m. the north-east wind shifted to south-east and the north-east trade winds now ceased. Our Lat. was 10° 43′ N., Long. 23° 52′ W. The thermometer indicated 83° F. at noon; at midnight in the open air 78° F.; below decks where the crew slept 82° F.

3*rd*. The wind, which had been gradually changing, now shifted to the east. We continued on a southward course at from $4\frac{1}{2}$ to 7 knots.

4*th*. We heard thunder from eastward from midnight onwards. There were heavy rainclouds, and sharp squalls swept across ahead and astern of the vessels, which, however, remained untouched by them; at night we observed a great deal of phosphorescent light on the surface of the sea proceeding both from very small points and large shining bodies. This impressive sight presents a striking spectacle. In the sky countless stars are seen and on the sea a mass of quivering sparks of light, which increase in brilliance in the neighbourhood of the ships and form a gleaming river of light astern. On beholding this sight for the first time, one is amazed at, and enchanted by, its rare beauty. The phosphorescent light is, as is well known, produced by vast numbers of tiny creatures (mollusca). In order to catch some of these sparks and larger shining bodies, we lowered a bunting-sack attached to a rope into the water from the stern of the vessel. On pulling it out again, we found a number of shining creatures of varying sizes; the *Pyrosoma*[1] especially attracted our attention by their brightness. They are sometimes as much as 7 inches in length, and $1\frac{1}{4}$ to $1\frac{1}{2}$ inches in diameter; one end is rounded and at the other there is an opening inwards which extends almost the whole length of the body; on the outside there are excrescences of various sizes. When lying still in the water, these creatures look as if they were made of glass and sometimes seem to lose their light. After a little time a light begins to shine from the excrescences and soon the whole creature appears lit up, after which the light gradually fades away, only to be renewed at the least quiver of the water; these changes go on continually until the creature dies, when the light vanishes. As an experiment we gave the cat a large piece of this *Pyrosoma* to eat; it ate it very willingly and seemed to suffer no ill effects. Perhaps it is not harmful therefore to human beings and might even prove to be nourishing.

During our voyage we always had a net hanging at the stern to catch such species of sea creatures. Curiously enough, they were caught only when it was dark, but during the day we very rarely saw any of them in the water. One might conclude from this that the *Pyrosoma*, having light of its own, avoids the light of the sun or the day, which they probably find unbearable, and therefore sink down during the daytime into the depths where the light does not affect them so strongly. I merely mention this at some length as we had no naturalist on board who, concerned only with his own subject, might have been able to give the whole of his attention to this matter.

5*th*. The frequent rainclouds and squalls which now accompanied us gave us warning of the end of the north-east trade winds, and at 6.0 a.m. of the following morning, when we were in Lat. $7°\,40'$ N., Long. $22°\,12'$ W., we encountered a light south-easterly wind in place of the trade wind. Although it was a fair wind, it was nevertheless

---

[1] At this date naturalists were beginning to pay considerable attention to phosphorescent forms of life. At sea it is chiefly the jellyfish (Medusae) and the combjellies (Ctenophores) which give rise to the larger flashes of light. *Pyrosoma* belongs to the latter class. The small "sparks" referred to by our author are due to many kinds of small flagellates, of which *Noctiluca* is the best known. The *Challenger* naturalists caught a specimen of *Pyrosoma* over 4 feet in length, of which Moseley writes: "I wrote my name with my finger on the surface of the giant *Pyrosoma*... and my name came out in a few seconds in letters of fire."

very light and consequently in the course of the next 24 hours we made but little progress. We took advantage of the fine weather to lower a boat. Mr Simanov and Mr Paryadin took soundings from it with a thermometer—purchased from Professor Norie[1] in London—attached to the lead. The difference in the temperature of the water appeared to be as follows:

$$\begin{aligned}
\text{At a depth of 290 sazhen (375 fathoms)} &= 79\tfrac{1}{2}° \text{ F.} \\
\text{On the surface of the water} &= 82\tfrac{1}{2}°. \\
\text{In the shade} &= 85°.^{[2]}
\end{aligned}$$

About noon the temperature was as much as 87° F., which was the highest we had as yet experienced. Although I had warned Mr Simanov not to touch sea nettles (*Physalia*) with his hands, nevertheless out of curiosity he did so and was stung much more severely than if it had been an ordinary land nettle. He had large blisters on his hands and suffered from excessive itch.[3] Two miles to leeward we observed a waterspout, and could clearly see the foam on the water in its vicinity. It is known that such waterspouts can be scattered by cannon balls and that even the vibrations of the air arising from the firing alone are sufficient to destroy this dangerous phenomenon.

6th. Before nightfall we observed several fountains produced by the spouting of large fish of the whale species. On dragging up the bunting sack which we had lowered into the water astern, we found a quantity of transparent globular organisms which emitted a light in the dark; they were up to about one-fifth of an inch in diameter.

7th. From this date onwards we found ourselves in the calms and light winds usually encountered near the equator. At noon we were in Lat. 7° 14′ N., Long. 22° 11′ W. The current had taken us off our course 10 miles to the north-west. At noon in the shade in the open air the mercury went up to 87° F.; at midnight in the open air it stood at 80° F. and below decks in the crew's sleeping quarters at 83° F.

---

[1] J. W. Norie was an authority on navigation. Besides publishing tables he wrote the *Epitome of Navigation*, published in 1803 and still in use in later editions.

[2] These figures would not be accepted now, the decrease of temperature with depth being much more marked. The error is due to the pressure of the water affecting the bulb of the thermometer. It was not until fifty years later that satisfactory temperatures at considerable depths were obtained. Applying the usual gradient the true temperature at 375 fathoms was probably about 55° F.

[3] The sting of the Portuguese man-of-war (*Physalia*) is very severe and has been described as giving rise to "a maddening pain which lasts for many hours".

These temperatures are also reached in St Petersburg in the summer, but only for a few hours in the afternoon, and then they are followed by beautifully cool evenings. Here, however, there is very little change night or day; during the evening the water on the surface of the sea is at times warmer than the air, and in the mornings the air is warmer than the water; as a result the average conditions are almost the same, and it is therefore impossible to escape from the great heat, equally oppressive in both air and water, especially during a long calm when there is very little movement on the surface of the sea, which is then filled with large numbers of various kinds of gelatinous organisms which, on decaying, vitiate the atmosphere.[1] In the locality in which we now were, clouds are brought up from both hemispheres by the trade winds; viz. by the north-east wind from the northern and by the south-east wind from the southern hemisphere. These clouds meeting produce what are known as the equatorial torrential rains, which slightly cool the atmosphere; the huge rain-drops, falling into the sea, produce at the same time some movement on the surface, changing for a time its absolutely motionless aspect, and they cleanse the water of all decaying matter.

8th. Owing to the calms which now commenced, we proceeded very slowly, and at noon on the 8th October, we were only in Lat. 5° 32′ N. and Long. 20° 53′ W. At 6.0 p.m. we let down the lead with a tin cylinder containing a thermometer attached. This cylinder had been made on board and resembled the instrument by which water is brought up from any depth. This test showed that at a depth of 310 sazhen (360 fathoms) the temperature of the water was 78° F.; the water at 80°.6 had a specific gravity of 1·0895; the same quantity of water obtained from the same spot on the surface of the water, at a temperature of 82°, had a specific gravity of 1·0883. Concerning this, it may not be superfluous to remark, that the water collected in the cylinder at a depth of 310 sazhen (360 fathoms) however quickly raised, may, in passing up through the water to the surface, have had time to be warmed a little, and also that, owing to possible imper-

---

[1] A prolonged calm with its absence of agitation of water against the air leads to an exhaustion of oxygen in the upper layers of the water and hence wholesale death for the plankton or floating organisms. Compare *The Rime of the Ancient Mariner*:

> The very deep did rot: O Christ!
> That ever this should be!
> Yea, slimy things did crawl with legs
> Upon the slimy sea.

fections in our cylinder, made on board, a little water from a lesser depth might have got in, thereby slightly changing the original density and temperature. In order to observe the current, a copper kettle of the capacity of 8 vedro (a vedro = 2·7 gallons) was let down to a depth of 50 sazhen (58 fathoms) to keep our long boat stationary, and by using a logline, the stream appeared to set us north-east 9 miles in 24 hours. During the calms, we made a few experiments to assure ourselves that it was possible to obtain water in a bottle from a depth of from 30 to 40 sazhen (35–47 fathoms) by the following means: Take an empty porter bottle, cork it carefully, attach it to the lead and lower it into the water to the above-mentioned depth. On bringing up the bottle, it will be found to be full of water and still tightly corked, the only difference being that the cork is inverted.

9th. The General Staff-Surgeon of the Fleet, Mr Leiton, had commissioned Mr Lazarev to try the above experiment. We lowered the corked bottle to a depth of 200 sazhen (230 fathoms), but as the bottle had not been tightly corked, the cork came out at that depth. This induced Mr Lazarev to try the experiment again. He corked the bottle himself, cut a cross on the outside of the cork, tied a fourfold thickness of cloth over the cork and lowered the bottle into a depth of 200 sazhen (230 fathoms). When raised, it was full of water, the top of the cover was torn, the cork was in its place but was upside down and driven so tightly into the neck of the bottle that it was hardly possible to pull it out with a corkscrew. I confess that at first this completely dumbfounded us all, but after many experiments made at different depths, we concluded that the warm air in the bottle, on its reaching depths at which the water is much colder, contracts, and that thereby the cork is sucked into the bottle, which then fills with cold water. During the raising of the bottle, under the action of the rising temperature of the water, the cold water in the bottle becomes warmer, requires more space and thus forces the cork back into position. As, however, the lower end of the cork is thinner than the upper and therefore occupies less space in the neck of the bottle, the cork is forced into the neck more easily upside down.[1] On repeating this experiment at different depths in the ocean, we convinced ourselves that this was the invariable result when lowered, as described,

---

[1] The explanation given is, of course, the correct one, except that he ascribes too much of the effect to change of temperature and too little to change of pressure.

to depths of 30–40 sazhen (35–45 fathoms), but that it does not occur at less than 30 sazhen (35 fathoms). We did not make any similar experiments in shallower seas where the temperature of the water at different depths has a different relation to that of the surface from that which holds in the case of the ocean, but probably similar results would be obtained there also on lowering the bottle to a greater or lesser depth. Such experiments, which at first sight may seem of little importance, may ultimately lead to discoveries of great moment, just as the apple falling from the tree gave the great Newton the idea of the system of gravitation.

As we were now approaching a position in which French navigators in 1796 reported having found a shoal, which is indicated on the Purdy[1] chart in Lat. 4° 52′ 30″ N., Long. 20° 30′ W., I thought it well to try and verify the existence of this shoal and fix its position. We ascertained that it existed only on the chart; both vessels passed directly over the position with a fair wind, then hove to and cast the lead, but at 90 sazhen (105 fathoms) there was still no bottom, nor could we see any change in the colour of the water, which usually marks the position of a shoal. Many such banks and rocks are indicated on the charts in the vicinity of the equator, but they do not exist in actuality; Mr Arrowsmith, the hydrographic publisher in London,[2] has therefore very wisely omitted the greater part of these from the new editions of his charts.

10th. We passed, on this date, an American three-masted ship which was making for America. We were carrying very little sail, as we were waiting for the *Mirnyi*, at that time a considerable distance astern of us. For three days we had had light variable winds, accompanied by frequent rains. We succeeded in shooting a few small storm birds, sometimes called weather-birds (*Procellaria pelagica*), as they flew near the ship. Their flight is similar to that of a swallow; in general, their feathers are black except for a white patch about 1½ inches above the tail; the upper mandible is not much bent, but the nostrils are of tubular shape; the legs are black, with yellow webbed

---

[1] Purdy was one of several firms of cartographers in London which, even after the establishment of the Admiralty Hydrographer in 1795, continued to collect information and publish charts in a semi-official capacity.

[2] Aaron Arrowsmith, 1750–1823, after serving in the firm of Cary, set up for himself as a map engraver, to be succeeded by his two sons and nephew, John, who was one of the founders of the Royal Geographical Society. Their charts, like Purdy's, had a semi-official character until the Hydrographic office of the Admiralty became firmly established.

feet.[1] The weather-bird is about the size of a swallow and receives its name from the idea that its presence near a ship is a warning of a coming storm. We observed on the contrary, however, that these birds flew around the ship when a calm set in and continued for some time. We shot a few weather-birds, skinned them and tried to preserve the skins for our return to Russia. Staff-Surgeon Bergh on the *Vostok* and Dr Galkin on the *Mirnyi* willingly undertook the work of preserving such rarities during the course of the voyage.

13*th*. The wind often shifted from south-east by south to south by west: rain fell and there was a heavy swell from the south, which predicted the speedy setting in of the southern trade winds. Land swallows accompanied us, fed on midges near the ships, perched at night in the rigging and not infrequently flew into the officers' cabins. The nearest land was about 600 miles distant. These birds cannot, therefore, be taken as an indication of the proximity of land. Whilst the calms continued, we experienced currents from various directions, a fact which showed that their irregularity was due partly to the prevailing winds of the adjacent localities, owing to the configuration of the African coast which was the coast nearest to us, and partly due to the unevenness of the sea bottom.[2] Whilst the vessels remained in this belt of calms, i.e. for twelve days, we experienced thunder, lightning and sheet-lightning almost daily. On account of the calm, the wind sails contributed very little towards ventilating the ships, and we therefore had fires lit on both between decks during the day. This is necessary near the equator during the calms, as the damp is so great that boots, kept even on the deck and in the officers' cabins, were covered with mould in two days. During the day in the hot climate, the poop, quarter-deck, midships and forecastle were protected from the sun's rays by awnings which were kept up from morning till night.

14*th*. On the 14th at noon, by which time we had reached Lat. 3° 10′ N., Long. 19° 19′ W., the calms and the variable winds came to an end; at first a light south wind set in and increased in force gradually as we approached the equator; then it shifted to eastward. We had passed out of the northern trade winds in Lat. 7° 14′ N., so

---

[1] This is Wilson's petrel (*Oceanites oceaniens*) and is met with all over the world, even as far south as 78° S. latitude.

[2] The idea of the configuration of the ocean bottom affecting surface currents seems a strange one to the present-day student of the sea, but it must be remembered that until deep-sea sounding began, some few years after this date, the profound depths of the ocean were not even guessed at.

that consequently the line of temperature equilibrium of both hemispheres was then in Lat. 5° 12' N. When Admiral Kruzenstern passed near this spot, the line of equilibrium of temperature was in Lat. 4° 45' N. and Mr Golovnin in the *Diana* found it in Lat. 4° 01' N. In several voyages accomplished at various times and in various parts of the equatorial zone the positions of temperature equilibrium are marked as irregularly distributed, but a mean curve drawn between these positions will give the true position.[1]

15*th*. We had become very tired of calms, heat, rain, thunder and lightning, and were delighted to reach at last the southern trade winds, which, besides cooling the air, refreshed and re-animated us all with the hope that we should speedily pass out of this sultry and exhausting zone. By the afternoon there were heavy clouds, followed by torrential rains. Near the vessel on the water a large number of creatures were floating of a beautiful blue colour like that of blue tinsel. They were about $2\frac{1}{2}$ inches in length and $1\frac{1}{4}$ in breadth, and on the middle of the upper surface transparent crystalline membranes, perpendicularly arranged, were set aslant like sails. The lower part of the creatures was shaped like an ellipse edged with a blue fringe, and in the centre were tiny yellowish nipples, the shape of the surrounding surface being concave like a knight's helmet. We recognized them as the little animals called *Velella scaphilia* by the traveller Peronne.[2]

17*th*. At noon we were in Lat. 0° 41' N., Long. 20° 52' W., the variation being 14° 09' W., on a course south-south-west-half-west. There was a fresh steady south-east wind. We carried topsails on all masts. The rain-clouds were coming up one after the other.

18*th*. At 10.0 a.m. we crossed the equator in Long. 22° 19' 56" W. after a twenty-nine days' voyage from the island of Teneriffe. The greater number of navigators agree with Captain Vancouver that the best point to cross the equator is near Long. 28° W., as at that point there are no calms such as are prevalent nearer to the African coast. Moreover, crossing in this longitude, one can use the winds from the Brazilian coast. I was the only one of the *Vostok* who had ever crossed the equator and, following the general custom of all sailors, we drew

---

[1] The "line of temperature equilibrium" is a phrase which has passed out of use. Such a line, like the belt of calms, must be irregular owing to the distribution of land and sea. It must also move across the latitudes owing to the seasonal movement of the vertical sun.

[2] *Velella* is related to the Portuguese man-of-war (*Physalia*), though much smaller.

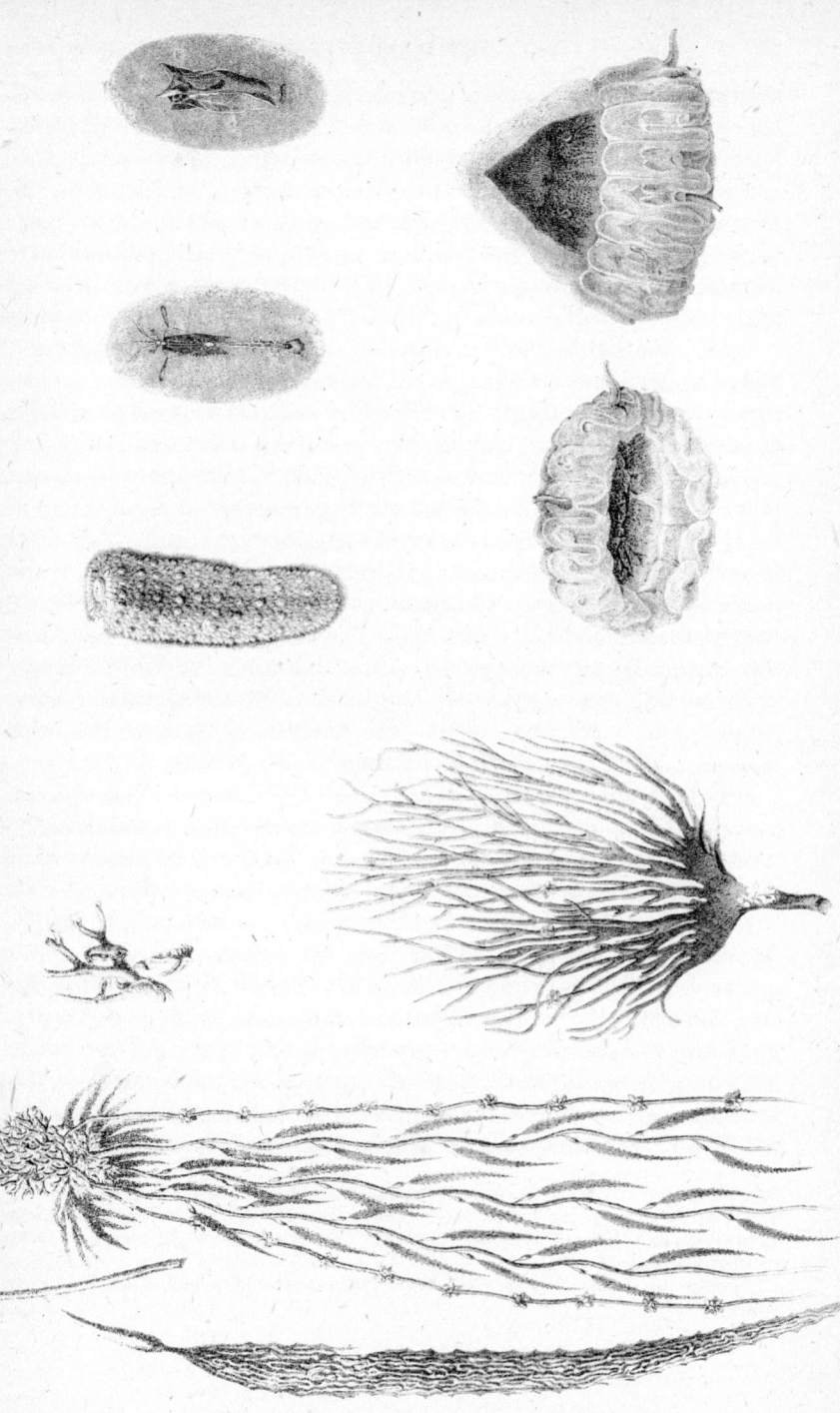

PLATE I

Seaweed and Plankton

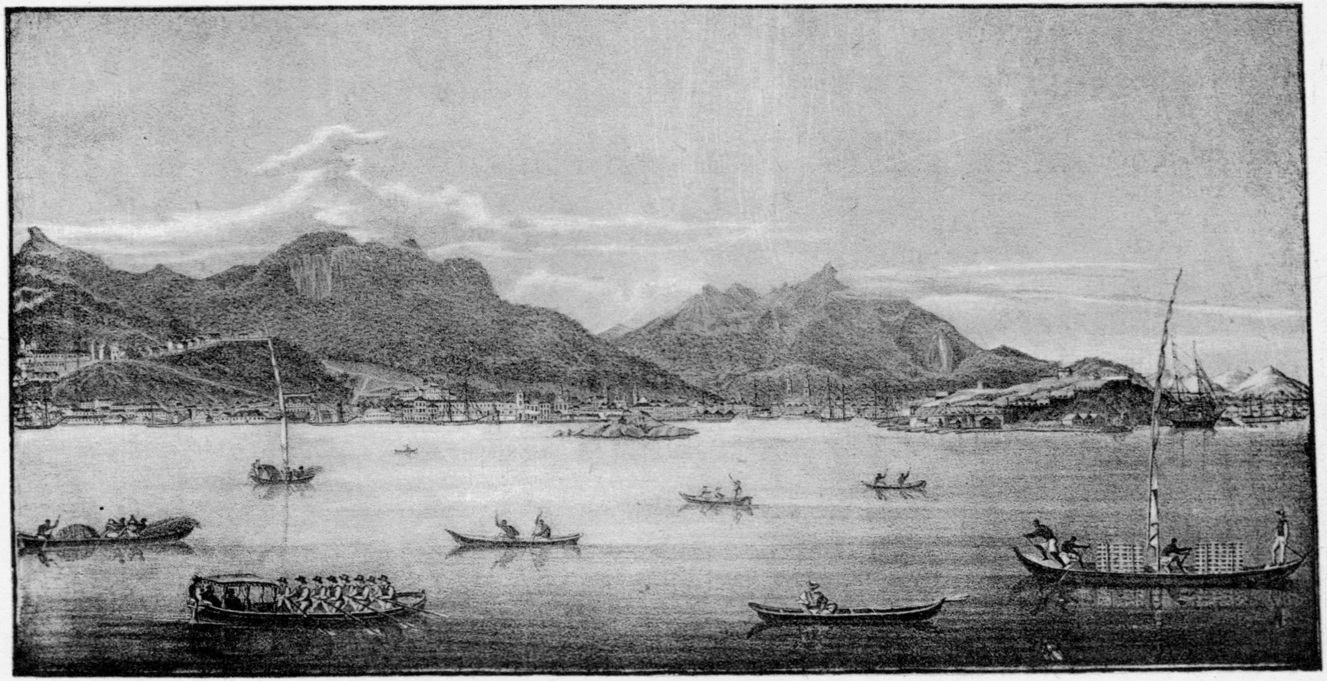

VOL. I View of the town of San Sebastian, Rio de Janeiro PLATE II up some water and I sprinkled the officers and cadets with it to introduce them, so to speak, to the waters of the southern hemisphere. The purser, who took part in this ceremony along with the others, performed it then on the crew with the difference, however, that instead of a drop, each man received a whole jug full in the face. They all submitted with the best of graces to the ceremony administered by the purser, and I then ordered a glass of punch to be served out to each man, in honour of the crossing of the equator, and to drink the health of His Imperial Majesty Alexander I, while salutes were fired meanwhile. The custom of celebrating the crossing of the equator in some especial manner may seem a matter of small importance and a perfectly childish amusement, nevertheless it makes a great impression on sailors. The tedious and monotonous voyage between the tropics is divided into two parts by the equator. Once there, the sailor, rejoicing to think that one half of the voyage is over, celebrates the event and hopes anew from that day, forgetting all the weary time which preceded it. It seems to him that the remainder of the voyage cannot be so long. He forgets the past tedious and stiflingly sultry days; and the happy sense of relief tends to preserve the general health of the crew.[1]

The atmospheric conditions at the equator were as follows: on the 18th at noon the mercury stood at 80° F. in the shade; in the morning at 6 o'clock at 78° F., at midnight at 77° F., in the lower deck where the crew slept at 81° F. Here I must observe that the greatest heat is not found exactly on the equator, where the south trade winds passing over it cool the air. The greatest heat is in the belt of calms between the north and south trade winds. On the 5th October, in Lat. 7° 14′ N., although the mercury rose to 87° F. by day, at night the temperature never exceeded 80° F.

From the equator we set a course direct for Cape Frio. As soon as the southern trade winds began to cool the atmosphere a little, we began work; amongst other things we caulked the outside of the ship. We chose such hours for this work as enabled the men to carry it out in the shade. On reaching the vicinity of Cape Frio, the outside of the ship as well as the deck had been caulked and painted, but not the

---

[1] On his first crossing the line in the *Nadezhda* Bellingshausen did not witness any particular function, as Kruzenstern writes in his narrative, "the usual farce with Neptune could not well be represented as there was nobody on board except myself who had crossed the Equator".

chains¹ as, at the speed we were going, it was impossible to hang out a cradle to paint the ship without risk of falling into the sea. As much of this kind of work as possible was done during the voyage so as to have less work in port and thereby to relieve the crew. The period of continuous fine weather gave us a good opportunity for undertaking astronomical observations. Messrs Zavodovski, Torson, Lyeskov, Demidov and the astronomer Simanov made observations with the sextant made by the well-known firm of Troughton of London, and I also used the same sextant. Navigating Officer Paryadin and his two assistants had the Dollond sextants. Lieutenant Ignatiev and Midshipman Adams had sextants made by Steving, a compass-maker of Portsmouth. We had besides two planimeters,² but on account of their weight we left them unused. On the *Mirnyi*, Messrs Lazarev, Obernibessov, Annenkov and Novosilski had sextants made by Troughton, and Mr Kupriyanov one by Burge; Navigating Officer Ilin and his two assistants had Dollond sextants. The two Steving sextants were divided to 20 seconds, all the others were divided to 10 seconds. Besides the above, Mr Lazarev had another sextant made by Banks, on the pattern of the Troughton instruments, but it was not used. With the exception of Mr Lazarev, Mr Zavodovski and myself, none of the officers on either ship had ever before had occasion to make astronomical observations; but during our stay in London each had bought the very best sextant and each endeavoured to excel the others, both in understanding the use of, and in exactly testing their instruments, and also in the measurement of lunar distances; and even before reaching Rio de Janeiro all had become good observers. Mr Lazarev praised Mr Kupriyanov especially for his skill. On the *Vostok* Lieutenant Ignatiev, through illness, lost the opportunity of taking observations.

27th. With a fresh south-east trade wind, we rapidly altered our position: at noon on the 27th we were in Lat. 15° 38′ S., Long. 33° 32′ W. At the same time the wind shifted to the east as we approached the Brazilian coast. With a south trade wind blowing since the 15th, the stream set us south-east to north-west in 24 hours;

¹ The lower ends of the shrouds are fastened outside the ship's bulwarks, overhanging the water, and these are known as the "chains".

² These planimeters, which were mentioned as having been bought in London, were obviously not instruments for measuring areas. They appear to have been some form of clinometer, capable of being used at sea, but heavy, rather after the style of the mediaeval quadrant or astrolabe.

when we reached Lat. 16° S., we received a southerly set along the Brazilian coast of 6 miles in 24 hours. From Teneriffe to Brazil our reckoning of the stream was as follows:

By reckoning on the *Vostok* N.W. 64° 51′ 24″ at the rate of 9 miles in 24 hours.
By reckoning on the *Mirnyi* N.W. 29° 19′ 24″ at the rate of 6 miles in 24 hours.

The average of these two reckonings is N.W. 47° 05′ 24″, rate 7 miles; the average rate during forty-three days was 5 miles in 24 hours. As this stream is produced by the constant trade winds, one may rightly call it the trade stream: flowing into the West Indian waters and Gulf of Mexico, it gives rise to the above-mentioned Florida Stream (Gulf Stream).

29th. The wind shifted to east-north-east and blew fresher than before; our speed was from 7 to 8 knots. We were then in the latitude of the Abrolhos Rocks.

30th. At 7 o'clock in the morning, when we crossed the parallel of Colvado,[1] the wind blew from the north with undiminished force. At noon we were in Lat. 20° 54′ S., Long. 37° 25′ 41″ W. Towards 8.0 p.m. the wind fell completely. At 9.0 p.m. there was a very light south-south-east wind with mist, and towards 10.0 p.m. a heavy squall of rain came up from windward in gusts, obliging us to take a reef in the topsails, and later we close-reefed them and struck the royal yards, the gallant yards and top-gallant masts. At 11.0 p.m. we sent up blue signals in order to indicate our positions to each other. We found that the *Mirnyi* lay 1 mile behind us.

31st. A strong wind continued until 6.0 a.m. of the 31st; we made more sail. At noon we were by observation in Lat. 21° 19′ 29″ S., Long. 38° 45′ 30″ W.

1st. The head wind continued, but more moderate, with a swell from the south. At 8.0 a.m. the depth was found to be 30 sazhen (35 fathoms), bottom fine sand. At noon our position was found by observation to be Lat. 22° 01′ 16″ S., Long. 40° 24′ 22″ W.; the depth on sounding was 28 sazhen (33 fathoms), bottom yellowish grey loose sand. From midday to 4.0 p.m. we had a dead calm; after 4.0 p.m. a light east-south-east wind freshened, and we were able to continue on our south-west course. At 6.0 p.m. we observed through the mist Cape Saint Thomas on the Brazilian shore bearing N.W. 66°. Favourable weather on the 29th and 30th October and 1st November

[1] This would appear to be the former name for this island of Escalvada, which is about 8 miles from the coast of Brazil in this latitude.

permitted us to take lunar distances. These distances were measured by Messrs Zavodovski, Simanov, Paryadin and myself to the number of 410, and the longitude of our position seemed to be a little farther west than indicated by the chronometer No. 518.

2nd. The night was clear and we proceeded on a south-west by south course at 5 knots; at 5.0 a.m. we altered course to west in order to pass round Cape Frio, which from seaward presented the aspect of two hills divided by a valley; this gives the Cape, from a distance, the appearance of two islands. From this point we proceeded along the low-lying sandy shore towards Rio de Janeiro. Later it appeared that, according to chronometers the difference in longitude between Cape Frio and Rio de Janeiro is 1° 11′ 30″. We had with us a book entitled *The Brazilian Pilot*, and in it we found the description of the sloping mountain called the "Sugar-loaf" (Pão de Assucar) forming the western side of the entrance to the bay. On approaching nearer, we observed the fortress of Santa Cruz on the eastern side of the entrance to the Bay. At 5.0 p.m. they spoke to us from the fortress through a speaking trumpet, addressing us in Portuguese, but as none of us understood Portuguese we replied in Russian, which was probably equally incomprehensible to them. Passing the fort of Santa Cruz, we proceeded on our way leaving to port a small fort called Dalageya erected on a small island.[1] An officer arrived from the first fort in a cutter and came on board. He asked the usual questions, whence come, whither bound, and how many days at sea? We informed him that our ships were bound on a voyage of exploration and that we were only touching here to lay in a store of fresh water and to rest the crew. The officer made notes of all this to report to the authorities. At 6.30 p.m. we anchored off "Rat" Island, in a depth of 15 sazhen (17 fathoms), the bottom consisting of mud.[2] The town of Santa Cruz lay on a bearing of S.E. 32″ from us: the Pão de Assucar S.E. 7°; the middle of the Dos Rolos fortress S.W. 44°. On the same evening all the rowing boats were lowered. The *Mirnyi* was anchored beside the *Vostok*.

We were very delighted to meet the *Otkryitie* and the *Blagonamyerenny* at Rio de Janeiro. They had left Portsmouth two days after us and had arrived one day earlier in Rio de Janeiro, as Mr Vasilev

---

[1] This fort, now called Lage, is so close to sea level that it is smothered with spray in stormy weather.

[2] Rat Island has now been renamed Fiscal Island, and accommodates the harbour offices.

had not touched at any port, while we had spent five days at Teneriffe. Sir Thomas Hardy,[1] commanding the two English ships *Superb* and *Vengeur*, sent a lieutenant to greet us on our arrival and to offer his assistance in obtaining wood and water. He knew already where these necessaries were to be found. We had been assured that, as our Ambassador was resident in Rio de Janeiro, we should be able to secure all necessaries, and therefore we merely thanked Sir Thomas Hardy for his friendly offer. An officer sent by Rear-Admiral Count de Vieno very soon came on board from the Portuguese ship-of-the-line, *John VI*, and congratulated us on our arrival. Like the officer from the fort of Santa Cruz, he put the same questions to us. Afterwards the Russian Vice-Consul, Mr Kilkhen, came to see us; we saw at the first glance that he was an obliging person and we requested him to send us provisions of fresh meat, green vegetables and fruit daily during our stay here.

At 7.0 p.m. our Consul-General, Ministerial Councillor Langsdorf,[2] came on board the *Vostok*. I met him again with very great pleasure. During my three years' acquaintance with him on the *Nadezhda* in 1803, 1804, 1805 and 1806, on a voyage round the world, when he was with us as our naturalist, we had become great friends. Mr Langsdorf, out of friendship for me, and by reason of his position, promised to do all in his power to obtain what we required. In the morning at 10.0 a.m. I went ashore with Mr Lazarev, where our Vice-Consul, Mr Kilkhen, was awaiting us at the quay with an open carriage. It was a conveyance on two large wheels, drawn by two mules, on one of which the coachman or driver was seated. We came ashore quite near the palace, and took our seats in the carriage; the driver cracked his whip and the mules galloped off along the narrow dirty streets. On our visit to our Ambassador, Major-General Baron de Teille von Seraskerken, we were received very kindly. He offered us all the assistance in his power and ordered the Vice-Consul to see that all our needs were supplied. Work was meanwhile being carried out on the *Vostok* under the superintendence of Mr Zavodovski. Both vessels

    Sir Thomas Hardy had served for many years with Admiral Nelson, and was flag-captain on the *Victory* in the Battle of Trafalgar. He was with Nelson on the quarter-deck when the latter received his mortal wound.

    George Henry Langsdorf—German naturalist and traveller—was born in 1774. He accompanied Admiral Kruzenstern on his scientific expedition round the world in 1803–6. Subsequently he joined the service of Russia and became Consul-General in Brazil. While occupying that post he did some scientific exploration in the interior of Brazil.

were moored; after which the crew washed all the linen, blankets, clothes, the decks and finally themselves.

The following day, by my wish, Mr Langsdorf obtained permission for us to encamp on the small rocky island, named "Rat" Island, near which we were anchored, in order to rate our chronometers. Tents were put up there on that very day. The astronomer, Simanov, and his assistants, Midshipman Adams and the non-commissioned gunnery officer, Kornilev, moved to the island. The following day they set up there the transit instrument, but at first with little success; the pedestal had been made from our cast-iron ballast; a wooden base had been placed on the top but, although very carefully fastened down by Mr Simanov, the wood had nevertheless warped under the rays of the sun and consequently the instrument had been shifted out of position. The chronometers were rated by observations of two equal altitudes and by observations at noon. The Bay of Rio de Janeiro (i.e. of the River Ianuarius) received its name from its having been discovered by Diaz de Solis in 1516 on the day of St Januarius. This bay at first glance resembles a river and hence, although a bay, was called Rio de Janeiro. The town of San Sebastian lies on the western shore of the bay on low ground.[1] This low ground extends to the foot of high steep mountains, covered with woods. Although the town is laid out very regularly, the streets are for the most part narrow. There are several fine squares and houses of two stories. The ground floors consist of shops or workshops, and in the upper floors are the living rooms of the inhabitants. Litter and all rubbish are thrown directly into the street; of an evening, when it grows dusk, it is impossible to walk near the houses without exposing oneself to the unpleasantness of being drenched with water from the upper floors. The town in general presents a disgustingly dirty appearance.

The summits of all the hills are crowned by monasteries which improve the external aspect of the town. Indeed, the inhabitants of the monasteries are almost the only people to have the benefit of fresh healthy air and the pleasure of fine prospects from the heights. During our stay we saw church processions almost daily in the streets and churches, which attracted crowds of people; judging by this, the

---

[1] James Henderson, in his *History of Brazil*, published in 1830, describes Rio as "centuries behind in the comforts and enjoyments of civilized life". According to his account the Brazilians were not noted for their friendliness or civility to foreigners. Bellingshausen seems to have been more fortunate, as he makes no mention of any inhospitality during his stay there. He also managed to re-victual without difficulty.

stranger inevitably infers a tendency towards idleness on the part of the population. There are no municipal schools in the town. The education of the children is for the most part in the hands of the monks. A well-built theatre is the only place in which the public foregather. A great number of country houses with gardens are built on both sides of the town along the shore, but across the bay, on the opposite shore, only a few buildings are to be seen. Two islands lie off the town; on one (Isla das Cobras) there is a fortress, in which the Admiralty stores are kept, and on which the flag of the port is hoisted. The other is a granite island named "Rat" Island. The town of Rio de Janeiro was built long ago, but it was only on the discovery of the diamond mines in its vicinity in 1730 that it attracted the notice of the Portuguese Government. Since then it has been almost always the residence of the Viceroy.

There are a few shops here for the sale of negroes, grown-up men and women, and children. On entering these abominable shops, one sees a number of scrofulous negroes sitting in rows, the small ones in front and the bigger ones behind. Each shop is superintended by one of the Portuguese owners or one of the negroes of a previous slave gang. It is the business of such an overseer to see that these unfortunate creatures present themselves to the best advantage and in the most cheerful manner when a purchaser appears. The master stands there with a whip or cane in his hand, and at a sign from him they all stand up and jump from one foot to another, singing a dancing song. Any one amongst them who, according to the proprietor's idea, looks insufficiently happy, and who does not dance or sing enough, is livened up with the cane. The purchaser, choosing the slave he fancies, has him brought out in front of the others, makes him open his mouth, feels his body and thumps him all over. If, after these tests, he is convinced of the strength and soundness of his negro, the purchase is completed. One was sold for 200 Spanish dollars in our presence. In the market for women, everything is arranged in the same way, with the exception that the negresses wear small aprons of blue cloth and, in some cases, the breasts are covered. An old woman and a young lady went into the shop at the same time as ourselves. They appeared to be Portuguese. Whilst bargaining for one of the negresses, they looked at her mouth, lifted her arms and bared her breasts; finally the old woman felt her all over with both hands; it was evident that the price named by the owner was too high and, instead of buying this negress, they went away to another store. The examination, the sale, the dirt, the odious smell coming from a number of slaves herded together, and the barbarous rule of the whip and the cane, all arouse a feeling of loathing towards the inhuman proprietors of these shops.[1] When we were in Rio, the Portuguese lived in hopes that the abolition of the slave trade would be deferred.[2] Accustomed from childhood to look on such degrading sights daily, they were so used to them that they looked on unmoved. An additional factor is the high profits of, and the need of labourers on, the plantations, which have been much enlarged since the arrival of the King from Portugal.

During our stay two Frenchmen arrived with the intention of taking up coffee planting. The great profits and the hope of becoming rich attracted even people with little capital. Mr Langsdorf told us that a great many such colonists had come out in a short time. The presence of the King of Portugal in Rio de Janeiro has attracted a great many people from other countries with different kinds of business to Brazil and, adding to the population and the trade, has raised Brazil to a flourishing position similar to that of the United States of America. The number of the inhabitants in Rio de Janeiro is assumed to be about 80,000.[3]

The King[4] sent for colonists from Switzerland on terms very

[1] Of the slave market in Rio Maria Graham makes the following entry in her diary of May 1st, 1822: "I have to-day seen the Val Longo; it is the slave market of Rio. Almost every house in this very long street is a depot for slaves. On passing by the doors this evening, I saw in most of them long benches placed near the walls, on which rows of young creatures were sitting, their heads shaved, their bodies emaciated and the marks of recent itch upon their skins. In some places the poor creatures were lying on mats, evidently too sick to sit up. At one house the half-doors were shut and a group of boys and girls, apparently not above 15 years old, and some much under, were leaning over the hatches and gazing into the street with wondering faces."

[2] The abolition of the slave trade was one of the provisions of the "Congress of Vienna", 1814, but slaves were sold and used in Rio de Janeiro until 1878, and it was not until 1888 that the total abolition of slavery was decreed.

[3] The present population is 1,730,000.

[4] It was really Napoleon who was responsible for the presence of the King in Brazil at this time. In 1807, he threatened to invade Portugal, and the Prince Regent and his Queen-Mother, Donna Maria I, were forced to fly to the Portuguese colony of Brazil. This is the only known instance of a colony becoming the seat of government of its mother country. The royal family were forced to leave Lisbon at the shortest possible notice.

The court was established at Rio de Janeiro, and the city was considerably developed during its residence there. On the death of Queen Maria, in 1816, the Prince Regent was proclaimed King of Brazil under the title of John VI.

In 1821, after the subjection of Napoleon, the King returned to Lisbon, leaving his son, Prince Pedro, as Regent of Brazil. He proved himself a wise and con-

advantageous to them. They are given land, cattle and other necessaries. A Hamburg ship had arrived from Europe while we were there, on which 400 men had embarked, of whom 130 had died on the way. The King was very indignant at this. Had these first settlers been brought on a warship or a large merchant vessel on which enough water could have been stored and had efficient ventilation been provided this would not have happened. The colonists are conferring a great benefit on Brazil by the growing of potatoes, onions, garlic and all sorts of vegetables, also by the rearing of cattle, butter-making and the cultivation of different fruit trees, etc. The natives do practically nothing of all this and obtain fruit and vegetables from the Europeans, and more particularly from English people, at high prices. The Brazilians are more interested in coffee and sugar plantations. Young coffee plants bear fruit in the fourth year, and each plant may be reckoned in round figures to bring in a franc or a rouble annually. As a rule these coffee plantations are planted on the slopes and are worked by negroes. One negro is reckoned for every three thousand bushes. These slaves are fed on manioc,[1] beans and dried beef; they are very rarely given any clothing.

Mr Kilkhen gave us the opportunity of seeing a waterfall, much praised by travellers, about 16 miles distant from Rio de Janeiro. In the morning carriages and saddle horses were awaiting us. All the officers and cadets and some of the local residents assembled. We proceeded very gaily, partly through beautiful cultivated country, partly over steep wooded hills, sometimes with cliffs on one side and deep ravines on the other. When still 5 or 6 miles distant from the cataract, it was no longer possible to proceed in the carriage, owing to the steepness of the rough road; so we got down and walked. The great heat and the hard work of descending and climbing the hills were very fatiguing. At last, one after the other, we dragged ourselves

---

scientious ruler and was most popular amongst his Brazilian subjects. The Portuguese Government, however, was corrupt and profligate, and the Brazilian people yearned for their independence. A revolutionary war broke out and continued for two years. Prince Pedro tried to act as mediator between the Portuguese and the Brazilian people, though his sympathies were strongly with the latter. Finally, in the year 1823, he was proclaimed Emperor Pedro I of Brazil, and his authority was recognized throughout the whole country.

[1] Cassava is the meal prepared from manioc, a farinaceous root-stock. The roots are cleaned, sliced and dried, and ground into meal, known in Brazil as farinha. When the starch is extracted from the roots and dried on hot plates it forms the familiar tapioca of commerce.

to the inn, half a mile from the waterfall; there we refreshed ourselves with lemonade and then continued our way by a narrow path winding along the slope to the cataract, the noise of which was already audible in the distance. The view of the cataract was wonderful, though it was hidden from our sight until we were quite close to it, the water rushing over the steep cliff in different directions between huge boulders over a width of 80 feet, and finally falling headlong into a wide valley, winding along it down to the boundless ocean, gleaming blue in the distance. All this impressed us the more as the high mountains rising on both sides of the waterfall shut out all other objects. On one of the cliffs and on a rock, flat like a table, were carved the names of a great number of visitors. Amongst these we noticed those of our compatriots, Captain Golovnin and of other officers; to these we added our own.[1]

The dinner ordered by Mr Kilkhen, and carried up by negroes upon their shoulders, was very much appreciated after such fatigue. Meanwhile, Mr Karnyev, the artist attached to Mr Vasilev's division, made a sketch of the waterfall. On the return journey we often became separated from each other, as some were mounted and others preferred going on foot in the difficult road. I was mounted, and Mr Lazarev, who elected to walk, was obliged at times, when going up hill, to lay hold of my horse's tail to help him along. Having covered 5 or 6 miles, we got into the carriages and drove back to town, where our cutters awaited us and we went on board again.

19*th*. The Ambassador presented to King John VI the following Commanders of the ships: Vasilev, Shishmarev, Lazarev and myself, and also the Consul-General Mr Langsdorf. The King was at his country palace, the road to which passes through marshes. At the entrance to the room in which His Majesty received us, we, following Mr Langsdorf, to whom the customs of the Brazilian Court were already familiar, made a low bow, took a few steps forward, made a similar bow and lastly a third. The King asked me a few questions about Rio de Janeiro, about the Roadstead, the purpose of our voyage, and, after the usual courtesies, bowed, when we again bowed low and stepped backwards without turning round, while the King, walking away from us, each time turned to acknowledge our bows. I once saw a similar bowing when I was on board the *Nadezhda* at Nagasaki in 1804. The Japanese brought the officials of the Dutch factories and two ship's captains on board the *Nadezhda* and, at the entrance to the

[1] Golovnin had been there just two years before *en route* to Kamchatka, via Cape Horn.

cabin, said to them, "Compliment for de grote Herr" (Salutations to the distinguished gentleman), upon which they all bowed low. After remaining for some time in this position, one of them, the doctor attached to the factories, said to the interpreter, "May I stand up?" The interpreter nodded consent, and all stood upright.

Our short stay in Rio de Janeiro, the considerable preparations on board ship for the new voyage and ignorance of the language prevented my making any detailed observations, and I have only noted what we had occasion to see.

20th. On the 20th all the provisions procured by Mr Kilkhen at my request arrived on board for our distant voyage, namely, two oxen, forty large pigs and twenty sucking pigs, a few ducks and hens; rum and castor sugar, lemons, pumpkins, onions, garlic and green vegetables, required for the use of the crew. On the same day we moved the chronometers from "Rat" Island back to the ships.

21st. The rates of the chronometers in Rio de Janeiro were as follows: No. 2110 was in advance of mean time by 2 hr. 22 min. 14·86 sec. and gained daily 2·514 sec.; No. 518 was in advance of mean time by 3 hr. 1 min. 39·360 sec. and gained daily 6·748 sec. No. 922 Barraud chronometer was in advance of mean time 2 hr. 40 min. 14·36 sec. and lost daily 7·487 sec. There only remained to get the hay which Mr Kilkhen had promised to obtain for the bulls and rams, and to settle our accounts. To do so Mr Demidov was sent into the town in the morning.

The wind in Rio de Janeiro, for the most part, is at night, a light wind blowing out of the bay until 8.0 or 9.0 a.m., after which the wind drops. From 10.0 or 11.0 a.m. there is a fresh sea breeze which continues until sunset, and towards evening the wind again falls; consequently, in order to reach the sea conveniently and with minimum damage, almost all vessels accomplish their departure in two stages. In the first stage they approach the exit of the bay, and on the following morning, the passage out to sea is completed. Following this rule, we weighed on the morning of the 21st, taking advantage of the fair light wind and, after 10.0 a.m., when the wind began to blow shorewards, tacked about and anchored near the exit to the sea in a depth of 14 sazhen (16 fathoms), bottom fine sand and mud. Later in the evening Mr Demidov arrived on board with Mr Kilkhen, with whom we went over all the accounts. The hay was delivered on board both vessels in the evening. After that all communication with the shore ceased.

CHAPTER III

Departure from Rio de Janeiro. Voyage to the Southern Coast of South Georgia. Discovery of the Marquis de Traversey Islands. Voyage to the Eastern Coasts of the South Sandwich Islands. Voyage in the Southern Antarctic Ocean. Arrival at Port Jackson. Report of the *Mirnyi* during her separation from the *Vostok*. Stay in Port Jackson.

22nd. At 6.0 a.m., with a light wind between south and east, I gave orders to weigh. We passed out between the fortress of Santa Cruz and the mountain named "Sugar-loaf". At 10.0 a.m. the wind blew from seaward as usual in the day-time, owing to which we were unable to proceed either beyond or east of Raza Island and, not knowing the passage between Raza and Redonda Island, I decided to go on a starboard tack towards the Brazilian coast. At 11.0 a.m. we again altered course, and on this course we passed Raza Island, at a distance of half a mile to the north, which is in Lat. 23° 05′ 18″. When both vessels had passed out of these narrows we directed our course southwards to South Georgia, on the route by which La Pérouse, Vancouver and Colnett had sought for Isla Grande, discovered in 1675 by Antonio de la Rochè in Lat. 45° S.* The position of this island is now altered on the charts.[1] At 4.0 p.m. the wind freshened, and we took in one reef in the topsails and struck the royal yards and mast: in the evening there was a heavy sea. We again took in a reef and took in the mizzen topsail. At night we sent up signals in order to indicate our position. The *Mirnyi* was following in our wake.

23rd. At 5.0 a.m. the wind dropped a little, some rain fell, and we made all sail. At noon we were in Lat. 25° 39′ 49″ S., Long. 43° 23′ W., at 6.0 p.m. in Lat. 26° 10′ S., Long. 43° 21′ W., variation 4° 36′ E. The night was fine; we continued on a direct southerly course.

24th. At 9.0 a.m. of the 24th we drifted in a calm. I ordered a boat to be lowered and sent Lieutenant Lyeskov to invite the priest and Mr Lazarev on to the *Vostok*. At 10.0 a.m. Mr Lyeskov returned bringing the priest, Messrs Lazarev, Galkin, Annenkov and Novosilski. The usual service was at once begun, and we prayed Almighty

---

* Vide *Chronological History of the Voyages and Discoveries in the South Sea or Pacific Ocean*, vol. III, p. 398, 1803–17, by Admiral James Burney.

[1] See footnote on p. 84.

God for a happy and successful end to the voyage which lay before us. After this I ordered Mr Lazarev to receive on board the *Mirnyi* twenty months' pay and also a sum of money to cover extra allowances for that time, in order that, should any misfortune happen to the *Vostok*, the officers and crew of the *Mirnyi* should not be left without necessary comforts, and I also gave him the following instructions in the event of our being separated:

"In pursuance of the instructions given to me, I beg you, with all on board the *Mirnyi* entrusted to you, to keep, during bad weather, 5 cables astern of the *Vostok*, and during mist nearer to her. During good weather, on the other hand, keep abreast of her at a distance of 4, 6 or 8 miles so that we may have a wider range of vision. At night, when we hoist a light on the *Vostok*, there must also be one on the *Mirnyi*, at the most visible point. It may happen that the vessels, although ordered to sail in company, become separated, and, as this is nearly always somebody's fault, I ask you to impress on all officers of the watch the necessity of being most vigilant; but, should the ships unexpectedly lose sight of each other, we must then search for each other for three days at the point where last seen, and make gun signals. If that does not bring us together, then act according to the instructions given to me, of which you have a copy. If this separation should occur before reaching South Georgia, then I appoint as rendezvous the head of Possession Bay, the ships waiting there for four days, and then acting according to instructions. But if we are separated near the Falkland Islands, and the season will allow, then keep to leeward of those islands and look for a harbour; enter it and wait there for six days, lighting a bonfire on the hills. After this return through Cook Straits to Port Jackson and await there the arrival of the *Vostok*.[1] In case of separation, all the above is to be followed equally by the *Vostok*."

At midday we were in Lat. 27° 38' 46" S., Long. 43° 32' 51" W. The direction of the current was S.W. 64°, 12 miles in 24 hours. We continued our course due south under all sail. At 7.0 p.m. I signalled to the *Mirnyi* to come astern of the *Vostok*, and when this was done, we wished each other the best of good fortune and then continued on

---

[1] This passage is obscure. It seems likely that a large part of the instructions has been omitted, and the concluding sentence inserted completely out of context. Cook Straits must refer to the passage between the North and South Islands of New Zealand.

our way. At 10.0 p.m. the wind again freshened and we took in a reef in the topsails.

25*th*. In the course of the night the sky became overcast and a strong east wind got up, bringing with it a heavy sea. The *Mirnyi* remained far astern. We were obliged to close-reef the topsails. At 2.0 p.m., when the *Mirnyi* had caught us up, we again set topsails. At 4.0 p.m. it began to rain and at 8.0 p.m. we encountered a strong but short squall from the north-west. After this we had a light north-east wind with dull weather. About midnight lightning unceasingly lit up the whole horizon towards the south-east and thunder was heard.

26*th*. The north-easterly wind, which had up to now constantly accompanied us from Rio de Janeiro, is the prevailing wind off the Brazilian coast from September to March. At 8.0 p.m. it veered to east by south with dull weather and rain, and increased so much that at daybreak we took in a reef in the topsails and struck the top-gallant masts.

27*th*. The dull weather, rain and heavy sea continued. The night was very dark. On sending up signals we got no reply from the *Mirnyi*, and at dawn she was not visible. Deciding that she must be astern, we shortened sail and at 3.0 p.m. we hove to, to look for our consort. Immediately the weather had cleared a little, we saw her north by east, and ran down to her. At 4.0 p.m., when the vessels were near each other, we again turned on a port tack on a south-west by west course. There was then a strong wind from south by east blowing in gusts; the sun appeared from time to time, and there was a heavy sea.

28*th*. In the morning the wind had fallen. We hoisted the mainsail, unreefed the topsails, and set the top-gallant sails. The temperature was 64·1° F. Towards midday we were becalmed, and the sky cleared completely. We found ourselves in Lat. 34° 19′ S., Long. 44° 41′ 09″ W. In the course of the 24 hours the current had set us S. 3° 14′ W. 56 miles. By measuring twenty lunar distances I made the Long. 44° 40′ 03″ W., Lieutenant-Commander Zavodovski placed us in 44° 55′ 50″ W., and Navigating Officer Paryadin 44° 40′ 31″ W. At 6 o'clock we were in Lat. 35° 04′ S., Long. 44° 44′ W., and the magnetic variation was 6° 15′ E. At 2.0 a.m. a squall blew up from the south-west, with rain and sleet, which necessitated our taking two reefs in the topsails. At daybreak the wind increased still more so that we took in the fore and mizzen topsails, furled top-gallant sails and struck top-gallant masts and stood under reefed main topsails and storm staysails. After this, when the crew had changed into dry clothes, they were given a glass of punch to hearten them. At midday we found ourselves in Lat. 35° 46′ 09″ S., Long. 43° 48′ 31″ W. At 3.0 p.m. a sharp squall of short duration with rain and large hailstones blew up from windward.

30th. During heavy wind, on that day, we were surrounded by petrels (*Procellaria*) almost the size of a duck;[1] back, tail and head light brown above and white underneath. During the day the horizon was clear and we were able to see 15 miles on all sides.

1st. On December 1st with a light wind we continued southward. In Lat. 36° 10′ S., Long. 42° 15′ W. we found the variation 7° 21′ E. In the morning we hoisted the top-gallant mast and sails and unreefed the topsails. At 11.0 a.m. a light wind was blowing from the north and at midday our position was Lat. 36° 17′ 56″ S., Long. 42° 00′ 37″ W.; the current had set us S. 76° E. 12 miles. In the afternoon the wind began to freshen and we proceeded at from 6 to 8 knots. At 11.0 p.m. we double-reefed the topsails and took in the mizzen topsail, in order to keep with the *Mirnyi*. In the course of the day a few albatrosses (*Diomedia exulans*) flew round us and the above-mentioned petrels. All through the evening and night there was sheet lightning towards the south and east.

2nd. At midday of the 2nd we were in Lat. 38° 59′ 33″ S., Long. 41° 48′ 23″ W.; the current had set us S. 54° E. 13 miles. There was a fog on the horizon, like that in St Petersburg when the Neva breaks up and the moisture from it is carried by the sea breezes over the town. Large fish of from 15 to 16 feet in size, of the whale family, surrounded our ships. Everyone went for rifles. Lieutenant Demidov succeeded in shooting one in the head; it rose perpendicularly about 5 feet out of the water, and, being wounded, sped away from the vessel, leaving traces of blood behind it. These fish have one fin on the back, a horizontal tail, and small breathing orifices on the head.[2] In the

---

[1] A vast number of petrels closely resembling each other haunt the southern seas, and it is impossible in many cases to identify them when they are so briefly described. Here and there where the descriptions are more accurate and detailed it is possible to do so.

The petrel here referred to is probably the Antarctic petrel (*Thalassoica antarctica*), first discovered by Captain Cook, which is widely distributed throughout the Southern Ocean.

[2] The description is not clear enough to enable the species to be named, but they may have been the Grampus or Killer whales.

evening we found the variation 8° 15' E.; from midday to midnight we had proceeded slowly.

3rd. At 11.0 a.m. the officer of the watch, Lieutenant Ignatiev, reported to me that breakers were visible to the west-south-west. I was very glad, and concluded that it was the land observed by La Rochè in 1675, in Lat. 45° S. I therefore gave orders to steer towards the breakers. But on approaching nearer we observed a dead whale over which the water was breaking, and a great number of sea birds were flying or swimming round it or sitting on it. Mr Demidov and Mr Bergh went in a boat to shoot some of the birds, and they succeeded in killing an albatross 2 feet 6 inches in length. From the tip of one wing to the tip of the other it was 7 feet 6 inches; the colour of the feathers on the upper parts of this bird was dark brown, the neck and underneath were white. At noon by observation we found our position to be Lat. 39° 48' 36" S., Long. 41° 44' 29" W., the current having set us S. 39° E. 15 miles. At 2 o'clock a large school of a small kind of porpoise with pointed head passed the ship. At 3.0 p.m. we drifted and, on sounding, found 200 sazhen (233 fathoms) and no bottom. From 4.0 p.m. until evening we observed numerous flocks of petrels flying or resting on the water. We were very anxious to bring one down, but were unsuccessful on account of their being so very shy. At 6.0 p.m. we observed towards the north-west a number of whales spouting. The weather continued splendid throughout the whole day and towards sunset heavy dew fell on the ship. The magnetic variation at sunset was east.[1]

4th. At 1.0 a.m. thick fog came up from windward which continued until 8.0 a.m. When it cleared, we observed flocks of birds of the same kind as we had seen the previous night. The wind rose gradually; towards midday we attained a speed of 8½ knots. Our position now was Lat. 41° 30' 55" S., Long. 41° 55' W. The mercury in the barometer began to drop in the morning, predicting high wind, which came on at sunset.[2] Although the fact of the birds flying round us made it seem likely that land was in our vicinity, during the whole day to our regret we were unable to see farther than 5 or 6 miles, as the whole horizon was covered by mist. At 8.0 p.m. the increasing

---

[1] The exact figures for the variation are not given in the original, but must have been about 7°.

[2] One of the notorious "pamperos" which blow in that region, many of which originate as cold south-west winds blowing across the great plains of Argentina.

wind from the west obliged us to stand under reefed topsails, foresail and mainsail. During high wind I found it best to carry the mainsail and not the foresail, because the *Vostok*, on which the foremast was stepped too far forward, always pitched forward a good deal with the foresail set, and was liable to labour and refuse to answer her helm.

5th. We had a strong south-south-west wind. At 2.0 a.m. we sent up signals, the *Mirnyi* replied, and we found she was near us. At dawn we had a high sea and the ship laboured considerably. The horizon was clear and distant, so that each half hour the men went up to the three look-outs and each gave a separate report to the officer of the watch of what they had observed aloft. This arrangement was carried out with exactitude from our departure from Rio de Janeiro to the end of the voyage, and the officer of the watch did not allow the men sent aloft to communicate with each other. Until afternoon the wind blew from the south-south-east; we went on the starboard tack. Our position at noon was found to be Lat. 42° 40′ 52″ S., Long. 41° 11′ 26″ W., the current having set us S. 49° E. 6 miles per hour.[1] The topsails were unreefed and the mizzen topsail set. At 2.0 p.m. we sounded and found 200 sazhen (233 fathoms) and no bottom. In the evening the wind dropped, but the sea still continued rough. All day birds of the kind reported on 3rd and 4th December flew round us. Mr Zavodovski shot down one small bird (*Procellaria pelagica*), but, as its head was completely smashed, it was of no use for stuffing.

6th. After midnight with a light east by south wind we again proceeded on a southerly course. At 3.0 a.m. the wind veered east-north-east and gradually freshened so that we travelled at the rate of 5 to 6 knots. During the night the sea was of a whitish colour. I suppose the change in the colour of the water during the night arose from great numbers of small phosphorescent creatures which, on a clear night, do not shine brightly and therefore do not give the sea the appearance of being on fire, as on dark nights. In the morning we hoisted the top-gallant sails and made all sail but, in consequence of heavy clouds, we were unable to see the sun and could not make the midday observations. At 3.0 p.m. the weather turned dull, with rain, and continued thus until midnight, making it impossible during the whole 24 hours for us to see farther than 5 miles all round. Mr Lazarev

---

[1] This must be a printer's error in the original; it probably should read, "6 miles in 24 hours".

shot a white albatross and took it on board. The albatross weighed 31 lb., the width from the tip of one wing to the tip of the other being 10 feet 7 inches.¹

7th. At night the sea appeared full of phosphorescent creatures, and we saw a number of whales, two of which spouted close to the ship. At 5.0 a.m. the wind abated and a little later we had a contrary south-south-west wind. We hove to with ship's head south-east. At 10.0 a.m. Mr Bergh succeeded in shooting one of the petrels flying round the ship. To pick it up we set the main topsail and lowered a boat. The length of the bird from beak to tail was 1 foot 6 inches. The upper part of the beak was curved at the tip; there was one nostril only, which was divided by a thin perpendicular membrane. The upper part of the head, the back, the wings and the tip of the tail were brown, the neck and lower part white, the legs short with three webbed toes and claws and one spur behind.² When they fastened the bird by a line to the stern of the boat and let it float behind, the other petrels collected all round it and plaintively mourned its fate. In a short time they were able to shoot ten more of them, after which we took in the boat and again made all sail.

At noon we found ourselves in Lat. $44°46'30''$ S., Long. $41°16'49''$ W. The set, in the course of 48 hours, was 9 miles; a contrary wind was blowing from the south and there was a heavy swell from the south-west. The barometer stood at 29·47; at 3.0 p.m. dull weather and rain set in, and then a squall, coming up quickly from the south-south-east, forced us to reef the topsails and strike the top-gallant yard and mast. We gathered two kinds of seaweed from the water here. The first kind had a stalk 1 foot long and $1\frac{1}{2}$ inches in diameter. On cutting it with a knife, we observed the inside resembles a horny substance. From the stem the branches spread out like a fan, of different sizes and thicknesses, all cylindrical and hollow in the middle; it has flowers of a dirty greenish colour. The whole plant was about 7 feet long. The second kind grew from a tufted root, straight, flexible stalks about two "lines" thick.³ The leaves are about 2 feet long, flat corrugated and indented, and are set on spindle-shaped, hollow branches; this seaweed varies very much in length. We occasionally spread it out over the whole length of the quarter-deck and poop, i.e. 70 English

---

[1] Probably a wandering albatross (*Diomedia exulans*).
[2] Probably the Antarctic petrel (*Thalassoica antarctica*).
[3] Two-twelfths of an inch.

feet; its colour is a dirty yellowish green and, like all weed floating on the surface, the plant is the home of mussels.[1]

8th. At 7.0 a.m. the wind veered south-south-west and we altered course with it. Towards the afternoon it veered aft and we lay to with ship's head south by east. Our position was Lat. 44° 36′ 43″ S., Long. 42° 51′ 02″ W. The current had set us N. 55° W. 27 miles. About 5.0 p.m. we crossed the parallel of 45° S. on which it is supposed that La Rochè discovered Isla Grande. The weather was beautiful, and we were able to see a long distance, nevertheless we had the same lot as La Pérouse, Vancouver and Colnett who, at different times and at different points on this parallel, had in vain sought this island, of which Burney in his *Chronological History*, vol. III, p. 397, says that La Rochè, rounding Cape Horn on the return journey from the Pacific Ocean, by a mistake in reckoning, was exposed to danger and, having extended his voyage to a late time of the year—to the month of April (which corresponds to October in the northern hemisphere)—observed land covered with ice and snow; finding depths of 20, 30 and 40 fathoms, he anchored. When the weather cleared, he saw that there was a mountain quite near covered with snow and a cape extending towards the south-east. He remained there for fourteen days. In an hour and a half he passed through a strait between this shore and a small island. He then sailed north-west and on the following day, by a storm from the south, was carried northward for three days. When the weather changed, he believed himself in Lat. 46°, whence he directed his course to the Gulf of All Saints (Bahia de todos los Santos) in Lat. 45°, came upon a great island, near which there was a good anchorage, and on the eastern side he found fresh water, wood and fish in abundance but no inhabitants were to be seen. La Rochè named the island "Grande".

From such a description it is not possible to know where La Rochè saw the land on rounding Cape Horn or which strait he passed through, and therefore it is impossible to fix the longitude of Grande Island. Some navigators and geographers suppose that La Rochè rounded Cape Horn from the eastern side[2] and that the land discovered by

[1] This particular kind of seaweed, of the *Laminaria* family, is now usually known as Kelp. It occurs in great profusion in the southern seas, growing in moderately deep water to a great length. Its presence off a bay or harbour often makes an otherwise risky passage for boats safe by its damping effect on the waves. It is also a sure indication of rocks below the surface.

[2] This passage is obscure.

him, covered with snow and ice, belongs to the Falkland Islands; others again believe that he sighted Willis Island and passed through one of the small straits, by which one might conclude that his landfall was the southern side of South Georgia. All these opinions fixed Isla Grande in different longitudes and therefore a course directed on one meridian can only by chance strike on this island.[1]

Approaching Lat. 45° S., we daily encountered great numbers of birds, fish and floating seaweed, such as are generally taken to indicate the proximity of land, which, however, we did not see.

9th. At 2.0 a.m., waiting for the *Mirnyi*, we took in a reef in the topsails and furled the mizzen topsail. At daybreak we scanned the whole horizon from aloft in a vain search for the vessel and I realized the disagreeable necessity of keeping to the agreement to look for each other in the place where last we had seen the other. Soon it began to rain and I still more began to lose hope of encountering the *Mirnyi*, but, on firing a gun signal, we heard a reply from astern. We therefore hove to at once to give Mr Lazarev a chance of coming up with us. We rejoiced greatly when, as the weather cleared, we saw the *Mirnyi* in our vicinity and promptly set all sail. At noon we found ourselves in Lat. 46° 24′ 57″ S., Long. 42° 27′ 47″ W.; the current having set us N. 74° E. 15 miles. After dinner it was possible to take some lunar distances. The longitude of our position at midday was fixed as follows:

Self, from 15 measurements	42° 22′ 01″
Lieutenant-Commander Zavodovski from 15 measurements	42° 22′ 52″
Lieutenant Torson from 15 measurements	42° 07′ 22″
Astronomer Simanov	42° 17′ 22″
Longitude by Chronometers, No. 518	42° 26′ 18″
No. 922	42° 25′ 02″

We found the variation to be 7° 48′ E. The weather improved, so we hoisted the top-gallant sails and continued on a southerly course.

---

[1] That a navigator should make efforts to discover an island reported 150 years before and never afterwards seen is a good instance of how difficult it is to remove from charts any island once entered on them.

The probable explanation is given by Burney himself, namely, that after being driven east of Staten Island Rochè entered one of the passages in the Falkland Islands and anchored there for fourteen days. Sailing from there on a north-west course he came to the headland between the Gulf of St George and Camarones Bay on the coast of Patagonia, in Lat. 45° S. Seen from the east this has the appearance of an island and it would afford the water, wood and fish mentioned by La Rochè.

10*th*. In the favourable weather we brought up all the crew's clothing and bedding and spread them out for drying. Up to that time, we had always, during the day-time, lit fires in the iron stoves on the lower deck which, when the fire had gone out, had been removed.

Coming now to a colder climate, I ordered the stoves to be fixed up permanently, with pipes passing out through the main and fore hatchways, these hatchways being closed in. In the main hatchway, for light, an opening of 4 square feet was cut in the cover and was fitted with glass to keep out the damp. The remaining part of the hatchway was covered over with tarred sail. The fore hatchway was reserved for passing to and from the lower deck; the main hatchway was only to be used as a passage in cases of emergency and, in order to lighten the upper part of the vessel, the four bow and stern guns were withdrawn and dismounted on the orlop deck.[1]

On the 10th, in Lat. 47° 52′ 04″ S., a few lunar distances were taken and our longitude at midday fixed as follows:

Self, from 20 measurements	42° 05′ 29″ W.
Lieutenant-Commander Zavodovski from 25 measurements	42° 04′ 13″
Navigating Officer Paryadin from 30 measurements	42° 06′ 10″
Longitude by Chronometers, No. 518	42° 15′ 44″
No. 922	42° 15′ 35″

On this day we shot three of the birds fluttering round the ship and took them on board. They belonged to the class of the petrels (*Procellaria*) and were 1 foot 11 inches in length, their beaks 1½ inches with curved point, their plumage being white marked with brown spots. These birds were recognized as the same as those referred to in Captain Cook's Voyage as "pintades"; we shall call them "pestrushki".[2]

The temperature had fallen noticeably and I therefore permitted the crew to wear the clothing specially provided for colder climates, such as flannel shirts, drawers and, over the shirts, cloth suits, etc.

---

[1] The orlop deck was situated below the lower gun deck. On it cables were coiled and sails stored.

[2] The Cape pigeon (*Daption capensis*), or "Spotted eaglet" as it is sometimes called, is easily recognizable by its spotted plumage and its curious raucous cry, so unlike that of most of its allies.

Shelvocke, in his *Voyage round the World*, describes them as follows: "We were constantly attended by Pintado birds about the bigness of a pigeon, the French call them Damier because their feathers being black and white are disposed in such a manner as to make their backs and wings appear chequered like a draught board."

11th. Up to 8 o'clock in the morning on 11th December we continued our course southwards with light south-south-east winds. We then turned towards the south-west, whence we faced a heavy swell. At noon we found ourselves in Lat. 49° 03′ 56″ S., Long. 41° 57′ 11″ W. The current was N. 12° E. 18 miles per day. The thermometer indicated 6° R. (45·5° F.) and the variation was 11° 32½″ E. At 4 o'clock the wind shifted to the south-west quarter and we brought the ship round again. During the day we saw several albatrosses, a number of pestrushki and crested penguins or jumpers.[1] We tried to shoot at least one of these, but failed owing to their extreme shyness. On this day a certain amount of seaweed floated past the ship.

12th. With a light wind from north to west and a heavy swell from the south, we continued our course to South Georgia. In the morning the wind freshened from the north-east and by midday we found ourselves in Lat. 50° 09′ 40″ S., Long. 41° 22′ 18″ W. In the afternoon it began to rain and we shortened sail so as not to let the *Mirnyi* fall too far behind us.

On this day all Russia was celebrating the birthday of the Emperor, Alexander Pavlovich I. We celebrated the date by hoisting the ensign and drinking to the Emperor's health; the crew gave seven cheers whilst a salute of twenty guns was fired from each sloop. To our regret, the fresh wind and high sea prevented the priest from coming on board the *Vostok* for the service, but we offered earnest prayers to the Most High for the health and prosperity of His Imperial Majesty.

At 7.0 p.m. on the evening of the 12th the wind backed to west-north-west. At midnight the temperature in the open had fallen to 3·7° R. (40·3° F.); below deck in the crew's quarters it was 6·8° R. (47·3° F.). Later on in the night we had rain and in the morning the entire horizon was grey and misty.

13th. At midday on the 13th we found ourselves in Lat. 52° 25′ 18″ S., Long. 40° 23′ 42″ W.; the stream set N. 57° W. 29 miles per day. On sounding here we found 250 sazhen (291 fathoms) but no bottom. The variation was 10° 48′ E. At 10.0 p.m. the wind set in against us south by east; we steered south-west by west. Throughout the day petrels of different kinds fluttered round and for the first time some blue birds appeared among them.

14th. While the contrary winds lasted we lay to and sent out a boat to shoot birds. In a short time we shot down two, one white

[1] These must have been the Macaroni penguin (*Eudyptes chrysolophus*).

and the other blue, both belonging to the petrel family; the first was called by Captain Cook the "Snowy petrel"[1] and the second the "Blue petrel". The latter were about the same size as a turtle-dove; their colour was blue, approaching azure; the wings had a brown bar across them, the tip of the tail was also brown, feet and beak being blue. I shall call them "blue storm birds" or blue petrels.

At midday of the 14th December, we found ourselves in Lat. 53° 10' 53" S., Long. 40° 08' 05" W.; the thermometer stood above freezing point, at 2·8° R. (38·3° F.) and, for the first time, some snow fell. At 7.0 p.m. we encountered a sudden squall from south-west by south with snow, so that we were obliged to shorten sail. Soon after the wind fell again, we let out a reef and hoisted the mainsail in order to reach South Georgia with the least delay; at 10 o'clock we had another squall with snow and the wind remained the same.

15th. The night was clear and a heavy swell was running from the south-west; the temperature in the open air was 1·4° R. (35·6° F.). At 6.30 p.m. we passed the parallel of Willis Island and then directed our course east-south-east. Curiosity made us all get up very early next morning in the hope of seeing South Georgia. Although the island was not yet visible at daybreak, the place where the shore ought to be was marked out from the rest of the horizon by a bank of heavy dark clouds. A large number of whales spouted in our neighbourhood. Blue and white and small black petrels, as well as 'pestrushki', flew about in flocks or rested on the water; here and there albatrosses appeared swimming or flying. Some pestrushki, more daring than the others, ventured close to the vessel. A number of crested penguins, jumping in the water and calling to each other, passed the vessel. Large quantities of seaweed of the kind known as *Fucus pyriformis* drifted past. At 8.0 a.m., when the weather cleared

---

[1] Dr Wilson writes as follows of the Snowy petrel (*Pagodroma nivea*), in the National Antarctic Expedition *Report* 1901–4: "This beautiful petrel is more strictly confined to the limits of the ice than any other—nothing could be more beautiful and less apparently fitting for the rigours of a storm-ridden climate such as the Antarctic than this little dove-like bird...the flight of this bird is exceedingly beautiful and dainty and from the whiteness of its plumage it is very easily lost to sight on the snow-covered pack or ice-floe, appearing now for a second and now as suddenly disappearing, and there is something almost ghostly in the silent flight and sudden appearance and disappearance of this bird...though the flight is so beautiful not only is the croaking guttural voice discordant but its gait upon the snow is equally unbecoming. The legs are set wide apart and the broad webbed feet are turned inwards giving it an ungainly straddle-legged appearance...."

a little, we saw Willis Island[1] and South Georgia about 21 miles[2] off with their pointed peaks partly hidden by the clouds and covered with eternal snow. By midday we approached Willis Island, lying 2 miles N. 37° E. from us. The midday observation showed us to be in Lat. 54° 05′ 23″ S. Accordingly the latitude of Willis Island is 54° 04′ S. The longitude given by two chronometers was 38° 22′ W., and by lunar observations on the 9th, 10th and 12th, made on the *Vostok*, 38° 17′ 18″ W.; according to the observations made by Mr Lazarev 38° 27′ W. This island is formed by a high mountain crest rising out of the sea.[3] It lies east to west and is about 4 miles long. Its summits were covered with clouds and its ravines filled with snow. At the north-eastern extremity are three isolated rocks rising out of the sea.

An extremely heavy surf from the west-south-west thundered against the cliffs. I kept along the coast of South Georgia at a distance of $1\frac{1}{2}$ to 2 miles. Going at the rate of 7 knots, we noted several bays in which there was probably good anchorage to be found. From one of these bays[4] a sailing boat, flying the British colours, came out. On their approach, we asked them to come up to us and hove to. In the boat was a steersman and two sailors. The former told us that they had not recognized us from a distance and, supposing that we also had come for whaling, they had intended to pilot our vessels into the bay, hoping that they would receive payment for their trouble. Two three-masted vessels, belonging to a British Whaling Company, one the *Indespensable*,[5] the other the *Mary-Ann*, under the command of Captains Brown and Short, were lying in the bay whence the boat had come. The depth at the anchorage was 18 sazhen (21 fathoms), bottom mud; a large brook of fresh water runs into the bay which is called Port Mary. The vessels had been there already for four months; the whalers extract the blubber from the seals; their work takes them into all the bays and, as a shelter for the night, they turn their boats

---

[1] Willis Island was named by Captain Cook after the seaman in the *Resolution* who first saw it in 1775.

[2] All miles are nautical miles unless otherwise stated. A nautical mile is 6080 feet or 1·15 statute miles.

[3] The summit of the island consists of two peaks, about 1800 feet above sea level.

[4] The name Port Mary given by these sealers appears to have died out and it may have been Undine harbour, still much used by whalers and sealers when hunting to the south-westward, or it may have been Queen Maud Bay of the modern chart, once known as Marian Bay. The sealing industry began in South Georgia soon after Cook had discovered it in 1775. By 1791 as many as 102 vessels were sealing in the South Atlantic Ocean.

[5] *Indespensable* is thus spelt in Lloyds' lists of February 22nd, 1820.

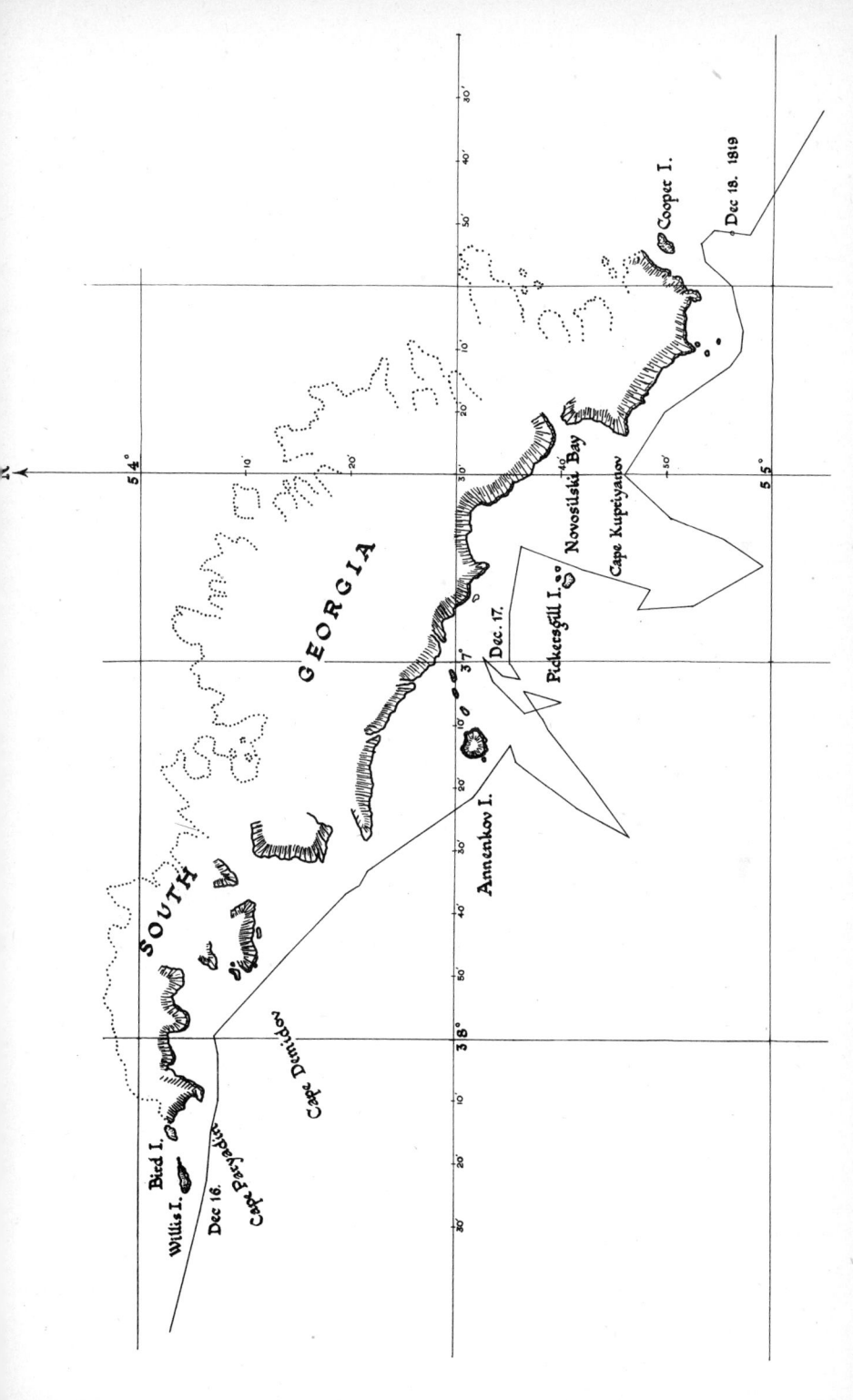

keel upwards and light fires underneath them. For melting the blubber of these animals they use as fuel the skins of penguins which frequent this part in very great numbers at this time of year. They also saw very frequently albatrosses and other sea birds, but of land birds only larks and a kind of pigeon, also called a sheath-bill.[1] The only plant life there was moss. In return for this information I ordered our guests to be given grog, sugar and butter. One of the sailors was a Russian who had deserted from one of our warships during her stay in a British port and had then drifted into this hard occupation to eke out an existence. After our visitors left us we set sail and shaped our course towards an island about 12 miles farther out to sea in front of us. We reached it by 9.0 p.m. but, on account of the darkness and low visibility, we turned to windward on the port tack. The depth at this point was 75 sazhen (88 fathoms), bottom small black stones. This island, in Lat. $54° 31' 30''$ S. and Long. $37° 13'$ W., I called Annenkov Island in honour of the second lieutenant of the *Mirnyi*. The shore of the island visible from our position consists of rocky hills, the tops covered with snow, and all the valleys filled with ice. Although we kept close in along the shore, we looked in vain, even with telescopes, for any vegetation. Excepting here and there a yellowish-green moss, we saw none.

For the more convenient description and survey of the main island, I named the various headlands after the officers of both vessels. Thus we gave the name Paryadin to the cape on South Georgia ending in the three sharp rocks, bearing S. $30°$ E. $3\frac{1}{2}$ miles from Willis Island. From Cape Paryadin the coast took a direction S. $69°$ E. $13\frac{1}{2}$ miles to a cape which I named Cape Demidov[2] and which is easily recognized by a high island lying off it on its western side. From this point to the East Cape at Maria Bay the coast takes a direction S. $47° 30'$ E. for a distance of 17 miles. Between Annenkov Island and South Georgia three large rocky islets show clearly, lying N. $67°$ E. Annenkov Island is practically round in shape, its circumference being $7\frac{1}{2}$ miles, and it

---

[1] The Sheath-bill (*Chionis alba*), or "Paddy" of modern seamen, is a tame bird and sometimes has even to be poked with a stick before it will take flight.

The "lark" mentioned is the South Georgia pipit, the only land bird on the island and the most southerly in its range of all land birds. It was mentioned by Captain Cook.

[2] These two names have been confirmed and now appear on the Admiralty chart. Bellingshausen's chart, reproduced from his "Atlas", shows what pains he and his officers took with their survey work, and until comparatively recently it remained the best chart of the difficult south-west coast.

rises to a height in the centre covered for the most part with snow and ice, with bare rocks showing in places. During the night the wind freshened and was accompanied by a high sea.

16th. We lay under reefed sails on account of the thick rainy weather. The temperature was 37·2° F. At 3.0 a.m., although it was still dark and rainy, both vessels got under weigh to proceed to the place where we had stopped in our survey the night before. Although at 7.0 a.m. we were within 8 miles of South Georgia and 5 miles distant from Annenkov Island, it was still so dark that we could not see either the one or the other: we had consequently to bring the vessels again into the wind and wait for the weather to clear. At 8.30 a.m. Annenkov Island was visible and we made straight for it. When at a distance of 4 miles I altered course N. 43° E. and at the end of an hour we found ourselves $3\frac{3}{4}$ miles from South Georgia; but the thick weather and snow again hid the shore from us and we had to work to windward. At 1.0 p.m. the snowstorm abated and we were able to see the shore once more, and steered along it. At 3.0 p.m. we passed between South Georgia and Pickersgill Island, which Captain Cook, on 20th January, 1775, named after one of the lieutenants on his ship. This island has a circumference of 3 miles, is fairly high and, between it and South Georgia, there lie two other islands and all three lie in a line only a little more than 2 miles long. Mr Lazarev had commissioned the above-mentioned English sealers to bring us penguins and eggs, but he was delayed thereby and remained so far behind that we lost sight of the *Mirnyi* while waiting for her, so that I was unable to take advantage of the favourable wind. For that reason and also because we were again overtaken by thick weather, I turned the *Vostok* into the wind at 3.0 p.m. The coast of South Georgia surveyed that day forms the continuation of the coast which we had seen the previous day; equally hilly, the tops of the mountains covered with snow, the valleys filled with ice. Only the steep rocks on which snow and ice cannot lie show a dark colour. Near the coast we observed some icebergs which probably had broken off from the shore. Meanwhile the wind had freshened with a high sea, and darkness, accompanied by rain, began to fall. We fired a gun signal from the *Vostok* every hour to let the *Mirnyi* know our position, but we heard no reply and only met at 8.0 p.m. when we bore to the south under reefed topsails.

At 1.0 a.m. we returned to the coast. The wind then shifted from west-south-west to west-north-west, accompanied by snow and rain. The mercury stood at 1° R. above freezing point (34·3° F.). At 6.0 a.m. we approached the shore opposite a bay which I named Novosilski Bay. It lies from Maria Bay S. 65° E., distant 22 miles.[1] On sounding we found 80 fathoms, mud bottom. From this point we held a course parallel with the island 2 miles distant at 8 knots. From Novosilski the coast runs in a direction south by east for about $5\frac{1}{2}$ miles until a sloping cape is reached, near which lie three low islands. I called this cape, Cape Kupriyanov;[2] from it to Cape Disappointment, so named by Captain Cook, the coast runs in a direction S. 50° 30′ E. for 10 miles and consists of high peaked rocky mountains between which all the gullies are covered with snow and ice. On the way from Cape Kupriyanov to Cape Disappointment, 4 miles from the former, there is a dangerous submerged rock $1\frac{1}{2}$ miles from the shore; in consequence of the high sea at the time there was surf breaking over it, but in calm weather this rock might be very dangerous. Near Cape Disappointment there are three islets: the first is a high rock close to the Cape itself and the last, called Green Island by Captain Cook on account of its colour,[3] lies 3 miles south of the cape. The mountainous coast runs for 5 miles S. 85° E. from Cape Disappointment and then turns to N. 40° E. At the change of direction lies the southern cape of South Georgia, lying in Lat. 54° 25′ S., Long. 36° 02′ W. At 9.30 we rounded this cape, where our survey ended, joining our survey of South Georgia up with the part of the island surveyed by Captain Cook forty-four years before us. Nineteen years before Captain Cook this shore had been discovered by the vessel *Leon* and had been named San Pedro, extending north-west and S. 61° E. to an extent of 92 miles.[4]

[1] The true distance is 42 miles. It is probably a misprint as it is correct on the chart in his "Atlas".
[2] Novosilski and Kupriyanov were sub-lieutenants of the *Mirnyi*.
[3] Actually there are four islets, low and flat, now known as the Green Islands, and they are covered with tussock grass.
[4] Dr H. R. Mill writes in his *Siege of the South Pole*: "The next incident in Antarctic History is the discovery by the Spanish merchant ship *Leon*, returning from Chile in 1756, of a high mountainous land covered with snow in 55° S. and far to the east of Cape Horn. This was named San Pedro after the Saint of the day and, though the longitude assigned by the discoverer is wrong by ten degrees, there is no reason to doubt that it was the island now known as South Georgia." Cook landed in Possession Bay on the north-east coast of the island in 1775. Whaling and sealing industries are now established on the island, but only certain areas have been thoroughly surveyed.

With very thick weather and rain, and at times with snow, the wind freshened and we were obliged to reef all but the two topsails and, under the lee of South Georgia, we waited for the *Mirnyi*. The wind increased more and more so that we struck the topyards. About midday the *Mirnyi* rejoined us. I had little hope that the weather would improve soon in order to look for a safe anchorage; moreover the land was inhabited only by penguins, sea elephants and seals; there were but few of the latter, since they are killed by the whalers. On sailing along more than half of the southern coast of the island, we saw not a single shrub nor any vegetation; everything was covered with snow and ice. To wait a week or more for better weather in order to survey the land, frozen and, so to say, dead as it was, seemed to me all the more useless as I should have missed the summer, which is the best time for navigation in the dangerous Antarctic Ocean. I therefore signalled to the *Mirnyi* to follow the *Vostok* and take a course south-east by east straight for the northern extremity of Sandwich Island, which I was anxious to survey from the eastern side since Captain Cook, during his survey of it, had only investigated the western side.[1] At 2.0 p.m. we shortened sail so as to remain as near to the *Mirnyi* as possible as she was scarcely visible on the dark horizon. Now and then, when the weather cleared for a few minutes, we saw Clerke Island, the position of which we fixed by bearings in Lat. 54° 55′ S., Long. 34° 46′ W. This island was discovered by Captain Cook and named after the first lieutenant on board his ship.

At 5.0 p.m. we were again obliged to proceed under the foresail only because the *Mirnyi* was falling behind and was lost in thick weather. At 8.0 p.m. the sun came out and we fixed the variation of the compass at 7° 29′ E., being in Lat. 54° 58′ S., Long. 35° 16′ W. At midnight, when Mr Lazarev again came up with us, we set fore and main topsails, close-reefing all the sails.

18th. At 6.0 a.m. the temperature was 34° F. Up to midday with a steady north-north-west wind, a high sea and thick weather we

---

[1] Captain Cook had discovered the group, now known as the South Sandwich Islands, from the southern end but, having had hazy weather, he was not certain whether they were islands or capes. He sailed up the western side of the southern four. After leaving the group, not having sighted the northernmost three, he summed up his opinions of his discovery in the characteristically cautious, yet wise, remark: "I concluded that what we had seen, which I named Sandwich Land, was either a group of islands, or else a point of a continent. For I firmly believe that there is a track of land near the pole which is the source of most of the ice that is spread over this vast Southern Ocean."

proceeded at 8 knots. The *Mirnyi* was to the windward and a little ahead of us. Then Mr Lazarev signalled to us that he had sighted land. On the *Vostok* we could see, through the mist, a mountainous shore, so we promptly turned to wait for clear weather without exposing ourselves to any risks by surveying the coast in the storm: we carried the main topsails close-reefed and the foresail and the mizzen staysail. The thermometer indicated 35·7° F. At 2.0 p.m. the weather was again so thick that we were unable to distinguish objects at more than a cable length.

19th. The unfavourable weather lasted until midnight and the thermometer stood at only 34·2° F. The vessels rolled so that we were forced to turn into the wind on another tack to the north. As the sea was brought on to the bow the excessive rolling was reduced. Close on midday we passed a dead whale which was surrounded by albatrosses and petrels flying round or swimming on the water. At noon we were in Lat. 56° 02′ S., Long. 32° 57′ W. The stream set N. 62° E. 39 miles in two days. With the fall of the wind we shot birds. Mr Ignatiev shot an albatross which measured 10 feet 5 inches from one wing-tip to the other. It was smoke-coloured and its head, neck and wings were brown. In its head, feet and wings it resembled the white albatross, with this difference, that the eyes were surrounded by a white band, one-tenth of an inch in width, and along the black beak it had narrow white streaks on both cheeks in a small depression on either side. The tail was pointed and longer than that of the white albatross.[1] Some of the officers wounded four penguins, of which two lived for a day. These, by their strange gait, waddling from one foot to the other, greatly amused the crew, who saw them close at hand for the first time. At 3 o'clock we observed ice east by north; it was this which, on the day before, in the darkness, we had taken for land. Some whales were spouting here and there. From 7 o'clock to midnight we passed through thick fog.

20th. With variable light winds and a heavy swell from the west, we took an easterly course and at daybreak found ice ahead of us at various points. Lieutenant Zavodovski shot two smoke-coloured albatrosses. At midday we were in Lat. 56° 13′ S., Long. 32° 25′ W. On sounding we found 260 sazhen (303 fathoms), but no bottom. Taking advantage of the absence of wind, we drifted and let down a thermometer of Mr Norie's to a depth of 270 sazhen (315 fathoms)

---

[1] A sooty albatross, carefully drawn by the artist, Mikhailov.

for ten minutes and found a temperature of 31·75° F. at that depth. On the surface the temperature was 48·75° F.[1] To my great regret, through the navigating officer's carelessness, this thermometer was broken; the loss was all the more unfortunate in that we had only one thermometer of this make. At 10.0 a.m. we passed an iceberg 1½ miles in circumference, standing 180 feet out of the water. On the north side the slope of the iceberg was covered with penguins. They were all standing flapping their wings. This immense iceberg, the like of which we saw for the first time, made a great impression upon us. We were then in Lat. 56° 04′ S., Long. 32° 15′ W. These great icebergs are common in the southern hemisphere. Captain Cook met ice in his voyage from the Cape of Good Hope to the south on the 10th of December 1772, in Lat. 51° 04′ S., Long. 22° 23′ W. In 1739 two vessels of the East India Company, sent on a voyage of discovery in southern latitudes,[2] saw ice in Lats. 47° and 48° S. Any intelligent reader will draw his own conclusion from these facts concerning the difference between the northern and southern hemispheres in this respect. During the day, penguins had been swimming and diving round about our vessels; some petrels and a few Egmont hens[3] also flew about.

21*st*. At midnight we had a light wind from south by east; a swell ran from the west. The temperature was 1·7° R. above freezing point (35·7° F.). At 3.0 a.m. the wind freshened and some snow fell, so we reefed the topsails. We observed an iceberg ahead which we passed at 8.0 a.m. At 10.0 a.m. we shortened all sail and struck the topyards. At midday we stood under two topsails and struck the topmasts. In the evening, to reduce speed, we turned the vessels into the wind to south-west by west. From 7 o'clock until midday it snowed.

22*nd*. We had a strong wind which raised a heavy sea; the moon was shining and the thermometer stood just below freezing point. During the night we encountered a line of drift ice in immense floes running east by north and south-west by south. In the morning we had a fall of snow. At daybreak we set our course east by south, but

---

[1] This figure for the surface temperature of the water is obviously wrong in the original, and cannot be accounted for except by remembering that the Fahrenheit scale would be unfamiliar to the Russians.

[2] This is a reference to the expedition led by Captain Bouvet of the French navy, in the *Aigle* and *Marie*, two ships lent by the French East India Company. In spite of meeting ice in 48° S. he succeeded in discovering the island named after him, in 54° S.

[3] An earlier and clumsy name for the Skua gull.

we could not keep it for more than an hour as the thick weather forced us to turn the ships into the wind. At 8.0 a.m. the weather cleared a little and we turned east-north-east. Snow continued to fall from time to time and obscure everything which, but for its presence, we might have observed. At 11.0 a.m., when it had cleared a little, an unknown island appeared about 13 miles to the northward. We headed for it with more sail, and tried to lie up as near to it as the wind permitted; we were anxious to fix the position of the island, but the thick weather interfered. Soon after noon the sun appeared from behind the clouds for a short time and Mr Simanov succeeded in taking an altitude of the sun, from which we fixed our position at midday as Lat. 56° 43′ S., Long. 28° 07′ W. At the same time we observed the island bearing, N. 24° W. distant 5 miles, which gives its position as Lat. 56° 41′ 30″ S., Long. 28° 10′ W. According to the observation made by Mr Lazarev, the position is Lat. 56° 41′ S., Long. 28° 07′ 40″ W.[1] The island has the appearance of a mountain standing sheer out of the water; its length being rather less than 2 miles and width about half that. Its southern extremity ends in a low hill, resembling a sugar loaf in form, which from a distance appears isolated from the rest. The whole island was covered with snow and, as it was so far unknown, I called it Lyeskov Island in honour of the third lieutenant of the *Vostok*.[2] At 4.0 p.m. we steered south-south-east in order to sight Candlemas Island, discovered by Captain Cook. We kept this course, having thick weather and snow, until 9.0 p.m.; then, owing to the extreme darkness of the night, with a light north-north-west wind, we hove to so as to await daylight. In the course of the day we were accompanied by great numbers of the various birds before mentioned and by penguins. The latter have a habit of raising themselves out of the water to call to each other as people do in a thicket.

23*rd*. At midnight the temperature was 0·8° R. (34° F.); we had a heavy swell from the west-north-west, from which we concluded

---

[1] As will be seen on the chart of comparative positions for the various islands, this was an extraordinarily accurate determination considering the bad weather.

[2] Lyeskov Island has been visited four times since this voyage, but no landing has ever been made. For the best description of all these islands, the reader is referred to the report on them by Dr Stanley Kemp and Lieutenant Nelson (*Discovery Reports*, vol. III) from which the following facts are taken. Bellingshausen's description is very accurate, though he does not seem to have approached closer than about 5 miles. Like the rest of the group, the island is certainly volcanic, but it is not established whether it is still active. The island is heavily cliffed and has three large caverns on the northern side.

that no large mass of land could possibly lie in that direction, at least not in close proximity to us. When the thick weather and snow had abated, we saw high land to the north-east, the summit of which was hidden in the clouds. At daybreak an island appeared in sight, quite clear of fog, with a high mountain in the middle of it, its summit and sides covered with snow; its steeper slopes, where the snow and ice could not lie, were dark in colour. The island is round, with a circumference of about 12 miles, but it is impossible to land on account of the steep rocky shore. Fine weather permitted us to take midday observations, and we found ourselves in Lat. 56° 44′ 18″ S., Long. 27° 41′ 51″ W. According to this observation, the position of the mountain in the middle of the island is Lat. 56° 44′ 18″ S., Long. 27° 11′ 51″ W. I named our discovery "Visokoi (High) Island", as it was distinguished from the other islands by its height.[1]

In the morning thick black clouds were visible ahead of us to the north which seemed to remain in the same position. This led me to believe that there must be land in that direction, and we at once set our course northward towards these clouds. Indeed, having proceeded a little way, we saw an island and, on approaching, we observed on the south-western side of the island a crater, from which a thick stinking vapour was continually rising. As we sailed with the wind along the island, this vapour formed an unbroken dense cloud and from afar resembled the thick smoke from the funnel of a steamer, only of much greater volume and density. I named this island, in honour of the captain-lieutenant of the *Vostok*, Zavodovski Island. The high mountain in the middle of the island with the sloping sides had the appearance of two Roman "SS" leaning against each other. In passing along the island, we noticed that there was some snow on the mountain, but very little on the lower ranges and none at all on the side of the crater.[2] Probably for these reasons the penguins had chosen the island for a dwelling-place, for from the base midway up the hill every spot was covered with them. The shore on the south-western side is sheer and inaccessible; the colour, like that of the mountain itself, is dark red with a yellowish tinge in parts. At 8.0 p.m., after we had gone round the island and finished our survey, we double-reefed the mainsails so as to remain here until

---

[1] Visokoi Island rises to 3000 feet.
[2] In spite of the mountain being a volcano, and therefore subject to change, this description would do for the present day.

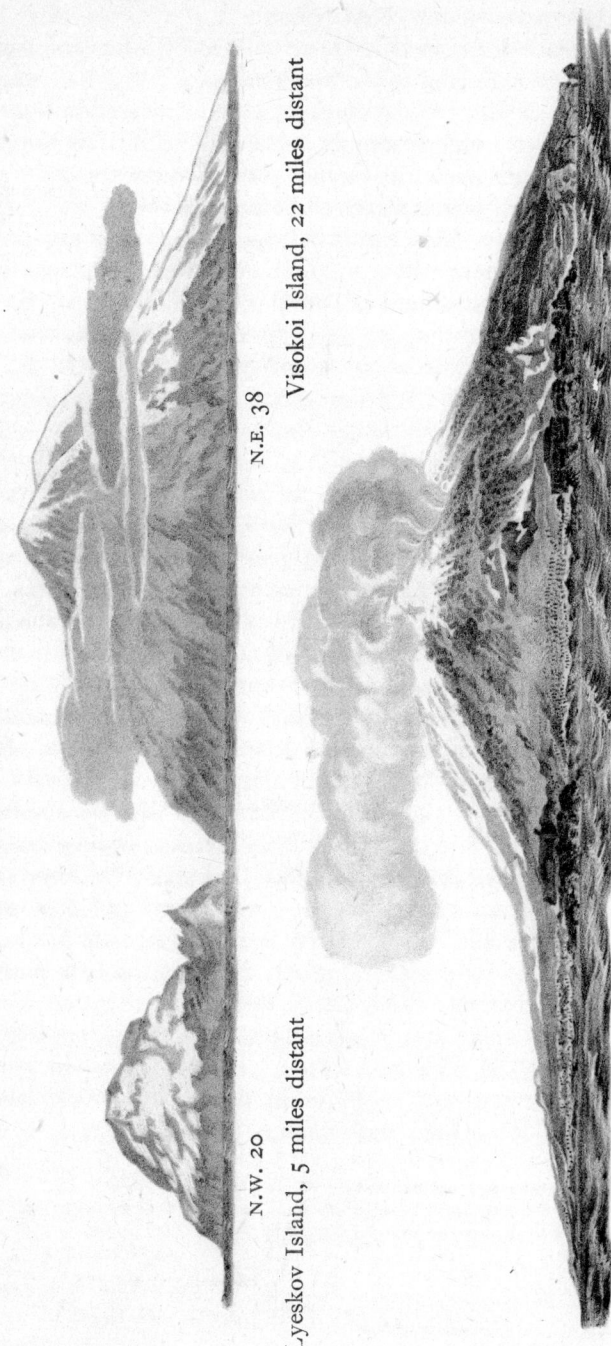

Lyeskov Island, 5 miles distant
N.W. 20
Visokoi Island, 22 miles distant
N.E. 38
Zavodovski Island, 2 miles distant
East
South-east
VOL. I
PLATE III

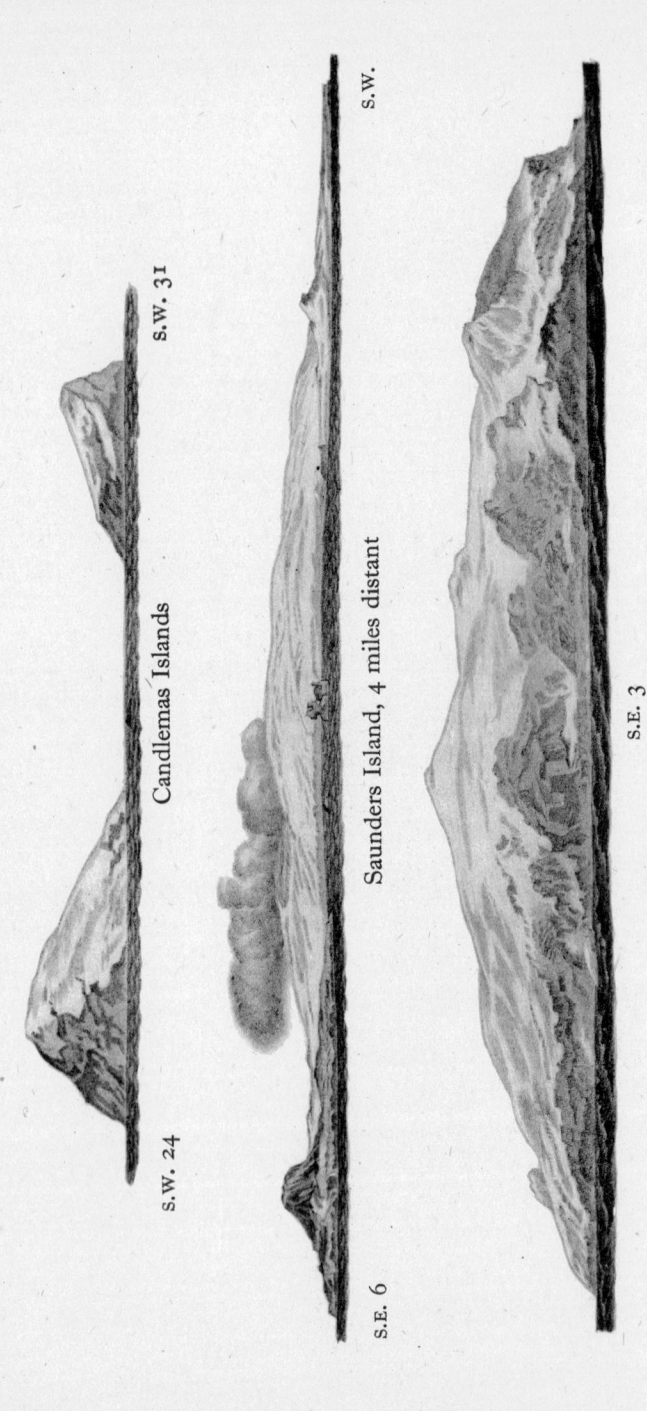

Candlemas Islands

Saunders Island, 4 miles distant

Montagu Island, 4 miles distant

PLATE IV

VOL. I

the following morning as I intended to survey the island from the shore.

24th. During the night the temperature was 33° F. and we set a course at 10.0 a.m. for the south-western cape of the island. At a distance of 1½ miles we lay to and lowered a boat, in which Mr Zavodovski, the astronomer Simanov and Mr Demidov went ashore. At the same time, on sounding, we found 110 sazhen (128 fathoms), but no bottom. Soon afterwards the *Mirnyi* came up to us and asked permission by signal also to send a boat ashore with officers. At midday we found ourselves in Lat. 56° 15′ 35″ S., Long. 27° 34′ 53″ W. At the same time Mr Zavodovski found by observations Lat. 56° 18′ S., Long. 27° 28′ 53″ W. The circumference of the island is 10 miles and the height of the mountain is 1200 feet above sea level. At 1 o'clock the boat returned. Mr Zavodovski reported to me that they landed easily amongst rocks, had climbed from 18 to 20 feet up the rocks and found great numbers of penguins sitting on eggs. They would not move out of the way except when struck with sticks. Our travellers had gone almost half way up the mountain and had found the ground warm. A particularly bad smell from the great quantity of guano from the penguins forced them soon to return to the vessel. They brought from the island nine Egmont hens, a few penguins and a few burnt stones.[1] The penguins brought were of two kinds; one kind was a little smaller and to distinguish it from the big variety we called it the "common" penguin.[2] They had black pointed beaks, the upper mandible curving downwards, the neck white underneath with a narrow horizontal black stripe, the back brown with blue-grey speckles, their flippers are the same colour on the upper surface as the back, while the belly is white and glossy; the flippers underneath are white, the feet flesh coloured and the eyes straw coloured with dark pupils. The other kind is larger and more beautiful than the smaller kind; the beaks, which are not of the same shape, are red, the eyes red with small black pupils; long yellow feathers grow on the head; rather shorter ones on the tail. We called these "Mandarin" penguins on

---

[1] At least three landings have now been made on Zavodovski Island and the survey by *Discovery II* has established its chief features. All who have visited the island have noted the strong fumes, and when Captain Larsen landed on the island in 1908 he was rendered seriously ill by them. The crater mouth is still on the western side as in 1819, and still recognizable are the two long fissures down the eastern side of the mountain described by our author as similar to two SS leaning against each other. His description of snow being abundant on the mountain but less so on the lower slopes still holds good. [2] The ringed penguin (*Pygoscelis antarctica*).

account of the colouring of their plumage.[1] They were the same that we saw before reaching South Georgia. The "common" penguins on the shore sat on two eggs only; they pursued our officers as they returned to their boats and were ready to attack them with their flippers, which deal fairly heavy blows. The "Mandarins" had each one egg only under them; in appearance they are prouder, quieter and more peaceful than the smaller penguins. At 30 or 40 sazhen (about half a cable's length) from the shore the depth was 25 sazhen (30 fathoms). I called this group of three islands discovered by me the Marquis de Traversey Islands, after our then Minister who had so kindly interested himself in us on our departure.

As we found ourselves close to a small ice floe I decided to avail myself of this opportunity; so we approached it and sent boats with a few men to hack out some ice and bring it on board. At the end of an hour and a half they had brought enough to fill six large barrels, some portable cauldrons and all the available powder barrels, after which the boats were hauled up and we set sail. Some of this ice I ordered, as an experiment, and without telling any of the officers, to be melted down as water for our tea, and all pronounced it to be excellent and the tea admirable. This assured us that when navigating amongst ice it would always be possible to have good water.

If there were any high islands to the north they should have been visible during the clear weather which had prevailed on the previous day from midday until sunset and again on this day, at least from the look-out, within 40 miles or more, but as we did not see any we concluded that the chain of these islands did not extend any further to the north and therefore decided to proceed to the Candlemas Islands.

At midnight the temperature fell to 0·8° R. below freezing point (29·8° F.). We tacked into a head wind from the south. I requested the *Mirnyi* by signal to send us the priest to conduct a service on the anniversary of the deliverance of Russia from the invasion of the French and their allies.[2] On ordinary days the crew had one half salt

---

[1] *Eudyptes chrysolophus*; called "Macaroni" penguins on account of their dandified appearance.

[2] Napoleon began his retreat from Moscow on October 15th, 1812. At the Battle of Beresina which lasted from the 22nd to 28th of November, the Russians completed the destruction which the cold had already begun. On December 18th Napoleon reached Paris and from that date the nations of Europe combined in a war of liberation against the despot. Probably in the last week of that year the Russian people were relieved from their dread of the tyrant, and that, together with the fact that December 24th was Christmas Eve, made it a suitable day for thanksgiving and rejoicing.

pork and one half fresh, but on this day they had the favourite Russian fare—cabbage soup with pickled cabbage and fresh pork and a pie of rice and minced meat. After dinner a half tankard of beer was served out to each; at four o'clock a glass of rum punch with lemon and sugar. After this the crew were as gay as if they had been in Russia on a feast day, instead of being far away from their own country in the Antarctic Ocean, surrounded by fogs in the darkness of continual night and snow. Mr Lazarev with his officers was entertained to dinner on board the *Vostok*, and the pleasant company remained together until the evening. Mr Demidov shot a petrel of a kind which we had not seen before; the back light blue, the tips of the wings white with black spots, white underneath. When it flies it extends its wings much farther than the other birds of this species; in size it was a little larger than a pigeon. We named this bird—as Captain Cook had done before us—the large blue petrel.

26*th*. From morning until midday we had a thick fog. At midday we were in Lat. 56° 32′ 12″ S., Long. 26° 26′ W. From 3.0 p.m. fog covered the horizon till night. At 6.0 p.m. we encountered a small ice floe, lay to alongside it and sent a boat to cut some ice and bring it on board, but as this ice was very brittle and some salt water got mixed with it, we could not make any use of it.

27*th*. At midnight the mercury stood at 32° F. and there was a slight fall of snow. At daybreak we saw to the south, at a distance which we estimated as 30 miles, some land which, owing to the thick weather and the snow falling at times, was sometimes hidden from view. At 11.0 a.m. we observed between the Candlemas Islands yet a third island. Captain Cook in his Voyage speaks of two islands only and of a rock lying between them. Owing to this similarity we assumed these islands to be the Candlemas Islands, discovered by this explorer. He named them after the day on which he saw them.[1] At 4.0 p.m., when a calm set in and the ships were stationary, we lowered an ordinary thermometer enclosed in a cylinder made of sheet iron into the water. This cylindrical case had been made on the vessel and had valves at both ends which opened as the case was lowered with the lead, so that the water flowed through. As it was brought up again,

---

[1] Bellingshausen's description of the Candlemas group as consisting of three islands has caused some interest since Cook definitely spoke of two, while Larsen and Filchner in 1908 and 1911 spoke of only one. Dr Kemp has provided the most probable explanation of Bellingshausen's mistake, namely, that the low snow-free part of the larger island looks, from a distance, as though it were separate from the higher snow-covered part.

the valves closed and the water which had flowed in at the lowest depth remained in it. Its temperature would not change much when the cylinder was drawn up with the necessary speed. The Réaumur thermometer was lowered in this way to a depth of 220 sazhen (256 fathoms); when taken out of the case, it registered a temperature of 1° R. below freezing point (29° F.). At the same time the thermometer showed ½° above freezing point on the surface. Although the raising of the cylinder from that depth took only 4½ minutes, even in that short interval the thermometer had time to become warmer passing through the water which, as is known, becomes gradually warmer towards the surface. Besides, we cannot guarantee that no water at all had got into the cylinder near the surface where the water is warmer and lighter. The specific gravity of the water brought up from that depth in this cylinder proved to be 1·1009, and on the surface at freezing point in the same place, it was 1·0997. This observation shows that the deep sea water is salter than that on the surface.

28*th.* Nothing of any importance happened. A head wind was blowing just as during the two previous days, with the only difference of continual changes of weather; sometimes thick, then clear, now snow fell in flakes, then for a time rain. We tacked about to the south.

29*th.* The thermometer at midnight stood at 1° R. below freezing point (29° F.); below deck it was 8·4° R. above freezing point (51·4° F.). At daybreak the wind went round to the south. At 8.0 a.m. we crossed the transit-line of the Candlemas Islands, both islands bearing 70° S.W. At 10 a.m. we left to port a large iceberg, round which a large quantity of ice floated. At 11.0 a.m. thick weather with snow set in from the north-west and I shortened sail to give the *Mirnyi* a chance of coming up with us.

As we had fixed the position of the very high Marquis de Traversey Islands in clear weather and as we could take no observations at midday, we fixed our position and the position of the Candlemas Islands from the Marquis de Traversey Islands. The most easterly of the Candlemas Islands is in Lat. 57° 09′ 45″ S., Long. 26° 44′ W., lying north-east to S. 50° W. with a circumference of 6¼ miles. The eastern side is higher than the western. The west island lies in Lat. 57° 10′ 55″ S., Long. 26° 51′ W., runs north-east and S. 60° W. with a circumference of 4½ miles. The third is in Lat. 57° 09′ S., Long. 26° 47′ 30″ W.

We proceeded at 6 and 7 knots through rain and sleet. The temperature at midday was 33·5° F. At 3.0 p.m. we observed through the thick weather the coast of Saunders Island in a south-south-west direction about 7 miles distant. It was also discovered and named by Captain Cook. We kept along the apparently inaccessible north-eastern side of the island, whose hills were hidden by clouds. Off the middle of this side lie great submerged rocks, extending for 2 miles. Passing at a distance of $3\frac{1}{2}$ miles, we found a depth of 42 sazhen (49 fathoms). The *Mirnyi*, passing along farther inshore, found a depth of 27 sazhen (31 fathoms), bottom small black pebbles. From the eastern side the island is high and sheer. It lies south-east to north-west and is $6\frac{1}{2}$ miles in length with a circumference of 17 miles; it is covered with ice and snow, though not so deeply as Torson Island,[1] although it lies farther south. This led us to think that this island perhaps also possessed an active volcano like Zavodovski Island, which was much freer of ice and snow than the others.[2] The centre of Saunders Island is in Lat. 57° 52′ S., Long. 26° 24′ W. Captain Cook fixed the position of this island as Lat. 57° 49′ S., Long. 26° 44′ W. The mean compass variation we found to be 4° 52′ E.

After 6.0 p.m. the shore was hidden by thick weather and the wind took us out of our course south by east for about an hour. We then steered once again direct to Cape Montagu, so named by Captain Cook.[3] At 10.0 p.m. we observed land and turned away from it and remained under shortened sail; but at 1.30 a.m. we unreefed the sails and turned again towards the shore in order to reach Cape Montagu by daybreak. At 5.0 a.m., when the weather cleared, we saw before us a high island, the north side of which turned towards us, presenting a high shore broken at three points, the valleys between the heights slightly sloping and covered with snow and ice; a good many large and small icebergs floated off the shore. The larger masses had a

[1] This appears to be a curious misprint for Lyeskov. Torson was another officer on the *Vostok*, of equal rank, and possibly the leader had been undecided as to which should receive the honour of having an island named after him.

[2] Bellingshausen discovered next day that he was quite right in his suspicion that Saunders Island had an active volcano. Although the main dome of the island, rising to 2640 feet, is covered with glaciers, it is in full activity, while near the coast are many fumaroles and warm areas where the snow melts immediately. In this island, in contrast to Zavodovski Island, there seems to be distinct evidence of change in the south-east point, where the high dark dome appears in the artist's drawing on Plate 3. This is now replaced by an area of volcanic ash, still warm, and at least one recent crater.

[3] It was called a cape by Cook because he thought it was a point projecting from land connecting it to "Cape Bristol".

regular shape, that is, they had a flat surface slightly convex, with sides perpendicular, as is usually the case near the shore. From this we concluded that large masses of ice had formed on the shore and had broken off from it by sheer weight. Keeping at a distance of 6 miles from the shore, we held a course parallel with the north coast. At 8.0 a.m. we passed the eastern headland, then turned southward along the steep east coast.

30th. The morning was beautiful: Saunders Island, cleared of clouds, presented a magnificent sight, with its majestic snow-covered summits gleaming in the sunlight. From a crater thick smoke was rising, spreading out in the air, and on the horizon here and there white scattered masses of ice were visible. Pursuing our course with a fresh wind through the broken ice, we reached, at 10 a.m., the southern extremity of the island, which had the shape of a sugar-loaf situated at the very cape. At 11.0 a.m., after we had gone a good deal southward, we sighted Cape Montagu from the southern side, so we had thus completed the survey of the whole island. This part of the coast, called "Cape Montagu" by Captain Cook, is therefore in fact an island, about 25 miles in circumference; the northern side of the island is higher than the southern; the whole is covered with ice and snow and there is apparently no good anchorage. I accordingly named this island "Montagu", as Captain Cook had named the Cape.[1]

At midday the sky was covered with clouds and the coast disappeared from sight. Captain Cook, being off Cape Montagu on 1st February, 1775, determined in clear weather its position as Lat. 58° 27′ S., Long. 26° 44′ W. We were not in a position to make observations at midday, and therefore accepted the latitude of the Cape as fixed by Captain Cook as the true one, correcting our own reading. At midday the thermometer stood at 33·9° F. Owing to the particularly thick weather, we were unable to see farther than 1½ miles. At 2.0 p.m. the wind shifted from west-north-west and we turned on a new tack to the north-north-east and reefed sails. At 3.0 p.m. we found a depth of 80 sazhen (93 fathoms) and no bottom. At 5.0 p.m., when the wind changed and blew from north-west by north, we turned to south-west by south, and for the rest of that day tacked under

[1] The keen powers of observation of the Russian captain in this account of the island are proved by the report and survey of it by *Discovery II*. The island is the highest of the group, its summit, Mount Belinda, being 4500 feet. The high conical point, compared by Bellingshausen to a sugar-loaf, is a very striking feature, 1600 feet in height.

shortened sails on account of the darkness and the broken ice which we tried to avoid so as not to be caught in it.

31st. At midnight, with a west wind with slight gusts and thick weather, we hove to. The thermometer stood at 0·4° R. below zero (31·1° F.); both decks where the crew slept had a temperature of 8·4° R. (50·4° F.). On sounding we had 150 sazhen (175 fathoms) and no bottom.

At 2.0 a.m. as the weather cleared, we sighted land to the south-south-west, called Cape Bristol by Captain Cook. We turned south-west in the direction of this land, passing through a great deal of brash ice in order to reach its western extremity and then with the favourable wind to pass along the northern shore. At 4.0 a.m. we passed a large flat ice floe. The thick weather shut out everything and only cleared a little at 9.30; then we saw three small islands off the western side of Cape Bristol. The most westerly of these islets, sugar-loaf in shape, we recognized as Peak Freezeland, which was fixed by Captain Cook in Lat. 59° S. We turned S. 17° E. so as to pass round the visible eastern extremity of the shore from Cape Bristol. At 10.0 a.m., 4 miles distant from it north-east by north, the shore and all the masses of ice in sight were lost to view in a thick fog. On sounding, we had 185 sazhen (216 fathoms) and still no bottom. The *Mirnyi* was still some distance off, so we reefed sails; after half an hour she came up with us, when we sailed south-south-east. After 11 o'clock, as the thick weather still continued, accompanied by a heavy sleet storm, and we constantly encountered very large masses of floating ice, we were obliged to turn into the wind on the port tack.

At midday the thermometer stood at 33·2° F. The *Mirnyi* was in our wake, and the heavy snowfall continued. On account of icebergs and broken ice, the crew was stationed along the side of the vessel to listen for the sound of surf breaking on the ice and warning us thereby of its neighbourhood. After 5.0 p.m. we heard very near us and to leeward the sound of unusually high breakers. Mr Zavadovski and some of the other officers believed that we were near a shore on which the sea was breaking. The snow was now falling so fast that we could not see farther than 15 sazhen (35 yards); in such circumstances it was extremely dangerous to remain in this position, and I therefore decided to turn on another tack. The *Mirnyi* was signalled to turn, which was done and we steered north-north-west. I hoped by doing so to get clear of the ice, for icebergs and large masses of ice were continually passing us. At 10.0 p.m. we encountered an impenetrable mass of brash ice and were forced to turn again and to remain under the topsails only so as to reduce speed. The sails were so much covered with snow that in order to shake it off we had constantly to turn the ships sharply into the wind and slacken the sails. All this time the watch were barely able to sweep up and throw overboard the thick cover of snow on deck. At last at midnight the snow stopped. In the next 24 hours we saw near the vessel a great number of different kinds of sea birds; penguins played about in the water or sat on the ice in large numbers.

1st. On the first day of the New Year we wished each other a happy escape from our dangerous position and a safe return to our dear home on the conclusion of the difficult voyage before us. The thermometer stood at 31·5° F. There was a fresh wind from the north-east by north, and a heavy swell was running from the north. We were just congratulating ourselves that the snowfall had stopped; but our joy did not last long, for at 2 o'clock instead of snow thick fog with wind set in. We found ourselves again amidst a quantity of small ice and the cries of the penguins were to be heard on all sides. Soon after 5.0 a.m. we saw through the fog many icebergs close to us to the north-east. The noise of the waves breaking on the ice and the screaming of the penguins created a most unpleasant feeling. After an exchange of signals the *Vostok* and the *Mirnyi* turned away from the icebergs on a starboard tack, and at the time of turning, when the sails slackened and shook the whole gear, icicles and the frozen snow from the rigging fell on the decks; the frozen ropes looked as if they were threaded through glass beads of a thickness of from $\frac{1}{20}$ to $\frac{1}{2}$ an inch. The crew during each watch knocked it off with spikes from the shrouds.

At 6.0 a.m. the thermometer showed 30° F. At 7.0 a.m. on the *Vostok* a signal was fired and at 8.0 a.m. a fog signal was sounded in order that the *Mirnyi* should reply giving her position; but with the dense fog and the roar of the sea breaking everywhere on the ice, the *Mirnyi* did not hear the signal, whilst we on the *Vostok* did not hear the *Mirnyi's* guns. At 10.0 a.m. the wind was blowing from the east. At midday we passed a number of icebergs and floating ice, to avoid which we were obliged now to keep close to the wind and then bear away. At midday the fog cleared a little, and as we could now see the dangers around us, we were able to avoid them more easily. We also saw the *Mirnyi*, about which we had become very anxious. On sounding we had 120 sazhen (140 fathoms) and no bottom. In spite of the bad weather and our dangerous position amongst unseen ice, all the crew dressed in parade uniform in the morning to celebrate the New Year. In the morning for breakfast we served out tea with rum; for dinner there was good cabbage soup with sauerkraut and pork; after dinner, besides the usual ration, all were given a glass of hot punch and, in the evening, before the rice gruel, a glass of grog. The crews of both vessels were well and cheerful; we only regretted that, owing to the dangerous position and the stormy weather, we were unable to pass the day in the company of Captain Lazarev and the officers of the *Mirnyi*. At midday the temperature was 33° F.; towards 1 p.m., as the *Mirnyi* was near us, we set the main topsail and took a north-north-east course. At 2.0 p.m., in order to equalize the speed of the vessels, we double-reefed the mainsail; until 5.0 p.m. we passed icebergs and floating ice. At 5.0 p.m. we turned on another tack to a west-south-west course. We saw whales playing about in the water, rising perpendicularly about one-third of their whole length out of the water and then diving again, showing their horizontal tails.[1] We again passed through a quantity of ice until 9.0 p.m., when the weather improved a little and we saw Cape Bristol S. 58° W. at an estimated distance of about 5½ miles. With the rough weather it was impossible to make any survey of the shore and we therefore stood away from it.

2*nd.* The wind continued to blow fresh from south-east by east. There was a strong swell from the west and the waves produced a good deal of pitching and rolling. There were 3° of frost. The fog shut out both shore and horizon. Our course took us straight for an iceberg, and at 2.0 a.m. we had to change to another tack, but at 4.30 a.m. we turned back to the former course. At 7.0 a.m. we once more encountered a huge iceberg, and to circumnavigate it had to turn northwards and then steer north-east by east again. Round this iceberg great numbers of white petrels were circling. At 8.0 a.m. the weather began to clear a little, and we could see the shores of both Cape Montagu and Cape Bristol and were thereby able to fix our positions. We turned towards Cape Bristol under full sail; by 11.0 a.m. we had passed six icebergs. Our course then took us past the eastern extremity of the

---

[1] These were probably Killer whales (*Orca*) whose habit it is, when in thick pack ice, to rear their heads high out of the water to look over the ice.

aforementioned headland and, approaching it about 11.0 a.m., we therefore turned on another tack so as to pass along the eastern side of the Cape, as Captain Cook had not surveyed it from that side. After three tacks we rounded the eastern cape on the fourth and observed that the coast, which runs in a north-west by west to south-east by east direction with a circumference of 17 miles, is uneven in height. At the southern extremity there is a pointed mountain completely covered with snow and ice, except a few particularly steep dark patches.[1] Proceeding on a S. 14° W. course for $4\frac{1}{2}$ hours, we observed the land extending S. 54° W., called Southern Thule by Captain Cook. At 6.0 p.m. we found ourselves in Lat. 59° 13' S., Long. 26° 13' W. and observed to port and ahead of us a great deal of pack ice, which we passed through in a direction S. 54° 30' W. At 10.30 p.m., as the ice was becoming much more frequent, we turned on another tack to pass the night under shortened sail.

3rd. At midnight the thermometer stood at 30·2° F. At 2.0 a.m. we passed one iceberg to starboard and one to port. At 3.0 a.m., at dawn, we turned again S. 40° W. with an east-south-east wind, going 6 knots; in the morning we proceeded under all sail to make the most of the clear weather. We passed through layers of broken ice, not unlike river ice, except that it was much thicker. The officer of the watch was stationed forward and guided the ship by ordering port or starboard helm to avoid the ice; on the port side the ice was quite impenetrable; from the top and the look-out nothing was to be seen but an endless icefield and in the middle of it here and there were icebergs of different shapes and sizes.

The Thule group consists of one high rock and three small islands, of which one is smaller than the other two. These islands are high and inaccessible and lie in Lat. 59° 26' S., Long. 27° 13' 30" W. The middle one, the largest, is about 6 miles long. I called it Cook Island in honour of the great explorer who had been the first to see this shore and who regarded it as the most southern land on the globe. The most westerly island is about 3 miles long and the smallest is about two-

---

[1] Captain Bellingshausen is very brief about this island, but nevertheless he manages to mention most of the characteristics which have now been investigated by *Discovery II*. The island rises to 3600 feet in Mount Darnley, which appears to be part of a large extinct crater. The whole of the island is covered with glaciers, including the "pointed mountain" in the south, which is 1900 feet high. This high dome and the large isolated rock of Freezeland Peak (900 feet) are the most striking features of the group.

thirds of a mile in length. Between the two largest islands lies a rock; all three are covered with snow and ice. Captain Cook, in consequence of the stormy weather, did not approach Thule and Montagu Islands, and therefore the ice between them appeared to him to be land, which he named in honour of the then First Lord of the Admiralty, Lord Sandwich.[1] Captain Cook saw these islands first, and therefore the names given by him must remain unchanged that the memory of this daring explorer may be handed on to posterity. Consequently I also call them the Sandwich Islands.[2]

We continued on our course S. 40° W., always amidst very thick pack ice, and at 10.0 a.m. we proceeded along the edge of an iceberg about 3 miles square. Its surface was quite level, the sides perpendicular and on the left, that is to the east, of a height of about 30 feet. We saw everywhere uninterrupted ice, formed of flat blocks piled one upon another in different directions; here and there in the middle of the field large icebergs of various forms stood out. Some of these were of a light blue colour; in my opinion, because the iceberg, having lost its balance, had turned upside down and had not yet had time to be bleached by the air.[3] To starboard to the west there appeared to be less broken ice but a great many icebergs. Proceeding from early morning through this ice, we could not avoid several times colliding

---

[1] John Montagu, fourth Earl of Sandwich, was born in 1718. Though a man of great talent and activity, he was unprincipled and profligate. On three occasions during his public career he was made First Lord of the Admiralty and once dismissed from that office in disgrace. At this time the British Navy had reached its lowest depths of corruption. Lord Sandwich retired into private life on the fall of the North Administration in 1782.

[2] These three islands, about which Bellingshausen is tantalizingly brief, are perhaps the most interesting in the whole Sandwich group. They have been fully investigated by *Discovery II*, and Dr Kemp very appropriately gave the name "Bellingshausen" to the most easterly of the three. This island, though described in the text and figured in the "Atlas", is not shown on the Russian chart, which is additional evidence that the charts were constructed by some one who was not on the expedition and who had not had access to the artist's drawings. As shown in the sketches in the *Discovery* report, the island has a large crater which is in the solfataric stage, but is only 500 feet high at the highest point. The sketch by the Russian artist is very similar to the modern one from the same point of view, though this can hardly be taken as evidence of no change since that time. The two larger islands, Cook and Thule, were shown by the soundings taken between them to be the remnants of the rim of a very large crater, the cauldron of which now forms a deep basin.

[3] This ingenious explanation cannot be accepted unfortunately, the true reason being that, in the normal Antarctic iceberg, the upper layers are compressed snow, rather than ice, while towards the bottom the lack of air inclusions gives it the true ice-blue reflection.

with it, and, scraping the whole length of the side of the vessel, it damaged the copper in places and tore away the heads of the copper nails. The damage, however, was slight, as there was no sea on, and the vessels proceeded smoothly.

At midday we fixed our position as in Lat. 59° 57′ S., Long. 27° 32′ W. The centre of Thule Island bore N. 13° E., 32 miles from us; Cook Island N. 32° E., 32 miles. The mercury stood at only 33·2° F.

At 2.0 p.m. we braced round the mainsails and topsails to give the *Mirnyi*, which had dropped astern, time to come up with us. Meanwhile, in order not to waste time, we sent off two boats to cut some ice and bring it on board. To take it in conveniently, we packed the ice in sugar sacks and then filled all the empty receptacles available, even filling the sacks with it, using them first. No ice was put directly into the barrels down in the hold lest it should cause damp, but the water melted from the ice was run into the barrels. We lay to until 7.0 p.m. By then we had had time to fill ten barrels of medium size, tubs and other vessels with ice. We found ourselves in Lat. 60° 3′ 33″ S., Long. 27° 39′ W., the magnetic variation being 7° 4′ E. At 7.0 p.m. the wind veered through south to the south-west quarter. We hoisted sail and, passing through small ice, in a direction S. 40° E., we pushed farther south with the object of circumventing the pack ice, which we had observed to eastward. Snow forced us to shorten sail and to proceed with the greatest caution. In the course of this day, we saw only a few whales, white petrels and penguins. The other sea birds which usually accompanied us daily had disappeared.

4*th.* At midnight we had 2° F. of frost; below in the crew's quarters it was 51° F. Snow fell until 2.0 a.m., when we hoisted sail and proceeded eastwards with a south wind. A little before 4 o'clock, in Lat. 60° 15′ S., Long. 27° 16′ W., we encountered impenetrable pack ice, amongst which were many icebergs. This icefield, probably a continuation of the pack ice near which we had found ourselves on the previous day, had a south-south-east direction. We therefore turned on the port tack and proceeded among many icebergs. In Lat. 60° 16′ 47″ S., Long. 27° 24′ W., we found the magnetic variation to be 7° 9′ E., with the ship at the time on a west-south-west course. At 6.30 a.m. we turned on a starboard tack and took a south-east course with icebergs and broken ice on both sides. At 9.0 a.m. it was impossible to continue on this course as we encountered to the east and south an extensive icefield; from the look-out nothing but unending ice and large icebergs was to be seen; we therefore turned on another tack. The weather was fine. At midday we were in Lat. 60° 25' 20" S., Long. 27° 38' 30" W., with a view from the look-out of 40 miles; no continuation of the Sandwich Islands towards the south could be seen. The icefield lay from south to west. Finding ourselves among floating ice and not seeing any possibility of passing round it to the southward during the good season, I considered it desirable to leave this locality betimes and to circumvent it on the north so as not to lose time uselessly nor to expose the vessel to damage on the first approach of stormy weather, a danger which we would certainly have run in that place surrounded by ice. We therefore turned to west by north past numerous icebergs and a great deal of broken ice. After 5 miles, we altered course to north by west with the object of passing round the western side of Thule, Cook and Bristol Islands. We kept on this course for 22 miles, having on both sides an horizon strewn with icebergs; then snow, hiding the ice from us, made navigation still more dangerous. At 5.30 we turned north by east, in order to pass again within sight of Thule and Cook Islands. Whilst on this course we noted penguins sitting on some of the icebergs and large blocks of ice. The weather got thicker, squalls accompanied by snow set in and forced us to shorten sail; the snow sometimes fell so thickly that, as we approached the ice, the ships scarcely answered the helm in time to clear it. After proceeding 30 miles, we turned northward and kept on this course for 9 miles up to 11.0 p.m. In order not to approach too close to Thule Island in the darkness and thick weather, as it was surrounded by icebergs, we turned to about north-east by east at 11.0 p.m. At several points during the day we had seen whales which, as it were, tried to amuse us by spouting water like fountains.

5th. In the course of the night, we proceeded at the rate of 5 to 6 knots; the temperature was 29° F. At 5.0 a.m. we made more sail. When proceeding from the west between the Bristol and Montagu Islands, we found, on a north-east course, a magnetic variation of 5° 52' E. At 6.0 a.m. we again passed over the meridian of Peak Freezeland, a high pointed rock on the western side of Bristol Island. It was discovered and so named by Captain Cook. Cape Bristol lay from us S. 30° E., and the Peak of the eastern extremity S. 37° E. Passing Peak Freezeland we fixed its longitude at 26° 29' 06" W. On the *Mirnyi* the magnetic deviation was found to be 6° 32' E. on a course north-east by east-half-east. From daybreak until midday we passed many icebergs and much broken ice. Again the officer on watch, stationed on the forecastle, had to exert the greatest care to avoid collision with the ice. At midday we were in Lat. 58° 39′ 09″ S., Long. 25° 51′ 55″ W. Peak Freezeland lay south-east from us, the end of Montagu Island N. 62° 30′ W. distant 20½ miles. Now that we passed in fine weather the place where, on the 1st and 2nd of January, we had been tacking in thick weather and among ice whose proximity we had only discovered by the noise, we were amazed at the great number of icebergs and at our luck in having escaped disaster.

The land discovered by Captain Cook and called by him Sandwich Land, as also the three islands discovered by me and called the Marquis de Traversey Islands, consist, it seems, of the summits of a mountain range, which is connected by the Clerke rocks with South Georgia and by the Aurora Islands with the Falkland Islands.[1] By the volcanic activity on the Zavodovski and Saunders Islands, the southern hemisphere is relieved in this part of subterranean fire, which does not appear to be very extensive. The northern hemisphere must, it seems, be everywhere warmer than the southern hemisphere, not only with regard to the atmosphere, as is well known, but also in respect of the interior of the earth. This is shown by the many volcanic eruptions at different points in the northern hemisphere, such as Iceland and the coast of Italy, the peninsula of Kamchatka together with the Kurile Islands near the Japanese coast, the Aleutian Islands, etc., compared with which the volcanic activity in the southern hemisphere is small. On Zavodovski Island there was little lava—such as is usually formed by eruptions—to be found, possibly because the substance below the surface of the island does not lend itself to transformation into lava.

At midday we altered course to S. 89° E. in order to get clear of the ice and to make a new attempt to penetrate southward at another more favourable point into high latitudes. By 5 o'clock we had made 32 miles, with icebergs on both sides of us at various distances from the ship. Observing that ice was becoming less frequent, I ordered

[1] More recent soundings have demonstrated the accuracy of this conclusion. The Sandwich group is connected with South Georgia by a low submarine ridge, nowhere more than 1500 fathoms deep, curving round from east to south. On the concave side the depths run to over 3000 fathoms, while on the convex side there is a "deep", long and narrow, of over 4000 fathoms.

the ships to turn southward again. In order to reach a higher latitude while at the same time keeping clear of ice, we turned east by south and after 26 miles we took a course south-east by east. At that time the ice had diminished still more and, in the course of 24 hours, we saw few sea birds, except penguins, of which great numbers were sitting on the ice or diving round the ships. To our delight the fine weather made it possible for us to dry and air the crew's clothes and bedding.

6th. With a top-gallant-sail wind, and with a temperature of 30° F., we held the same course for 24 miles until 6.0 a.m. We passed a few icebergs and then turned to S. 46° E. and at midday we had proceeded 27 miles in that direction.

For the celebration of the feast of the Epiphany the priest from the *Mirnyi* came aboard at my invitation, and we held a service. At 1.0 p.m. we took him back to the *Mirnyi*. At 2 o'clock we were again under sail when, with the wind, thick weather and snow set in. At 2.30 p.m. we passed a large ice floe on which a great number of white petrels were sitting. The surface of the ice was quite flat. When the *Mirnyi* had come up with us, we set more sail and until midnight held on different tacks, passing ice on both sides of us.

With variable light wind and rather thick weather, the temperature was 30·2° F. We went slowly east and at break of day saw blue petrels. At 4.30 p.m. thick fog set in, and we shortened sail to enable the *Mirnyi* to keep in touch with us. At 6.0 a.m. we had 29° F., and at 10.0 a.m. we observed a whale close to the vessel. In order to indicate our position to the *Mirnyi* we signalled by gunfire, but received no reply. On the gun being fired, the whale immediately dived. At 11.0 a.m., to ascertain the drift, we lowered a boat and kept it stationary by means of a kettle lowered to 50 sazhen (58 fathoms) but no drift was observable. At midday the mist rose and we saw the *Mirnyi*. At 4.0 p.m. a fresh wind blew from south by east with snow, so that we made little headway southward. Until 6.0 p.m. after passing some ice we lay to near a low ice floe on which a great many penguins were sitting. Mr Simanov and Mr Demidov started off in a boat to catch some of them; while they caught some with their hands and stowed them in sacks, the others remained sitting; only a few dived into the water, but without waiting till the boat had gone they jumped back on to the floe, helped by the wash of waves. Our booty consisted of thirty penguins. I ordered a few to be sent to the mess, a few to be prepared for stuffing, and the remainder were kept on board and fed on fresh pork, but this appeared to be injurious to them, as they soon sickened, and died after three weeks. The crew skinned them and made caps of the skins, and used the fat for greasing their boots. The penguins were cooked for the officers' mess and we proved that they are good for food, especially if kept for several days in vinegar as is done with certain kinds of game.[1] There was nothing in sight but the unbroken monotony of ice and sea, and the penguin hunt therefore proved a welcome occupation and incidentally provided us with fresh food. We had it stewed together with salt beef and gruel and seasoned with vinegar; the crew liked it, seeing that the officers' mess too pronounced favourably upon it. Fifteen of the penguins were given to the *Mirnyi*.

After the hunt we hoisted the boat and set sail. In the evening when we were in Lat. 59° 49' 50" S., Long. 20° 47' W. the magnetic variation was found to be 2° 34' W. We saw up to twenty-five icebergs and a good deal of broken ice, whilst blue and white petrels and one albatross flew round us continually.

8th. At midnight we had 3° of frost. We kept to a south-easterly course so as to reach a higher latitude. The wind changed from south by west to south-west and at 3.0 a.m. the horizon was completely invisible. Between daybreak and 10.0 a.m. we passed twenty-two icebergs and a large quantity of small broken ice. We approached one of these icebergs on which we could see a great many penguins. We lay to and lowered the boats to cut the ice and to catch as many penguins as we could. Mr Simanov, Mr Lyeskov and Mr Demidov went for the hunt, taking with them part of a fishing net. By midday they had caught thirty-eight. In the meantime the others were cutting ice with which they were able to fill sixteen barrels and all the tubs and cauldrons. We placed the penguins in the chicken runs and in a bath tub placed on the poop for that purpose.

At midday we were in Lat. 60° 06' 08" S., Long. 18° 39' 51" W. The set of the stream during three days was S. 89° E. 39 miles. Owing to heavy snow and a great deal of ice we had to proceed on a different tack until 6.0 p.m. At this time by observing eight lunar distances, we fixed the longitude of our position at 18° 12' 07" W. The wind

[1] Penguin meat is generally regarded as very good and slightly preferable to seal. That it receives only grudging appreciation here is due rather to the natural conservatism of the seaman than to any unusual taste in the meat.

Bristol Island, 7 miles distant

Cook Island, 15 miles distant

Thule Island

PLATE V

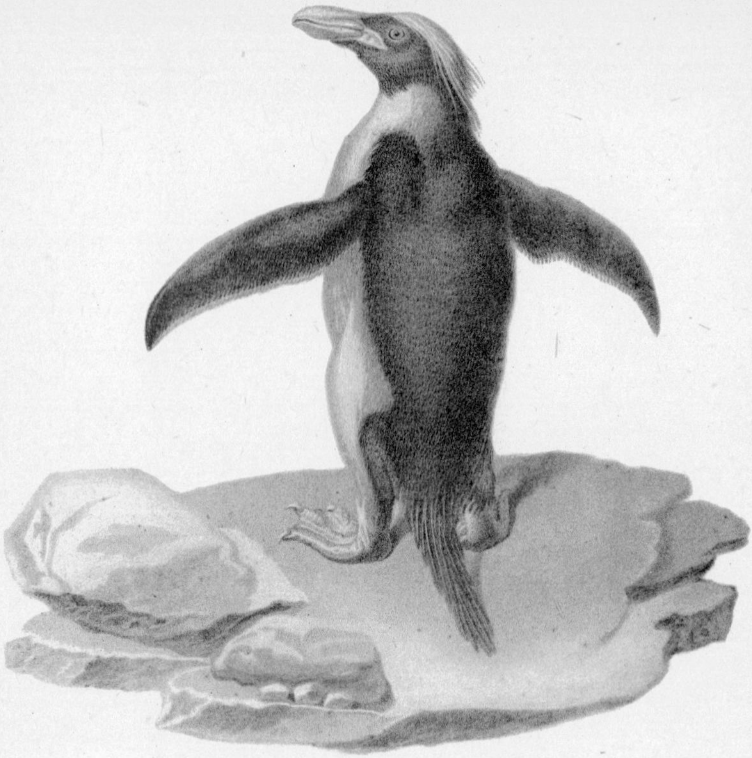

Macaroni Penguin

Ringed Penguins

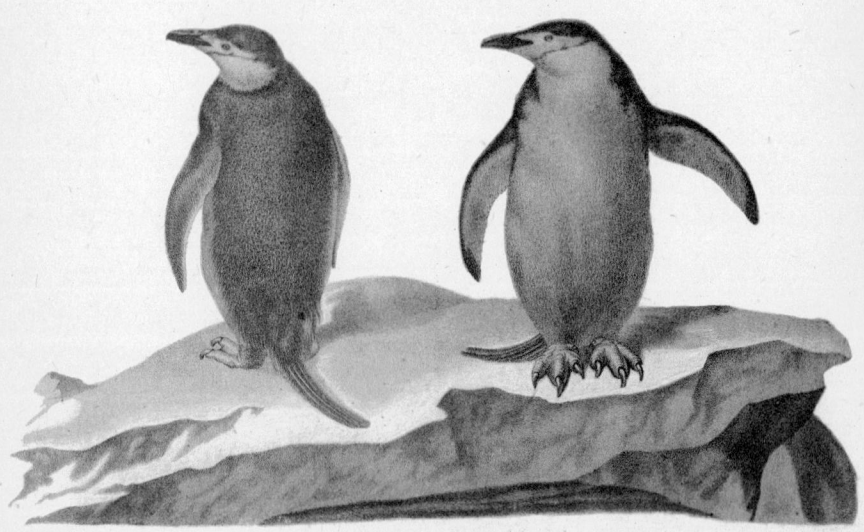

had veered to the west. Soon after 6.0 p.m. we saw on the low flat ice a sea animal; we made for it to see what kind it was and with luck to shoot it. Mr Ignatiev and Mr Demidov, considering themselves fine shots, loaded their guns. The *Mirnyi*, at the same time, went direct towards this ice floe and, as soon as she came within rifle shot, an attack was made from both vessels. The animal was wounded in the tail and in two places in the head. The ice was covered with blood. The hunters disputed in a friendly way as to whom the booty should fall, but the dispute remained undecided. Mr Mikhailov drew a sketch of the animal. It was 12 feet long and measured 6 feet round the body; its head somewhat resembled a dog's, the tail was short, the upper part of the body was a greenish-grey colour and the underneath was yellow.[1]

Among the crew of the *Vostok* there was a sailor who came from the town of Archangel. He told us that in that district these animals are called "utlyuga". It seemed to be a species of seal. May one conclude, on encountering such animals in the polar seas, that there is land near or not? This question remains unsolved, all the more as these animals may perfectly well breed, change their coats and rest on these ice floes as we saw them. The nearest land known to us was the Sandwich Islands, which were 270 miles away.

After hoisting the boats, we set all sail and turned east-south-east. At 7.0 p.m. we observed pack ice to the south; at 9.0 p.m. we had sleet. We could see about fifty icebergs besides a great quantity of broken ice which, at 10.0 p.m., in Lat. 60° 22′ S., Long. 17° 18′ 51″ W., obliged us to set our course east and to shorten sail for the night. Up to midnight we passed through a great deal of ice.

9th. With a fresh west wind, fog, sleet and snow, we continued on an easterly course, continually forced to change our course by the great quantity of floating ice. The thermometer stood at 33·5° F. At 12.30 p.m., in order to reduce speed, which had been 6 knots, we took in one reef in the topsails and two reefs in the mizzen topsail. At 1.0 p.m. the thick fog increased the danger of navigating so that the ship scarcely answered the helm in time to clear the ice; but fortunately for us towards 2.0 p.m. the fog lifted and we saw ourselves surrounded

---

[1] It is curious to find reluctance on the part of the officers to recognize this as a seal. Identification would be easy had the teeth been described but, being too large for a Crab-eater seal, it must have been a Leopard seal (*Stenorhynchus leptonyx*), especially as it was solitary. It is often found on the pack ice far from land, as too is the Crab-eater seal.

by icebergs and floating ice. An icefield extended from north-east to south-south-west, in the midst of which were wedged a number of large flat icebergs. I proceeded to the north by east, the *Mirnyi* following in our wake. I signalled to alter course to port. Although the fog had lifted a little, we were still unable to see much round us; we continued our way until 5.0 p.m. amongst a great quantity of small ice, constantly working the helm from side to side. After proceeding 16 miles in this manner, the weather fortunately cleared, and we observed ahead, from north-north-west to north-east by north, an icefield, surrounded on all sides by small ice. The wind now freshened; it was not possible to turn to the south, nor was there room to turn the vessel to the west. However, from the look-out I saw a narrow passage to the north-east between this field and the other, which we had seen at 2.0 a.m., extending to the point where we now were and surrounded by a large number of icebergs and quantities of small broken ice. I decided, therefore, with the changing wind from south by east, to advance into the ice and we turned to the north-east at 8 knots. To avoid collision with the smaller ice floes, the officer of the watch steered the ship by command, stationing himself on the forecastle. The *Vostok* had the great merit of answering the helm quite well, and thereby several times avoided collision with the floating ice. When we had proceeded $8\frac{1}{2}$ miles to the east, the look-out reported that it was a little clearer to the north-north-east-half-east. After proceeding for $7\frac{1}{2}$ miles through small ice, we found ourselves at 7.30 a.m. out of visible danger. We took another reef in the fore topsail to wait for the *Mirnyi*. During this time we had alternate rain and fitful sunshine.

At 9.0 a.m. in Lat. 59° 47′ 27″ S., Long. 15° 30′ W., we found a magnetic variation of 3° 48′ W. on an east by north course.

We passed near a large iceberg looking like a couch with the back reclining and decorated with carvings. All the ice had a great variety of shapes, though the flat floes were, for the greater part, uniform in appearance.

At 10.0 a.m., with a strong wind, we were obliged to reef again and remain under reefed topsails and strike the top-gallant yards. At midday we found our position by observation to be Lat. 59° 35′ 51″ S., Long. 15° 01′ 35″ W. The wind freshened very much from the south and brought with it high seas; the temperature was 35° F.; the stream set N. 11° W. 7 miles in these 24 hours. We proceeded on an east by north course from 9.0 a.m. to 5.0 p.m. at $7\frac{1}{4}$ knots, and in order not to get into lower latitudes we kept a course due east.

At 6.0 p.m., passing under the lee of a large iceberg, we noted that the thermometer, which was standing at 31° F., fell to 30° F. but, when we had passed the iceberg, the mercury rose again to 31° F.

10*th*. We continued on the easterly course until 4.0 on the following morning, making 7 knots and passing several large high icebergs with flat surfaces. These icebergs lay in a line south to north. In the morning, in Lat. 59° 15′ S., Long. 11° 19′ W., we found the magnetic deviation to be 4° 8′ W., both ships being then on an east-south-east course. At 4.0 a.m. the wind fell and during the afternoon our speed decreased to 1 knot. At midday we were in Lat. 59° 12′ 46″ S., Long. 10° 41′ 46″ W., the stream setting N. 6° E. 18 miles in 24 hours. At the previous midnight we had a temperature of 30° F., at midday it was 33° F. The weather was fine, and on the horizon we could see, at different points, a number of icebergs and ice floes; but in spite of this, to avail myself of the fine weather, I turned again first to the south-east, shaking out the reefs and setting all sail, later to the south-south-east. A light wind was blowing from the south-east, the swell from the previous high seas continuing from the south, from which we concluded that there was less ice to the south than we had previously encountered. From midday to 6.0 p.m. we passed fifteen icebergs. In the evening, in Lat. 59° 27′ 33″ S., Long. 09° 50′ W., we found a magnetic variation of 7° 06′ W. on a south-south-east course.

At 9.0 p.m. the sky was covered with clouds and mist spread over the horizon. There were many icebergs in sight and the wind blew from the north-west. Towards night we shortened sail and proceeded under topsails only. Soon afterwards we had a snowstorm which prevented our seeing an immense ice floe in the near distance, though we knew it was near by the noise of the swell breaking over it. At 10.0 p.m. the snow stopped. At 11.0 p.m., in order to reduce speed, we took in another reef in the fore topsail.

11*th*. Very soon we had snow again and 3° F. of frost. At 1.0 a.m., owing to darkness caused by the heavy snow, I ordered the ships to turn on the port tack to the north-east. At 2.30 a.m., when it got lighter, we saw that there was no ice in our neighbourhood, but a good deal to the south-east of us. We turned to an easterly course for 27 miles, passing a few icebergs with small ice falling from them, and noted that the swell, which had come from the north-west, was now setting in from the south-east. Thick weather with sleet continued from 9.0 to 10.0 a.m. We steered one point more into the wind to pass to the south of five large icebergs lying in our route. At 10.0 a.m., having passed these, we turned south-east under all sail; the existence of a swell from that point suggested that there was little, if any, ice in that direction.

At midday we were in Lat. 59° 43′ 55″ S., Long. 8° 11′ 24″ W.; the stream set N. 82° E. 5 miles in 24 hours. The temperature was 35° F. The wind shifted to the south-west and we set our course south-east by south. About 4.30 p.m. we were in Lat. 60° 07′ 07″ S., Long. 7° 18′ W., the magnetic variation being 9° 12′ W. From midday to midnight, we made 6 to 7 knots under a fresh south-west wind. The weather continued overcast and from time to time snow fell.

12*th*. The wind dropped a little, there was a swell from the south-west, and the temperature was 35° F. We proceeded on a south-south-east course. Towards 5.0 a.m. we were in Lat. 60° 50′ S., Long. 5° 52′ W., magnetic variation 10° 37′ W. From morning until midday in Lat. 61° 21′ S., we passed eight icebergs; the wind freshened a little. The horizon was still hidden by the haze and the temperature was 36° F. At 5.0 p.m. we passed an iceberg with a steeply rising top and at 6.0 p.m. we had rain but it was not for long. At 9.0 p.m., on account of the darkness and thick weather, we shortened sail so that the *Mirnyi* should be able to come up with us.

13*th*. At midnight the mercury stood at freezing point, but below, where the crew slept, it was at 50° F. There was a fresh wind from the west, the horizon was hazy, and at 3.0 a.m. and at 7.0 a.m. we passed icebergs on a south by west course. In Lat. 63° 18′ S., Long. 3° 53′ W., we found a magnetic variation of 9° 55′ W. We proceeded at the rate of 8 knots and at midday we were in Lat. 63° 49′ 21″ S., Long. 2° 36′ 42″ W. We continued on a south by west course until 5.30 of the following morning—14th January—when, with a change of the wind to the north, the whole horizon was covered with a haze and snow and rain were falling. Fearing still worse weather, I ordered the main topsails to be close-reefed and turned the ship on the starboard tack. At 8.30, on account of the high wind and considerable pitching and rolling, we struck the topyards.

15*th*. At 7.0 a.m. on the following morning, although the weather remained unchanged, I did not hope for any improvement, and therefore proceeded again on a south by west course. Up to midday, we passed three icebergs; we were then in Lat. 66° 53′ 42″ S., Long. 3° 03′ 54″ W.[1] At 4.0 p.m. we saw three blue petrels.

16th. The thick weather, with snow and ice and high north-west wind, continued through the night. At 4.0 a.m. we saw a grey (smoke-coloured) albatross flying near the ship. At 7.0 a.m. the wind changed to the north, the snow ceased for a time and the blessed sun now and then broke through the clouds.

At 9.0 a.m., in Lat. 69° 17′ 26″ S., Long. 2° 45′ 46″ W., we found a magnetic variation of 8° 48′ W. Proceeding south, at midday, in Lat. 69° 21′ 28″ S., Long. 2° 14′ 50″ W., we encountered icebergs, which came in sight through the falling snow looking like white clouds. We had a moderate north-east wind with a heavy swell from the north-west and, in consequence of the snow, we could see for but a short distance. We hauled close to the wind on a south-east course and had made 2 miles in this direction when we observed that there was a solid stretch of ice running from east through south to west. Our course was leading us straight in to this field, which was covered with ice hillocks. The barometer fell from 29·50 to 29, warning us of bad weather. We had 2° F. of frost. We turned north-west by west in the hope that in this direction we should find no ice.[2] During the last 24 hours we had observed snow-white and blue petrels and heard the cries of penguins.

17th. The thick weather and snow continued through the night. At 2.0 a.m. both ships put about on to the port tack. At 6.0 a.m. we observed right ahead of us an iceberg which we only just succeeded in avoiding. The thermometer stood at freezing point; at the same time the wind began to freshen and we were forced to double-reef the topsails. At 8.0 a.m. the *Vostok*, turning to the wind, joined up with the *Mirnyi*. Towards midday the sky cleared a little of snow clouds and the sun appeared. We were able to take midday observations and

---

[1] It is to be noted as curious that no mention is made of this, their first, crossing of the Antarctic Circle, usually a great event in polar expeditions.

[2] This day must be accounted an unfortunate one for the Russian expedition for we know now that they must have been within a few miles, not more than twenty at most, of the coast of what is now called Princess Martha Land, discovered in 1929–30 by the Norvegia expedition. It is even possible that the "solid stretch of ice running from east through south to west" was indeed the land ice which, everywhere along this coast, marks the edge of the continent. In any case, a few hours of clear weather on this day would have certainly antedated the discovery of land here by 110 years.

found our position to be Lat. 68° 51′ 51″ S., Long. 3° 07′ 06″ W., the stream having set N. 20° W. 13 miles. We did not, however, enjoy the sun for long; in these latitudes it is so rarely visible. Fog and snow, the travelling companions of the navigator in the Antarctic, again overtook us.

In these high latitudes, into which we extended our voyage, the sea is a most beautiful blue colour, which in some measure serves to indicate the great distance of land. The penguins, whose cries we heard, are in no need of land. They live just as comfortably, and indeed seem to prefer living, on the flat ice, far more so than other birds do on land. When we caught penguins on the ice, many dived into the water but, without even waiting till the hunters had gone, they returned to their former places with the help of the waves.[1] Judging by the form of their bodies and their air of repose, one may conclude that it is merely the stimulus of seeking food that drives them from the ice into the water. They are very tame. When Mr Lyeskov threw a net over a number of them, the others, not caught by the net, remained quite quiet and indifferent to the fate of their unhappy fellows who, before their eyes, were put into sacks. The suffocating air in these sacks and careless handling while catching, transferring and taking the penguins on board the vessels, produced a sickness amongst them, and in a short time they threw up a great quantity of shrimps, which evidently form their food.[2] At this point I may add that we had so far not found any sort of fish in the high southern latitudes, excepting the different species of whale.

At 8 o'clock the *Vostok* waited for the *Mirnyi* and, joining her, we passed to windward on a starboard tack so as to draw away from the ice and lie to during the foggy weather. The wind blew steadily from the north with occasional snow. The whole horizon was in a haze. Since our arrival in these higher latitudes we had always the same sort of bad weather with north winds, but with the wind from the south we had dry weather with a clear horizon.

[1] In several places Bellingshausen refers to the waves assisting the penguins to jump out on to the floes, a misconception due to the extraordinary suddenness of a penguin's leap out of the water so that it appears to be propelled. The bird swims under water at a fast rate and at the appropriate distance elevates its tail sharply which causes it to rise steeply out of the water with a shower of spray. Usually it allows a large margin for the height of the ice above water level and therefore jumps much higher than is really necessary to clear the edge of the floe.

[2] Practically the only food of the smaller types of penguins is a small reddish crustacean, *Euphausia*, which is also the food of whales in the Antarctic seas.

18*th.* At midnight we turned on to the port tack. The thermometer in the open air showed a temperature of 33° F.; below deck where the crew slept 53° F. At midday the wind fell almost completely, but continued from the north. The weather cleared, but the horizon still remained hazy. There was no ice in sight. We were in Lat. 68° 35′ 28″ S., Long. 2° 33′ 51″ W. The barometer stood at 29·13.

Profiting by the calm and clear weather, we invited in the morning, by signal, Mr Lazarev and all the officers of the *Mirnyi* who were not on duty, to dinner. They arrived at 1.0 p.m. and did not return to the *Mirnyi* until 11.0 p.m. The weather was clear and calm with a light north wind. This day corresponded exactly to the 18th July in the northern hemisphere;[1] the thermometer showed 33° F.

Mr Lazarev, amongst other things, reported to me that on the 9th instant at 2.30 a.m., when passing through a narrow passage between icefields and floating ice, the *Mirnyi* struck against a fairly large flat ice floe with such force that everybody rushed on deck. The result of the collision was that a timber, about 4 feet long and 1 foot wide, below the water level was forced out of the stern. Such a shock probably startled even the bravest. The watch was at that time being taken by Lieutenant Obernibessov. He was on the forecastle, and from there gave orders for the helm.

We passed the day in friendly conversation, talking over the dangers and adventures we had encountered since our last meeting, and quite forgetting for a time that we were in a region, uninhabited save for whales, penguins and other birds, and where thick fogs and frequent snow prevailed.

19*th.* It remained calm until 3.0 a.m., and then a light wind with snow blew up from the south-east by east. We steered on a starboard tack in a north-easterly direction. It was my intention to work a little to the east and then to return southward to push at a new point into the higher latitudes. At 6.0 a.m. the wind from east-north-east freshened. We reefed the top-gallant sail and took in a reef in the topsail. At 8.30 a.m. we turned to port and set the mainsail. At midday we found ourselves in Lat. 68° 36′ 36″ S., Long. 1° 43′ 59″ W., with the temperature 1° F. above freezing point. On sounding, we had 100 sazhen (116 fathoms), still no bottom. The snow continued

---

[1] The meaning here is somewhat obscure but apparently refers to the fact that they were almost on the Greenwich meridian.

to fall during a contrary east wind. We endeavoured to proceed on our course on short tacks and encountered no ice. On that day for the first time we succeeded in bringing down a "polar bird", so named by Captain Cook. It was the size of a hen, the feathers on the back, wings and top of the head were brown, the neck and breast much lighter in colour, tail and under part of the body white. The upper tail feathers were brown at the top; the colour of these tail feathers was regularly divided, i.e. the underside of each feather was brown and the upper part of it white. The eyes were dark with black pupils, the beak and feet were dark, the membrane between the claws being a muddy dark colour, the legs still darker. This bird resembles in all particulars the other petrels and therefore I shall call it the "polar petrel".[1]

20*th*. At 4.30 a.m., after tacking to the eastward for 30 miles and seeing the persistence of contrary winds from that quarter, I was convinced of the truth of Captain Cook's observation that in the higher southern latitudes there are always easterly winds. I therefore decided to make straight for the south, until it should be quite impossible to continue navigating farther, and then to return to lower latitudes. From there we should get farther to the east under the prevailing west winds and then turn again to higher latitudes. And so I turned southward, in thick weather, snow falling steadily until 3.0 p.m. At 7.0 p.m. we observed an iceberg of about $\frac{3}{4}$ mile circumference and up to 70 feet high, the sides perpendicular. There was a heavy swell from the east, with wind, all of which were indications to us that there was probably little ice in our neighbourhood towards the east. A few snow-white and polar petrels, also some storm petrels, flew near the ship. These latter we found in all latitudes from the equator to the ice regions and called them, during the voyage, "Jews of the Sea", because, like the Jews on land, these birds have no abiding place but roam over the ocean in all latitudes.

21*st*. We still continued southward with a light wind from the south-east by south and clear weather. Whales spouted and polar and snow-white petrels—a warning of the vicinity of ice—flew round the ships. Towards the south it became lighter from hour to hour. At

---

[1] Antarctic petrel (*Thalassoica antarctica*). This bird is plentiful in the pack ice in summer and ranges farther north in the winter. It was not until 1912 that their nests and young were first discovered, by the expedition under Sir Douglas Mawson, on rocky islets close to the mainland.

View of Ice Islands

Ice Islands

PLATE VIII

VOL. I

1.0 a.m. we saw ice ahead and, farther south at 2.0 a.m., found ourselves among broken ice; farther to the south there were about fifty icebergs of various sizes enclosed in the middle of the field. As we surveyed the extent of the icefield around us to the east, south and west, we were unable to see its limits; it was precisely an extension of that which we had seen in thick weather on the 16th, but had been unable to examine properly on account of the mist and snow.[1]

At this point we found it impossible to proceed farther south. We were then in Lat. 69° 25' S., Long. 1° 11' W.; the air was dry and we had 6° F. of frost. On sounding we found 100 sazhen (116 fathoms), no bottom. Turning on another tack to north-east by north, we much regretted that the wind did not allow us to pass along the ice, or at least to go parallel with it to the eastward, in order to penetrate at another point into higher latitudes.

In the morning in Lat. 69° 00" S., Long. 0° 48' W. we found a magnetic variation of 11° 28' W., both vessels being on a north-east by north course. Although, on the deck where the officers and crew lived, we lit the stoves every day, wiped the ceiling (on which the damp collected in drops) three times a day and dried the damp clothes as far as possible in the open air, nevertheless the continuous thick fogs, snow and sleet had reduced us to a condition which made us feel the absolute need of fine weather. That day, during fine and dry weather such as we had not experienced since our departure from the South Sandwich Islands, bedding and clothing were carried on deck to be dried and aired. The crew were not permitted to go below deck and an endeavour was made to dry the lower deck as far as possible. At midday, when the horizon cleared towards the west, we observed an iceberg; we were then in Lat. 68° 54' 01" S., Long. 0° 09' 58" W., with a temperature of 31° F. We did not long enjoy clear weather. At 6.0 p.m. the sky became overcast and at 8.0 p.m. we had thick weather with snow and hail, and a fresh wind from the south-east which obliged us to double-reef the topsails. At 10.0 p.m. the *Vostok* closed up to the *Mirnyi* for the night.

22nd. At 10.0 a.m. I signalled to the *Mirnyi* to make more sail. Owing to heavy snowfalls we were unable to take any midday observations. At 4.0 p.m. the *Vostok* shortened sail so that the *Mirnyi* might come up with us. From the heavy swell from the south-east we concluded that there was no ice in that direction. A great many white,

[1] The ships were again probably within 30 miles of the continent.

polar and snow petrels, and one grey albatross,[1] flew about the ship. At this time we saw only one whale.

23rd. The night was fairly light. We had 8° F. below freezing in the open air, but in the crew's quarters there was a temperature of 35° F. At midday we were in Lat. 67° 15′ 40″ S., Long. 2° 59′ 22″ E. The stream in the last 24 hours had carried us N. 12° W. 23 miles. At 5.0 p.m. on sounding we found 268 sazhen (313 fathoms) and no bottom. A light east wind and calm lasted until 5.0 a.m. of the 25th. We saw a few polar petrels, grey albatrosses and two whales.

25th. The horizon was clear and there was no ice in sight. We endeavoured to beat up to the eastward, and to work a little northward in the hope that, in the lower latitudes, we should sooner get a westerly wind which would enable us to proceed some degrees to the east. Being in Lat. 66° 12′ S., Long. 3° 12′ E., we fixed the magnetic variation at 15° 57′ 30″ W., the course of the ships being then northeast. This morning we succeeded in taking some lunar distances from which we determined the longitude at midday.

Self from 40 lunar distances	2° 26′ 25″ E.
Lieutenant Zavodovski from 40 distances	2° 28′ 10″ E.
Navigating Officer Paryadin from 20 distances	2° 27′ 50″ E.
The mean longitude from the chronometers Nos. 922 and 512	2° 42′ 47″ E.

Our latitude at midday was fixed at 65° 58′ 19″ S. The thermometer registered 33° F. At 1.0 p.m., by invitation from Mr Lazarev, I and some of the officers dined on the *Mirnyi*. Mr Lazarev showed us the pestrushki and polar petrels, quite beautifully stuffed by Dr Galkin.[2] For the rest of the day we had a light south-east wind; the sky was clear and the sea smooth. Soon after we had returned on board the *Vostok* at 11.0 p.m., the wind veered south-south-west and we turned on an easterly course. During the day only a few polar birds and snow-white petrels flew round the ship; we also saw two whales.

26th. The night was clear with stars and there was 3° F. of frost. We were proceeding under a light north wind and, at

---

[1] This would be a Giant petrel (*Macronectes giganteus*), as the true albatross never goes so far south as 68° S. It is known to sailors as the "Stinker" or the "Nelly" and to sealers as the "Glutton". It is a large, powerful bird, equalling some of the smaller albatrosses in size. It is widely distributed in the Southern Ocean where it was discovered by Captain Cook. There is a wide range of colour throughout the species varying from sooty black to a light greyish white.

[2] The surgeon on the *Mirnyi*.

midday, we were in Lat. 65° 51' 45" S.; we fixed the longitude as follows:

Self from 90 lunar distances	4° 05' 52" E.
Lieutenant Zavodovski from 65 distances	4° 09' 40" E.
Navigating Officer Paryadin from 75 distances	4° 06' 29" E.
The average longitude from two chronometers	4° 27' 19" E.
From the *Mirnyi* from 234 distances	4° 20' 48" E.
By chronometer No. 920	4° 43' 45" E.

In the morning we observed ahead of us, to the east, four large icebergs and, as I had been waiting for some time for fine weather to lay in a supply of ice, I lay to near one of them. The sky was clear and there was a light wind blowing with a slight swell from the south-east, a state of things which rarely occurs in this part of the open ocean. Unless the wind has dropped completely, it is impossible to lie alongside an iceberg on account of the surf breaking on the ice. Making use of the favourable weather, we rounded the iceberg to the port side and hove to to leeward of the bergs. Such ice is not always good since, having floated for some time on the surface and being low, it has been continually washed by the waves and becomes friable and contains a certain amount of salt. Nevertheless, in case of necessity, it can be used after it has been treated as follows: Having taken up the ice, leave it for 24 hours in the sacks so that all the salt water in it can drain off. In the Antarctic Ocean a great deal of high ice is to be found from which pure ice can be cut which requires no such treatment. The iceberg from which we obtained the ice was 200 feet in height on one side and only 30 feet on the other. In appearance it was smooth with a sloping surface, in length about 125 sazhen (300 yards) and about 60 (140 yards) in width. It was with difficulty that the men could keep a footing on this frozen mass and, as it was both difficult and dangerous to cut the ice at the edges, I decided to give up the attempt and ordered the boats to return and stand by. Meanwhile I had ordered the carronades to be loaded, and having set sail, we turned and stood off the corner of the high ice cliff, reefed the main topsail and then ordered shots to be fired at the very corner. The shock of the shots not only broke off a few fragments of ice, but shook the whole mass of ice to its foundations, so that large pieces of it fell with a huge crash into the water, raising a vast spray, a third of the height of the iceberg itself and producing for some little while a considerable swell. All this and in addition the sudden appearance of a shoal of whales, which we had not before observed, presented an exceptionally impressive spectacle such as is only possible in the Antarctic. When the iceberg, after some swaying, righted itself, the top of the lower part was level with the water, that is the lower side of the iceberg which had been 30 feet out of the water, and the other side was raised correspondingly.

The second lieutenant of the *Vostok*, Mr Lyeskov, celebrated his birthday that day. The captain of the *Mirnyi*, Mr Lazarev, and some of the officers stayed with us until evening. On the suggestion of Mr Lazarev, we fired gun shells from the carronades at the swimming whales. However, partly owing to their very brief stay on the surface of the water, and partly owing to the nature of these guns, which are not well adapted for target practice, our shots missed, falling sometimes wide and sometimes short, and the whales dived, showing their broad horizontal tails. Whalers call this kind of whale "sperm whales" and recognize them solely by their spouting. They reckon that only those which spout twice per minute belong to that species. Whalers were unable to give us any distinguishing features of these whales.[1]

We at once sent the cutter and two boats to cut the ice from the floating blocks. For the quicker despatch of the business, all the crew were set to work. The ice was taken up on both sides and broken into small pieces in a tub (placed for that purpose on the poop), so that it was possible to fill the barrels through the bung holes without having to enlarge the opening. The boats continually brought the ice alongside and, after each trip, the hands at the oars were changed in order to lighten this work, which had to be carried out in the cold and wet. As soon as it was finished all were ordered to change into dry clothing and all were given a glass of hot punch to refresh them. From 3.0 p.m. to 10.0 p.m. forty-nine barrels of medium size were filled with ice, as well as all kettles, cauldrons and a few sacks for immediate use. All the barrels filled up with ice were distributed about on the poop, on the deck and on the forecastle, but none were placed in the hold or on the lower deck, in order to avoid the cold, damp air which is given off by the melting of the ice. At last, after hoisting the boats, we turned to the east until 3 o'clock of the following morning, with a little rain.

[1] Sperm whales very rarely wander as far south as this and it seems more likely that they were members of the Rorqual family of whales which, in those days, were not hunted by whalers.

27*th*, 28*th*. At 9.0 p.m. with a change of the wind, which was now blowing from the north, wet snow fell. At 11.0 p.m. the whole horizon was shut out by thick mist. From 8.0 p.m. until 5.0 a.m. of the following morning, the rain and sleet continued. From this time on the wind became completely contrary. In order to get a more favourable wind for getting farther eastward, we turned back to the north, because the farther we got away from the higher latitudes, the stronger were the westerly winds. At 7.0 p.m. the east wind began to freshen, forcing us to take in two reefs in the topsails, and soon raising a heavy sea. When the sun came out for a little while, we succeeded in fixing our position as Lat. 65° 49′ 39″ S., Long. 9° 42′ 27″ E., the magnetic variation being 19° 58′ W. Sleet fell all day. We observed a grey albatross, petrels, some pestrushki and a few polar petrels. Towards night we clewed up the fore- and mainsails, and drew near the *Mirnyi*. At midnight there was 1° F. of frost.

29*th*. At midnight the high wind fell somewhat, and a heavy swell ran from the south-east. At 4.0 a.m. we set more sail but, in consequence of the strong contrary swell, it was impossible to carry much sail. Towards midday the wind fell, but after dinner the wind blew again from the north-east and by 8.0 p.m. it freshened so that we were forced again to take in two reefs in the topsails. On that day pestrushki and some black sea birds about the same size as a white petrel were flying round us, but they did not come near enough for us to see them well.

From 9.0 p.m. heavy snow fell which we had continually to shovel overboard; as a consequence we were unable to see anything ahead of us. I fired signals to the *Mirnyi* to turn to a northerly course. The *Vostok* turned in the same direction and we felt certain that we were free from danger, because we were taking a course on which we had not encountered any ice before.

30*th*. The sea was so heavy that it forced us to lower the top-gallant mast and yards. At night the wind blew with heavy snow squalls so that we were obliged to close-reef the topsails and take in the mizzen topsail at 2.0 a.m. The ship yawed a good deal. The mercury in the barometer fell to 28·25. At 10.0 a.m. the wind fell a little. At midday the temperature was 33° F. All day long the mist, rain and snow continued uninterruptedly. Sea birds such as white and grey albatrosses, large and small pintades, blue pestrushki and large black petrels in great numbers flew round the ship, but we did not succeed in shooting even one. Owing to the heavy sea raised by the strong east wind and the north-north-west swell, we pitched and rolled heavily. At midday the wind veered to the south and we turned on an easterly course. At midday we were in Lat. 64° 26′ 31″ S., Long. 12° 04′ 15″ E. and we found the magnetic variation to be 22° 39′ W. We were going at the rate of 6 knots. Towards 7.0 p.m. the wind changed through south to west, and I ordered a more southerly course so that, whilst changing the longitude, we might reach a somewhat higher latitude.

1st. In the course of the 24 hours the sun broke through several times and snow fell. The same kind of birds flew round us. In order to take full advantage of the wind, I signalled to the *Mirnyi* to make all sail. In the evening a sea animal rose for a moment out of the water and then quickly disappeared so that we did not succeed in getting a good view of it. We did not observe any ice.

We continued on an east by south course, with the same, but light, wind, the night being dark. The ship pitched and rolled a good deal due to the two swells running, one from the east-south-east, the other from the north-west by west. In the morning we shook out the reefs in the topsails and made more sail. At midday we were in Lat. 64° 30′ 09″ S., Long. 15° 49′ 46″ E. To-day Mr Demidov shot a large black bird, about the size of the smaller kind of albatross. By the look of it it was a species of petrel.[1] In the evening the wind blew from the north-east quarter. We continued on the port tack to the south-east. At this time, as in previous cases of a north-east wind, we had a good deal of thick weather. As we got farther away from higher latitudes, we saw no ice and only the polar petrels remained with us.

2nd. At midnight we had ½° F. of frost and a steady head wind. We had by then succeeded in getting to a more easterly longitude and therefore I once more decided to turn southward, to try how far the ice would let us proceed. Therefore we continued close to the wind on the port tack. Towards 7.0 a.m. the wind had attained a force which obliged us to reef the mainsails and take in two reefs in the topsails and, towards midday, we were close-reefed. The sea became so high, the mist and the steadily falling snow so thick, that we could not see farther than 50 sazhen (120 yards), so we turned to the north with the wind. I did this as a precaution against running on to the ice or on

---

[1] Probably a Giant petrel (*Macronectes giganteus*), which shows all variations of colour from dark brown to white.

to unknown land. A great deal of snow had fallen on the ship and the sails and rigging were all white. Towards 7.0 p.m. the mist was no longer so thick and the snow had almost stopped; so we once again turned with the wind to the south. The sky cleared after this, but not for long, and the night was dark. The mercury stood at freezing point.

3rd. In the morning we loosened two reefs in the topsails and we continued southward with the same fresh gusty easterly wind, in spite of incessant and sometimes very heavy snowfalls. By morning, in Lat. 65° 45′ S., we again observed petrels. At midday we were in Lat. 66° 00′ 56″ S., Long. 17° 35′ E.; the magnetic variation was 22° 59′ W. At 10.0 p.m. we crossed the Antarctic Circle for the third time and shortened sail so as to give the *Mirnyi* an opportunity of coming up with us. She had remained behind at a considerable distance from us. We saw no ice in the course of the 24 hours. Polar, blue and black petrels and pestrushki flew near the ship. At midnight we had ½° F. of frost.

4th. The weather continued thick. The wind blew fresh and gusty with high seas. The sky was covered by thick clouds and heavy snow fell, so that the sails and rigging, as well as the ship herself, were entirely covered and, as from time to time sleet fell and then froze, the sails and rigging were soon covered with ice. At midday we were by dead reckoning in Lat. 67° 16′ S., Long. 17° 00′ 45″ E. We found the magnetic variation to be 23° 14′ W., on a southerly course. There was 1° F. of frost at the time.

5th. The night was clear and soon after midnight the wind fell a little. At 2.0 a.m. we passed ice to starboard of us. At 3.0 a.m. we shook out a reef, but the sea was still high and the ships rolled and pitched. At 9.0 a.m. on the horizon towards the south a vivid brightness appeared which indicated dense pack ice. Towards midday the mist cleared and the dry snow, which had fallen at times, ceased, but the sky remained cloudy. There were 5° F. of frost in the open air.

Before midday ice was observed to south from the look-out, and before 1.0 p.m. we were able to make out from the forecastle that it was detached icebergs. Towards 3.0 p.m. we were already passing through ice and then the waves abated perceptibly; the farther we proceeded, the more dense became the ice until about 3.15 p.m., when we observed a great many large high flat-topped icebergs, surrounded by small broken ice, in places piled up high. The ice towards the south-south-west adjoined the high icebergs which were stationary. Its edge was perpendicular and formed into little coves, whilst the surface sloped upwards towards the south to a distance so far that its end was out of sight even from the mast-head.[1] We noticed several whales spouting among the broken ice at different points. Judging from the icebergs now before us, their surface and edges so like the surface and edges of the large extent of ice just referred to, we concluded that these and all similar masses of ice become separated from the main mass either by their weight or for other physical reasons and are carried away by the wind and float over the Antarctic; then other icebergs break off from them. When storms or other causes break off small pieces from the large icebergs, these latter lose their equilibrium and float with this or that edge or angle standing out of the water or even turn turtle. Hence the great variety in their appearance. Small broken ice is formed of the fragments detaching themselves from the larger masses, and thus to leeward of each iceberg a great deal of this broken ice is to be found. Near the ice we shot a few petrels, polar snow petrels, storm petrels and weather birds; this last bird is to be found in all latitudes. We saw one Egmont hen, a grey albatross and many blue petrels.

6*th.* After midnight the sky became overcast, we had a light south-east by east wind and a slight swell from the south-east. We had 6° F. of frost.

At 4.0 a.m. we were close to small broken ice. I decided to pass through it as far as possible in order to reach some distant icebergs, so as to examine them more closely. We were obliged to alter our course constantly so as to avoid heavy collisions with the ice. The floating ice resembles that found in bays, i.e. it was flat and from an

---

[1] In this characteristically cautious way does the captain record, what he himself did not suspect apparently, but what we now feel must have been the case, the first discovery of the main Antarctic continent by man. It was a bare three weeks earlier that Edward Bransfield saw Trinity Land, the northern extremity of the long Graham Land peninsula, in Lat. 64° S. The narrative does not give the exact position at this time, but the position next day is plotted on the chart attached. From this it will be seen that he was distant about 50 miles from what was plotted by the *Thorshammer* in 1931 as Princess Ragnhild Land. The description of "little coves" in "a perpendicular edge" leads one to suspect that he was considerably closer.

His mention, on the next page, of "ice-covered mountains similar to those mentioned above" further confirms the suspicion that he was not sure whether he was looking at a mass of ice alone, parent of the mighty icebergs round him, or at an ice-cap, resting on land, whose form was responsible for the peaks and domes which sloped upwards to the south.

Wandering Albatross

Sooty Albatross

VOL. I PLATE IX

Petrel

Petrel

VOL. I   PLATE X

inch to 4 feet or more in thickness. The water round it thickens and is covered with a thin top ice which then, compressed by the wind, forms the beginning of the ice mass. If the swell does not reach the spot at the first calm, the surface of the water turns to solid ice, and the first north wind, bringing high seas with it, breaks the ice into pieces. At 6.0 a.m. the broken ice had become so dense and thick that the attempt to continue farther to the southward at this point was impossible. A mile and a half from there we could see blocks of ice piled one on top of the other. In the farther distance we saw ice-covered mountains[1] similar to those mentioned above and probably forming a continuation of them. We were then in Lat. 69° 06′ 24″ S., Long. 15° 51′ 45″ E. We found, on sounding, a depth of 180 sazhen (210 fathoms), still no bottom, and we had 9° F. of frost. We turned into the wind and tried to steer so as to avoid collision with the floating ice. We steered northward to get out of this narrow space, but during the passage both in entering and leaving we could not prevent small ice blocks from passing under the head of the ship and scraping along the sides; but as the ships proceeded slowly, no great damage was done, except that the heads of some of the copper sheathing-nails were torn off almost to the main chains. The *Mirnyi* was in our wake and turned astern of us to get out of the ice. When the ice became less dense, we brought the ships close to the wind on a starboard tack to the north-east by east, with a fresh top-gallant-sails wind from south-east by east.

On the previous evening, as an experiment, I poured some sea water in a small tub to see if it would freeze in that temperature and hoisted the tub on a stay; in the evening we had 7° F. of frost; at midnight we had 6° F. of frost; at 6.0 a.m. we had 9° F. and the water froze. When this ice was removed from the tub and allowed to melt, the water from it was fresh. There can be no doubt that the ice which we found in Lat. 69° was formed and much increased by snow, besides which the perpetual moisture which spreads over the ice freezes and by this continuous action forms the large masses. If now, in Lat. 69° in the summer season, we had 9° F. of frost, it is probable that, when the sun ceases to warm these parts, the quantity of floating ice masses

---

[1] This important phrase has also been rendered by different translators as "ice-peaks", "mountainous ice" and "mountain ranges of ice". There seems little doubt that again they were looking at the rolls of ice-covered land typical of the continental fringe.

must increase twofold with the more intense cold. That day the sun did not even appear, so, as on the previous day, we had no opportunity of taking observations. At midday we had 6° F. of frost. After dinner, having invited Mr Lazarev to come on board, I informed him that, in the course of our projected farther voyage to the Lord Auckland Islands, I was determined to make another attempt to go southwards in Long. 60° E., and then for safety to return northward in order to visit the Auckland Islands. Mr Lazarev reported that, if our voyage were to be continued, he would find himself entirely without wood. For some little time this shortage had also made itself felt on the *Vostok*, and therefore I decided to take measures to avoid having to resort to breaking up our water or wine barrels for firewood.

At 8.0 p.m., as we were passing close to a large flat-topped iceberg, we hove to and fired ten shots at the middle of the mass, but were unable to break off a sufficient quantity of ice to fill the barrels, so we ceased drifting and continued on our former course. In the evening Mr Lazarev and the two officers who had accompanied him returned to the *Mirnyi*. A number of different kinds of petrels flew round the ship, and a great many whales were swimming about in the neighbourhood and spouting. There were even more whales near the ice. At midnight the temperature was 3° F. below freezing. Although the ice was a long way off, we nevertheless observed a reflected light from it not unlike the light at dawn;[1] from time to time snow fell. At 6.0 a.m., when the wind shifted to east-north-east, we found that by turning to the south-east it was possible to gain a little in longitude, and then to push on to higher latitudes. I therefore steered a course S. 27° E. At 4.0 p.m. we again met continuous ice consisting of small horizontal blocks of ice. In the midst of them seven large icebergs with flat surfaces were wedged in. From the look-out we could not see the end of the ice to southward, so that we were forced to turn on another tack to north-east, and again to proceed to the north to find a westerly wind and then to turn eastward.

At the time of turning we were in Lat. 68° 05′ S., Long. 16° 37′ E. We had 8° F. of frost and the mercury in the barometer stood at 29·20. The wind was blowing steadily from the east.

To-day, besides snow and polar birds, a few birds about the size of turtle-doves flew over the ships. Their beaks and legs were red,

---

[1] A phenomenon now usually referred to as ice-blink, particularly marked when there are patches of sunlight coming through stratus clouds.

the tail was long and forked like a swallow's; they kept the wings bent back at the joint and thereby differ in their flight from the petrels; they flew at a great height, with piercing cries and, for the most part, circled round the pennants. To discover to which species they belonged, we wanted to bring down at least one of them. We sent a sailor up into the look-out with a gun, but to our great regret our sniper did not hit a single one. We had observed similar birds near South Georgia Island.[1] In the course of the day we saw one Egmont hen, and many whales spouting. The reappearance of these birds and of the Egmont hen gave ground for the suggestion that there might be land fairly near, as we had never seen these birds out in the open sea.

At 8.0 p.m., in consequence of the darkness, we took in the top-gallant sail and one reef in the topsails. At midnight there were 6° F. of frost and we could see the reflected light of ice to southward. On the following morning we once again made more sail and continued on our course northward, keeping to the east as much as the wind, which continued fresh as before, allowed. All the officers and crew greeted the reappearance of the sun, which we had not seen for seven days. They all came up on to the quarter-deck and forecastle in order to enjoy its reviving rays.

At midday we were in Lat. 67° 25′ 05″ S., Long. 19° 02′ 41″ E. The magnetic variation taken from several observations was found to be 24° 44′ W. on a north-north-east course. There was 2° F. of frost. On the last three days of Shrove Week, following our Russian custom, I ordered for the crew's dinner fried pancakes made with flour which the sailors ground in mortars from rice. During these three days, in addition to their usual rations, a glass of good punch, and a glass of beer made from essence, were served out to each man. I considered it necessary to observe on both vessels, as far as possible, everything that concerned all religious ceremonies and the customs of our country. On feast days all dressed in full uniform, and on festivals, besides the ordinary rations, fresh pork with pickled cabbage was served out with punch or grog and wine. Securing contentment in this way, I warded off the boredom and weariness, which can so easily be fostered during such a long period by the daily round, added to the dangers while ice,

---

[1] Probably this was an Arctic tern (*Sterna para disca*). It ranges more widely than almost any other bird, as it nests in the Arctic and frequently winters in the Antarctic. Its chief characteristics are a blood-red bill and legs and its short harsh cry—"kleeah".

continuous snow, fog, rain and sleet were our constant companions. Who does not know that cheerfulness and contentment contribute to good health, whereas weariness and dejection create idleness and that want of cleanliness which helps to produce scurvy? About midday, we again saw pestrushki, blue petrels and grey and common albatrosses, whilst a few whales were spouting. Mr Lazarev, Mr Kupriyanov, Mr Novosilski and Dr Galkin paid us a visit and remained with us all day.

9*th*. The night was very dark and a great deal of snow fell. The wind blew stronger, raising a heavy sea, so that at about 2.0 p.m. on the 9th February we found it necessary to close-reef the topsails and take in the top-gallant yards. We saw a number of whales and piebald porpoises, shoals of which continually crossed the bows of the ships. The mercury stood at freezing point. The rigging and sails were white with the heavy snow. At dawn on 10th February the wind went down a little. We set all sail and proceeded eastward.

10*th*. On the morning of the 10th, our Lat. was 65° 44′ S., Long. 23° 18′ E., and the mean magnetic variation was 29° 55′ W. At 4.0 p.m. we observed flying near us some large birds, so far unknown to us; in size a little larger than the pestrushki, with head and back dark brown, wings and under part white. The evening was bright and therefore without shortened sail I ordered the course to be kept eastward.

11*th*. A swell had set in from north-east by east. At midday we were in Lat. 65° 12′ 48″ S., Long. 28° 15′ E. The mean magnetic variation was 32° 11′ W. and the thermometer stood at 37° F. Up to 2.0 p.m. the weather continued fine but then the wind veered round to west-south-west. Wishing to profit by this change, I signalled to the *Mirnyi* to make more sail. Black birds about the size of a pigeon, such as we had already met near ice when passing the South Sandwich Islands, were flying round us. Mr Lazarev shot one of them down. Its feathers were dark brown, almost black, beak and feet white, and it appeared to belong to the species of petrels. I shall call them, as we had called them before, the small black petrels. We also saw some of those birds we had observed the previous day. I supposed that they lived on the small islands lying to the southward of the Cape of Good Hope. These, as well as the other birds, rarely came within range of our guns. We also saw small blue petrels and two albatrosses.

Towards evening the wind freshened and snow fell. We close-reefed the fore topsail so as not to get too far ahead of the *Mirnyi* and also for safety during the night, which was dark and only cleared now and then.

12*th*. At midnight we shook out the topsail, our speed being 6 knots. The *Mirnyi* did not overtake us until 4.0 a.m.; then we loosened two reefs in the main topsail and one reef in the fore and mizzen topsails. A swell running from north-east by east made the ship pitch a good deal. At 7.0 p.m. we sighted on our beam away to the southward an iceberg which we soon passed. Having a favourable wind for navigating eastward, and not meeting with any ice there, I ordered a south-east course, so as to reach higher latitudes and longitudes, and to ascertain on the way whether the position of the ice was still the same there as Captain Cook had found it on his voyage forty-seven years before. In 1773, 6/17 January, the great navigator, in Long. 39° 35' E., reached Lat. 67° 15' S., whence, finding impenetrable ice, he turned back to lower latitudes without attempting navigation farther to the south.[1] On the following day we proceeded at 8 knots with a fresh gusty south-west wind accompanied by high seas. The sky was covered with snowy clouds and, from time to time, snow and hail fell. Flights of small blue petrels flew round us, a few grey albatrosses and one Egmont hen. At 8.0 p.m., owing to the extremely dark night, we close-reefed the topsails. I was afraid of encountering ice as it was impossible to see it. At 11.30 I signalled to the *Mirnyi* to proceed close-hauled on a starboard tack so as not to go ahead until daybreak. There were 7° F. of frost. At midnight we observed towards the south-west on the horizon a faint brightness resembling dawn and extending vertically almost 5°. As we proceeded southward this light extended farther upwards. I concluded that it came from large masses of ice; however, as the day broke the light paled, and when the sun rose there were only white, very dense, clouds to be seen; there was no ice in that position. We had not, so far, observed any phenomenon of this kind.[2] At 2.30, which was daybreak, both vessels got under way, set more sail and proceeded on the former south-easterly course with the same but less strong wind, heavy seas from the west, and some snow. At 7.0 a.m. the snow ceased and we found ourselves in Lat. 66° 59' S., Long. 37° 38' E., the varia-

---

[1] As noted by Dr H. R. Mill, in his *Siege of the South Pole*, this was an important occasion in history, since it was the first time the Antarctic Circle had been crossed by man.
[2] Almost certainly an aurora.

tion being 35° 33′ W. At midday our position was Lat. 66° 53′ 17″ S., Long. 38° 12′ 20″ E. Although the sun often appeared from behind the clouds we still had 4° F. of frost at midday and 7° F. at 6.0 p.m. In 48 hours the current had set us N. 26° E. 19 miles. After midday variable light winds from south and south-east with heavy snow continued until 9.0 p.m. Then the wind again veered to the south-west quarter and at midnight I altered course to the east. The *Mirnyi* was astern of the *Vostok*.

13*th*. On the following day we noted a number of whales spouting, grey albatrosses, polar and little black petrels, as well as a few of those birds which we had observed on the 7th. These birds are about the size of a turtle-dove, and have red, awl-shaped beaks. The top of the head and the neck are black; from the beak to the eye the feathers are greyish black, the rest being a light grey colour, except underneath the neck and wings where they are a little whiter. The tail is entirely white and forked. When the wings are closed, the longer wing feathers extend an inch and a half beyond the tail. The feet are sharp with three toes and sharp claws and are webbed like those of all water birds and have one spur at the back. When in flight they utter continual cries like woodcocks. They have long wings, bent at an obtuse angle, which they bear in a distinctive manner different from all other sea birds, which stretch out their wings almost in a straight line and move them imperceptibly and gently. These birds to all appearance belong to the species known as the sea swallow. I have already remarked that we had never met similar birds in the open sea at a long distance from land. If they could live near ice, we should have encountered them before and after we actually met with them; and therefore I concluded that there must certainly be land somewhere in the vicinity. The nearest known islands are Prince Egmont, Desert Island and Kerguelen Land,[1] lying 1200 miles to northward of us. Considering this distance it was impossible to believe that these birds had flown from the above-mentioned land. Speaking of all this, I must also add that the farther we went into higher latitudes and continuous ice, the greater the number of whales we observed, so that their increasing numbers indicated to us the vicinity of ice.

14*th*. On the 14th the night was dark. Towards the south on the

---

[1] "Prince Egmont" is a misprint in the Russian text for Prince Edward. "Desert Island" must be East Island, one of the Crozet group, named "L'Ile Aride" by its discoverer, Marion du Fresne, in 1772.

horizon there was a broad line of light and we had 8° F. of frost. At this time we were crossing Captain Cook's course. The bright streamer visible to the southward seemed a reliable proof that even at present there was a great deal of ice in that region, from which Captain Cook on 6/17 January, 1773, turned back to lower latitudes. He encountered then an immense expanse of ice here, composed of floating blocks piled up one on the top of another. It is probable that in the course of the last half century various changes due to stormy weather have taken place in this ice. Some of the masses of ice have disappeared and new ice has been formed in their place. But whatever changes may have occurred the region in which Captain Cook encountered impracticable ice, now distant from us about 30 miles to the south, is still covered by vast quantities of ice. At 2.15 a.m. the day began to break and we set more sail. When it had fully dawned we counted towards the south-east up to ten icebergs together with a great deal of small broken ice.

In the morning we were in Lat. 66° 49' 05" S., Long. 41° 26' E. and found the variation to be 40° 13' W. Captain Cook at the same point found a variation of 29° 30', from which it appears that, in the course of the last forty-seven years, it has altered 10° 43' more towards the west. From midnight until 9.0 a.m. we had a light wind blowing between south and east, then a calm and later a light wind between north and east. I set a course S. 60° E. Before midday, passing a small ice floe, we slackened sail and sent two boats to procure some ice. We were then in Lat. 66° 52' 53" S., Long. 40° 55' 36" E. Although, owing to high breakers from the north and a swell, it was difficult to collect the ice, I sent the boats back again after they had brought some; but they had only just reached the ice when the wind veered to the east and began to blow in squalls. The horizon was shut out by fog and therefore I signalled to the boats to return. They did so immediately and were hoisted.

At the same time that the boats pushed off from the *Vostok*, two set off from the *Mirnyi* towards the ice and loaded up. But as the ice was sodden when brought on to the ship and was found to be soaked with salt water, Mr Lazarev ordered it to be thrown overboard. The wind continued to increase and was accompanied by fog and wet snow. At 7.0 p.m. we found it necessary to close-reef the topsails and strike the top-gallant yards and mast. We had 4° F. of frost. The whole rigging, the sails, and the ship herself were covered with ice, and we could not keep even the running tackle and the deck clear of snow. With such a strong wind, thick fog and snow, it was very dangerous to be in the midst of icebergs.

We proceeded on a course N. 20° W., carrying very little sail, to get out of the visibly dangerous position before night. The seas were high. The darkness was increased by the fog and thick snow which limited visibility to the smallest distance. Many icebergs lay on our course. By great good fortune by 10.0 p.m. the wind abated, but during the night so much heavy snow fell that it covered the sails and rigging and froze on everything, and it was only with difficulty that we succeeded in clearing it away.

15*th*. The variable wind, accompanied by thick weather and wet snow, became a strong contrary east wind. The vessel laboured dreadfully and dangerously because a heavy swell was running from west-south-west, meeting and uniting with the seas coming from the east, and rising into appallingly high breakers from which the wind blew the seething white foam and carried it through the air. These seas were a danger to the ships because the sides of the waves, owing to the contrary forces, were almost perpendicular. The vessel, coming up on such a wave, encounters a great mass of water on one side, whilst at the same time, from the other side, the same wave forms a deep hollow, into which the vessel tends to heel over. During the course of this perilous night, neither ship saw or heard any light or gun signals made by the other. Up to 3 o'clock the wind remained changeable; we had 4° F. of frost, and the mercury in the barometer stood at 28·80. Supposing that the *Mirnyi*, as usually happened, had fallen behind, I wore ship after midnight so as to meet her at daybreak. A separation would be awkward for both of us because, according to the instructions which I had given to Mr Lazarev, we had to search for each other for three days at the point where the separation took place, by which we would both lose three days, being in danger amongst icebergs and thick weather, high winds and unceasing snow. To our mutual joy we soon saw our consort, joined up and proceeded north.

Although the health of the officers and crew was of the very best and permitted us to continue the attempts to the south, Port Jackson, the nearest port at which I could lay in a store of wood, water and fresh provisions, was distant 120° of longitude and 31° of latitude, that is to say, by the shortest possible route, we should still have to

travel 5000 miles and our voyage from Rio de Janeiro had already
lasted thirteen weeks. The weather in the approaching late season was
stormy and the frost about latitudes of 67° was 8° F. In view of all
these circumstances I thought it expedient to withdraw from the high
southern latitudes where we constantly found contrary east winds and
return far enough northward to encounter a fair wind, proceeding
with this wind eastward as far as Lat. 61° S., Long. 90° E. By this
arrangement I intended to survey that part of the Antarctic Ocean
which remained as yet unexplored. Captain Cook had left this to
future navigators, and had himself directed his course to lower latitudes
to examine the land which not long before had been discovered by the
French Captain Kerguelen,* which many took to be a cape of the
southern mainland.

When the day had fully broken no ice was visible on the horizon
and the *Mirnyi* presented to our eyes the usual wintry picture—all
covered with snow. Towards midday the wind fell a little and we
unreefed the topsails. In consequence of the mist, we were not able
to make any observations at midday. At 4.0 p.m. we observed towards
the east-south-east two masses of ice in the far distance.

16*th*. The night was dark, with 2° F. of frost, and calm. The
violent labouring due to the cross swell continued. A great deal of
snow fell between midnight and morning. At midday we had 6° F.
of frost. Our position was 65° 48' 31" S., 41° 44' 19" E. The variation
was 40° 33' W. The wind shifted to the north, but was light. We kept
on our easterly course and observed a large high mass of ice ahead of
us. Having reached it at 5 o'clock, we lay to and fired a salvo at it,
but owing to the ship's labouring, hit it only with difficulty. We found,
however, a few blocks of ice on the other side and these we brought
on board. In the meantime the *Mirnyi*, which had dropped astern,
had now come up with us. This iceberg was more than 150 feet in

---

* Monsieur Kerguelen, commanding the vessels *Fortuna* and *Gros Ventre*, started
out from Mauritius or Ile de France Island at the end of 1771. On January 31st,
1772, he observed two islands and called them "Fortuna", and on the following day
yet another island which he called "Round Island" on account of its appearance.
Then he observed still more land, which he called "La Terre de Kerguelen".[1]

---

[1] The footnote in the original text was evidently taken from a Russian source
as it uses the Old Style date and the account of the discovery is much condensed.
Actually Kerguelen saw the western islets and thought he had discovered a new
continent which he named La France Australe. He returned again in 1773 and,
disappointed that it was only a large island, renamed it Terre Désolation. The name
Kerguelen was given to the island later.

height. When we approached it all the wind was taken out of our sails. It had apparently half turned turtle, because the part which had been submerged was out of water as was evident from the colour of the ice. The part washed by the surf was bluish, whilst over the large masses of ice now projecting below water, a surf of a greenish colour was breaking. While the ice was being brought on board, Mr Zavodovski succeeded in shooting a penguin which was diving near the ship and weighed 13 lb. It belonged to the class of little or common penguins like those which we had caught on the ice. For some time we had not seen these birds and did not know to what to attribute the presence of this one—to the vicinity of land, or perhaps to the fact that this one had lost its companions; there was no ice in the vicinity on to which it could easily have clambered.[1] At 10.0 p.m. we hoisted the boats and turned northward with a contrary wind from east-north-east.

17*th.* At midday of the 17th we were in Lat. 65° 05′ 20″ S., Long. 41° 21′ 34″ E. The variation was 38° 09′ W.

18*th.* Snow fell accompanied by thick weather almost throughout the whole 24 hours. We proceeded on our former course northward until 4.0 a.m. of the 18th so as to get away from Captain Cook's route[2] on which we proceeded against our will in consequence of a contrary east wind. We altered course south-east by south, but on this course we only continued until midday. The wind became very strong, and therefore for safety we again altered course northward. The wind caused enormous seas and blew the snow and spray on to the ship. These immediately froze, so that the sails and rigging and the tackle were covered with ice more than an inch thick. The *Mirnyi* found herself taken aback but towards 5.0 p.m. she closed us. Mr Lazarev, guessing that we were to leeward and unable to see us owing to the thick fog, fired four shots, and did well, for we could indeed see him only with difficulty. It was not easy to keep a look-out to windward in consequence of the very keen wind (with 2° F. of frost) and the thick snow and flying spray which blinded our eyes. In these circumstances I bore away with the wind upon the quarter and opened out to such a distance as to be safe for the night. The *Mirnyi* was quickly

[1] Almost certainly a young Adelie penguin (*Pygoscelis Adeliae*). The adults would still be at their rookeries farther south at this date.
[2] It will have been noticed already that Bellingshausen endeavoured on all occasions to supplement Captain Cook's discoveries by going south where Cook had turned north and vice versa.

out of sight. We had just luffed again when there was a shout from the forecastle, "Iceberg ahead, a little to windward". I ordered the helm to be put hard over, but the slow action of the helm increased our horror. The weather with the thick snow was so stormy and thick that, even if we had encountered ice, we should not have been able to sight it until within three-fourths of a cable's length. I went forward with the officers and with the utmost care we peered in all directions, but could see nothing and came to the conclusion that the look-out had only seen, in the thick weather, the foaming crest of a wave and, as the eyes of nervous people are unreliable and tend to exaggerate, that he had mistaken it for an iceberg. Feeling quite certain that there was no ice, or if there were, it was impossible to see it in this weather, I gave orders to resume our course. All the same, this occurrence brought vividly home to us the dangers to which we were exposed: the uncertainty about ice, the storm, the sea with its deep hollows, the enormous waves, thick fog and snow shutting everything out from our view and, at the same time, the darkness of night drawing on. It seems shameful to feel fear, but even the hardiest man prayed within himself, "Lord, save us!" Towards night additional look-outs were put on when it was necessary, with orders to notify the officer of the watch of the slightest indication of danger.

19*th*. At 8.0 a.m., when the fog cleared for a short time, we saw with joy that there was no ice anywhere in view. The *Mirnyi* lay N. 60° E. of us, under reefed storm staysails. We also observed some polar petrels flying near us which we had not previously noticed north of the Antarctic Circle. Probably these birds had been driven from their natural home by the force of the storm.

20*th*. Accompanied by fog and wet snow the storm raged, and it did not cease until 4.0 a.m. of the 20th. Even then wet snow continued to fall.

At 5.0 a.m. we set the foresail and at 9.0 a.m. the topsails, which had been close-reefed. At 10.0 a.m. we again saw the *Mirnyi*. During the forenoon we had a glimpse of the sun for a little while and found our position to be Lat. 63° 20′ 44″ S., Long. 40° 18′ 50″ E.

This morning we were very perplexed by observing in the sea quite near to windward of us two boards, like the foot-boards of a boat. As they were fairly new, not yet overgrown with moss and shells, we concluded that one of the boats on the *Mirnyi* had been smashed by the high waves or that some European had recently suffered shipwreck in these latitudes, as neither the currents nor the waves could have carried these planks to such a high latitude before they were covered with moss, shells and seaweed. The incident made us ask each other the question—was it possible that, besides our two vessels, someone else was making a voyage to these regions? In the evening it was all explained. We discovered that the planks had been torn away from our own vessel under the windward net. Here it will of course strike the reader that many travellers, meeting with similar phenomena and not knowing the exact cause, often draw quite unfounded conclusions, in the same way as we had done.

In the course of this storm we saw very few sea birds; from the *Mirnyi* only one penguin and one spouting whale were observed.

21st. It was a moonlight night, the stars were shining and we had 2° F. of frost. The day began to break at 4.0 a.m., the wind gradually fell and shifted south-west by west. I altered course due east with the intention of proceeding in that direction until we should meet some insurmountable obstacle.

We were now in Lat. 62° 44′ 47″ S., Long. 41° 31′ 05″ E. In this latitude I hoped to avail myself of a favourable wind, because in the middle southern latitudes the prevalent wind is westerly.

Owing to the long period of uninterrupted damp and cold, snow, sleet, thick weather and storm, the damp had penetrated into all parts of the vessel. Fine weather was absolutely necessary to us. In order to counteract the bad effects of these conditions, I ordered the fires in the stoves to be lighted to dry the lower deck where the crew lived, while the officers' cabins were dried by means of cannon-balls brought to a red heat. To use this method of drying during a violent storm would be very dangerous.

We hoisted the top-gallant mast and yard and shook out a reef in the topsails. It was impossible to carry more sail in consequence of the heavy after-swell of the storm and also because the *Mirnyi* had fallen behind.

In Lat. 62° 50′ S., Long. 42° 05′ E., we found the variation to be 39° 02′ W. At 10.0 p.m. we passed close to an iceberg which we had already seen ahead of us. Had it not been moonlight, one or other of the vessels could hardly have escaped an accident. The *Mirnyi* was abeam of us to northward. In the course of the day snow fell at times. We saw some whales, grey albatrosses, one white and many blue and black petrels and pestrushki.

22nd. With a fresh south by west wind we continued our course eastward. The night was cloudy, but for our comfort, the moon broke through now and then. Our speed was 7 knots. In the darkness of the night we had to look ahead constantly with telescopes from the forecastle so as not to run into ice. The *Mirnyi* was astern of us. During the 24 hours there were gusts of wind from time to time, snow clouds and a sharp fall of hail.

23rd. At midnight we had 2° F. of frost. We proceeded with the same wind under reefed topsails only, at 7 knots. I waited impatiently for daybreak because I longed to avail myself of the favourable wind to reach New Holland quickly, as this was essential for the health of the ship's company.

At midday the sun peeped out from behind the clouds and we fixed our position as Lat. 62° 27′ 58″ S., Long. 52° 26′ 41″ E. While in that latitude, but in Long. 53° 12′, we found a variation of 44° 04′ 05″ W. During the day we passed close to seven icebergs, about which masses of ice floated to leeward, probably broken off from the bergs by the force of the recent storm. The *Mirnyi* kept station northward of us at a distance of 4 miles and towards night as usual came astern of us so that we should not separate.

24th. At midnight we had 5° F. of frost. The sky was covered with clouds through which the moon shone from time to time. Our speed was not more than 4 knots.

From 3.0 a.m. the wind veered from south-west to west and began to freshen, and at 5.0 a.m. blew from the north. The horizon was shut out by mist and heavy snow fell. In consequence of the darkness, we could not see far and therefore we remained under topsails only, spilling the wind out of the mizzen sail, so as to reduce our speed.

At daybreak, owing to fog and thick snow, we could not see the *Mirnyi*. I gave orders that a gun should be fired each half hour, the last shots with cannon-ball. The *Mirnyi*, however, did not hear them. At 7.0 a.m. when the snow ceased for a short time we saw our consort ahead of us. She had passed us when we had shortened sail to wait for her. At 3.0 p.m. Mr Lazarev informed me by signal that he had observed a sort of bird which rose from the water and flew westward. We were then in Lat. 62° 32′ S., Long. 57° 41′ 17″ E., and at 10.0 p.m. we heard the cry of a penguin. That and the other might be indications of the proximity of land, particularly the former, because the cormorant or shag, on account of its heavy flight, cannot fly far out to sea. The nearest known land was Kerguelen Island, which lay 800 miles from us to the north. Such a distance I considered to be too great for the flight of a land bird, but perhaps strong north winds might have carried it from Kerguelen Island far out to sea. During the course of the day, we had a fresh wind with fog and thick wet snow. We proceeded at 8 knots. Although our visibility was extremely limited, in consequence of the fog and snow, up to midday we saw and passed three, and after midday, four icebergs. Probably, had the weather been clearer, we should have seen many more.

25th. With the same strong wind from north-north-west, with fog, wet snow and 2° F. of frost, we continued eastward during the night, reefing the mizzen topsail so as to reduce speed. At 4.0 a.m. by means of light signals both vessels showed their positions. The *Mirnyi* kept in our wake. Mr Lazarev in his report says: "Although we kept a look-out ahead with the utmost care, it still seemed to me unwise to go on in the thick night at a speed of 8 knots." I was of the same opinion as Mr Lazarev and I was not altogether happy during such nights; I was, however, not concerned merely with the present, but was planning our future arrangements to achieve the desired object of our enterprise without having to remain in the ice region at the time of the approaching equinoxes. In the morning we made more sail so as to avail ourselves of the favourable wind, but soon after midday we stood again under topsails only close-reefed to give the *Mirnyi* time to catch up with us. At 4.0 p.m. we observed a few icebergs to starboard. At 9.0 p.m. the wind blew from north-west by west with strong squalls, mist, wet snow and rain. In this bad weather we could not see anything ahead of us, which obliged us to alter course and proceed on another tack until the following morning.

26th. At 2.0 a.m. we had again a strong west wind, with thick weather and snow. Black clouds sped across the sky. We turned on to the port tack, then ran close to the wind until daybreak and took in the mizzen.

At 4.30 we set an easterly course. At 6.0 and at 10.0 a.m. we passed two icebergs, the former was 4 miles to southward of us and the latter was 3 miles off in the same direction.

At 8.0 a.m. the sky began to clear. The day became bright and the weather was beautiful and we were able to verify our navigation. Although it was not very easy to take altitudes on account of the heavy rolling, we none the less did so as far as possible. We hung out all the clothes of the crew to dry them thoroughly, also the hammocks and spare sails; of this they had long stood in need because they had been incessantly exposed to damp air.

At midday we were by observation in Lat. 62° 47′ 46″ S., Long. 68° 50′ 28″ E. The variation in the same latitude and in Long. 68° 43′ E. was 48° 09′ W. We were then passing near an iceberg 200 feet in height, and three-quarters of a mile in circumference.

The wind had fallen at midday and gradually shifted east. At 8.0 p.m. we had a contrary east-north-east wind and we turned for the night towards the north because in this direction I supposed that we should meet less ice. During the frequent strong winds and high seas the tiller slackened in the stays so much that, to reduce as far as possible further damage and relieve the rudder, I carried little sail. We refitted the tiller, but it still remained unsteady. Some large and small black petrels, pestrushki and grey albatrosses flew round the ship.

27*th*. Strong wind, thick weather, snow and rain continued. At 7.0 a.m. we passed near an iceberg. The wind fell at midday. The swell from the previous gales caused a heavy pitching and rolling of the vessel. The mist, wet snow and rain, sometimes varied by fog, did not diminish.

Our unsteady tiller was a source of anxiety. I again gave orders to refit it, but when we removed it, to our astonishment we found that half of the end, being rotten, remained in the rudder head. We had therefore to put in a spare tiller as quickly as possible. The spare iron fittings did not fit it. This unreliability of the tiller, so necessary for the safety of the ship, proves the carelessness of the shipbuilder who, forgetful of his sacred obligation to the service and to humanity, had exposed us to destruction. I cannot pass over in silence the fact that in the course of my service I have often heard strong expressions of opinion by naval officers about shipbuilders delivering unreliable fittings to vessels.

To-day we used all our remaining ice. Owing to the recent stormy weather we had not been able to lay in a store of it, although we had often encountered icebergs.

Apart from the birds which we had seen daily and have often mentioned, birds of the size of a raven flew at some distance from the vessel, their undersides being white and all the upper part black. We had seen them a few times before but had not succeeded in bringing a single one down. From the *Mirnyi* they saw two penguins. During the whole night the fog and ceaseless snowfall continued. Our navigation was uncomfortable owing to the meeting of swells from different directions. We had 2° F. of frost.

From daybreak till midday the weather remained changeable, sometimes clear, sometimes thick with snow falling, shutting out everything from us. We collected snow and melted it for the use of the pigs and sheep. At midday we were in Lat. 62° 04′ 14″ S., Long. 68° 15′ 40″ E. The mean variation was found to be 45° 19′ W. At midday with a light east wind we reached a lower latitude. In the evening the sky was absolutely clear of clouds, and we had the indescribable pleasure of seeing the constellations of Orion and the Southern Cross, which for several months had been hidden by fog, thick weather and snow clouds. From both ships we saw three penguins, besides which the *Mirnyi* saw some divers[1] exactly like those we had seen near South Georgia. They proved the proximity of land. Among these birds there were flocks of pestrushki, black petrels, a few blue ones and grey albatrosses.

At 9.0 p.m., towards night, we took a reef in the topsail. The sky was again overcast and a little snow fell.

29th. At 4.0 a.m. the wind shifted so far to the south as to permit us again to take course eastward. At daybreak we saw the *Mirnyi* very far behind, and therefore shortened sail. At 6.0 a.m. the mercury in the thermometer stood at freezing point. At 11.0 a.m. the *Mirnyi* was still far behind us. We shortened sail, but she was lying to to bring in an Egmont hen which had been shot, and I gave her a gun signal to get under way. At midday we were in Lat. 61° 21′ 40″ S., Long. 69° 36′ 57″ E. The variation on both compasses was 45° 26′ W. The cold was moderate and we saw heavy snowstorms on either side of us at some distance. There was no ice in sight. At night we stood under reefed topsails so as to reduce speed. When the snow clouds had passed we could see two cables ahead. In the course of the day penguins appeared, grey and white albatrosses, pestrushki and blue petrels. Of these latter there is yet another such species considerably larger, of the size of a raven and with dark wings. They did not fly near to the vessel and we saw them more rarely than the others. They have a more rapid flight and are more beautiful than any of the other known petrels.

[1] This seems to be a case of faulty identification; there could have been no ducks here.

Blue Petrel

Antarctic Petrel

Seal 8½ feet long (Crab-eater Seal)

Seal 9½ feet long (Leopard Seal)

Our voyage, reckoning from our departure from Rio de Janeiro, had taken just a hundred days. We included this day among the number of feast days, which the officers distinguished by treating each other to chocolate made with milk, specially preserved by Mr Hamble. For the crew a pig was killed and a soup was prepared with pickled cabbage and pork, and afterwards, in addition to the usual ration, a glass of good hot punch was served out.

During this night we carried a fair amount of sail because of the light wind and equally because we had not met a single iceberg. In the darkness of night we saw the surface of the sea gleaming, which we had not seen in the higher latitudes because these phosphorescent creatures do not go beyond a certain latitude.[1] There is probably a degree of cold which they cannot bear, like all life on the globe we inhabit.

1st. At midnight both vessels indicated their position by sending up lights. The *Mirnyi* was following in our wake, not far from us. The wind changed to south-south-east, and we continued on a starboard tack close-hauled. The night was dark. At 2.0 a.m. we shortened sail owing to the strong wind and took another reef in the topsails.

In the course of the 24 hours we had heavy squalls and the clouds brought fine dry snow and hail. We had 8° F. of frost at 6.0 a.m., at midday 6° F. of frost, and at 6.0 p.m. we had again 8° F. In the evening, when on the approach of night we reefed the foresails, the running gear in the foretack could not be moved, because the spray, which constantly dashed over it, had frozen it stiff. All the rigging on the bowsprit was also thickly covered with ice; this ice, although formed by the salt spray, was not salt. We observed a large flock of black petrels, one large white albatross with black wings, and a whale. About midday, small porpoises with white sides in large numbers swam constantly across the bows of the ship. They swam at least at $1\frac{1}{2}$ times the rate of the vessel, which was then making $6\frac{1}{2}$ to 7 knots. From the 1st of March we began to reckon the second hundred days of our voyage. The officers and crew were in perfect health. Throughout all this time only one sailor had died, on the *Mirnyi*, from rheumatic fever. Despite all endeavours of Dr Galkin to give him all possible help, his efforts proved vain in consequence of the hard climate. The sails and running rigging on the boats were rotting from the frequent and continual wet. The stocks of wood and water were running low,

---

[1] This is now known not to be the case.

especially the former. I intended to lay in a store of water when we should meet an iceberg, if only the weather permitted.

2nd. We continued on an easterly course, with a keen strong wind from the south-south-west. The weather was dry and there was 6° F. of frost. At times the hurrying clouds driven by the wind brought dry fine snow and hail. Navigation was not easy owing to the swell from the south. I endeavoured, during the night, to go at the lowest possible speed. The sails were braced round, but in spite of all this we made 5 knots. To my extreme regret we had to close-reef the topsails and proceed under very little sail so that the *Mirnyi* might keep with us. These unequal speeds of the two vessels, in spite of all the skill and care of Mr Lazarev, caused the greatest difficulty in carrying out our plans and hampered the successful navigation of the vessels entrusted to me. I repeatedly thought of leaving the *Mirnyi* definitely behind, and would have made up my mind to it had it not been for the instructions which forbade our separating in the higher southern latitudes.

At midday we were in Lat. 60° 45′ 44″ S., Long. 76° 51′ 31″ E.

At 2.0 p.m. we saw ahead of us icebergs, and, after an hour, we were among them; along the horizon there were as many as ten, possibly more but, owing to the thick weather, we could not see far. In order to pass round one of these icebergs we were obliged to bear away; the violent bitter wind and high sea forbade any idea of obtaining ice from them. All day Mr Lazarev kept 7 miles to northward of us and towards night followed in our wake. We continued until midnight to make 8 knots but, on account of the darkness, we spilled the wind from the main topsail in order to reduce speed. In the course of the day the icebergs encountered led us to conclude that we should meet them very often. The approach of night, the sharp wind and the high seas still more increased the dangers of such an encounter, because it was very difficult at night and with a good speed to distinguish between the icebergs and the seething foam on the waves. Moreover, a sudden encounter with an iceberg with a gale blowing and heavy frost could easily create great difficulty in the handling of the ship. Each rapid change of course demanded great exertions, because all the running rigging on which any movement of the ship depended was so hardened by wet and frost that it was extremely difficult to work it.

The mercury in the thermometer stood at night at 27° F. The officers of the watch had only just changed, when we observed a flashing light which appeared from time to time, the cause of which we did not know. Finally, at the close of the second hour after midnight when the clouds became less dense, we beheld one of the most beautiful and impressive phenomena of nature. To the south there appeared two columns of a whitish-blue colour similar to phosphorescent fire, flashing from clouds along the horizon with the rapidity of rockets. Each column was as broad as three diameters of the sun. Then this amazing spectacle spread along the horizon over about 120° and passed the zenith. Finally, towards the end of the phenomenon, the whole sky was covered with similar pillars. We enjoyed and admired this extraordinary sight. The light was so strong and penetrating that opaque objects threw shadows exactly as in daylight when the sun is covered with clouds, and it was possible to read even the smallest print without difficulty.

The phenomenon faded gradually, but lighting the whole horizon throughout the whole night, it was most helpful to us, because though for the past few days it had become quite light from time to time even on the cloudiest nights, the cause of which we had not understood, this light allowed us to proceed much more boldly. The last phase of this display appeared at first as a small bluish-white ball, from which instantly bands of the same colour spread over the vault of the heavens, some extending to the opposite horizon, others reaching the zenith and passing beyond it. Sometimes across the whole of the sky there were feathers of light and sometimes the whole of the sky and even the horizon to the north were covered with light. With the dawn the magnificent sight gradually faded away.[1]

There was a strong south-westerly wind blowing; we proceeded to the east. At daybreak we observed four icebergs ahead of us. The high seas broke with fury against the iceberg nearest to us. The spray was dashed up and carried by the wind over the berg which looked like a lighthouse. Before midday we passed thirteen icebergs and some floating ice. At midday our position by observation was Lat. 60° 49′ 11″ S., Long. 82° 22′ 16″ E. The average variation was 48° 04′ W. From the afternoon until twilight we passed many icebergs, which from hour to hour increased in number. In the evening a sharp squall blew up from the west. Owing to the darkness of night and the heavy snow we could not see more than 5 cables ahead; consequently at 10.0 p.m.

[1] This is a very vivid description of what must have been an unusually bright aurora. It is very rarely that auroral displays enable one to read small print.

we were forced to turn close to the wind northward and proceed in that direction until dawn.

4th. During the night the wind continued to blow in sharp gusts with an extremely heavy snowfall, but as soon as the snow ceased to fall, the southern aurora showed in all its magnificence and brightness, quite different from that which we had seen the previous night. The whole vault of the heavens except 12° or 15° from the horizon was covered with bands of rainbow colour which, with the rapidity of lightning, traversed the sky in sinuous lines from south to north, shading off from colour to colour. This spectacle, surpassing all description, aroused in us the greatest wonder and saved us, it may be, from misfortune. When the snow clouds had cleared and the sea was lit up by the aurora, we observed that we were passing close to a huge iceberg to leeward: we considered ourselves fortunate not to have run into it.

Later Mr Lazarev related to me that a few of the sailors in his ship during this strange spectacle uncovered and exclaimed, "Heaven is on fire and is already drawing nearer". I was not surprised, because I think that such a sudden sight might have astounded even a professor lecturing on this subject if he had not happened to have seen such phenomena before.[1]

At 4.30 a.m., as soon as it was clear, I bore away on a course S. 70° E. and we observed twelve large icebergs in our vicinity. By 8.0 a.m. the squalls with heavy snow ceased but the wind continued as before. The icebergs became more numerous and many of them were of enormous size.[2]

At 10.0 a.m., when the number of icebergs had become so great that they constituted a danger, I altered course to the north-east and signalled to the *Mirnyi* to turn four points to port.

We were then passing an iceberg looking like an ancient castle. Lieutenant-Commander Zavodovski found by sextant its height to be

---

[1] A close parallel to this story was the behaviour of the Russian groom taken by Captain Scott in 1910 to look after the Manchurian ponies. At his first experience of an aurora he ran into the hut and hid his head in his bunk, saying the sky was alight and about to explode.

[2] The special frequency of the icebergs at this stage of their voyage has an explanation. Owing to the prevalent winds near the Antarctic continent being from the south and east, the icebergs tend to drift northwards to lower latitudes. At about the latitude of 60° they meet the great westerly drift due to the prevalent westerlies which pass unhindered round the globe. The icebergs therefore tend to collect along this line, drifting towards the east.

357 English feet above the surface of the sea. Mr Mikhailov sketched it.[1] Mr Lazarev, in his first interview after this with us, told me that, when the *Vostok* was passing near one of these icebergs and was about 5 miles distant from the *Mirnyi*, it seemed to him that the height of this huge iceberg was three times that of the *Vostok's* masts and spars. From that he concluded that the iceberg rose 408 feet into the air. This height above the surface of the sea is the mean between the spires of the Petropavlovsk Cathedral in St Petersburg and St Michael's in Hamburg. The former is 385 English feet and the latter 429 in height. This iceberg ended in a sharp peak. The *Mirnyi*, being a considerable distance from us, did not at once carry out the order, and so the signal was repeated with two gun shots with ball.

At midday we were in Lat. 60° 29′ 35″ S., Long. 86° 06′ 05″ E. The variation taken as an average of a number of observations was 49° 40′ W. From early morning until 5.0 p.m. we passed icebergs and floating ice. We hove to near one huge iceberg from which the waves had broken off blocks of ice, and lowered boats, filled up ten barrels with ice, then hoisted the boats, double-reefed the topsails for the night and directed our course N. 40° E.

Whilst we lay to, Mr Lazarev came on board. I explained to him my intention to withdraw from the high latitudes, partly on account of encountering so much ice, and the approach of the equinoctial gales, and also because of the darkness of the nights and the unceasing snow. I told him that instead of the Auckland Islands to which I had been instructed to go, I should proceed to Port Jackson, where we should be able to obtain stores of all fresh provisions, which would not be possible in the Auckland Islands; wood also would be more easily obtainable in Port Jackson. In consequence of this change of plan, I told Mr Lazarev that the ships should separate at the point where Captain Cook broke off his course. The *Mirnyi* was to proceed on a parallel, 2½° to 3° S., of Captain Furneaux's course until approaching Long. 135° E. Then, on reaching Lat. 49° 30′ S., to continue to the eastward on that parallel so as to locate Royal Company Island, indicated on the Arrowsmith Chart in Lat. 49° 30′ S., Long. 143° 04′ E. Then, after surveying the stretch from this island to the southern

---

[1] An unusually high iceberg; they are very rarely more than 200 feet high in the Antarctic. The added testimony of Mr Lazarev, however, supports the measurement. It is possibly the berg illustrated by the artist on Plate 7 with the *Vostok* in front of it.

extremity of Van Diemen's Land, to proceed to Port Jackson. The *Vostok* would navigate $2\frac{1}{2}°$ or $3°$ northward of Captain Cook's course, so that both vessels should traverse and survey a stretch of ocean which had not yet been examined by any known navigator over a length of $55°$ by a width of $8°$. Reaching Royal Company Island, I intended to survey it and then proceed to Port Jackson. I also informed Mr Lazarev that, when the moment of separation should come, I would let him know by signal.

During the night we continued on the same course under shortened sail. Twice we had sharp squalls from the south-west accompanied by such heavy snow that it was impossible to see anything at all at 10 sazhen (24 yards).

5*th*. At 3.0 a.m. we proceeded through large masses of floating ice, but fortunately for us the southern aurora lit up the sea at this time, so that we were able to see everything and steer clear of all the ice. In the course of an hour we passed into a clear part.

At daybreak we saw up to eleven icebergs in different directions from the ship. All the following day we were amongst icebergs. At midday we were in Lat. $59°\,00'\,31''$ S., Long. $88°\,51'\,09''$ E. The variation averaged $48°\,02'$ W. By evening there were not quite so many icebergs. In the course of the day a few heavy snow clouds passed, and as the equinox was approaching I had no hope of any better chances for cutting ice; so the fallen snow was collected into tubs and later on used for the pigs and sheep.

On the *Vostok* the crew was much larger than on the *Mirnyi*, and therefore to make it possible for them at the beginning of Lent to fulfil their Christian obligations I took the priest from the *Mirnyi* on board until our meeting again in New Holland. Both vessels lay to and the priest came over to us.

After hoisting the boat the vessels proceeded on their former course, N. $40°$ E. Soon after, with a salute of seven guns, I instructed the *Mirnyi* by signal to proceed on the course laid down for her, wished her all possible success and appointed Port Jackson as our place of meeting. Mr Lazarev replied with a salute of twenty guns, signalled us all success and then turned on a course N. $79°$ E. At 7.0 p.m. the darkness hid our consort from us and we separated from her for a long time. From evening we stood under reefed topsails. With a fresh south-south-west wind we proceeded on a course N. $70°$ E. 7 knots, encountering a few icebergs. Thick snow prevented our distinguishing objects, and therefore as a precaution from time to time I reduced speed, taking the wind out of the sails.

6th. At midnight there was 3° F. of frost. The southern aurora, which to some extent gave us security in navigating, continued from 10.0 p.m. to 3.0 a.m. At daybreak I looked from the stern for the *Mirnyi* from force of habit. As I came on to the quarter-deck and there was no sign of our consort, it was borne in upon me that we were indeed alone. Many icebergs were in sight; we made more sail, but we could not escape from the dreary solitude. The pestrushki, black and blue petrels, and grey albatrosses were now the only witnesses of our voyage. The number of icebergs diminished. In the course of the day, whilst making a good rate of speed, we met not more than ten of them. At 7.0 p.m. the wind shifted to the west and a little snow fell. For the night we took in the studding sails.

7th. From midnight to 4.0 a.m. the southern aurora assisted us on our way. At daybreak we set the studding sails, the wind shifted to the north, with a slight mist, rain and snow. The mercury in the thermometer stood at freezing point. At 7.0 a.m. we passed ice lying to port. I had for some time wished to replenish our store of ice, but had always been prevented either by too high winds, or favourable winds that I did not wish to miss, or the heavy swell had made it impossible to heave to and keep boats near the ice. On that day at 10.0 a.m., approaching quite close to an iceberg, we fired five shots at it with ball. We broke off enough ice, lay to, lowered both boats, and sent crews to pick up the ice.

Whilst hove to we had time to replace the old tiller ropes, which had rotted, by new ones. At noon we were in Lat. 58° 21' 48" S., Long. 97° 28' 38" E., the variation being 42° 51' W. The ice being stored and the boats hoisted, we set sail and steered on a course N. 80° E. with a fresh north-west wind. We were going at a rate of almost 8 knots. From afternoon till evening we saw only two icebergs in the distance. At 8.0 p.m. we took in the studding sails for the night. At 10.0 p.m. we again passed near ice. The mist cleared and at 11.0 p.m. the southern aurora appeared again, extending from south-west to north-east.

8th. At 9.0 a.m. the wind from the north freshened and obliged us to take in the top-gallant sails and reef the topsails. At 2.0 p.m. we lowered the top-gallant yards. After 3.0 p.m. the horizon was covered by mist. At 5.0 we close-reefed the fore and mizzen topsails and took in the last reef in the mainsails. At 9.0 p.m. we took in the mainsails. At 11.0 p.m. we passed by an iceberg and observed a few more ahead of us. The wind freshened more and more and forced us to alter our course.

9th. At midnight the wind was already so strong that we stood under reefed main topsails and storm staysails. At 2.0 a.m. the storm staysail falls broke; we replaced them by new ones and hoisted the staysail again. At 5.0 a.m. the main topsail and the main and mizzen staysails suddenly split. The position of our ship was such as only those who have experienced it can imagine. Although the topsail was quickly taken in and the staysails lowered, they were none the less of no further use. The fore staysail alone stood. I ordered it to be taken in quickly in order to have at least one sail for an emergency. The wind howled and the seas rose to an extraordinary height. Sea and air seemed to mingle and the labouring of the ship drowned all other sounds. We remained now under bare poles at the mercy of the furious gale. I ordered some of the sailors' hammocks to be hoisted on the mizzen shrouds in order to keep the vessel to the wind. Our only comfort was that we had not yet encountered any ice in this appalling storm. At last at 8.0 a.m. there was a cry from the forecastle, "Ice ahead!" This filled us all with horror and I saw that we were being driven straight on to one of the masses of ice. Immediately the fore staysail was hoisted and the rudder set hard up. But all this had not the desired result and the ice was already close to us; nothing remained to us but to watch our approach. One mass was carried past under the stern and another lay right amidships. We awaited the shock which seemed bound to follow, when fortunately a huge wave, rising under the vessel, carried the ice some yards away and rushed it past the quarter gallery to leeward. The ice might have stove in the side or carried away the bulwarks and the masts. At 11.0 a.m. the storm raged as furiously as ever. The crest of one of these enormous waves struck the end of the bowsprit and broke the weather hooks, stays and cathead stays. In these circumstances I was indebted to the energy and resource of Lieutenant-Commander Zavodovski, to whom was entrusted the task of fitting preventer rigging. The prompt execution of this task enabled us to relieve the strain on the bowsprit and masts. During the storm we did not see any birds except a grey albatross, which sheltered itself from the gale in the hollow of the waves and maintained itself there with outstretched wings whilst it paddled with its feet. At 2.0 p.m. the force of the gale diminished somewhat. At 3.0 p.m. we saw a large iceberg 3 miles distant from us. In the afternoon the wind shifted through north to north-west. Setting the fore staysail, we turned and set a course N. 80° E. By 6.0 p.m. we were able to carry reefed fore- and mainsails. We then observed an iceberg bearing north and a few pestrushki. They were still hard put to it to maintain themselves on the surface of the water between the waves. The approach of night increased the dangers around us, because we knew by experience that navigation amongst icebergs during a gale can be disastrous, especially when the darkness of night prevents you seeing the ice until you are within the very shortest distance from it; owing to the force of the wind it is sometimes impossible to steer the ship as you wish. It may happen that there is no chance of either passing to windward or of bearing away, and then destruction is inevitable.

10th. At midnight the gale still blew furiously, as before accompanied by rain and snow; each oncoming wave raised the ship on its crest and then plunged her into the trough. The ship for one moment was in an upright position, then listed to port or to starboard; the perpetual motion and the groaning of all parts of the ship were most disagreeable.

We observed an iceberg to windward which we could not hope to pass farther to the windward and we therefore kept to leeward. At 3.0 a.m., passing close to this iceberg, we encountered some of the blocks broken off from it. Very fortunately we succeeded in passing through them without striking one of them. At first we had been misled into thinking that these pieces of ice were only foam formed on the waves. At 11.0 a.m. the wind again shifted to north-east. We turned to north-west so as to be driven as little as possible to the southward, where there was the danger of encountering more ice. On turning, we observed two huge icebergs, one bearing south-southwest distant 3 miles, and the other N. 60° E., also 3 miles distant. The mist clearing away soon revealed a third, 4 miles to the north-east.

Towards evening the wind began to fall. At 7.0 p.m. we bore away to the south and passed an iceberg.

At midnight the wind had completely fallen; there was snow and rain. The seas caused the vessel to yaw tremendously and carried us with them on their course. This position was no less dangerous than the previous one because it was equally impossible to steer the ship.

By morning the torn main topsail was replaced by a new one and, because of the excessive rolling and the fog, we stood under reefed topsails. The incessant falling of wet snow made the work of the sailors very difficult.

At midday the wind blew from west-north-west. I again set our course north-north-east so as to get quickly beyond the ice, but a very heavy swell, due to the gale, prevented our taking full advantage of this wind. By evening there was again a strong northerly wind which forced us to go eastward. We then had only the main topsail close-reefed and a reefed foresail. There were $2\frac{1}{2}°$ F. of frost.

12th. At 2.0 a.m. we sighted an iceberg to leeward. With the sail we were carrying I could not hope to pass to windward of it and I therefore turned to leeward. At 7.0 a.m. we passed through ice again. Throughout the whole night and up to noon snow fell, but it ceased at midday; the sky then cleared and to our delight the sun came out. By observation at noon we found ourselves in Lat. 58° 39' 57" S., Long. 108° 16' 15" E., the current in the course of six days having set us south 62 miles. About midday the force of the wind had somewhat diminished and towards evening it blew from the north-west; setting therefore the fore top- and mainsails, we took a north-easterly course.

13th. Up to midnight the moon appeared from time to time, breaking through the clouds, and after 1.0 a.m. our friend the southern aurora shone brilliantly, if fitfully.

On that day also we passed near a few icebergs, one of which was 250 feet in height. At one end stood a pillar of ice looking like an obelisk.[1] At 8.0 a.m. in Lat. 57° 33' we passed an iceberg which had the appearance of a volcano, and this was the last we saw on our way to Port Jackson.

14th. Owing to a strong wind we reduced sails for the night and stood under reefed topsails only. We made $7\frac{1}{2}$ knots. The night was dark, at times we had mist and a little snow and we could not see anything ahead of us. Under these circumstances I reefed the main topsail in order not to make more than 4 knots. In the morning we made more sail and went all day at $8\frac{1}{2}$ knots on a course N. 77° E. From evening, owing to the darkness resulting from thick weather,

---

[1] This iceberg appears to be the subject of one of the drawings on Plate 8. The height given for the berg must be treated with reserve, even though with their customary caution the officers doubtless took sextant angles.

and an overcast sky and rain, we ran before the wind and remained under main topsails, fore staysails and mizzen staysails. The wind was blowing hard, and an exceptionally heavy swell caused considerable rolling. At 11.0 the sky cleared and the moon lit up the horizon: we then hove to. The mercury in the thermometer stood at 37° F.

15*th*. At daybreak we let out a reef in the main topsail and set the fore topsail and the mizzen topsail with one reef. The day was fine, the best that could be hoped for in the southern ocean.

At noon we were in Lat. 56° 41' 40" S., Long. 124° 10' 07" E., variation 21° 05' W. The current had apparently carried us in the last three days S. 62° E. 77 miles. As a result of the high seas our observations of compass variation were unreliable, since the variation cannot be determined with accuracy whilst the compass is very unsteady. Nor can the sun's altitude be taken with accuracy, since the vessel rises and sinks with the waves and the line of the horizon itself changes. In the afternoon I altered course to N. 40° E. in order to reach a lower latitude, but we only kept on this till 9.0 p.m., when a head wind blew up from the north-east. In the course of the day we observed blue petrels, pintades and one white albatross and, towards evening, we observed an Egmont hen.

16*th*. The night was dark, foggy and rainy. The thermometer stood at 39° F.; at 3.0 a.m. the wind blew from the north-west, we therefore altered course to north-east by east. The wind continued to rise and by 8.0 a.m. forced us to take in sail until we could only carry with difficulty one reef in the mainsail; at 3.0 p.m. we took this sail in as well and stood then under one mizzen staysail. During this gale the wind veered to the west about 10.0 p.m. and then fell considerably; so we set the storm staysails and foresails and turned north-east. The mist soon cleared away and the moon lit up the whole horizon.

17*th*. Towards morning the wind fell and we made all sail. Owing to the gales, we had not been able to do this for a long time and the sails needed drying after the soaking of nine days' continuous storm. All the clothes of the crew were also hung out to dry. At noon our observation showed that we were in Lat. 55° 03' 37" S., Long. 129° 07' 51" E., variation 8° 45' W.

18*th*. We had a favourable west wind throughout the whole day; towards night for a short time it shifted to foul. At 1 o'clock it had shifted again to the west and we continued on another tack in a north-easterly direction. At noon we were in Lat. 54° 28' 54" S., Long.

131° 09' 52" E., with a current setting eastward 17 miles a day. We passed seaweed floating on the surface. In the afternoon the wind blew from the north-east with mist and fog. As I was anxious to reach a lower latitude quickly, I turned to the north-west.

19th. From midnight the wind unexpectedly changed through east to south-east and, from the morning onward, rose to a stiff gale. It was very difficult for the ship to make headway against the swell, which carried away our martingale. From 7.0 a.m. the wind turned to the south-west and rose to a gale. We were making 10 knots and often passed seaweed. At noon we were in Lat. 53° 01' 58" S., Long. 135° 09' 42" E.

Until 6.0 p.m. the gale raged, driving the spray from the crests of the waves and filling the air with it. The sun's rays penetrating through the clouds and refracted in this spray, formed before our eyes numberless small rainbows over the surface of the water. The seas were very high and the vessel pitched and rolled uneasily. Pestrushki and grey and white albatrosses, besides the blue, and the usual black petrels, accompanied us. Towards midnight the wind fell a little and shifted to the west.

20th. We proceeded on a course N. 50° E. by the moonlight which shone through the clouds. At 8.0 a.m. the wind blew from east-north-east with rain and I altered course to north-west. The sea from the south-west still continued and caused a heavy roll. In the afternoon the wind shifted again to north-east and south-east, and so to-day we made very little distance towards the north-east. We saw a little seaweed and ten penguins.

21st. After midnight the wind, accompanied by rain, blew so hard from the south that we were able to continue on a course N. 56° E. at from 7 to 8 knots. At 6.0 a.m. the wind was blowing hard with heavy squalls. It brought high seas, causing the ship to labour dreadfully. We carried the main topsail and foresail close-reefed.

It is well known that, in the course of any long voyage, owing to storms or heavy rolling and pitching or through other causes, the men, when going aloft, sometimes fall and injure themselves and sometimes even perish in the sea. During the whole course of the voyage such a misfortune only happened once, as follows: on the 21st at 10.0 a.m. the ship in the heavy sea heeled so unusually far that the priest, who was talking in the ward room, could not keep his feet. Navigating Officer Paryadin wished to help him but, through his clumsiness, was thrown down with him, struck his head on the long bulkhead in the ward room, smashed the partition and fractured his skull. The priest was more fortunate because he fell on the navigating officer and on getting up was astonished to see the latter still lying on the floor. Doctor Bergh at once rendered assistance, but Mr Paryadin did not completely recover until our arrival in Port Jackson.

22nd. At noon we were in Lat. 49° 44′ 37″ S., Long. 142° 29′ 39″ E. The fresh west-south-west wind continued; the weather in the morning was foggy, which turned to rain from time to time. We were not able to see more than 6 miles. From noon onwards I set a north-easterly course so as to approach the latitude of Royal Company Island, which lies in Lat. 49° 30′ S. After proceeding 9 miles to the north-east, I set a course N. 85° E. This course, according to the Arrowsmith chart, must have passed through the above-mentioned island, but though I kept on this course for another 17 miles until 5.0 p.m. we sighted no land. I expected also to encounter the *Mirnyi*, which was also due to pass through this neighbourhood, but we neither saw the island nor met the ship. If the latitude of Royal Company Island was not correctly fixed, it would be very easy to miss it in the thick weather we were having and I therefore altered course for the night at 5.0 p.m. N. 18° E. for the southern end of Van Diemen's Land. I leave it to some more fortunate explorer than I to find Royal Company Island. On turning on to this course we found the variation to be 6° 53′ E. We saw two Egmont hens. As we were continually meeting seaweed, divers and a few penguins and Egmont hens, we had some evidence of the vicinity of Van Diemen's Land and were probably not far from a few small islands which, however, we were unable to see.[1]

At 11.0 p.m., in consequence of strong squalls from the north by west, we close-reefed the topsails.

23rd. After midnight the wind shifted towards the west and blew hard with mist and rain, so I altered course north-half-east. We travelled at 9½ and 10 knots.

24th. At noon we were in Lat. 47° 18′ 26″ S., Long. 144° 45′ 53″ E. With a strong wind and squalls from west by south, with rain and high seas, we proceeded on a north by east course. At 1.0 a.m. in Lat. 45° 40′ S. we observed flashes of lightning, which we had not

[1] This seaweed probably came from the Kerguelen group of islands and not from Tasmania since the drift is from the west.

seen during our sojourn in the higher latitudes of the southern hemisphere. At 4.0 a.m. a squall blew up accompanied by rain and snow. At midday we were in Lat. 44° 10′ 14″ S., Long. 146° 13′ 13″ E.

Soon after 2.0 p.m. the man who had been sent aloft to look out for land called out, "Land in sight!—Land in sight!" The officer of the watch repeated, "Land in sight!" and joy was expressed in every face. We then set a course parallel to the southern shore of Van Diemen's Land and soon passed the high rock situated on the western side of Cape Pedra Blanca.[1]

There was a strong wind from the south-west with squalls; heavy clouds gathered and rain fell from time to time. There was a heavy sea which made the ship labour heavily. The temperature was 48° F. We were going at the rate of 10 knots. At 7.0 we struck the mainsail and foresail and turned N. 50° E.

25th. The night was very dark and it rained from time to time. The foaming sea was filled with sparks of light. After midnight we set our course N. 18° E. and took in the main topsail. At 7 a.m. the wind changed and blew from the west; we set the main topsail and the mizzen topsail, and reefed the fore- and mainsails.

At noon we were in Lat. 42° 04′ 40″ S., Long. 149° 24′ 25″ E. We all felt a great change. The sky was cloudless, a light wind blew from Van Diemen's Land, the temperature was 61° F. The barometer rose to 30, which had never happened in the high southern latitudes. We thoroughly dried the sails, which were very damp and for a long time past had required drying. I gave orders to open all hatches again, and to set to work to put the ship in better order. At 5 o'clock in the afternoon in Lat. 41° 41′ S., Long. 149° 37′ 25″ E. we found the variation to be 11° 22′ E.

26th. During that day and the whole of the night we had a favourable wind. At noon of the 26th we were in Lat. 39° 02′ 19″ S., Long. 149° 46′ 50″ E. At 7 a.m. we saw to the west the shore of New Holland;[2] we were then in Lat. 37° 17′ S., variation 8° 34′ E. The wind almost failed.

---

[1] Pedra Blanca is a high white rock at the southern extreme of Tasmania, so named by Abel Tasman, who says, in his log for November 29th, 1642: "We sailed along the coast which extends here East and West. Towards midday we passed two cliffs, the Western of which resembles the Pedra Blanca near the coast of China."

[2] This would be the high land behind Cape Howe and Gabo Island, the south-eastern corner of the continent.

On the following day the crew were busy washing and cleaning the vessel to prepare for Easter Sunday. The fine weather put new life into everybody and all faces were radiant. After being continually wet from snow, rain, sleet, fog, etc., it was a pleasure to all to get their clothes thoroughly dried.

On the first day of the Easter festival all dressed themselves in clean holiday clothes as is customary with our countrymen.[1] We said matins and all the prayers. The crew had Easter cakes for breakfast. Since the morning a light wind from the south eased the ship very much. We sailed in sight of the high hills of New South Wales, and already imagined that we should be in Port Jackson by the next day and enjoy ourselves in various ways, but the wind fell and a foul wind from the north set in.

29th. We beat up in sight of shore, all the crew enjoying the beautiful weather, joking, playing and amusing themselves. They brought out clothes, books, cards, etc., cleaned the sextants and cleaned the lenses of the telescopes so as to see objects on shore more clearly; in a word, all were pleasantly busy. Yet only three days before no one had come on deck unless he had to, and the thermometer at noon had shown not more than 50° F. All bolts in the interior of the ship were sweating from the previous cold, and had to be constantly wiped, and this continued until the hull of the ship had acquired a temperature equal to the temperature of the surrounding atmosphere.

At noon we were in Lat. 35° 57′ 42″ S., Long. 150° 57′ 51″ E.; the height on the coast of New Holland called the "Pigeon House" then bore S. 87° 30′ W., and a projection of the shore, the headland "Perpendicular Cape", bore N. 6° 46′ E.; thereby the position of the above-mentioned height, Pigeon House, works out at 4′ farther south and the Perpendicular Cape 4′ 30″ farther west than in Flinders' Atlas.[2] At this time the coast line visible to us was 20 miles away. At 2 o'clock, when 6 miles south of George's River, we put about. On the low-lying shore opposite to us was a line of yellow sand, beyond

---

[1] Phrases such as this show that the author was expecting his book to be read by other nations, though by the irony of fate it was to be more than a century before it was fully translated into any other language.

[2] It is evident that the ships were provided with the atlas published officially in 1814 from the surveys made by Matthew Flinders in the *Investigator* from 1798 to 1803. The Pigeon House is a prominent hill near the head of the Clyde River and Perpendicular Cape is the cliffed northern point of the entrance to Jervis Bay. Bellingshausen's corrections to the Flinders chart are accurate in the main.

which forests could be seen everywhere, and not far from the sea a little white house.

Towards 9 o'clock in the evening, after a brief calm, the wind changed and a light fair wind set in. We set our course north by east. At 7.30 a.m. we sailed past Botany Bay, as Captain Cook called it on his first voyage. At the entrance to Port Jackson a pilot came alongside in a boat and we took him on board to take us to a clear berth. To our first question as to the arrival of the *Mirnyi* he replied that she had not yet arrived but that there had been two Russian sloops in the port, the *Otkryitie* and *Blagonamyerenny*, commanded by Captain Vasilev, which had left for Kamchatka about three weeks previously. I had supposed that as the course of the *Mirnyi* took her for the greater part out of the ice zone sooner and was attended by fewer dangers than ours she ought to have arrived before us, and not finding her I concluded that Mr Lazarev had probably lain to more frequently at night during the gales so as not to miss any so far unknown land. At 10 o'clock we passed between Middle Head and the surf which breaks over a sunken reef.[1] The green shores of Port Jackson are surrounded by forests, and the beautiful valleys here and there, with yellow sands in small bays, seemed to us an enchanting view after the clouded, monotonous horizon, with the scattered icebergs washed by the raging sea, where the hungry petrels, cleaving the air, hunt for food. In those dark, harsh climes it seems as if men's hearts grow cold in sympathy with the surrounding objects, men become gloomy, depressed, harsh and to a certain extent indifferent to everything, but with a clear sky, the beneficent influence of the reviving sunshine, and the various beauties of nature to gaze upon, man rejoices in her gifts and values them to the full.

Half-way up the bay to the town of Sydney the Captain of the Port, Mr Piper, most courteously came to meet us and proposed that we should anchor in the road opposite the town.[2] We availed ourselves of this suggestion, and at 11.0 a.m. anchored off the town of Sydney in $6\frac{1}{2}$ sazhen ($7\frac{1}{2}$ fathoms) with a bottom consisting of mud, fine sand and small shells, having been 131 days under sail from the time of our departure from Rio de Janeiro. The newly built fortress on Cape

---

[1] The reef was known then, as now, by the name of the Sow and Pigs.

[2] Mr Piper reigned for another ten years as Captain of the Port, an office which included in its duties the collection of customs. But he seems to have succumbed to temptation as did so many of the earlier colonial officers and he was finally superseded because his "accounts were in disorder".

View of the town of Sydney at Port Jackson

Natives of New Holland

Benelong[1] lay 3 cables S. 14° E. from us. This anchorage was all the more agreeable to us because all foreign vessels had to anchor in the so-called Neutral Bay, where had lain the captains of the French Fleet, Baudin and Freycinet, sent by the Government for various investigations and possible discoveries. We furled the sails and put down the boats.

Mr Piper, leaving the vessel, proposed that I should go ashore with him to visit the Governor, General Macquarie. I did so with pleasure as soon as we had finally anchored. A few days before our arrival at Port Jackson, blue spots had appeared on the feet of two of the sailors, an undoubted symptom of scurvy. One was an elderly Tartar, and the other a Russian, a young and excellent topman, but unfortunately of weak constitution. Mr Bergh gave them a decoction of essence of fir cones. Considering this remedy to be insufficient, I ordered their feet to be rubbed with lemon juice and gave them half a wineglass of this juice to drink; but by this remedy, which had been recommended to me on our departure by Vice-Admiral Greig, we were only able to arrest the disease to a certain degree. We endeavoured in every possible way to prevent and arrest this disease, but during the 130 days' voyage in a cold, damp and stormy climate it overcame all our efforts. I considered that we were fortunate not to have lost a single man on the whole voyage.

Owing to the damp and cold the pigs and sheep had also contracted scurvy and a few of them had died during the voyage. Their hoofs and gums became blue and swollen, so that the sheep on our arrival in Port Jackson were unable to eat with comfort the fresh grass owing to pain and the weakness of their mouths.

I considered it my duty to give all due praise to the officers for having contributed to the successful completion of our voyage by their energy and the thoroughness with which they carried out all their duties, without which we could not have brought our long and difficult cruise to so successful a conclusion. I am particularly beholden to Lieutenant-Commander Zavodovski, who, as first lieutenant of the ship, had given me the benefit of all his experience and devotion. Without his help I should have had to bear the whole weight of this

---

[1] Named after a native who became so civilized that Governor Phillip took him to England as a personal servant when he retired from his Governorship. The anchorage was slightly to the east of the pontoons for the ferry boats which, until the bridge was built, crossed from Circular Quay to the North Shore.

anxious voyage, or would sometimes, to lighten my burden, have had to signal to Mr Lazarev to go ahead as a reconnoitring vessel; I was able to avoid this throughout the whole voyage since his vessel travelled badly and was not able to carry much sail, and our progress would have been very slow. When, however, the *Mirnyi* kept astern at the requisite distance she acted on my signals with the desired results.

We found in Port Jackson the 40-gun British transport, *Coromandel*, under the command of Navigating Officer Downey of the Royal Navy. He had brought out convicts from Britain. On the return journey to Europe he was instructed to touch at the Bay of Islands in New Zealand to take in wood. Another similar vessel, *Dromedary*, had not long before left for the same place. They had orders to take timber suitable for masts of 74-gun warships from New Zealand.

The tender, *Mermaid*,[1] under the command of Lieutenant King, who is making a survey of the northern part of New Holland, is soon to sail to complete the survey. Besides these vessels, we found up to twelve merchant vessels, the greater number from India and Canton, whence the shops in Port Jackson obtain their Chinese and Indian goods.[2]

About midday a family of natives arrived on board, in a dirty European boat from the north shore. They spoke a little broken English, bowed very low to the Europeans, and made grimaces to express their delight. One of them wore the worn-out trousers of a British sailor, and on his forehead there was a plaited band, decorated with red clay and mud, on his neck he wore a copper plate, in the shape of a crescent moon, with the inscription:

BOONGAREE
Chief of the
Broken—Bay—Tribe
1815

This plate was attached to a strong copper chain. From this inscription we knew who our guest was, and he added that he had accompanied Captain Flinders and Lieutenant King in their voyages off the coast of New Holland. Boongaree presented his wife Matora

---

[1] The *Mermaid* was a cutter of 84 tons burthen.
[2] By this date the colony had freed itself from the earlier restrictions on trade, and in 1823 for instance Sydney was importing as much as 15,000 tons in the year in fifty-five vessels. The trade was in the hands of about a dozen firms of importers, who dealt primarily with goods from England but also from India and China.

to us. She was partially attired in a dress of English frieze, and had adorned her head with kangaroo teeth. A daughter was almost half white, handsome in face and figure, which gave evidence of European blood; the son, like his father, was dark; all were naked. Boongaree, pointing to his companions, said, "These are my people". Then pointing to the whole north shore, "This is my Land". I ordered that they should be given a glass of grog each and of sugar and butter as much as they wished. Seeing this liberality they begged for tobacco, old clothes and ropes, and whatever they happened to notice. I ordered him to be given some Brazilian tobacco twist, and told him that they would receive clothes and ropes if they brought fish, live birds, a kangaroo and other animals. His reply to all this was "Oh yes, yes". They left the ship half drunk, shouting horribly. Matora, who called herself "Queen", behaved with even greater vulgarity than the other guests.

I promptly went ashore, taking with me Mr Demidov as interpreter. We went immediately to the house of Captain Piper, who accompanied us to the Governor, Major-General Macquarie, whom we found sitting in the garden of his small country house.[1] He received us very kindly, at once gave permission for us to establish an observatory on the north shore of the harbour opposite our anchorage, and sent orders to the administration to meet our needs. As our ship had suffered no considerable damages which our own men were not able to repair I thanked the Governor for his kind intentions and only asked for permission to cut down such wood as was necessary for our use, on the northern shore of Port Jackson Bay.

31st. The day after our arrival I sent a tent to the foreland which had been selected as the site of our observatory and Mr Simanov was

---

[1] The Governor was at this time almost at the end of his term of office, being succeeded by Governor Brisbane in November 1821. He had succeeded Governor Bligh (of the "Mutiny of the *Bounty*" fame) in 1809 after his stormy reign. Macquarie appears to have been very vain and inclined to be arrogant, but the colony advanced greatly in population, extent, and resources during his twelve years of office. He was finally superseded as a result of the friction caused by his policy. As Rusden says in his *History of Australia*, Macquarie considered "that the colony was created for the benefit of convicts; he scorned the assumption of virtue by the unconvicted...he essayed the harder task by making gentlemen out of convicts". To this end the Governor did his utmost to discourage free immigration and openly associated himself with the convict class. His patronage of exploration and his passion for building was of great service to the young colony, but it was largely paid for by practices such as selling monopolies which were precisely what he had been sent out to Australia to stamp out.

detailed to erect the transit instrument.[1] This instrument had, owing to our lack of experience, been set up badly at Rio and had therefore been of no use to us. This time, to set up the instrument, we took a small cast-iron stove without its chimney, fixed it firmly on the rock, filled it with sand and through the opening where the flue is attached we poured lead, making a covering of $2\frac{1}{2}$ inches. On this firm foundation Mr Simanov erected the instrument and during the whole of our stay at Port Jackson it was in daily use, in day-time for observation of the sun, and at night to observe the transit of the southern stars across the meridian. Mr Simanov himself undertook the night observations, all the more eagerly as, since the observations taken by the astronomer de Lacalle at the Cape of Good Hope, no one had carried out similar observations in the southern hemisphere. Scientific men will understand and appreciate the praiseworthy efforts of Mr Simanov and his labours in the interest of astronomy. He chose as his assistants two navigating petty officers and the artillery lieutenant, who were instructed how to record the time observations from the chronometers.

As their guard and for the purpose of cutting brushwood for brooms required on board we employed the two sailors who had shown signs of scurvy. The blacksmith and a portable forge were also transferred on shore.

In the neighbourhood of the tent where the observations were taken, we put up another two, one for the guard, who at night stood by with loaded rifles, in case of an attack by wild beasts or to meet any temptation which the convicts might feel to steal. The other tent was used as a bath. In this latter we built from our metal ballast an oven with chimney. While the bath was being heated, the tent was opened and the oven made red hot with wood, the water being boiled partly on the stove and partly in another place by means of heated cannon-balls. When everything was ready, the tent was closed and water was poured continually with the fire-engine over the tent to prevent the steam produced by pouring water over the heated ballast from escaping through the tent cloth. Many of the officers and crew preferred this bath to the ordinary baths, explaining that the air in such a tent bath is much less stifling than in rooms built of wood or stone.

[1] This foreland, now known as Kirribilli Point, had been used for a similar purpose in 1793 by a Spanish expedition under the command of Don Alexandro Malaspina.

1st. After the erection of the bath on April 1st the crew spent two days in washing all their linen, bed linen and pillows in the bath. To people who are accustomed since childhood to take a steam bath several times a week it becomes a necessity; but when afloat this is impossible to carry out. Nevertheless, during the last voyage in the high southern latitudes, once every fortnight ice water had been heated to summer heat, i.e. to about 60° F., and I had ordered everyone to wash. I may say that bodily cleanliness went no small way towards the preservation of the health of the crew in our long voyage. At 1.0 p.m. the Governor and Vice-Governor, Lieutenant-Colonel Erskine, commanding the regiment, came to call on us; we met and received them with all honours laid down in Admiralty regulations.*

All empty barrels to be repaired, and all movable articles were removed to the tents in order to lighten the vessel as much as possible. It was necessary to raise the ship in order to repair the copper plates which had been torn by minor collisions with the ice, and to replace the copper nails torn out of the sheathing by others.

On Sunday the day was beautiful and the crew did not work on the ship. I divided them into two groups; one half went ashore until dinner time, and the other on the return of the first party after dinner, to wander about in the woods near the tents or, as I might term it, our "dockyard", because I thought it better for them to wander about the woods than to be exposed to temptations, only damaging to their health, by visiting the town.

On Monday morning the joiners and carpenters were sent to cut down such wood as was necessary for repairs on board, and fifteen sailors with the quartermaster were also sent to cut down firewood for the voyage. We began the repair and setting up of the rigging which through the frost and damp had become extremely taut and had then, through the warmth at Port Jackson, become so slack and weak that it had to be reset up and in large measure respliced.

On the invitation of the Governor I and all the officers went to his house at 8.0 a.m. After breakfast he proposed to show us the newly erected lighthouse. Two of us, Mr Zavodovski and I, drove, and all

* On the arrival of a Major-General on board a man-of-war, a guard is mounted under the command of an officer. He is saluted by beating the drum. On departure the guard salutes again, and as they push off from the side, the sailors man the yards, whence, at the word of command, three cheers are given from the crew, and after a similar response, two more cheers, then seven shots are fired as a salute from the ship. For a Lieutenant-General the salute is nine guns and for a full General eleven.

the other officers with the Governor's Adjutant went by sea in the cutter. The road to the lighthouse was very fine. It runs along the rocky heights parallel to Port Jackson Bay, which with all its bays remained in view for the whole of the way, with a few cottages along the shore and on the right lay Botany Bay. As we approached the lighthouse, I was overjoyed to see the *Mirnyi* beating up into the bay. From Sydney, the drive to the lighthouse takes about fifty minutes.

It is erected near the mouth of the harbour on the southern side, where there are steep cliffs. Its height above the surface of the sea is 427 feet, the lighthouse itself being 70 feet high.[1] Buildings for the housing of the overseers, the workmen and the storage of materials are added. In the cupola there are nine reflectors, lit by lamps, which are distributed in threes at the angles of a revolving pyramid. This pyramid completes its revolution once every six minutes, and each of the three groups of reflectors shows seaward for a period of two minutes.

A revolving light is here considered preferable to a fixed one to prevent vessels coming in at night because of the danger of confusing the lighthouse with the shifting camps of the natives who are never without fires and light them everywhere.[2] Having inspected the lighthouse, we returned, Mr Zavodovski going in the cutter, as he wished to return by water. About midday the wind, which had been foul for the *Mirnyi*, changed and blew in from the sea, and in a short time she lay at anchor near the *Vostok*. The reunion of the officers of both ships was a great delight to all.

The very light winds on the eastern side of New Holland had delayed Mr Lazarev for seven days. All were well on board with the exception of one sailor who had indications of scurvy. He was a very hard worker, and had injured himself at work. He had therefore been unable to get sufficient exercise, and in consequence had contracted scurvy.

The *Mirnyi*, after separating from us, had followed the course ordered, and had, like ourselves, passed by that spot where, according to the Arrowsmith chart, the Royal Company Island lies, alleged to have been discovered by the Spaniards. Nothing had been seen either

---

[1] These figures are not quite accurate, the height of the light was only 300 feet.
[2] By the kindness of the Librarian of the Mitchell Library in Sydney, the Editor was able to inspect the voluminous personal diaries of Governor Macquarie. It was disappointing to find that only bare references to the Russians were made, on this and other meetings with them.

of this island or of any new land. Mr Lazarev made the following report of his voyage to me:

"On March 4th, in the afternoon, as we hove to near an iceberg to fill our empty water barrels with ice, I availed myself of the opportunity of visiting the *Vostok* and learned that you had decided, as the season was advancing, to give up the attempt of going farther south, and to proceed direct to Port Jackson. In order that all the expanse between the routes traversed by Captains Cook and Furneaux, which is not less than $65°$ in length and $8°$ in width, should not remain unexplored, you instructed me to proceed on a route parallel with the course of Captain Furneaux, at a distance from it of $2\frac{1}{2}°$ to $3°$, and then to continue on the parallel of $49° 36'$ as far as the meridian of $138°$ east longitude, or, if more convenient, to continue the course eastward, to survey the island marked on the Arrowsmith chart as Royal Company Island, which is alleged to have been discovered by the Spanish ship *Rafaelo*. After that I was to proceed to the southern cape of Van Diemen's Land, and finally to hasten with all speed to Port Jackson, the appointed place of meeting. On my returning to the ship, I found that the ice brought on board was so soft and so much impregnated with salt water that even after remaining on deck for $4\frac{1}{2}$ hours in order to let the salt water drain off it was still unsuitable for use. The taste of the salt remained. No doubt, had the ice remained on deck all night we might have had fresh water from it, but neither the weather nor circumstances permitted this, as the whole quarter-deck was obstructed. I was very sorry, though we were not desperately in need of fresh water, and with care we had sufficient water for all ordinary purposes for about three months, even if all on the ship drank as much as they wanted. In the morning, all the crew drank tea and, after supper, we served out a glass of weak punch to each man during our stay in the higher latitudes. I regretted the uselessness of the ice chiefly on account of the wasted labour of collecting it, which always entailed considerable trouble and the sailors engaged on the work, who got soaked with cold water, were constantly exposed to catching cold. The water obtained from the ice is useful on board, because the health of the crew depends largely on personal cleanliness and on clean underwear, and they used the water from the ice for washing themselves and their clothes. It seems well to note for the future that not all ice taken from the sea is equally quickly suitable for use, but only that which is still hard and has only recently been broken off from the larger masses. At night we saw the southern aurora in all its splendour. This extraordinary phenomenon is often the salvation of mariners in the ice, since it sheds so strong a light as to show up large icebergs 5 or 6 miles off, and it sometimes enabled us to set a perfectly safe course. We proceeded at about 5 knots under topsails only, and as soon as the sky was lit up by the magnificent belt of light we observed about twenty small icebergs ahead of us and on both sides which we could not clear to windward. By the light of the aurora, however, we were able to continue our course through the ice, as if it had been day, and only received a few shocks from it. At this time the *Vostok* lay at a distance of about 2 miles on our port beam, and had probably passed the ice on her beam. On this occasion I could not but confirm the truth of Captain Cook's statement that small ice is more dangerous than large, because the latter can be observed even on dark nights about $\frac{1}{2}$ mile away, by the light that it gives out. But what I call 'small' ice, because there is no comparison between it and large bergs, is nevertheless of sufficient size to cause disastrous damage to the submerged portion of the hull. Very often these masses protrude very little above the water so that even in the day-time, if the wind and sea are high, it is not possible to see them until you are quite close to them.

5*th*. "When day had fully dawned, we saw around us eleven icebergs and towards 7.0 a.m. up to twenty lay ahead of us. We were then in Lat. 59° 34′ S., Long. 88° 32′ E., the variation, according to several azimuths observed by Nachthaus,[1] being 48° 40′ W., which was the highest value observed from the *Mirnyi* in the course of this voyage. As we proceeded eastward, it began to diminish. At 5.0 p.m., after exchanging signals with the *Vostok* and signalling our mutual good wishes for success, we stood away and proceeded under all sail. The point of our separation was in Lat. 58° 50′ S., Long. 89° 51′ E. It was a great satisfaction to me that this separation was effected on Captain Bellingshausen's own desire and solely for the success of the common enterprise, and not in any way by other unforeseen causes which might have easily been encountered, such as fog, mist or ice, for up to now we had not separated. I must attribute such an unusually fortunate circumstance to the zealous execution of duty on the part of all the officers of the watch, whom I mention here with feelings of

---

[1] This name is not mentioned in the list of officers on the *Mirnyi*, so presumably it must be one of the crew.

especial gratitude and pleasure. I must further add, as the best proof of the justice of this appreciation, that the superior speed of the *Vostok* had necessitated our going under all possible sail, and that since our departure from Russia none of the royal yards nor even the studding sail booms had been carried away, all of which shows the skill and foresight of the officers of the *Mirnyi*.

"At night there were clouds with hail. We set an east-north-east course under very little sail, our rate being $6\frac{1}{2}$ knots, and at midnight we passed very close to one of the icebergs. The thermometer then indicated 7° F. of frost. The coldness of the sea water itself was very noticeable, but we had long since become accustomed to this and we found it quite bearable.

6th. "On the morning of the 6th, in Lat. 57° 25' S., Long. 90° 59' E., we calculated from several azimuths taken by Nachthaus that the variation was 42° 50' W. At this time there were only two icebergs visible and from the look-out there were two more to be seen ahead of us and a quantity of broken ice. I steered north-north-east so as to reach Lat. 55° more quickly, after which we should be able to continue our voyage on a course parallel with that of Captain Furneaux. It rained in the afternoon; for almost two months we had not seen any rain, although hail with snow had occurred almost daily. The pestrushki, long our fellow-travellers on both sides of the Antarctic Circle, disappeared and only a few grey albatrosses, with the broad white mark above their eyes, and blue petrels accompanied us. We saw the latter daily.

7th. "At 6.0 a.m. on the 7th a penguin was observed and we heard the cries of two others. At 8.0 a.m. we were 156 miles from Captain Furneaux's course and we steered eastward, under a variable wind which shifted from west to north. With this change the sky began to be overcast, since these two conditions always go together in the higher latitudes. As far as we could judge in the course of our expedition in the Antarctic, north and east winds always bring an overcast sky, with mist and snow. On the other hand, with south and west winds, the weather is always clear. At noon we were in Lat. 55° 16' S., Long. 94° 23' E. and there were only four icebergs in sight. By midday a great deal of seaweed of the Kelp species floated past us. On the following day we saw the same sort of seaweed in different places. The north wind gradually blew stronger, and maintained the rainy and misty weather. The seas became heavy. At midday we found it necessary to close-reef the topsails, take in the mizzen topsail and strike the top-gallant mast. We found our latitude to be 55° 24′ S., longitude 98° 36′ E. After midday the wind began to veer to the east, with heavy snow, and continued to blow with the same force until midnight, when it dropped suddenly, and blew from the north-west. This lull was transient; in an hour the wind again rose suddenly to such a force that we were obliged to take in the topsails and lower sails and stand under storm-reefed trysails. The wind shifting with such violence through nine points, caused a cross sea in which the vessel laboured heavily. The waves, meeting near the vessel and breaking against each other, threw great quantities of water on the deck. About 2.0 p.m. the gale still continued with such fury that our new fore staysail was torn to small shreds. I am convinced that no storm sail fitted to a stay or a yard could possibly withstand the force of such a gale, but the gaffed trysails made at Kronstadt on my suggestion held throughout the gale. We had there a clear proof of the advantage of these over the usual storm sails and it would therefore be very useful to introduce them into use in the fleet, if not both, at least the main trysail, which might be used instead of the mizzen staysail and might replace the mizzen staysail and the mizzen topmast staysail. The barometer about this time fell to 28 inches. It must be noted that, of the three Dollond barometers which were on board, two were completely useless, owing to the extraordinary fluctuation of the mercury, and the third was of very little service to forecast either impending storms or fine weather, since the mercury always rose or fell several hours after fine or bad weather had set in. It was cheering to know that our ship was of such strength that she could withstand a gale of such violence, accompanied by such a confused sea. A small leak which, in calm weather, made about 2 inches in 24 hours, had not opened out in the least. We owed this to the careful survey in Kronstadt when the ship was strengthened and refitted. How heavy the pitching was which we experienced (which is doubtless the main reason of the weakening of the different members) could be seen from the great quantity of seaweed with which, at dawn, we found the ship's head covered. Probably every time the head of the ship struck the water the seaweed had been thrown over, instead of under, the taffrail, for the lower part of the head was so well fenced up by a grating that not even a single stay was broken and with all this the vessel had rolled easily throughout, and the bowsprit had rarely dipped water, although I know that many larger ships have lost their bowsprits by heavy seas washing them away. All this tends to show that the *Mirnyi*, besides being roomy and comfortable for the officers no less than the crew, had also the great quality of sea-worthiness. One defect, and rather a serious one, which we felt during the whole voyage, was that she was very slow in answering the rudder, which was due to the thick lines of the under-water parts of her hull.

"At 8.0 a.m. the gale seemed to decrease; after an hour the wind suddenly fell and we bore away east by north with a heavy sea on the beam, having set reefed topsails and foresail. In spite of all our endeavours to keep our people as dry as possible, the cold and frosty weather and the gales had caused cases of feverish catarrh and rheumatism. Owing to this I ordered, besides the usual midday issue of vodka, and the weak punch with lemon and sugar, an extra ration of vodka to be served out after breakfast. The results showed that this addition had helped to maintain the good health of the personnel. At midday we were in Lat. 55° 35′ S., Long. 100° 38′ E. About 6.0 p.m. the wind shifted to north by east and began to blow stronger; the direction in which the clouds began to move quickly across the sky warned us of the approach of the storm of which the barometer on the ship gave no indication; but since, as I have mentioned earlier, we could not rely on the barometer, I gave orders to reef the fore topsail and mizzen topsail and stood under the mainsails and reefed trysails.

10*th*. "During the night there was a very strong wind in fierce gusts and at 6.0 a.m. on the following morning it again turned to a gale and obliged us to reef the main topsail. Towards afternoon the wind began to fall, the sun appeared, and the mist cleared away; but the seas were still very high. I do not ever remember having seen seas so massive or of such excessive height. It seemed when the ship plunged from the top of the wave into the trough as if we were hemmed in by hills of water. By observation we found ourselves to be in Lat. 56° 04′ S., Long. 103° 30′ E. Soon after midday we observed an iceberg to the south-east from the top. I thought it could not be more than 6 miles off, but the high seas did not allow of any observations from the quarter-deck. We had the greatest good fortune during this gale in not meeting any large masses of ice which might have been disastrous for us, and now the above-mentioned icebergs appeared just when the equinoctial gales which had been blowing with such violence were beginning to abate a little. The *Vostok* was in my opinion in a most dangerous position, because if Captain Bellingshausen was 3° south of us, he would probably encounter more ice—a contingency which I thought of more than once with the greatest uneasiness.

11*th*. "There was a heavy sea from the north, but a moderate wind and clear weather, in which, I might say, all the sick amongst us recovered. At 7.0 a.m. in Lat. 56° 11′ S., Long. 104° 04′ E. the variation was found to be 37° 26′ W. from a few azimuths. Soon the wind began to shift to north-west and I altered course to north-east by east so as to make up for the setback due to the recent gale, during which the course imposed on us had taken us almost one degree farther south than I had wished. On that day we were able to air the ship and to re-establish the ventilation which we had enjoyed practically for the whole voyage from Kronstadt. The stoves between decks were relit and all the clothing and bedding of the crew were aired and dried. At night we had frequent squalls accompanied by hail, after which the clouds again cleared away and the sky was cloudless. The southern aurora appeared three times with great brilliance. Since parting from the *Vostok* I had tried to the best of my powers to follow the wise rule of Captain Flinders, which was that, in order not to miss anything, he laid it down as his principle to travel during night not more than 40 miles so that the visual field ahead at nightfall should still be visible at dawn astern. As we had a considerable distance to cover, this rule was sometimes broken on clear moonlight nights when the horizon was visible with night glasses for not less than 10 miles. Had there been any land on our track, it would undoubtedly have been high ground and in consequence visible even from a great distance.

12*th*. "On the following day the wind blew from the north-west until midday with strong squalls and very sharp hail. While it fell, it was curious to observe how the blue petrels tried to shelter from it between the waves. At midday the wind began to fall and the sky cleared completely. By observation we found ourselves in Lat. 55° 13′ S., Long. 108° 48′ E., and in the afternoon in Lat. 55° 03′ S., Long. 109° 33′ E. The variation by azimuths was 31° 16′ W.

13*th*. "With a steady north wind I set my course east-north-east under all sail. At 7.0 a.m. in Lat. 54° 49′ S., Long. 113° 07′ E., the variation was 27° 49′ W. About the same time we observed a great deal of seaweed and two divers, exactly like those which we had noticed within sight of South Georgia. These indications led us to think that we were at no great distance from land, but it was very difficult to decide in which direction to look for it. I therefore decided to hold on my former course. We again saw diving birds and a great deal of seaweed torn away from rocks. I did not doubt that some bare rocky islands were not far off, for the diving petrels, as far as we gathered in the course of our voyage, never fly away from land.* The nearest known land was the south-western end of New Holland, almost 1200 miles distant, near which no one had ever seen diving petrels. Previous experiences proved beyond a doubt that these birds indicate the proximity of land. Captain Cook, who on his third voyage searched for Kerguelen Land and fixed its position with great accuracy, saw diving petrels from 150 to 350 miles from its shore. Kerguelen Land lay 1600 miles away from us. Captain Cook saw these birds also 100 miles from Tierra del Fuego, and 150 miles from Conquest Island, one of those discovered by the French Captain Crozet; he also saw them near South Georgia and New Zealand. In view of these examples we were obliged to conclude that we were near some bare island, and I therefore took all possible means of sighting it, by keeping a man constantly on the look-out and offering a reward to the man who should first sight land. The sequel showed that the discovery of land in these regions was reserved not to us but perhaps to navigators more lucky than we were.[1] I thus continued our course east-north-east and at noon by observation we found ourselves in Lat. 54° 36′ S., Long. 140° 02′ E. In the afternoon we again saw divers and a great deal of seaweed. From 8.0 p.m. we proceeded under topsails only and at midnight the wind began to shift to the northward with misty weather and rain.

14*th.* "On the following morning the wind continued from the north-north-west, with misty weather and rain. We again observed divers and seaweed. Towards noon the weather did not change but the wind blew stronger and the sea increased. These obstacles to sighting land, which however I could not suppose to lie to the north

* We saw these diving birds near South Georgia, New Zealand, and Macquarie Island. Not far from the latter one of these birds was shot and we were then able to convince ourselves that these were uncommon divers which somewhat resembled petrels.

[1] No other land has been discovered: the seaweed must therefore have drifted from the Kerguelen-Heard group of islands and it is now known that the divers wander farther than Cook or Lazarev suspected.

of us, decided me not to lose the favourable wind, which was now very strong. We therefore let out the reefs of the lower sails, took down the top-gallant mast and mizzen topsail and fitted preventer braces. We proceeded at 8 knots with a heavy beam sea which repeatedly struck us very hard. I had sufficient reason to hasten on our journey since I knew that Captain Bellingshausen intended to leave Port Jackson in the beginning of May, so as to pass as much time as possible in the tropics, to verify the position of certain islands. I knew that, thanks to the *Vostok's* higher speed, he would reach Port Jackson long before us and that his crew would enjoy for a longer time fresh provisions, which are so necessary for recuperating after so long and so laborious a voyage. To lose more time in searching for a barren island and thereby to arrive late at Port Jackson, would have been unwise, all the more so as we had been at sea for 114 days already. In the afternoon masses of seaweed broken away from rocks floated past the ship four times, but we did not see any divers; black petrels as well as a new species of the latter accompanied us. I think this new species of petrel must be that which Captain Cook calls the "large blue petrel". At 11.0 the wind became moderate and began to shift to the west, which cleared the sky. The night was fairly clear with moonlight so that I was able to proceed on an east-north-east course under all sail. At 6.0 a.m. the wind lulled and the sky cleared completely, still there was a strong swell from the north-west which caused the vessel to yaw considerably. At 9.0 a.m. we hoisted the top-gallant mast and set the top-gallant sails. We again had indications of the proximity of land in the reappearance of divers and a great quantity of seaweed. Clouds near the horizon repeatedly took shapes which to many of us appeared like land, but sooner or later this imaginary land disappeared again. By observation our position at noon was fixed at $53°\ 41'$ S., Long. $123°\ 03'$ E. and $3\frac{1}{2}°$ south of Captain Furneaux's course. We did not enjoy for long the clear weather which the west wind had brought. At 6.0 p.m. the wind again blew from the north and rain fell. Towards 9.0 p.m. it blew so hard that we were obliged to shorten sail more quickly than we had made it in the morning when everything had pointed to continuous fine weather. Towards midnight we were carrying the topsails close-reefed and the top-gallant mast and yards were lowered.

16*th*. "Towards noon of the following day the wind gradually rose and developed again into a gale, with mist and rain; we were obliged to take in all topsails, mainsails and foresails quickly and stood under reefed trysails only. During two hours, from 4.0 to 6.0 p.m., the wind reached the force of a hurricane, and although the weather continued clear and there was no rain, the force of the gale blew the water from the crests of the waves and drenched us in a rain consisting entirely of salt water. All this time it seemed as if we were in a snow-storm such as one usually sees on the steppes, when with perfectly clear weather it is impossible to see farther than 1 mile. This gale continued until 8.0 p.m., when we set the main topsails to reduce the rolling produced by the increasingly high seas, and towards 10.0 p.m., as the wind shifted to the north-west and gradually fell, we made more sail: the pitching of the ship, however, continued to be very heavy.

17*th*. "The morning of the 17th did not give promise of clear weather owing to the presence of thick clouds on the horizon, but to our great delight soon after midday they entirely dispersed and the day was fine. I must confess that I had been waiting with much impatience for such weather to dry the crew's clothing, which in the last few days had been soaked so that they had nothing dry left. The air on the lower deck was very thick, since we had not been able to light a fire or open the hatchways owing to the rolling and the waves which broke over the vessel; but before midday I had the satisfaction of seeing that everything was all right and that there was no illness on board. Mentioning illness, I should not forgive myself if I did not here testify to the zeal of that most worthy man, Dr Galkin, who, with a skill proved in his art, looked after the sick on board. He combined a wide knowledge with an unabated devotion, untiring work and extreme care for the preservation of the health of all on board. I wish to express to him here the sincere gratitude which will always remain in my heart. At midday by observation we fixed our position as Lat. $52° 26' 41'' $ S., Long. $128° 09' 30''$ E. and at 5.0 p.m. we were in Lat. $52° 15'$ S., Long. $129° 12'$ E.; the variation we found by a few azimuths to be $8° 48'$ W. Various species of petrels and grey albatrosses with white marks above their eyes flew near us in great numbers throughout the whole day. It is worthy of observation that these latter are to be found over a wide expanse of the southern ocean, because we observed them on both sides of the Polar circle, between the parallel of $50°$ and almost $70°$ S. One may certainly say that this species of albatross roams over a wider area than any other bird with the exception of that small black petrel which we had seen also in the northern hemisphere, at the equator and in the highest southern latitudes. I have heard that they are found even near the North Cape. One of the officers very fittingly gave them the name of "Jews" because, like them, these birds wander all over the globe.

18th. "The night was fairly clear, and we awaited a lunar eclipse which should have begun about 2.0 a.m., but we waited in vain because just before the hour of the eclipse the moon was covered by clouds. Only the end of the eclipse was fairly clearly visible towards 5.0 a.m. Some of the observers of the eclipse on board, following Captain Vancouver's method, took observations with a sextant in a reversed position, bringing the horizon to the star, which is much more convenient if the vessel is rolling because the star can be kept more easily in the field of view, but if there is not much motion in the vessel, a good glass may be used with greater success because the star is much more clearly visible through it. Besides, Captain Vancouver refers only to solar eclipses, which can probably be observed with greater accuracy by his method than lunar ones. In general, it may be said, that the determination of longitude by lunar eclipses has not the required accuracy, especially at sea, where it is almost impossible to set up a large achromatic telescope. Even with such a telescope the covering shadow is never clearly outlined, and the edge is always darkened and surrounded, as it were, by an atmosphere, thereby appearing different to different observers at the same time.

"The observations of the eclipse with the sextant differed so much from each other that we discarded them; from the observations our position appeared to be as follows: according to my observations, 130° 10′ 45″ E., according to those of Sub-Lieutenant Kupriyanov, 110° 20′ 15″ E. Our true position at that time was Long. 120° 50′ 25″ E. At 7.0 p.m. we saw a penguin, resembling those which we had seen in the South Sandwich Islands, that is with a red beak and a yellow tuft on the head. The appearance of this bird again led us to expect land because this species of bird never wanders far from land, and the seaweed which floated by from time to time still more strengthened my hopes. In the afternoon the wind began to shift to the east, the weather became misty, and I therefore turned northward. Very soon after we had a heavy fall of rain which continued with the light northerly breeze until 2.0 a.m. on the following morning when the wind changed to the south and soon freshened. I steered on an east-north-east course under all sail. At the same time I ordered an inspection of all the crew, to assure myself that there were no signs of scurvy amongst them, which might be expected after seventeen weeks at sea, with continuous severe cold and wet weather. To my great satisfaction Dr Galkin pronounced everybody perfectly well. Our stores, taken on at Rio de Janeiro, had been so plentiful that neither officers nor men had any lack of fresh food. On this day we killed a pig and boiled some of the pork with peas, which provided a meal eaten with great relish by the crew. The recent gale had deprived us of several of the pigs, which we had taken on board at Rio de Janeiro; for they died from injuries due to the rolling.

"At noon we found ourselves in Lat. 51° 16' 51" S., Long. 132° 07' E. Wishing to reach the parallel of the island discovered by the Spaniards, at least 4° west of its charted position, I altered course again northwards. This precaution was very necessary because all the islands discovered by the Spaniards, when verified by other navigators, are proved to have been marked on the charts incorrectly by several degrees, not only in longitude but also latitude, and it is therefore very difficult to verify such Spanish discoveries. In the past much time has been spent on this without any success. Many have come to the conclusion that the Spaniards during their discoveries purposely invented false latitudes and longitudes to prevent other naval powers from making use of them, but I believe that the inaccuracies were due entirely to lack of proper instruments and perhaps also to lack of knowledge on the part of the commanding officers of the vessels. What advantages, indeed, could the Spaniards hope to gain by concealing the position of some barren islands, or more correctly speaking, rocks, which could be of use only to sea birds?

"The wind gradually shifted to the west and on the 20th blew from the north-west with fairly clear weather. By observation at noon, it appeared that we had been carried out of our reckoning 22 miles to the east. This arose not only from the current but, to some extent also, from the extremely high westerly seas. At noon we found ourselves in Lat. 49° 59' S. and Long. 136° 19' E. and we fixed the mean magnetic variation from some azimuths at 1° 10' W., and some afterwards by amplitude at 0° 52', also west. At 6.0 p.m. the wind fell, and lulled for about two hours, then a favourable westerly wind again set in, and soon blew steadily from the south-westerly quarter.

21*st*. "At 2.0 a.m. we fixed our latitude at 49° 46' S. by a moon meridian altitude; though according to reckoning we were 49° 44' S.

After two hours, finding ourselves almost in the same latitude as the islands we were looking for, I gave orders to keep due east by the compass, supposing that the variation here was nil, or if there were any, not more than 1° E. At 8.0 a.m. we saw two Egmont hens which were flying straight above us and settled on the weather-vane. These birds, named by Captain Cook, may also be taken as indicating land, particularly when there are two or three together. From 8.0 a.m. till the afternoon the wind rose steadily, but for all that the barometer not only did not fall, but actually rose slightly, and towards midday the wind, accompanied by mist, rose to such an extent that we were obliged to take in with great difficulty all sail, and in a very heavy sea to heave to under single-reefed trysails. This was all the more necessary because, as there was no possibility of taking observations at noon in the misty and stormy weather, we might miss the aforesaid island, whilst, if it really existed, we might easily be exposed to danger since we could see only 5 miles ahead. I decided to remain in this position until midnight, and then if the weather were a little more favourable to be able to look back on our track at daybreak.

22nd. "From midnight until 8.0 a.m. the weather was fairly clear but we saw nothing. From 8.0 a.m. until midday a fine rain fell with hazy weather. I did not hope for an opportunity of taking noon observations, which under the circumstances would have been extremely necessary. But at last just before midday the weather cleared, the sun came out, and we fixed our position in Lat. 49° 56′ 34″ S., Long. 142° 00′ 00″ E., 11 minutes west of the centre of the island, as marked on the Arrowsmith chart, and 16½ miles south of its southern extremity. For this reason I gave orders soon after noon to bear to the north so as to reach the latitude of the island, and continue our voyage to the eastward in the same parallel. Towards 3.0 p.m. we reached this parallel, that is Lat. 49° 39′ S. At this time it was so light that the island, which was high, would have been visible from the look-out within 30 miles or more. But all our efforts to catch a glimpse of it were fruitless, although we did see some Egmont hens and seaweed. At 6.30 p.m. in Lat. 49° 39′ S., Long. 142° 47′ E. we lay to. By that time we were in the very position in which Royal Company Island is marked on the Arrowsmith chart with the two other islands to the west of it.

23rd. "At daybreak on the following day as soon as it was possible to distinguish objects at some distance, we made all sail and continued our voyage eastwards. At noon by observation our position was Lat. 49° 07′ S., Long. 145° 03′ E., from which it appeared that the current in the course of the 24 hours had carried us N. 47° E. 39 miles; and as we had passed through the actual place where the island referred to was marked and had proceeded 2½° farther east without seeing any land, I decided not to continue the search and took a course towards the south-western cape of Van Diemen's Land, which I wished to sight in order to regulate the chronometers, as twenty-five days had passed since we had had an opportunity of taking lunar distances. During the night we observed on the surface of the sea bright patches such as I had noted on my first voyage in 1804 on the approach to Van Diemen's Land. Captain Hunter, on both his voyages to New Holland, comparing these lights to lamps scattered about the sea, states that these floating glows may be regarded as a reliable indication of the vicinity of Van Diemen's Land. I found that Captain Hunter's remark was well founded; we were not more than 250 miles from the above-mentioned land and had not seen these luminous patches on the water before. It is noteworthy that they are much larger than those which may be encountered in other parts of that ocean. The strong south-west wind continued with squalls, hail and rain, and forced us by its fury to run before it. The sea on the beam was very heavy and, each time it broke on board, covered the upper deck with more than a foot of water. For the first time it happened that we were carrying a great deal of sail for such weather, and I confess that but for our desire to end our voyage as soon as possible and rest the tired crew even for a little it would have been better to heave to and wait for better weather. At noon observation showed that we were in Lat. 46° 33′ S., Long. 145° 17′ E. The marked easterly set continued; during the last 24 hours at the rate of 16½ miles, and on the following day at midday, in Lat. 43° 50′ S., Long. 145° 18′ E., we found that the current had set us 31 miles to the eastward in 24 hours. The continuous westerly wind blowing with such unusual violence was evidently the cause of such currents.

25th. "Since we were now only 18 miles south of the south-western cape of Van Diemen's Land, I changed the course to a more easterly direction. At 2.0 p.m. we observed a merchant vessel which was also making for the land. She was British, and was proceeding to the Derwent River with cargo. At 4.30 p.m. we saw the south-western cape almost due east of us and set our course more to the south-east. When we came to the meridian of the cape, which lies according to the best known calculations in Long. 146° 06′ E., we established the fact that our chronometers had given us a position only 42′ E. from the true longitude. The difference was very small in such a long voyage, and all the longitudes mentioned in this report are accordingly corrected by frequent lunar distances and in conformity with the rate of our chronometers at Port Jackson. At 7.0 p.m. we shortened sail; the sky all round us was covered with clouds foreboding a bad night; I therefore stood away to the south for a few miles and at daybreak set all sail and turned to a north-east course. At 11.0 p.m. we sighted Cape Tasmania, bearing N. 17° W. At noon it was 35 miles distant from us, bearing N. 41° W. At 1.0 p.m., when we were 34 miles south of Cape Pillar, we checked our chronometers by an altitude observation and found the same error in longitude, i.e. 42′.

27th. "The 27th of March was a beautiful day, and all our difficulties, dangers and discomforts were forgotten and indeed we had not had such a fine day ever since we had left Brazil. Only navigators who have finished such a voyage as ours and have seen the rocky snow-covered cliffs of Peter I Island and Alexander I Land, and then looked upon the fertile shores of Van Diemen's Land, covered with beautiful vegetation, can sympathize with our emotions.[1] Our delight on this occasion can only be understood by those who during almost four and a half months have experienced unceasing cold and wet with 7° to 8° F. of frost and now rejoice in 55° of warmth. It seemed that the southern extremity of Van Diemen's Land was the boundary line of the terrible gales and seas with which we had so often wrestled during these last weeks.

28th. "On the 28th, in Lat. 40° 26′ S., Long. 150° 53′ E., the variation was found to be 10° 26′ E. by an average of a number of azimuths. On the following day, by observation at noon we were in Lat. 37° 32′ S., Long. 151° 39′ E. and it appeared that the current during the previous 24 hours had set us 24 miles N. 37° E. At 1.0 p.m. the wind fell and continued calm until midnight when, to our satisfaction, a light breeze sprang up from the south-east and we set a northerly course, hoping that we should reach Port Jackson on the following day; but at about 7.0 p.m. the wind shifted to the north-

---

[1] It was not until the next year that the Russians discovered Peter I Island and Alexander I Land, so the slight anachronism proves that Mr Lazarev's report was written after the return to Russia.

ward and deprived us of this hope. This light adverse northerly wind continued until 9.0 p.m. of the following day and then, after a short calm, changed to the south and we again turned northward.

2nd. "At daybreak on April 2nd we sighted the coast of New Holland, bearing N. 55° W. I concluded that this land was Cape St George, near Jervis Bay. At 8.0 a.m., when we were within 14 miles of it, we found our conclusion confirmed because the curiously conspicuous Cape Perpendicular was visible on the bearing N. 51° W. The current which had set north and north-east in the vicinity of the coast of New Holland takes then an almost entirely opposite direction; we were set S. 19° W. 33 miles during the 24 hours, and to-day by observation at noon it appeared that we had been set 37 miles due south during the previous 24 hours. Capes Perpendicular and St George were in line S. 35° W., and we were distant from the former only 6 miles. The latitude was 35° 00′ 21″ S., Long. 151° 03′ 30″ E.

"The south wind began to fall in the afternoon and at 8.0 p.m. we experienced a calm. At night we were off Red Bluff, so named by Captain Cook on his first voyage.[1] We saw a light on shore for a time, probably a fire lit by the wild natives of New Holland, as in that part of the country there was no British settlement.

3rd. "The following morning in Lat. 34° 27′ S., Long. 151° 13′ E. the variation on an average of many azimuths was 9° 20′ E. and by a rising amplitude 9° 06′ E. The depth on sounding was 70 sazhen (82 fathoms), bottom white sand. At noon the southern headland at the entrance to Port Jackson was visible bearing N. 21° W. distant 20½ miles. A light wind blew from the north-east and we tacked in for the land. When in 35 sazhen (41 fathoms) we turned on another tack, Cape Banks and Red Bluff being in line S. 25° W.

"The changeable light winds, the calms, and the streams going south prevented us from reaching Port Jackson until the night of the 6th and, after passing a little beyond to the above-mentioned foreland and being becalmed, we came to anchor in the inner bay in a depth of 17 sazhen (20 fathoms), the bottom being white sand. At this time the fine new lighthouse was 2 miles distant from us, bearing S. 20° W.[2] At 8.0 a.m. of the following morning, with a north-west wind and flood tide, we weighed anchor and beat up into the bay until 2.0 p.m.

---

[1] Now known as Bellambi Point, a little south of Bulli.
[2] From the bearing given, this anchorage must have been just within North Head.

The wind, shifting suddenly, enabled us very soon to drop anchor near the *Vostok*; but we had not yet come to anchor before we had the still greater pleasure of seeing Captain Bellingshausen. He came on board and told us that he had arrived at Port Jackson only six days before us and that all the officers and crew were in even better health than when we had left Kronstadt. On a repeated examination of all the men on the *Mirnyi*, we found them also all well, with the exception of one who had been injured and had therefore been unable to move about, a fact which probably was the cause of blue marks on his feet. The maintenance of good health in these damp cold climates, at sea which constantly demands exposure in the open air, is a matter of concern to all seafarers."

Here the Report of Captain Lazarev ends.

The *Mirnyi*'s tents were put up near ours, the sick bay, the blacksmith's forge, live stock and all superfluous material were landed there. Mr Lazarev was particularly anxious to repair his damaged stem as soon as possible. His carpenters therefore at once set out to search for timber and to look for a good tree, but his trouble was in vain because, in such proximity to the town, there were no trees suitable for the purpose.

The trees are large, but being on rocky soil, the heart of all the trees is twisted, and moreover the timber is too hard and heavy to be joined to the pinewood of which the *Mirnyi* was built. Of all the varieties of wood growing in New Holland, cedar wood is the most suitable and most easily worked for shipbuilding and we used it for repairs.[1]

13*th*. With the permission of the Governor, Mr Lazarev brought the *Mirnyi* into the first bay on the western side of the tents and beached her at high tide; when the tide ebbed and the damaged part became visible, we saw that a whole timber was crushed to splinters over a length of $4\frac{1}{2}$ feet. In order to complete the repairs speedily, I sent a joiner and a carpenter to assist; the latter was also an excellent borer. On the 16th the repairs of the stem were completed, and she was floated off. Later on Mr Lazarev anchored out in the road and began to get his vessel ready for the resumption of the voyage.

The repair to the copper sheathing on the *Vostok* was finished by

---

[1] Nearly all the natural timbers of Australia are hardwoods. At that time, however, there was plenty of cedar to be found in the coastal valleys in the Bulli district, some 30 miles south of Sydney.

the 13th after the ship had been much lightened forward. A crack was found in the stem of the bowsprit and this was strengthened by thick iron bands on both sides and was supported by two long slanting knees. I believed that after this the stem would be really as strong as any new one, which could have been constructed only with great trouble; in addition suitable wood was not to be had in the neighbourhood or from the local resources of the dockyard.

16th. Taking advantage of the hospitality and kindness of the Governor, Mr Zavodovski, Mr Lazarev and I visited the town of Parramatta, about 15 miles distant from Sydney, in his carriage, while the other officers went by boat.

The drive was beautiful; on both sides were little houses, villages and every sign of human industry. Nearing the town of Parramatta, we observed that the hills were of a gentler slope and therefore more suitable for settlements and agricultural work, etc. The woods consisted of strong, sparse timber which a carriage could pass through everywhere. The town of Parramatta lies in a fertile level valley, near the river of the same name. Its streets are wide and even and run at right angles to one another. The houses for the most part are of wood, clean, and having gardens or orchards running down to the street; which keeps the air in the town fresh, and gives to the place a pleasant rural appearance. A few of the inhabitants have already stone, instead of wooden, houses. We passed through the town to the Governor.[1] He received us most cordially, led us through the garden, showed us the house and then took us to the upper story, reserved for the use of guests; he assigned separate rooms to Mr Zavodovski, Mr Lazarev and myself and a double room to our astronomer, Mr Simanov, and to our artist, Mr Mikhailov, observing that science and art should be closely allied. The other officers put up for the night at the inns. We remained with the Governor for three days. His house was not large, consisting of two stories; it stands on a hill and is surrounded by a garden. It was built by Phillip, the first Governor to come out from England. After breakfast we went and spent some time in the town with the Governor's Adjutant, Lieutenant Macquarie. He showed us

---

[1] At that period the Governor had a country house at Parramatta, on a hill known as Rose Hill. The house is still there and now forms part of The King's School, which was founded in 1832. The garden, so fully described below, has now been greatly reduced in size, but the main part of the house is unchanged. The Editor recently had the privilege of sleeping in the room used by Captain Bellingshausen on this occasion.

the hospital and the stone barracks which were almost ready for the military garrison; women are employed at the place in the day-time, where they spin and weave clothes for the convicts, who are employed in public work for the Government. At night the women return to houses in the town. This arrangement was the occasion for the local clergyman, Mr Marsden, to make representations in England, accusing the Governor of not trying to stop the evils arising from the dissolute life of the convicts, and suggesting that a large new factory should be built where the women, at the close of the day's work, should be housed for the night under lock and key. Mr Marsden's proposal was taken into consideration.[1]

Meanwhile Governor Macquarie had intended for some time to erect such a factory and foundations had been laid, the only difference being that provision was now made only for unmarried women; those who had husbands should return to their homes at night. Mr Macquarie's energy and disinterestedness had won the hearts of all the inhabitants, who spoke of him with the greatest praise.[2]

From the women's factory we went to the school for the girls of the natives of New Holland. They are neatly dressed and are taught to read, write, draw and sew. On the completion of their education they are free and can marry Europeans by mutual consent. A similar school exists for the native boys of New Holland.

We were told that it was extremely difficult to persuade the parents to permit their children to be educated at these schools. Their habits of freedom and the nomadic life in a splendid climate were precious to them, just as in Russia, in a severe climate, the wandering Tzigani (Gipsies) have no wish to change their restless lives for a settled and quiet existence, choosing at their own will from among the climates which prevail between the northern latitudes of 42° to 70°.

Farther on we came to the Parramatta River, as it is called by the natives, and passed a dam built to keep back the water in times of drought and to prevent it mixing with the salt water during flood tides. We then passed by a new building which had already been carried up as far as the roof, intended for female convicts sent out

---

[1] Mr Marsden had begun his representations in 1815, but they did not come before the Secretary of State until 1819. In the meantime they had given rise to much bad feeling and were the cause of several vindictive acts towards Marsden by the Governor's friends.

[2] This was not strictly true of the emancipated section of the inhabitants; see footnote above, p. 163.

Matora

Boongaree

Chief of the Broken Bay tribe and his wife

Prince Regent Bird (Magpie)

Abbott Bird (Leatherhead)

from Britain every year for various offences. The weaving mill, of which mention has been made, is to be transferred to this building.

The day was exceptionally fine and warm, and the changes of temperature so great that we all felt weary and were very glad to return to the house. Our hospitable host fortified us with a glass of Madeira and water.

17th. On the following day after breakfast at 8.0 a.m. the Governor invited me to go for a drive with him on the Windsor Road. Horses were provided for the other officers. This road is beautifully laid out and on a sloping hillside little houses and gardens and behind them green cornfields could be seen. The woods in the vicinity had been burnt in order to prepare the ground for sowing. In the midst of this wild country we met everywhere with evidences of the taste, intellect, and labour of Europeans. Flocks of white parrots continually flew across the road with shrill screams. Small birds flitted from tree to tree gladdening us with their song. Red lories with variegated rose-coloured plumage, and the particularly fine Blue Mountain parrots were perched in the trees in pairs or in flocks. Having proceeded for 7 miles, the Governor, who noticed the weariness of my officers unaccustomed to riding, ordered that we should turn back.

On arrival at the house, after a rest, we walked about in the garden with the Governor's wife. The garden at the back of the house terminates on one side in a fairly steep semicircular hill covered with woods, on top of which is an alley of lemon trees $3\frac{1}{2}$ feet in height recently planted and carefully pruned. Along the hedge surrounding the garden masses of yellow downy Mimosa flowers were growing.[1] These trees contribute greatly to the beauty of the garden; at the foot of the hill part of the ground has been levelled and planted with fruit trees and laid out as a kitchen garden. Different kinds of European fruits are grown here, such as apples, pears, peaches, currants, gooseberries, strawberries and raspberries.[2] The other side of the garden extends to the Parramatta River. Out of this we passed into another garden, called the "English garden", which lies in the front of the house. We wandered through the winding paths, between the orange and lemon trees, each of them showing its fruits in the various stages of their growth; the bright yellow fruit, the still green fruit, the aromatic

---

[1] Known locally as "Wattle".
[2] Parramatta later became the centre of the fruit industry, and was noted for its orange orchards.

white flowers and finally its bare bud. Yet however impressive this glorious flourishing nature, the excessively sultry climate, the heat of the sun and the very scent of the flowers awoke in us a preference for a cool autumn evening in our own land, with its birch and lime groves and their barely perceptible perfumes.

18*th*. In the morning we went to see Mr King, Lieutenant in the British Navy.[1] He is in command of a small warship tender and is here for the purpose of exploring the northern coasts of New Holland and Van Diemen's Land, of which he has already surveyed one half. The Government of New Holland may be proud that so important a task has been entrusted to one who has been born and bred in these new colonies. Lieutenant King is the son of Philip Gidley King,[*] former Governor and Commander of Norfolk Island, and was born in that island and educated in the five continents of the globe. He combines a wide knowledge with charming manners and forethought for others.

On Sunday we went to church with the Governor. All the inhabitants of the town of Parramatta and the neighbourhood attended the service to thank God for the past and to implore his help for the future. The singing was accompanied by a choir rendering ecclesiastical music. With their little prayer books in their hands and with eyes uplifted to heaven the children of the native inhabitants, educated at the aforementioned school, sang in the service. All the girls were modestly dressed in white. The British education had taught them morality and formed their minds. Their dark faces were the only signs of their origin.

The Governor does not dine before 6.0 p.m. so, as there was still time, he took us for a walk in the woods. He showed us the old winding gullies, washed out by the rain and formed by Nature herself. These impassable stream beds had greatly impeded communication between the settlements; so the practical Governor had made convenient roads and restored others in order that the surplus produce which each

---

[*] In 1788, on February 12th, Gidley King was appointed Governor of Norfolk Island.

[1] Phillip Parker King had entered the navy in 1807 and rose to be rear-admiral in 1855, though he had retired from active service in the Navy in 1830, and spent the rest of his life in Australia. The survey work which he was just about to resume was completed in 1822 and published in 1827. His father, after being in command at Norfolk Island, later succeeded Hunter in 1800 as Governor of New South Wales.

settlement had at its disposal should not be wasted, but could be distributed amongst the villages requiring them, where formerly very high prices had had to be paid for these commodities. All the overflow produce of the surrounding settlements is now seen in the market at Sydney, where it is brought for sale on account of its being the chief centre of population and because of the number of vessels calling there requiring all sorts of provisions. Every settler hopes to sell his wares better there and to buy in exchange luxuries brought from China, East Indies and the Cape of Good Hope.

19*th*. On Monday, after thanking the Governor and our charming hostess for their kindness and hospitality, we returned to the ship in the cutter via the Parramatta River. There is a flood and ebb tide in the Parramatta. The current was favourable and we made good speed. Near the town itself the river is narrow and is blocked by a dam to keep the sea water at the flood tide from mixing with the fresh river water. The river water is used by all the inhabitants. Outside the town, the girls' orphan school, a fine two-storied building with two wings, stands on the high left bank, which has been levelled and covered with a pleasant turf. Mrs Macquarie herself undertook all the work of patroness of this praiseworthy philanthropic foundation. As the result of some unpleasantness which had occurred in the past, Mrs Macquarie had refused to allow any visitors, and we had therefore no opportunity of looking over it. In this institution the children are taught the Bible, reading, writing, arithmetic and drawing and different kinds of manual work. Proceeding farther, we noticed that the river widens and that houses with beautiful orange and lemon groves are built along its banks. These trees have been introduced into New Holland and do very well there. Farther on, midway between Parramatta and Sydney, on the sloping left bank, we noticed fine cultivated fields sown with wheat and other grain. This district is known as the field of Mars because this was the land handed over to the soldiers on their first arrival in New Holland in 1788. On the right bank there are farms and the salt works. The remaining part of the river does not in any way appeal to the eye, but is only a succession of rocky banks of greyish yellow sandstone with a layer of light yellow sandy soil. Down by the river these rocky banks are bare; on the top there are woods of large trees, for the greater part frequented only by the natives, who roam there seeking their daily food. These woods give the shore a wild and dismal appearance.

We called on a brewer who resided on the bank of the Parramatta River. I asked him to send us several barrels of beer and a quantity of cabbages, which he delivered on the following day.

On our return on board, we found that the preparations for proceeding to sea again had progressed satisfactorily. Every day we went ashore to the place where we had set up our little observatory and dockyard on the foreland. Boongaree and his family were encamped in the wood not far from this spot. We often visited them on our walks. Although he called himself "King" of this place, his title was "Chief of Broken Bay". His "palace", however, did not correspond to this high title, since his dwelling consisted of a semicircular wall, built of fresh branches 4 to 5 feet in height. This wall was always thrown up on the side from which the cold wind or bad weather comes. The roof of Boongaree's dwelling was the blue sky above him. Both men and women were naked except those who had a frieze blanket wrapped round them. Those in a position to do so buy tobacco. There is always a fire of dry sticks; on this fire they cook their fish without removing the entrails and devour it greedily. They also eat mussels and crayfish, animals of all sorts and birds, snakes and other reptiles found in the woods.

During our stay a great many trees of the *Banksia* species were flowering. The native women go into the woods to collect the blossoms in large baskets of bark and then suck the honey from them. Sometimes it is extracted from them by soaking the blooms in troughs with fresh water; after throwing out the sodden material, they drink the sweet liquid, which is very probably nutritious.[1]

Governor Macquarie, anxious to break the natives of their nomadic life and to accustom them to a fixed dwelling-place, presented Boongaree with a house and garden in Broken Bay specially built for him, and gave him the title of "chief" of the place, hanging round his neck the copper plaque with the inscription, "Chief of the Broken Bay Tribe". But the magic charms of drink and tobacco, the greatest of all temptations to these natives, are stronger than all the joys of a fixed, plentiful and quiet life and still attract them to the town of Sydney.

Boongaree has a boat given to him by the Government for his family. Other natives too are given boats by the inhabitants of Sydney, on condition that they shall give up a part of their daily catch

---

[1] The large yellow flower heads and stiff cones of the *Banksia* are illustrated in Plate 16. The honey from them is plentiful but is too coarse for human consumption.

of fish. They go out daily in these boats and, having given up the portion due, exchange the remainder for drink or tobacco.[1]

On their return from town to their camps on the northern shore, they had to pass near our ships, and every evening they came back drunk, shouting savagely and uttering threats: and often their quarrels with one another ended in a fight.

They also fish a good deal from the rocks near the shore with long spears made of the stem of the gum tree, ending in a fork.[2] To the prongs of these forks small sharp serrated bones are fastened, and, as the stems of the gum trees are not sufficiently long, they are lengthened by the addition of other similar stems, joined together with strong bark fibre, the joints smeared with resin from different kinds of trees.

Out of these fibres, called by the British "stringybark", they twist ropes for their canoes, which are a proof how far this race is removed from any aptitude for inventing anything better. To make a canoe a strip of bark is taken, 11 or 12 feet or more in length and 3 to $3\frac{1}{2}$ feet in width. This strip is bent up at the sides; some distance from either end stretchers are placed, and the ends themselves are tied up with the sort of rope described above. They move about in the bay in these poorly constructed canoes in which they always carry a fire.

Once Boongaree came on board to exchange his fish for a bottle of rum. In answer to my question, "Who has broken your head?" he replied indifferently, "My people when they were drunk", from which his power over his so-called tribe may be estimated.

At night we once went out of curiosity to see in what way our friends disposed of themselves for the night and how they slept. At our approach their faithful dog barked and they immediately awoke. Boongaree, on seeing us, got up and came towards us, but the others remained in the position in which they had been lying. Some small fires were smouldering and between them they quietly slept, the men not separated from the women. The fires kept them warm on both sides, and this group represented the family of Boongaree. The aborigines of New Holland are of middle size and very thin, legs and

---

[1] Boongaree himself had played his part well in the early days of the colony when he went as interpreter with Flinders all round Australia and later with King.

[2] This is the grass-tree shown in the foreground in Plate 13. It was called the gum tree by the early settlers on account of the yellow gum it exudes under the leaves. The trunk of the tree itself is usually blackened by bush-fires, hence the colloquial name of "blackboy" for the plants. It is the hard woody flowering stem, from 4 to 6 feet long, which is used for the spear.

arms especially bony; the head compared with the size of the body is large; the colour of the body is a little lighter than in the case of negroes, the hair is curly, the nose broad and for the most part hooked like a parrot's, the mouth large and the lips thick. Some of them have the little finger of the left hand cut off. They give as a reason for this curious custom that the little finger interferes with the winding of the fishing lines and therefore it is cut off in childhood. Part of their bodies is painted in parallel lines and smeared with a red colour. White stripes are painted on the face and body; a piece of wood is passed through the cartilage of the nose. When they wander in the forests, they are always armed with a spear made of the stem of the gum tree.

At my wish Boongaree procured for me a set of native weapons, a shield, a spear and a fork for catching fish. All these articles were sketched (Plate 14). They show that the aborigines of New Holland are a few centuries behind the other islanders of the southern seas. The backwardness and lack of manual skill of the New Hollanders appears in some measure to be due to the vast extent of the country inhabited by them, their lack of sufficiently numerous communities, the rare contact with neighbouring races, the sufficiency of food which they obtain without any effort of mind or great labour, or interference by climate or neighbours. All these causes hinder the development of the natives of this vast country.

To the delight of all on board the symptoms of scurvy in our two sailors disappeared. The pigs and sheep had even more quickly recovered from this illness. The swelling and the livid blue marks on their legs had disappeared, and we had to keep them tethered to prevent them from running away into the woods.

The officers went ashore daily, for the most part to go shooting on the north shore. They always returned with their game bags full of birds, chiefly red parrots, quails and various kinds of swift flying birds, of which the largest were of a beautiful colour and are known as "King-fishers".

As the refit of the vessels neared completion, we sent the crew ashore to wash all the linen and clothes, and made them frequently have a bath, usually in two detachments. As I proposed, when all preparations on board were complete, to go to sea at once, I had the observatory, all the instruments, and the birds and animals, both our former and our new stock, brought on board. The position of our observatory, as mentioned above, was on the northern shore of Port Jackson Bay, on the cape directly opposite Sydney Bay.

Latitude and Longitude of the Observatory

Average of 5 observations taken at about midday	33° 51′ 12″ S.
Average of a number of meridian altitudes	33° 51′ 08″ S.
Mr Zavodovski on 12 observations taken at the Observatory	33° 51′ 24″ S.
Longitude fixed by me from 125 lunar distances	151° 16′ 58″ E.
By Mr Zavodovski on 125 lunar distances	151° 23′ 28″ E.
By Navigating Officer Ilin on 120 lunar distances	151° 16′ 54″ E.[1]

Variation of Compasses

On the *Vostok*	8° 03′ 00″
On the *Mirnyi*	8° 28′ 08″

H. W. F. and C. 9 hours 2 minutes.

The highest range of tide was 4 feet 5 inches on 17th April and 15th May, at noon.

The large Arnold chronometer No. 518 was in advance of mean time by 2 hours 17 min. 16·79 sec. In 24 hours it gained 5 min. 10 sec.

The Barraud chronometer No. 922 was in advance of the mean time 1 hour 13 min. 20·79 sec. In 24 hours it lost 10 min. 31 sec.

The small Arnold chronometer was in advance of mean time 2 hours 20 min. 53·79 sec. In 24 hours it gained 6 min. 8 sec.

---

[1] The result of the observations by the Spanish expedition under Malaspina in 1793 was as follows: Latitude 33° 51′ 28″, Longitude 151° 18′ 08″. It is not at all certain, however, that they used the same observation station, though they were on the same headland.

CHAPTER IV

Departure from Port Jackson for New Zealand. Stay in Queen Charlotte Sound. Navigation of the Pacific Ocean. Discovery of the Russian Islands. Arrival at Otahiti.

7th. With the intention of putting to sea on the following day we unmoored in good time, hoisted boats, and at 5.0 p.m., firing a salute, we hoisted the jack on the fore-royal top-gallant mast. The pilot arrived in answer to this signal at 7.0 p.m. from the shore, and slept the night aboard, so that we might weigh at daybreak on the following morning.

8th. There was a west wind throughout the night with rain and starlight by turns. At 7.0 a.m. we weighed and made sail. The *Mirnyi* took station astern of the *Vostok*. About 9.0 a.m. we were clear of the harbour and dropped the pilot. No pilot came on board the *Mirnyi* and Mr Lazarev proceeded out of the bay without one.

As we were leaving the harbour we met a heavy swell which produced considerable pitching; and when we had got some distance from the land the wind shifted through south and blew fresh from south by east, which obliged us to close-reef the mainsails, take in two reefs in the topsails, and strike the top-gallant yards. On the first day we shaped a course N. 86° E. so as to get away quickly from the land and then ran before the wind. According to my instructions we were to proceed northward from New Zealand to the Society Islands. As I did not think there was any possibility of making discoveries in the vicinity of New Holland, I decided to proceed by the north of New Zealand towards Oparo Island, discovered by Captain Vancouver in 1791, choosing a course which had not been followed by other explorers. I decided to make Oparo Island the rendezvous in the event of our ships being separated. Thence I intended to continue, after passing to the east of the Society Islands, between that part of the ocean which Roggewein called the "Stormy Sea" and the Dangerous Archipelago, discovered by Bougainville. These names, so unpleasant to the nautical ear, have caused ships to avoid all these seas and therefore I counted upon finding islands or shoals as yet undiscovered. The discovery of either of these is always of service to mariners.

11th. At noon we were in Lat. 32° 13′ 43″ S., Long. 157° 39′ 06″ E.

Banksia, Blue Tit, Honeyeater

Waratah

VOL. I PLATE XVII

PLATE XVIII

From the very first moment of finding ourselves again under sail the wind had blown fresh with rain at times. At 7.0 p.m. it was blowing contrary from the east by south. We altered course to the south in order to wait for the wind to shift. To our great regret our smith, Gumin, died on this date, from injuries received in Port Jackson on the 2nd of May when he had fallen from the bunt of the main yard whilst serving the mast with copper at this part, to prevent the mast being worn by the trusses. This loss was all the more distressing to us in that he had proved himself a most efficient smith and a kindly man. I had been anxious to leave Gumin in the town hospital before our departure from Port Jackson, but the Staff-Surgeon had assured me that all danger was past and that his recovery was certain. To our regret, this hope was not fulfilled and I felt that when it is a matter of life or death it does not do to be too certain.

12th, 13th. On the 12th and 13th we tacked about with a head wind. I arranged that we should not go far to the southward in case the north wind should later detain us on this side of New Zealand. We saw an albatross, blue petrels and pestrushki. At noon of the 13th we were in Lat. 34° 08′ 55″ S., Long. 158° 36′ 26″ E. When we were five days out from Port Jackson the crews were medically examined, and it appeared that there was one case of venereal infection on the *Vostok* and several cases amongst the crew of the *Mirnyi*. During our stay in Port Jackson we had taken every possible precaution to avert contagion, but in vain. The disease was rife in Port Jackson and was constantly being brought by convicts transported from England.

After washing and drying all the ropes, they were stowed below. I was always most careful to take this precaution as wet cordage invariably produces a bad, damp air which often causes serious illness on board.

15th. On the 15th the wind shifted more to the northward, and blew with varying force. The port tack was the better one for us; we altered course somewhat to the eastward and southward. The sky remained overcast until the following morning and we had not a single gleam of sunshine.

16th. At noon we were in Lat. 36° 01′ 25″ S., Long. 163° 30′ 59″ E. The mean variation appeared to be 10° 36′ E. Mr Lazarev, with some of the officers, paid us a visit and we spent a very pleasant day, despite the tediousness of beating against the continuous head wind.

18th. Until the afternoon of the 18th the wind allowed us to advance on a direct easterly course. I say "advance" because we proceeded only very slowly, steering close-hauled into the wind, which was blowing fresh, with an overcast sky and rare intervals of sunshine during the day and a moon at night. Our position according to dead reckoning was Lat. 35° 51′ 58″ S., Long. 166° 37′ E. The sky and the horizon were misty, fine rain fell and the wind increased. We took in a reef in the topsails and struck the top-gallant yards.

19*th*. The north-east by north wind increased hour by hour, accompanied by thick mist and rain; in the afternoon we were forced to close-reef the topsails and soon stood under reefed main topsails only. Next we took a reef in the fore and mainsails, but later, owing to the force of the wind, we furled them. From 4.0 p.m. we had a storm with thick weather and rain, during which we stood under main and mizzen staysails, and as the latter was somewhat torn, we took it in. By this time there was a very heavy sea and the night was quite dark.

A storm from the north was most unpleasant for us but not dangerous because each of the officers had, in the course of his service, repeatedly experienced such storms. About 8.0 p.m., however, the night being then very dark, a momentary calm set up such violent rolling that the *Vostok*, although she stood high in the water, shipped so much water on the windward side through the gangway netting that there was about a foot of it on the lower deck and from 13 to 20 inches in the hold. The gangway netting was completely carried away. Nothing could be done during the calm. Expecting a repetition of such unpleasant incidents, I ordered that all covers on the hatchways should be carefully battened down to keep the water from getting into the lower deck. I was relieved to find that the crew all responded to the roll call and that none of them had gone overboard.

When the officer of the watch ordered all hands on deck, Mr Zavodovski too was hastening up the main hatchway. The water poured in like a cascade. Struggling through the water Mr Zavodovski so seriously injured his shoulder, that it got inflamed and was swollen for several days. Lieutenant Lyeskov happened to be at hand at the moment near the exit to the gangway, but he managed to hang on to a rope and thereby saved himself, to our great relief.

Hardly had the wind shifted to the south-west than I ordered the crew to furl the main staysails and set the foresails, to bring the head of the ship against the heavy seas and ease off the excessive labouring.

We shook out the main topsails so as to increase our speed, but the soundness of the main mast was doubtful. Some cannon balls had escaped from the shot-lockers and rolled violently from side to side hindering the work, already difficult enough. By turning into the wind I hoped to save our excessively heavy rigging, which we had had no time to reduce owing to the haste of our departure from Kronstadt. To complete the unpleasantness the officer of the watch reported that the anchors had shifted. I gave immediate orders to secure them with additional lashings. This was only done with the utmost difficulty as the whole forecastle was continually under water and the work could be carried out only at great danger to life. The rain had soaked everybody, so we served out grog to the crew to prevent their health being affected. During the whole night on both the *Vostok* and the *Mirnyi* we had to signal constantly by sending up blue lights and by gun fire; but these signals were neither seen nor heard by the other vessel. At daybreak from the top we observed the *Mirnyi* east-south-east of us.

20*th.* In the morning there was a light north-west wind with a heavy swell from the north which made the ship labour very heavily. The remains of the iron stanchions of the network were found to be in position. I gave orders for all possible repairs, hatchways to be opened, decks to be cleaned and aired, and all wet clothing and canvas to be dried. On the *Mirnyi* they had already begun to do so. At noon we were in Lat. 37° 09′ 56″ S., Long. 168° 21′ 49″ E. The mean variation was 14° 16′ 46″ E. By 7.0 p.m. the two ships had again closed and we proceeded on an eastward course with a north by east wind.

21*st.* It was a moonlight night with lightning to west-north-west. The wind increased towards 8.0 a.m. so that we were obliged to take a reef in the topsails. Much against our will we found ourselves driven daily farther south, and indeed had already reached latitude 37° S. Sea birds, such as albatrosses, pestrushki, large black storm birds and others, usually found in the higher latitudes, were met in great numbers. Owing to the steady adverse north wind I began to doubt whether we should succeed in passing to the north of New Zealand.

22*nd.* At noon we were in Lat. 37° 32′ 42″ S., Long. 169° 34′ 03″ E. The mean variation appeared to be 12° 18′ E. Owing to the force of the wind we were obliged to take two reefs in the topsails and I gave up all hope of being able to wait for a favourable wind. I therefore decided to direct our course through Captain Cook's Strait. At 4.0 p.m. I signalled to Mr Lazarev that as the wind made it impossible to pass to the north of New Zealand, we should make our rendezvous in Queen Charlotte Sound. Towards evening the wind, accompanied by mist and rain, increased in force, and we were obliged to close-reef our topsails. There was a heavy swell from the north and the night was misty; the sea was lit up everywhere by phosphorescent creatures. They appeared to be cylindrical in shape, such as we had already seen. At night the temperature in the open air was only 56° F.

That night the ships sent up blue lights to indicate their positions to each other. Seeing that the *Mirnyi* was far astern of us, we shortened sail. At 4.0 a.m. toward the west lightning was playing over the dense clouds near the zenith, whilst away to the opposite side the moon and stars shone fitfully through the clouds.

23rd. At noon we were in Lat. 37° 54′ 37″ S., Long. 172° 10′ 38″ E.

Although the wind had shifted to the north-west and was blowing very strongly, there was a heavy swell from the north and we could profit by it as little as if it had been a head wind. And so, having already wasted much time in waiting for a favourable wind, I decided not to risk any further similar failures. At 2.0 p.m., after signalling to the *Mirnyi* to follow the *Vostok*, we bore away to Captain Cook's Strait, which divides New Zealand into two parts, the North and the South Islands.*

24th. Towards midnight the wind fell a little. It was a clear night with stars shining, but there were thick clouds towards the east on the horizon and lightning from time to time. We conjectured that the clouds were lying over land.

During the night we observed various lights, not far distant from the ship. The land proved to be nearer than we had reckoned, therefore we altered course a little towards the south and steered parallel with the shore. At daybreak we sighted New Zealand covered with clouds.[1] Although it was easy to distinguish the majestic Mount Egmont, its

---

* Captain Cook found this strait on his first voyage round the world on January 13th, 1770, and between that date and the 7th of February traversed its entire length.

[1] The Maoris called the North Island of New Zealand Aotea-roa, Aotea meaning "white cloud", which was the first sign of land as they approached on their early voyages.

summit was covered with clouds, snow being visible below them. The gently sloping shore surrounding this southern giant was partly covered with forests and undergrowth. The morning dew was glistening in the valleys, and on the shore we could see smoke rising in the air, the only indication of inhabitants.

25th. At noon our position proved to be Lat. 39° 47′ 38″ S., Long. 174° 58′ 56″ E., and the position of Cape Egmont would accordingly be Lat. 39° 19′ 40″ S., Long. 173° 47′ 45″ E. By observations made on the *Mirnyi*, the position of the Cape was Lat. 39° 24′, Long. 173° 57′ 30″. The difference in the figures is probably explained by the fact that Cape Egmont is round in form and has no special outstanding feature. Mount Egmont is in Lat. 39° 14′ 40″ S., Long. 174° 13′ 45″ E. By observation on the *Mirnyi*, the position of this mountain was found to be Lat. 39° 15′ 30″, Long. 174° 14′. Until 4.0 p.m. the wind remained favourable, but at 4.0 p.m. it shifted to the southward, freshened and forced us to tack.

A great many small divers were swimming and diving near the ship. The variation near the entrance to the strait was found to be 13° 01′ E.

26th. On the morning of the 26th the wind began to increase so that at 8.0 a.m. it was blowing in gusts from south-east by south, and forced us to take two reefs in the topsails. We then altered course to the south-west. By observation we fixed Cape Stephens in Lat. 40° 43′ 10″ S., Long. 174° 03′ 20″ E. On Captain Cook's own chart, Stephens Island is marked in Lat. 40° 36′ 10″, Long. 174° 53′ 40″. The difference is rather considerable. Probably this position was fixed by triangulation when passing it and not by astronomical observations.[1] The southern shore of Cook's Strait consists of several bays full of islets and rocks. The shores of these bays consist of pointed mountain ridges rising one above the other. The highest are covered with snow, but the parts near the sea, especially the gorges, are overgrown with forests and undergrowth. At 12.30 p.m. we turned on a north-east course on passing near the outer rocks lying off Admiralty Bay. At 4.0 p.m. Mount Egmont became clear. It was 87 miles distant from us and we therefore only saw the lofty silvery

---

[1] Stephens Island is a small island to the north-east of Cape Stephens, and Bellingshausen's figures are almost the same as on modern charts. The discrepancy of 50 minutes of longitude in Captain Cook's figure is certainly considerable, and marks both the improvement in chronometers between the two voyages and the value of Bellingshausen's recent departure from a well-determined station like Port Jackson.

summit rising above the horizon. Captain Cook on his second voyage round the world rounded this Cape on the 6th of October, 1774, and says: "We saw Mount Egmont, which was covered with everlasting snow, bearing S.E. ½ E. 8 leagues."

"This mountain has a majestic appearance, and is not lower than the well-known Peak of Teneriffe, whose height is 12,199 feet, according to the Chevalier de Borda."

Mr Forster, who accompanied Captain Cook as naturalist, says: "In France in about 46° of northern latitude, the line of eternal snow is found at the height of about 3280 or 3400 yards, above the level of the sea." But as Mr Forster knew from experience that in the same latitudes of the southern and northern hemispheres, the cold is more intense in the former, he compares the climate at Cape Egmont, which lies approximately in Lat. 39° S., with that of France in Lat. 46° N., and therefore infers the snow-line on Mount Egmont to be at a height of 3280 yards; and, as a third of the mountain was covered with snow, its height, in his opinion, would be 14,760 English feet. I believe that such a comparison of the height at which the snow begins on mountains in different hemispheres lacks foundation. For it is known that in summer time, on the shores of Greenland in the northern latitudes, snow lies perpetually at sea level; on the mountains of Norway, in exactly the same latitudes and at exactly the same time, there is no snow. I happened to encounter sea ice on May 27th, 1805, when navigating off the Island of Sakhalin in Lat. 48° N. This latitude corresponds to that of the Bay of Biscay, where probably nobody has ever seen any floating ice. Anyone can see from these examples that it is impossible to fix the height of a mountain by the ice and snow on it.

Captain Cook himself, as well as our compatriots in the Russian-American Company's vessels, did not observe any ice in Captain Cook River, or the so-called Kenaiski Bay. On the contrary, in Greenland, in the corresponding latitude, there is snow as far as the eye can see, and a great deal of floating ice on the sea. These examples show the variations of atmospheric temperature over the sea in the same latitude of even the same hemisphere, and therefore I have come to the conclusion that it is not possible generally to fix the height of a mountain by the snow-line, except in the case of mountains situated on closely adjacent islands.

In the same way, if one mountain be situated on an island and the other inland on the mainland, the snow-line of these will vary in height above sea level, because the land is warmed during the day by the rays of the sun and gives off heat to the surrounding air, thereby raising the snow-line on the inland mountain. On the other hand the sea absorbs little, and reflects little, of the heat of the air and consequently the snow-line of the mountain near or actually on the shore will be lower.

Mr Forster, basing his theories on these incorrect comparisons in the two hemispheres, determined the height of Mount Egmont to be 14,760 feet, which is much in excess of the actual height. On this occasion, during our passage through the strait Mr Zavodovski computed the height of Mount Egmont to be 9947 English feet above the sea, a result obtained by measurement of the height taken by sextant and distance of the mountain based on astronomical observations. Mr Lazarev makes the height of this mountain 8232 feet. Comparing these measurements, although differing considerably, we note all the same that the actual height of the mountain is much less than that assumed by Mr Forster and Captain Cook, who compared it with the Peak of Teneriffe.[1]

27th. In the evening the wind fell. All night and all the following day, i.e. until Thursday the 27th, we endeavoured to keep to the middle of the Strait as rain was falling and the shores were hidden by mist. At 2.0 p.m. two green parrots alighted on the *Vostok* and amused us a great deal; they also visited the *Mirnyi*, but no one could catch them and they finally flew back again to land. We noted one penguin, many little divers, and a few porpoises.

28th. From morning onwards the wind settled in the south-eastern quarter. We tacked successfully under all sail, with a very favourable current. The weather conditions also allowed us to determine the position of Cape Koamaru to be Lat. 41° 05′ 10″ S., Long. 174° 26′ 46″ E. Cape Jackson is in Lat. 40° 58′ 20″ S., Long. 174° 23′ 50″ E.[2] We tacked about boldly, relying on the special chart of Queen Charlotte Sound drawn on Captain Cook's first voyage. At 4.0 p.m., with a direct head wind and current and gathering darkness, I anchored off the north-western side of Motuara Island in a depth of 9 sazhen (10½ fathoms), mud bottom. We were then surrounded

---

[1] The height of Mount Egmont is now estimated at 8260 feet.
[2] These capes are the eastern and western headlands respectively at the entrance to Queen Charlotte Sound.

by high, steep mountains, covered for the most part by forest. Towards the north, the southern shores of the North Island, also fairly high, appeared blue in the distance. We observed a fenced-in place on the western side of the island which appeared to be inhabited. Soon afterwards two canoes quickly made their way out to us, twenty-three men in one and sixteen in the other, which was a little smaller. These canoes carried at the bows open carvings with spiral lines and the representation of a human head, with the tongue hanging out and eyes made of shells. The poop rose up at right angles and ended in a pole about 6 feet high. The oars were paddle-shaped, similar to those of the South Sea Islanders. The whole was stained a dark red colour.[1] The people sat in pairs rowing and the canoes stopped within a few sazhen of the ships. One man stood up and, in a sonorous voice, delivered a speech, gesticulating with his arms. We did not understand a word and I replied with signs, common to all peoples, expressing peace and good will, waving a white handkerchief and motioning them towards me. The natives then took counsel amongst themselves, and then quickly drew near to the ships. I invited the old man, the speaker, who was apparently the Chief, to come on board, which he did, trembling with fear and almost beside himself. I treated him with all respect and offered him a few trifles such as beads, a mirror, some printed linen and a knife. He was very delighted with these gifts. I then told him that I was very anxious to obtain fish; the word in the New Zealand tongue is "Ghika" (fish).[2] He understood at once, laughed aloud and informed his companions of our wish, pronouncing the word "Ghika". All the people in the canoes seemed pleased, repeating the word and expressing their readiness to serve us. As it was now beginning to grow dark, they hastened back to the shore. All the New Zealanders wore a piece of cloth reaching almost to the knee, fastened in front with a bone or a piece of basalt. They all wear a piece of rope round the waist, and over this dress a piece of cloth is thrown over the shoulder resembling a "burka".[3] All these garments are made of the New Zealand flax which grows here plentifully. The faces of these islanders are tattooed with lined figures in a blue-black colour; and this decoration is evidently the privilege of

---

[1] The description is that of a small type of coastal canoe used for sea-fishing.
[2] The modern Maori word for fish is "ika".
[3] A woollen cloak used by the Circassians.

the older and more notable men. Their knees are unusually thick, probably because they always sit with their legs crossed.

The *Mirnyi*, having only a moderate speed, did not succeed in making the Gulf until it was dark; she beat about outside under a fresh head wind. When it became dark, I gave orders for two lights, one above the other, to be hoisted on the *Vostok* and for blue flares to be shown from time to time, so that Mr Lazarev should not confuse the shore, where the natives had lighted fires, with the *Vostok* and so miscalculate his tacks. The current running out of the Sound had hindered him considerably, but when it turned, he tacked a few times and finally, at 11.0 p.m., anchored close to the *Vostok* in a depth of 11 sazhen (13 fathoms), bottom green mud.

I ordered that the men on watch should be provided with loaded firearms and be prepared to use them. This precaution was necessary on account of the well-known treacherous character of the New Zealanders, who wage incessant war on one another and eat the flesh of their enemies.

29th. There was a fresh south by east wind blowing all night with overcast sky and fine rain. The temperature was 48° F.

Our anchorage did not promise perfect safety from the strong north-west winds which blow here. There would also be much difficulty in getting our water-barrels filled as the supply was at some considerable distance from the anchorage. It was almost 9.0 a.m. before the ships weighed and beat up between the Long and Motuara Islands, with a strong head wind from the south. The depths between the islands diminish from 10 to 7 sazhen (12 to 8 fathoms). After twenty-five tacks we came to anchor at noon behind Motuara Island in a depth of 12 sazhen (14 fathoms). The western end of Motuara Island was bearing N. 16° E., and the southern headland of "Ship's Cove" S. 37° W. The anchorage was perfectly safe, sheltered from all winds, no great depth, and offering the possibility of getting under way in any wind. Wood and water were both at hand, and we were near enough to Hanka Island not to need a tent for rating the chronometers. As we were beating up, two canoes filled with natives were trying to approach us. They were rowing after us, following each tack of the vessels across the Sound, apparently not understanding our movements. When we anchored, our guests of the previous day came on board the *Vostok* bringing their fish for sale. On my orders, the commissariat officer concluded a bargain for seven pood (250 lb.) of fresh fish in exchange for a number of ropes of beads, mirrors, nails and other trifles. There was a further exchange made for specimens of their handwork.

The old man to whom I had made such lavish presents on the previous day appeared to us to be the Chief. I received him with all the courtesies of the South Sea Islands; we embraced and, by rubbing noses,[1] confirmed our mutual friendship, which we maintained on both sides throughout our stay in Queen Charlotte Sound. As it was our dinner hour, I invited the Chief to come into the cabin and dine with us. We seated him in the place of honour between Mr Lazarev and myself. He examined with astonishment all the table utensils and fingered them, but would not make use of them to eat with until someone gave him an example; then he very cautiously and clumsily began to put his food into his mouth with a fork. He did not seem to care to drink the wine. After dinner we renewed our assurance of friendship for one another by signs and by means of the few words that I knew. But when, wishing to give him a further proof of my good will, I made him a present of a beautiful, well-polished axe, he jumped up from the table overjoyed, and asked to go on deck, whither I accompanied him. There he rushed at once to his compatriots and then embraced me with great delight shouting, "toki! toki!" (axe! axe!).

We regaled the other New Zealanders on the quarter-deck with biscuits, meat, gruel and rum. They all ate very heartily, but one glass of rum was sufficient for all of them. Such sobriety serves to prove that they can only have been visited rarely by the enlightened Europeans who, wherever they settle, always teach the natives to drink alcoholic liquors, and to smoke and chew tobacco; then, when these ignorant people begin to show the bad effects of strong drink, they start to explain to them how disgraceful it is to give way to drunkenness and other evil habits.

The New Zealanders, at the close of the meal, sat down in two rows facing each other and began to sing some quite tolerable songs in perfect harmony. One of them always intoned and then all the others joined in and finished in a very sonorous and abrupt finale; then the same man again began to intone; and in the same manner the others joined in and brought the song to the same abrupt conclusion. It seemed to us that their songs in some measure resemble our own folk-

[1] This mode of salutation, common in the Pacific, is better described as "pressing noses".

songs, and that they consist of a number of short couplets.[1] At first our drums and fifes did not attract their attention, but then they listened with some satisfaction to the sounds of the instruments and the Chief explained to us that they also had a musical instrument which sounded rather like the fife.[2] Mr Mikhailov made a sketch of the Chief.

After staying some considerable time, the New Zealanders started out to return to the shore and were extremely delighted with the results of their barter. They had provided sufficient fresh fish for supper on both ships. When starting ashore they invited us to join them and as an additional attraction made us understand by signs that we should be entertained by the fair sex.

After dinner I ordered a few shots to be fired from the *Vostok* and at nightfall a few rockets were sent up to announce our presence to the natives inland, expecting with confidence that they would collect to visit us in larger numbers on the following morning. On this day we lowered the boats of both vessels and set up the rigging, as it had been slackened by the constant beating against strong head winds. We also put up the portable forge in order to have new gangway netting made, in place of that which we had lost when the calm set in suddenly after the gale.

30*th*. On the following morning the same native boats approached the *Mirnyi* to visit her, and one party came on board the *Vostok*. The old Chief was amongst those visiting the *Mirnyi* and there were also some other notable elders. Mr Lazarev entertained them all to dinner; they preferred beef to anything else and even swallowed greedily some meat that was beginning to go bad.

Meanwhile the running rigging and tackle on the *Mirnyi* was being dried and the crew were getting up casks from the hold. The New Zealanders with pleasure and the utmost zeal assisted in the work and tailed on to the ropes, uttering loud, fairly harmonious shouts to keep time. When it happened that the rope broke and they all suddenly fell, they burst out into loud laughter.

After this they amused themselves by one of their dances, con-

---

[1] It is unusual for a European to appreciate Maori music which has not the definiteness of tone which characterizes ours. A Maori will break into a chant to illustrate an oration, the leader intoning on the note most suitable to his voice and moving his companions to join in.
[2] Simple types of flutes, a short mouth flute (*koanan*), a nose flute, and a wooden flageolet (*putorino*), a longer instrument, were played by the Maoris.

sisting of various grimaces with loud singing and stamping of feet and waving of arms. They made such hideous faces that it was unpleasant to watch and sometimes rolled their eyes up under their foreheads. This dance seemed to be a war dance, exhibiting their contempt for, and triumph over, their enemies.

Mr Mikhailov made a sketch of this dance. He represented all the grimaces, the rolling eyes, the positions of the various parts of the body, and the extraordinary muscular contortions. He also made a sketch portrait of one of the elders; for this purpose he invited him into the cabin and seated him on a chair to keep him quiet and occupied his interest with a variety of objects, new to him. The canoe, in which his wife and family were sitting, was brought round to the stern so that he could see them.

With some of the officers, I spent some time in the afternoon in Ship Cove searching for a suitable place to obtain water. As we were approaching the cove, the exquisite singing of land birds, which sounded like harpsichords and flutes,[1] charmed our ears, which had for so long been deprived of such a pleasure. We moored the boat in the bay and clambered over the rocks. At a distance of a few sazhen we observed a tiny stream, with sparkling fresh water, which flowed down from the top of the mountain through the dense impassable forest consisting of thick jungle and the network of liana* creepers twisting themselves from tree to tree with their shoots of the thickness of wild vine.

We observed a small wigwam, made of leafy branches, on the edge of the forest near the stream and in it found some fish and a great quantity of mussels, known as "Ushi" (Ear†) mussels. This wigwam

---

* The liana is a special kind of plant indigenous in America and the Antilles Islands, where it is used instead of ropes. The liana plant grows creeping round the trees and sometimes reaching the very top; then growing vertically down to the ground, the plant takes fresh root and climbs up again. Thus constantly growing up, down and intertwining, they gradually form an impenetrable forest. The liana grows as thick as one's arm, and sometimes twines round the trees with such force that they are withered or even killed. Several species of the plant have so poisonous a sap that arrows dipped in it retain for more than a year their fatal power. *Note of the appendix to Captain Cook's Second Voyage.*

† The Japanese called these mussels "Avabi". They remove the mussels from the shells and dry them for use.

---

[1] Captain Cook's men were much struck by the morning choruses of the Bell-birds heard at the same place, and they describe thousands of these birds singing together towards morning, the sound seeming to arrange itself into scales, like a peal of bells running down octaves. As the sun rose the singing ceased.

seemed to be the home of a small family. The officers who accompanied me shot a few cormorants with a bluish eye membrane like a coloured tinfoil, and a few other small birds, probably of the species described in Captain Cook's Voyage by the two Forsters. After remaining some time ashore, I returned on board and at once sent armed boats ashore from both vessels to obtain water. We were not impeded in our work by the presence of natives who, as it happened, were all on the other side of the impassable mountain. Fishing nets were put down here but very little fish was caught. On my arrival on board Mr Zavodovski told me that he had been anxious to buy some of the green stone objects made by the natives.[1] These articles resemble small paddles, but as the vendor asked for Mr Zavodovski's overcoat in return, the deal was not made.

31*st*. In the morning I invited Messrs Mikhailov, Simanov, and some of the officers of the *Vostok*, together with Mr Lazarev and officers of the *Mirnyi*, to visit the islanders. We started out in two cutters, on each of which we placed a swivel-gun, each of us also carried a gun and a pair of pistols. With such an armament we had no cause to fear any treachery of the natives. We made for the nearest village behind the first cape to the north of Ship Cove, the exact spot where Captain Cook on his first visit had observed human flesh. The inhabitants dispersed: only one of them approached us, with marked signs of timidity. But when we patted him all the others came out to us. The Chief, a man well advanced in years, sat on a mat in an open hut, and I at once went up to him. The natural curiosity of the women-folk overcame their timidity. First his wife appeared and then his daughter and both sat down on the mat. I made a few presents to the Chief and his wife, and to the daughter, who was quite pretty, I presented a mirror so that she might be able to compare herself with the other women to her own advantage. I was at once presented with a piece of material woven from New Zealand flax with a figured border; the Chief's wife suggested the exchange, to which I readily agreed. All the settlements were small and squalid and, after staying a short time, we went more to the northward to visit my friend the old man. He met us, we greeted each other and rubbed noses. The old man was very pleased to see us. We all went ashore, leaving only a guard for the boats.

This greenstone, a form of jade, is found only in a few localities in the South Island and was much valued by the Maoris for its hardness and beauty.

Towards the sea the village was protected by palisades, a little more than a man's height. We entered the settlement through a small gate in the stockade. A little stream ran through the village between the dwellings, which were scattered about without any idea of order. The bank of the river was edged with cobble-stones; and we crossed it on planks to the Chief's house. I did not enter but only looked in; the structure consisted of three rows of posts. The centre row was twice the height of a man and on each of them a human figure had been roughly carved and decorated with red colour. On these posts and the outside rows, which were little less than shoulder high, beams were laid for supporting the roof, consisting of poles covered with leaves. A space of about 6 feet at the entrance was cut off as an antechamber. The whole interior was neatly covered with fine matting. The floor, on which the inhabitants usually sit and sleep, was also covered with matting. Spears, about 24 feet in length, decorated the walls, also a mace, various insignia of the ruler, and human figures carved out of wood and painted red.[1] The other huts were not so elaborately decorated. Farther in the forest, into which we penetrated out of curiosity, we saw a small hut erected 20 feet from the ground on thick trees whose branches had been cut away. We did not find out what was inside, as it was impossible to look into them and we were ignorant of the language and could not ask. The skin of an albatross stretched on a hoop and some tufts of black and white feathers were hanging below the hut; probably these objects were used on the occasion of councils of war. Farther off we saw the straight trunk of a tree, the top of which had been cut down to about $2\frac{1}{2}$ times the height of a man and $1\frac{1}{2}$ feet in diameter: the top was carved with the figure of a human being. I thought that we had perhaps hit upon their cemetery, but there were no mounds or other indications of graves. Whether this statue had some connection with their religion I am unable to say owing to the shortness of our stay.[2]

On our arrival on shore we had been met by some of the men, but later on women also joined and mixed with the crowd. My friend the old Chief, probably remembering my presents to him when he visited the ship on the first two days, wished to show me equal

---

[1] It has been suggested that all Maori carvings take their basic pattern from a much conventionalized human figure, which is recognizable even when elaborated to the grotesque or reduced to intricate spiral designs.

[2] The "statue" was probably a "Rahui" post, marking a prohibited area. "Rahui" is a form of tapu for the protection of products of stream or forest.

hospitality and consideration. He selected a fairly young but repulsively ugly woman and offered her to me as a temporary wife; I declined, patting the old man on the shoulder. Very likely Europeans who had visited this place before us had given the New Zealanders occasion for offering such services and for trading in their women, a barter which, procuring for the natives many priceless things, encouraged them to pursue these shameful profits. Forster comments on this in the following words: "Our sailors carried on their former amours with the women. One of them had tolerable features and something soft and feminine in her looks. She was regularly given in marriage by her parents to one of our shipmates who was particularly beloved by this nation, for devoting much of his time to them, and treating them with those marks of affection which, even among a savage race, endear mankind to each other. To-gheeree, for so the girl was called, proved as faithful to her husband as if he had been a New Zeelander, and constantly rejected the addresses of other seamen, professing herself a married woman (*tirratane*). Whatever attachment the Englishman had to his New Zeeland wife he never attempted to take her on board, foreseeing that it would be highly inconvenient to lodge the numerous retinue which crawled in her garments and weighed down the hair of her head. He therefore visited her on shore, and only by day, treating her with plenty of the rotten part of our biscuit, which we rejected, but which she and all her countrymen eagerly devoured. Mahine, the native of Borabora, whom we had on board, had been so much accustomed in his own country to obey every call of nature that he did not hesitate to gratify his appetites in New Zeeland, though he was too clear sighted at the same time not to perceive the vast falling off from his own countrywomen. The force of instinct triumphed over his delicacy, and can we wonder at it when our civilized Europeans set him the example?"

On the way back to our anchorage we observed a half-open hut in which there was a great variety of different wooden fish-hooks and fishing lines; we concluded that all this gear must be the common property of several families as there was far too much of it for any one family, and to trade in these fishing utensils was impossible because each could easily make them for himself.

During our stay at this village we obtained some of their weapons and specimens of their handicraft by barter.

When we were saying good-bye, the old man detained me. By his orders, his men brought a mace 8 feet in length, the top being halbert-shaped, carved and inlaid with shells like eyes, the lower end being shaped like a narrow paddle. I thought that he was making me a present of the mace but, on my accepting it and being about to place it in the cutter, the old man seized it with both hands and I then understood that he was not giving it to me but wished to exchange it. To gratify him I gave him two arsheens ($1\frac{1}{2}$ yards) of red cloth; he was very pleased with his profitable deal and told all his fellow natives about it at the top of his voice.

Returning to our ships we proceeded along the shore and noted that there was cultivated ground lying fairly high on the headlands. We landed at one point and there saw a long row of baskets of potatoes, just dug up. We took some of them with us; on boiling them we found that they tasted very good and were not inferior to English potatoes.[1] Proceeding farther, we touched at Motuara Island. I was anxious to obtain some seed of New Zealand flax to grow it on the southern shores of the Crimea, where there is a similar climate and soil. I hoped to render no little service to the inhabitants of that region and to our native land. Although I did not find the seeds I wished to obtain, I did not regret going ashore there as we found wild cabbage and celery on the shore, enough for all the officers and crew to have "shohi" (cabbage soup) of the fresh vegetables.

1st. Mr Zavodovski went ashore at Ship Cove. When he returned on board, he told me that he had been joined by Mr Lazarev and that they set out together up the stream, making their way with great difficulty through the overgrown and intertwined masses of liana, and in spite of all their efforts were unable to proceed farther than 1 mile. It was doubtful if this part had ever been trodden by the foot of man, as it was so densely overgrown that they had to cut their way through at every step. The birds they had met were so tame that a sailor caught one in his hands quite easily. Mr Zavodovski shot a black bird with greyish down round the neck and two white curled tufts on the breast; it was as large as a European blackbird, and its song resembled that of the nightingale. They did not see any New Zealanders ashore.

The wind shifted to the westward on the evening of June 1st and later to north-west; the shores were hidden by thick clouds.

[1] As stated below, these potatoes were descendants of those given to the natives by Captain Cook in 1773.

Principal settlement of Queen Charlotte Sound, New Zealand

War Dance, Queen Charlotte Sound, New Zealand

PLATE XX

VOL. I

2nd. Towards 11.0 a.m. of the 2nd the wind began to blow up in sharp gusts from the passes of the mountains between Motuara Island and the shores of the western mainland. At 3.0 p.m. the cutter and boat, which had gone to Ship Cove under command of Lieutenant Lyeskov to fill the barrels with fresh water, returned. Mr Lyeskov reported that when he had got into the broken water between the mainland and Motuara Island, from which direction the wind was blowing, the boat began to fill and therefore, wishing to lighten her, he threw overboard fifteen casks, each containing $13\frac{1}{2}$ gallons of water, and removed the timber which had been fitted to increase the height of the hatch coamings on the upper deck. Past experience in gales had shown that the hatch coamings are always made too low and have to be rectified at sea, a matter which is attended by considerable difficulty and inconvenience.

From hour to hour the squalls increased in force and the topgallant masts and yards were taken down; we were riding with 70 fathoms of cable. The *Vostok* dragged a little with each strong gust. In order not to approach too close to Long Island, we let go another anchor, which steadied the ship greatly. The velocity of the wind reached such a degree that near the shore opposite the direction of the wind whirlwinds were formed which ploughed up the sea with extraordinary force and squalls struck the vessels on all sides. During this time we had heavy rain and lightning. The peals of thunder reverberating in the mountains seemed unusually loud. A little before 7.0 the rain ceased and at 7 o'clock the wind dropped. The clouds disappeared and the moon and stars shone out.

3rd. Early on the following morning Midshipman Adams went in the cutter in search of the barrels thrown overboard from the boat and found nine of them; some had been broken up and the hoops removed by the natives, but on our demanding them, they were returned without protest. We weighed and returned with a favourable wind, under staysails, to our former berth. I then set out in a boat accompanied by Mr Lazarev, to explore the interior of the Sound. We landed at different points and gathered a good deal of cabbage, celery and a salad cress. We went some 13 miles along the inner parts of the Sound and found some deserted temporary huts scattered in different places. Probably when the natives from the western shores of Motuara Strait come into the Sound, they take up their quarters in these huts. We did not see any villages as the locality would not be convenient for obtaining food which, amongst the New Zealanders, consists principally of fish and which is always obtained very easily in shallow water near the mouths of the rivers; while the depth in the inner part of the Sound is everywhere 25 fathoms. The farther in we went, the more mountains we saw; they have little vegetation and many patches of a yellow colour. Woods were confined to the lower ranges, nearer to the water level. We shot a few gulls on the way and returned to the ship at night. Had the weather detained us we should certainly not have starved, as Mr Lazarev had not forgotten to bring plenty of provisions, while everybody carried a gun, powder and smallshot, and green vegetables, as I have said, were obtainable in quantities everywhere.

On our return it was reported to me that the natives had arrived on board both vessels, and had bartered their goods as before. They had brought spears, various carved boxes, fish-hooks, maces, various ornaments for chiefs, balls made of green stone, axes, different sorts of clasps and ornaments of green basalt which they usually wear round their necks. They also brought some of their woven stuffs. All these objects, made by them with great labour out of hard stone and wood, they tried to exchange for axes, chisels, gimlets, strings of coral, shirts, mirrors, flints and glass beads.

4th. In the morning we were ready to weigh but the New Zealanders hastened to visit us, wishing to barter their goods for trifles which were very precious to them. I made a few more presents to the Chief and gave him to understand that we were leaving them. He expressed his unfeigned regret and all of them asked us to come back to them. When they observed that we had already weighed, the Chief embraced me and said farewell, mournfully exclaiming, "Eh! Eh! Eh!" One of the young men was very anxious to accompany us, but all the others implored him not to go and finally persuaded him to return ashore with them. I left it to his discretion.

The inhabitants at Queen Charlotte Sound are of medium height, strong and fairly well built though their knee-joints are somewhat heavy. Their faces and bodies are a dark tawny colour, their eyes black and very quick; their hair is also black. All of them have their ears pierced and the greater part of them their noses also. Their faces are marked with painted, curved but regular lines in a blue-black colour, people of importance being more decorated than the others. In the case of some women, the lips only were painted. In this respect they bear a close resemblance to the inhabitants of the Marquis de Mendoza Islands; moreover their language is akin to those of the groups of the Friendly, the Society or the Marquis de Mendoza Islands. The habit from childhood upwards not to restrain themselves and to follow their natural inclinations, good or bad, makes the New Zealand natives very warm-hearted in friendship, but inconstant and inclined to quarrel on the slightest provocation with occasionally fatal results. The New Zealanders are very agile in all bodily movements and, it seems, ever ready to fight, although they never picked a quarrel with us. While the Chief was dining with me I asked him if he ate human flesh and indicated my hand. He replied that he ate human flesh with great pleasure, and there seems to be no doubt about it as Captain Cook saw with his own eyes that the New Zealanders greatly enjoyed eating the flesh of their enemies killed in battle. In 1772, the unfortunate Marion and seventeen of his companions fell victims to this loathsome vengeance; their companions set off in a boat to assist them but returned reporting that they had found remains of the bodies of their shipmates, parts cut up for feasting and other parts already roasted. In 1773, the English naval officer, Rowe, and ten men belonging to the English vessel, *Adventure*, fell victims to this terrible revenge of the natives as the result of a needless outburst of one of the sailors against one of the natives who had stolen his jacket. Those sent ashore in search of them found only the clothing, the remains of the bodies, the heads and the intestines of their comrades.

The natives of Queen Charlotte Sound cover their bodies from a little above the waist to half-way down the thigh with a piece of white woven material secured by a narrow belt. A piece of white or red material with a dark-coloured border is thrown over the shoulder and fastened across the chest with pins, 4 or 5 inches in length, made of green basalt or bones, probably human or of dogs, for dogs are the only large animals which have been seen on the islands by travellers.[1] These pins hang by fine cords to prevent them being lost. When it is cold they put on besides a rough cloak, similar to the Circassian "burka".* My friend, the old Chief, was dressed as I have described,

---

* The Circassian burka (made of a kind of felt of which the rough side is always turned out) is generally black and is worn hanging from the shoulders, fastened round the neck either by a strap or a silver cord. The burka reaches almost to the knee and is sleeveless, the best being made of Angora wool.

---

[1] The native dog (Kuri) is now extinct, but it appears in many Maori myths and songs.

but younger men wore only one of the above-mentioned garments from the shoulders; the youths wore nothing but the short open cloak. They adorn their heads by dressing the hair on the crown of the head in tufts, into which they stick a few white feathers. They pierce their ears and pass through them pieces of birds' skin with white down on them. On their breasts they often wear ill-shaped human images,[1] or a clasp or a sort of knife made of green stone or in some cases simply of bone. They are always ready to barter these objects away so that it is impossible to believe that they can be idols. They are armed with fine, straight, pointed spears made of strong dark wood, up to 30 feet long;[2] and also with short hurl-bats called "Petu", which they make out of the bones of a whale or of green stone, carved, about 15 to 18 inches long and about 4 inches wide and 2 inches thick. The end is smoothed all round and towards the handle it becomes narrower so that it can be easily grasped. The handle has a hole drilled through it. The hurl-bat is usually held by a cord passed through this hole. The New Zealanders have two other weapons made of the above-mentioned strong dark wood. One is about 8 feet in length broadening a little at the lower end, the top halbert-shaped with a distorted human face carved on it, coloured green, the eyes being composed of shells. The other weapon resembles an axe and is about half the length of the former. These objects appear to form part of the Chief's insignia and are used for his defence.

Captain Cook measured some of the large war canoes of the New Zealanders, and found them about 63 feet long, but we saw none longer than 47 feet and $4\frac{1}{2}$ feet in width. On these canoes, as on those mentioned earlier, there are the carvings of human faces, with long tongues hanging out and eyes made of the shells called sea-ears and all coloured green. Behind this face there is a scroll of open-work carving resembling what is usually known as filigree work. The poops of these long canoes rise like a crest upwards to a height of about 5 feet. The hull of these boats is hollowed out of one tree, and to the upper edge of it two boards of a width of 7 inches are added on each side, joined to each other and to the submerged part by cords. To prevent leaking reeds are placed along the seams and are kept in

---

[1] The best known of these decorations was the "tiki", which is a grotesque-looking object generally made of greenstone, representing the human embryo, and therefore worn by women only.
[2] The longer spears were for fishing, not for battle.

position inside and outside by long strips of bark, $2\frac{1}{2}$ inches wide. The upper strakes, the carvings at the bow and the crest of the poop of these rowing boats are all painted a dark red colour. Although these boats do not indicate the same skill in construction that Captain Cook noticed in those of the northern part of the island, described on his first voyage, the dexterity and patience expended on this work may well—considering the lack of iron tools—fill a European with astonishment.[1] The islanders still look upon a nail presented to them as a great acquisition and will barter for one nail one of their "Petu" weapons on which they expend so much time and labour, or for their beautifully carved oars usually up to $5\frac{1}{2}$ feet in length. When they pursue anyone they use these standing erect in their boats and propel them thus at a better speed. Captain Cook, during his first sojourn in Queen Charlotte Sound, found on the shores of the Sound some tribes composed of about 400 men. During his second voyage he touched at the same place and writes as follows: "It may be that a great part of the people, which inhabited the country near this Sound in the beginning of the year 1770, have been since driven out of it, or have of their own accord wandered elsewhere. I can definitely state that by 1773 the number of inhabitants had decreased by two-thirds as compared to their former number. Apparently their settlement on the point of Motuara had been long deserted: and we found many forsaken habitations in all parts of the Sound."

At the present time, in the month of June 1820, there are certainly not more than eighty inhabitants. Such a reduction of a race existing in small families and continually at war amongst themselves is not surprising. It is probable that Captain Cook overrated the number of inhabitants on his first visit to the Sound and that he unwittingly included visitors coming from neighbouring settlements out of mere curiosity, to see the big vessel that had come. Moreover the islanders may well have hoped, without loss to themselves, to capture or kill some of the Europeans; for they probably knew by tradition that two large vessels had once come to "Massacre Bay", where they succeeded in capturing and eating some of their men. The Dutchman,

---

[1] The war canoe, used for longer voyages and for war, was sometimes up to 80 feet in length, hollowed out from the huge Totara or Kauri trees, a relatively soft timber. Nevertheless the fashioning and carving of such a canoe with stone tools often took at least twenty years.

Abel Tasman, left Batavia on December 13th, 1642, having under his command two ships, the *Heemskerk* and *Zeehan*; he sighted unknown land and called it Staten Land; at a later date this discovered land was renamed New Zealand. On the 18th Tasman anchored in Massacre Bay ("Meerdersbai") and the natives killed three of the crew of the Dutch vessels. Captain Cook believes that the bay in which Tasman anchored is that same bay which lies 18 miles to eastward of Cape Farewell, closed from seaward by a low-lying sandspit.

The opening named Blind Bay by Captain Cook on his first voyage, lies to the south-east of Tasman's Massacre Bay.

The New Zealanders, in consequence of their small numbers, cannot suffer from scarcity of food. The roots of ferns, large quantities of fish, which they catch daily, and shellfish are sufficient for them. Every day our own men caught enough fish for both vessels. The natives have now added to their provisions splendid potatoes, which are certainly not inferior to those cultivated by the English in their kitchen gardens. On May 29th, 1773, Captain Cook, on his Second Voyage, showed a New Zealander a potato plant planted by Navigating Officer Fanning of the *Adventure*, which was then doing well. Probably the natives at Queen Charlotte Sound, realizing that such a vegetable would be of use to them, planted some and have cultivated them ever since. Although in the course of forty-seven years they have been spread considerably, it is not possible to obtain any from the New Zealanders, as they plant only sufficient for their own use. But as a matter of justice the name of Navigating Officer Fanning will remain for ever connected with any description of New Zealand and its inhabitants. At the same time other sorts of garden vegetables, sown at the foot of the mountain near the sea, are growing wild.

During our stay in Queen Charlotte Sound I gave my friend the Chief and other elders seeds of different vegetables which might be of use to them, such as turnips, mangel-wurzels, carrots, pumpkins, broad beans and peas. I showed and, as far as I could, explained to them how to plant these seeds in the ground and to what use they could put the fruits of them. The islanders understood me perfectly, were well pleased with them and promised they would sow them in their patches.

The Rev. Samuel Marsden from New South Wales has now a home

in the northern part of New Zealand.[1] His intention is to preach the divine message of the Gospels for the enlightenment of the New Zealanders. A few of the New Zealanders have been kept as hostages in Parramatta for the safety of the preachers who come from there. Not only do some well-made weapons, woven materials, and carved boxes give proof of the skill of the New Zealanders, but they are actually employed with success in Parramatta in the cloth-weaving industry.

Rather a small breed of dog, of which Captain Lazarev bought two specimens, was the only kind of quadruped seen. They are not large, have thick tails, erect ears, a broad muzzle and short legs.

It is probable that seals visit the rocks lying off New Zealand, as I bought from the New Zealanders a sort of jacket made from the skins of this animal.

At the time of our departure on the 3rd of June, corresponding to the 3rd of December in northern latitudes, all the trees still retained green leaves. We had seen no signs of approaching autumn. During our stay the thermometer had registered a varying noon temperature of between 68° F. and 72° F. and at midnight it was always 48° F. The barometer never rose above 30·10 or fell below 29·51 inches. We fixed the place of our anchorage at Long. 174° 23' 52" E. Captain Cook made a longer stay than we did and therefore may have been able to fix the position with greater accuracy. According to his observations the longitude is 174° 25' 15" E.

Whilst we were passing through the channel between Motuara and Long Islands, the wind increased in force and obliged us to reef the top-gallant sails. After clearing the submerged rocks, which we could not see, we tacked in various directions towards the south-east to pass out of the Sound; we were soon off Cape Terawhiti[2] and were rejoicing over our successful passage when, towards evening, the wind suddenly shifted ahead to the south with mist and rainy weather and then increased so much that we were obliged to beat about in the strait with topsails close-reefed.

---

[1] Mr Marsden came out to New South Wales as a chaplain in 1793, but his energy led him into many other fields. He was a very successful farmer, he promoted schools and public works and was prominent in all affairs of the colony. He began his missionary settlement in New Zealand in 1814 and combined with it a certain amount of trading. He died in 1838.

[2] The cape at the south-western extremity of the North Island, which was often a difficult point for sailing ships to pass.

5th. By midnight the wind had increased still more and was blowing in strong gusts with rain, snow and hail. At times the lightning, accompanied by thunder, lit up the shore and showed us its proximity and our danger. The gusts of wind brought very heavy clouds, and besides waterspouts, we experienced all that the atmosphere of the southern hemisphere can possibly produce. Towards daybreak the wind increased still more and blew with the utmost violence all day, bringing heavy clouds, sometimes with rain and sometimes with snow and hail, so that at midday we could not see anything at all, although we were in a narrow channel with land on both sides. During the day the fore staysail was carried away and the fore braces parted so that we had to take in even these sails. Towards night the wind rose to a heavy gale, the squalls blew with such violence across the narrow channel that it sounded sometimes like the roll of thunder. At rare intervals during the night the moon and stars shone through the driving clouds; we burned blue lights, but the *Mirnyi* did not reply. I concluded that she must be nearer the northern shore of the strait.

6th. At noon we were by observation in Lat. 40° 16′ 15″ S., Long. 174° 05′ 46″ E. From this it appeared that the gale had carried us back some 65 miles into the Sound. In the afternoon the wind decreased in strength but remained ahead. We set all sail; the *Mirnyi* did not come in sight until daybreak the next morning.

7th. At noon we had a light fair wind from the south-west. I again set a direct course for the entrance of the Sound. The wind blew fresher and the ships proceeded at 8 and 9 knots. At 10.0 p.m. the wind fell and was variable during the night.

8th. At 4.0 a.m., when we were just at the entrance, again a strong south-easterly head wind with snow, hail and rain set in. We again struggled against the fierce wind, which prevented us so long from getting clear of this wild dangerous strait, and delayed our voyage to warmer and more favourable regions. The high wind from the open sea rebounded from the shores of the narrow sound and rushed along it with tremendous force. Up to 9.0 a.m. we were kept in the narrows and had turned about five times. The sea ran very high. As evidence of the violence of the gale, the ships had to close-reef all sails or risk losing the masts. I bore away through the interior of the Sound under reefed topsails and beyond Cape Stephens ran before the wind under storm staysails. Mr Lazarev was following our example, but when he

Wife of New Zealand chief

Native of Arakcheev Island

New Zealand chief

Native of Oparo Island

View of the coral island of Moller

bore away his ship was travelling at such a speed that she would not answer the helm and was making straight for the shore, until they reefed the mizzen and main topsails.

9*th*. About 3.0 a.m. the following morning, the wind fell. At 6.0 a.m. with a light west wind we again set a direct course to pass out of Queen Charlotte Sound and observed breakers over some submerged rocks. They lay on a line joining Cape Jackson to the mountain behind it, on a bearing of N. 24° E. from the former.

At 4.0 p.m. I gave orders to shorten sail so as not to outrun the *Mirnyi*, which had fallen far behind. I was afraid that the light uncertain wind might again shift to the south-east. At this time heavy black clouds were gathering on the horizon.

The narrowest part of Cook Strait, between Capes Terawhiti and Koamaru, is 15 miles wide. Beyond Cape Terawhiti, at the exit from the strait, lies a wide bay and it seemed to us that an island, overgrown with woods, lay inside it, but at such distance that we were unable to examine it.[1] Beyond the high central headland and Cape Palliser lies another bay. These shores appeared suitable for agricultural land and for European settlements. On the central headland a big fire was burning; probably the inhabitants wanted us to visit them.

10*th*. At midnight Cape Palliser bore N. 18° E., distant 11½ miles. A light wind was blowing from the south which towards morning began to fall. Whilst it was dark I had repeatedly sent up blue lights from the main yard-arm, but the *Mirnyi* did not reply as she did not see our light. It was not until 10.0 a.m. that we saw her on the horizon to the south-west.

At noon the position of the *Vostok* was in Lat. 41° 51′ 04″ S., Long. 175° 50′ 28″ E., with Cape Palliser bearing N. 70° W. Of the two snow-capped mountain ranges near the mouth of the strait, the farther lay S. 70° W. and the nearer S. 62° W.:[2] the soundings were 255 sazhen (296 fathoms), no bottom. White and grey albatrosses with white marks over the eyes were flying near the ship; we also noted some large white storm birds and pestrushki.

13*th*. From noon of the 10th until noon of the 13th we proceeded with a west and south-west wind and a heavy swell from the south. We passed some seaweed on the way, probably torn away from the

---

[1] This is the present Port Nicholson, the harbour of the city of Wellington. From the strait the peninsula of Miramor, with its low isthmus, looks like an island.

[2] These were the two Kaikoura ranges with mountains up to 9000 feet in height.

submerged banks off New Zealand. We were in Lat. 40° 09′ 06″ S., Long. 177° 53′ 34″ W. The variation was 10° 21′ 30″ E. During an almost perfect calm Mr Lazarev came on board with some of the officers; in pleasant conversation we did not notice how time was flying until evening and we regretted having to break up our party.

14th. From noon until 9.0 p.m. there was a variable wind, but at 9.0 p.m. it began to blow fresh from the north-north-east. The ships proceeded on the port tack close-hauled until noon of the 15th.

15th. From time to time gusts of wind struck us with fine rain. We were in Lat. 40° 38′ 52″ S., Long. 174° 48′ 39″ W. We saw a good deal of floating seaweed pass us. From all three look-outs we kept careful watch for land but did not see any. The wind shifted to the north-west quarter, and freshened; rain clouds and showers passed frequently; there was a heavy swell from the north-west which made the vessel labour considerably, and we altered course to the north-east. In doing so I was careful to avoid a track already gone over by former navigators.

17th. At noon we were in Lat. 39° 14′ 16″ S., Long. 170° 56′ 00″ W.; the variation was 10° E.[1] At 5.0 p.m. there was a light wind from the north-west and south-west and I continued on the course N. 70° E. Some pestrushki were flying near the ship. During the 21st and 22nd there was a strong wind with rain squalls.

23rd. By 75 lunar distances we fixed our longitude at noon on the 23rd at 157° 58′ 42″ W., but according to chronometer No. 508 it was 157° 45′ 16″ W., that is 13′ 26″ farther to the east.

On this day we observed pestrushki for the last time.

On both ships we were very busy repairing the sails which we used in the higher southern latitudes and, as the *Vostok* laboured heavily under the weight of her very large masts and yards, I reduced the area of the sails at the same time. We had now some free time and were in a fine climate so we were able to devote ourselves to reducing both sails and yards; I had the main yard reduced by 6 feet and the remainder in proportion.

The shipbuilder, Stoke, who had built the *Vostok*, had fitted very low coamings round the hatchways on the upper deck, with the result that water penetrated frequently into the lower deck; these and similar

---

[1] In the Russian text longitudes are reckoned eastwards and this meridian for instance is printed as 179° 04′ 00″ E.; for the convenience of modern readers these have been converted to west longitudes in each case.

mistakes are due to shipbuilders never going to sea in their own ships and consequently a vessel rarely leaves their hands in a perfect condition. Having obtained timber in New Zealand, we were able to remedy these defects. At 5.0 a.m. the westerly wind dropped to a calm which lasted 4 hours. Then a fresh south-south-east wind sprang up and we continued our favourable progress. At noon we were in Lat. 31° 49′ 42″ S., Long. 155° 35′ 18″ W. In the evening and during the night we saw a good deal of heat lightning. Almost all the time since leaving New Zealand we had had a heavy swell from the south.

26th. From noon the wind again shifted to the south-west and freshened with squalls; there was a swell from the south which caused the vessel to roll and pitch a good deal. We made use of this wind until 8.0 a.m. of the 28th, when we were able to proceed on our course helped by the trade wind. At noon we were in Lat. 28° 04′ 56″ S., Long. 146° 32′ 28″ W. The variation was 7° E. The thermometer stood at 63° F. in the shade and at midnight it was reading 60° F. The barometer indicated 30·13 inches. This moderate warmth in the open air helped to maintain the health of the crew of both ships, who were occupied in altering the rigging during the day. In the evening I ordered all up on deck in the fresh air, where they sang songs, played games and danced Russian, Cossack and gipsy dances: some amused themselves with an English country dance which they had learnt on board, and others played leap-frog.*

28th. These amusements helped to preserve the health of the men as much from the contentment they brought as from the exercise itself, both being necessary to bodily well-being. I therefore always endeavoured to secure both for the men under my command. From midday we set a course nearer the parallel and steered N. 63° 45′ E. with a gusty south by east wind accompanied by rain. The swell from the south produced considerable rolling.

29th. From midnight we kept still closer to the parallel of Oparo Island[1] and maintained a speed of 5 knots. During the night we

---

* Through the shocks caused by the racing about during these games, the fine needles on which the fly of the compass is balanced are apt to be damaged. On these occasions the compasses manufactured by Mr Steving of Portsmouth proved superior to all others, because the fly with a fine copper needle rests on a highly polished hemispherical agate plate, and therefore no damage can be done to it by any shocks such as may be caused on board through racing, games, gun fire, etc.

[1] Oparo or Rapa Island, one of the much scattered Tubuai or Austral group. It was discovered in 1791 by Vancouver.

observed heat lightning playing all along the horizon; towards morning the wind fell. At 6.0 a.m. just as day broke we sighted Oparo Island N. 88° E. at a distance of 16 miles; it seemed to us to be fairly high with four separate hills or peaks.

The wind shifted more to the eastward and no longer helped us to reach the island. I hoped to reach it by beating but the natives forestalled us. Before 1.0 p.m. we saw their canoes coming towards us from the shore. I gave orders to furl the main topsails. We did not have long to wait as the canoes, each manned by five, six or seven men, approached very quickly. They stopped at first at a little distance from the ship and one of them delivered a passionate address in a loud voice. When I showed them a few objects and made signs to them to approach they immediately resolved to come on board. I greeted the most important among them by touching noses and made them a few presents. Some time later a very tall, well-built, thickset man came on board. His appearance, and the respect shown to him by all the other islanders, showed him to be the Chief and he also introduced himself as such. I invited him to come into the cabin, to which at first he would not agree, but later he entered very timidly and was delighted with all he saw. I presented him with an axe, a mirror and a few arsheens of printed linen. The inhabitants of Oparo Island showed a great tendency to theft and endeavoured to steal everything that came within their reach. The sentries with loaded rifles had to keep the most careful watch. One of the islanders, finding himself in the wardroom, succeeded in stealing the back of a chair and disappeared into the water with it. As soon as we had noticed this we levelled a rifle at him; he was thoroughly frightened and returned the stolen object. The action of firearms was familiar to them and inspired them with great fear. When the *Mirnyi* fired her guns, they all dived from the side. The islanders brought nothing except shellfish, small taro roots, and hard, stale dough wrapped up in leaves ready for use. We exchanged for these a few pails and water-scoops, which they used at once for baling the water out of their canoes. After staying some time on board our guests returned on shore; they had come in fifteen canoes. Mr Lazarev was farther out than we were and therefore the islanders did not visit him. At 1.30, when they had all left us, we made more sail. Towards night we altered course to the westward, in order to approach the island again in the morning.

30*th*. There was a very light southerly wind and a slight swell;

the sky was brilliant with stars. We were unable to approach the island closer than 4½ miles during the day owing to the wind having fallen light. At 8.0 a.m., when we lay directly off a bay, the natives again came on board. Although on the previous day I had asked them to bring fish, pork and poultry, by pointing to those which we still had with us, they did not carry out my wishes and brought only a small quantity of shellfish and taro. The islanders were astonished at the size of the ship and all the things, which were quite new to them. One measured the length of the ship on the upper deck with the span of his arms, by lying down on the deck each time to stretch out his arms to their full extent. He also measured the width of the quarter-deck. Our guests did not leave the ship by the companion ladder but dived straight into the water and then climbed into their canoes. I gave various trifles, ear-rings, mirrors, tinder-boxes, knives, etc., to them all. To-day as many as twenty canoes came alongside the ships; as the two vessels were lying close to each other, the natives having received presents from me, hurried off at once for the same purpose to Mr Lazarev. Having received some from him they returned to me, stretched out their hands and by signs indicated that they had not yet received anything. After remaining more than an hour on the vessel, they all suddenly dived in great haste into the water one after the other, with the exception of one, who begged to be allowed to stay, which I permitted him to do. He stood on the gangway, watching his compatriots, who tried to persuade him to return with them. The islander would not consent for a long time; finally he appeared about to yield to their persuasions and entreaties, but still stood rooted to the spot, the struggle of his feelings showing plainly on his face. On one hand, some kind of bitterness against his fellow-islanders, on the other the natural human love towards one's own race fought a hard fight within his heart. But when this latter praiseworthy feeling overcame his anger against his fellow-countrymen, he begged me to allow him to return to them. I did not try in the least either to keep or to drive him away, but left him entirely to decide for himself. After waiting a little, he took leave of me, dived into the water and joined his fellows. Mr Lazarev explained to me the reason for the sudden and hurried departure of the islanders from the ships. One of them, whilst on the *Mirnyi*, taking advantage of a convenient moment when the sailors were busy shortening sail, pulled out an iron stanchion together with a rope ladder and dived into the water with it. He had evidently informed all his friends of his intention beforehand, for they all dived one after another into the water from various parts of the ship; only an old man whom his age prevented from following after them was left behind. Mr Lazarev ordered him to be put under restraint in full view of all the islanders. The canoe with the stolen object was pointed out to him and it was explained to him that on the return of this object he would be released. The islanders displayed perfect obedience to the old man from which it would appear that he was one of their chiefs. On this order the canoe which had been pointed out to him approached, and after a little conversation the old man announced that there was no stolen article in it. When those in the canoe discovered, however, that Mr Lazarev had every intention of getting back the stolen object and that without t he would not release the old man, the one who had taken the stanchion and rope ladder showed the latter and asked in apparent bewilderment if this was the object they wanted. As soon as he produced the rope ladder they were convinced that the stanchion too had been stolen by the same native and therefore insisted on its return. The culprit searched all round the inside of the canoe feeling with his hands, dragged up a broken basket, a few pieces of reeds, and finally raised his open palms, to indicate there was nothing further to be found. At last, seeing that all this served no purpose, he produced the stanchion, jumped with it into the water and brought it back on board. Then all the islanders began to shout and apparently abused him, especially the old man who, with an expression of delight on his face, rushed towards Mr Lazarev and several times rubbed noses with him. All this abuse was mere pretence; probably the old man himself was the chief culprit or at least the theft had been carried out in connivance with him, and if they had not succeeded in detaining him, he too would have dived overboard and managed to swim to one of the nearest boats. Mr Lazarev, however, did not show any suspicion towards the old man and gave him a nail with which he was very pleased, then he dived into the water and swam to his boat, together with the other islanders.

Oparo (Rapa) Island was discovered by Captain Vancouver in 1791 on his voyage from Dusky Bay (in the southern part of New Zealand) to the Society Islands, and was named "Oparo" because the natives constantly pronounced this word. Captain Vancouver did not find a suitable anchorage anywhere near it. In consequence of light contrary winds we could not approach nearer than 4½ miles, but we examined the island, which has the appearance of ridges of steep, fairly high mountains, lying in an east to west direction. The low-lying part and the foot of the mountains were covered with forest; the parts which were bare were yellowish red in colour.[1] On the northern side there were small patches of light red colour, probably red ochre. On the north-eastern side a waterfall fell into the sea over the cliffs. On the north-western side there is apparently a navigable bay.

The island is about 6 miles in length along the parallel and 3½ miles in width; it has a circumference of about 15 miles. On some of the summits of the mountains there appeared to be structures looking like fortresses, which are accessible only by footpaths.[2] The position of the island was fixed by observations as follows:

On the *Vostok*		On the *Mirnyi*	
Latitude	27° 37' 45" S.	Latitude	27° 36' 40" S.
Longitude	144° 14' 55" W.	Longitude	144° 25' 15" W.
Variation	5° 21' 00" E.	Variation	6° 24' 00" E.

In 1791 (December 22nd) Captain Vancouver fixed the position as follows:

Latitude	27° 36' 00" S.
Longitude	144° 01' 32" W.
Variation	5° 40' 00" E.

The islanders who came on board the ships were for the most part of medium height, but a few were fairly tall, almost all were strongly built, many of them stout. They were adroit and quick in all their movements. They had curly hair and bright black eyes. They did not shave their beards; face and body were dark red in colour; their features were pleasant and not disfigured by tattooing as is the case with many of the inhabitants of the Pacific Islands. One of the natives of Oparo, about seventeen or eighteen years of age and very slimly built, had light reddish hair, blue eyes, a rather aquiline nose and the fair skin of the natives of northern Europe. There is little room to doubt that he was the offspring of an Oparo woman and some European traveller.

---

[1] The island is volcanic and the ochreous patches mentioned are stretches and cliffs of bare lava, decomposed.

[2] Extract from Admiralty Sailing Directions: "All the principal passes from one valley to another are commanded by well-constructed, hard-cemented stone forts, generally built in the form of flat terraces and each commanded by a tower." Some at least of these stone works are ancient irrigation terraces. The highest mountain is 2070 feet high.

Mr Mikhailov made a very good sketch of this islander as well as of some others. Wanting to get some presents, the islanders made various grimaces and stretched out their hands; they thereby made the sailors laugh and obtained from them some trifles of European workmanship. They constantly invited us to go ashore, but it was dangerous to venture ashore at such a distance and the light head wind prevented us from going closer in. As there are no other islands in the vicinity, it would seem that the islanders, living in this beautiful climate and not lacking any of the necessities of life, might live in eternal peace; but the fortified places on the summits of the mountains, within which huts could be seen, led us to the conclusion that the islanders are divided into different factions, have their own reasons for breaking off friendly relations among themselves and are compelled in that case to find refuge and protection within these fortresses. We did not succeed in seeing any samples of their handiwork beyond the canoes in which they came out to us; probably owing to the lack of trees of sufficient thickness these craft were made of planks bound together by ropes made of the twisted fibres of the bark of trees. Some are as much as 25 feet in length, but have a width of no more than 1 foot 2 inches: on one side they carry a beam about $3\frac{1}{2}$ inches wide, which tapering at the ends like a canoe helps the craft to keep its balance. Owing to the narrowness of the canoes it is impossible for the fat islanders to sit down in them, but they fasten boards across at certain points and sit there quite comfortably. Mr Lazarev obtained a model of these boats for the Imperial Admiralty Department's Museum. The oars, and the water-scoops, for baling the water, resemble those of the New Zealanders, except that the scoops have handles and are without carving; the water-scoops are more like those used by Europeans for baling the water out of rowing boats. We saw a few small white birds with forked tails. As it was not worth while waiting for a fair wind, to touch at the small islet off the northern shore of Oparo Island, or to run into the bay on the north-western side[1] (where it looked as if there might be a convenient anchorage), I continued, after the natives had left, on an easterly course until twilight and reached Lat. 27° 36' 30" S., Long. 143° 43' W. Throughout the whole day we had beautiful weather, a cloudless sky, a clear horizon and, had there been any islands equal in height to Oparo Island to the eastward or in any other direction, we would have seen them at a distance of

[1] The bay of Ahurei which affords the only reasonable anchorage at the island.

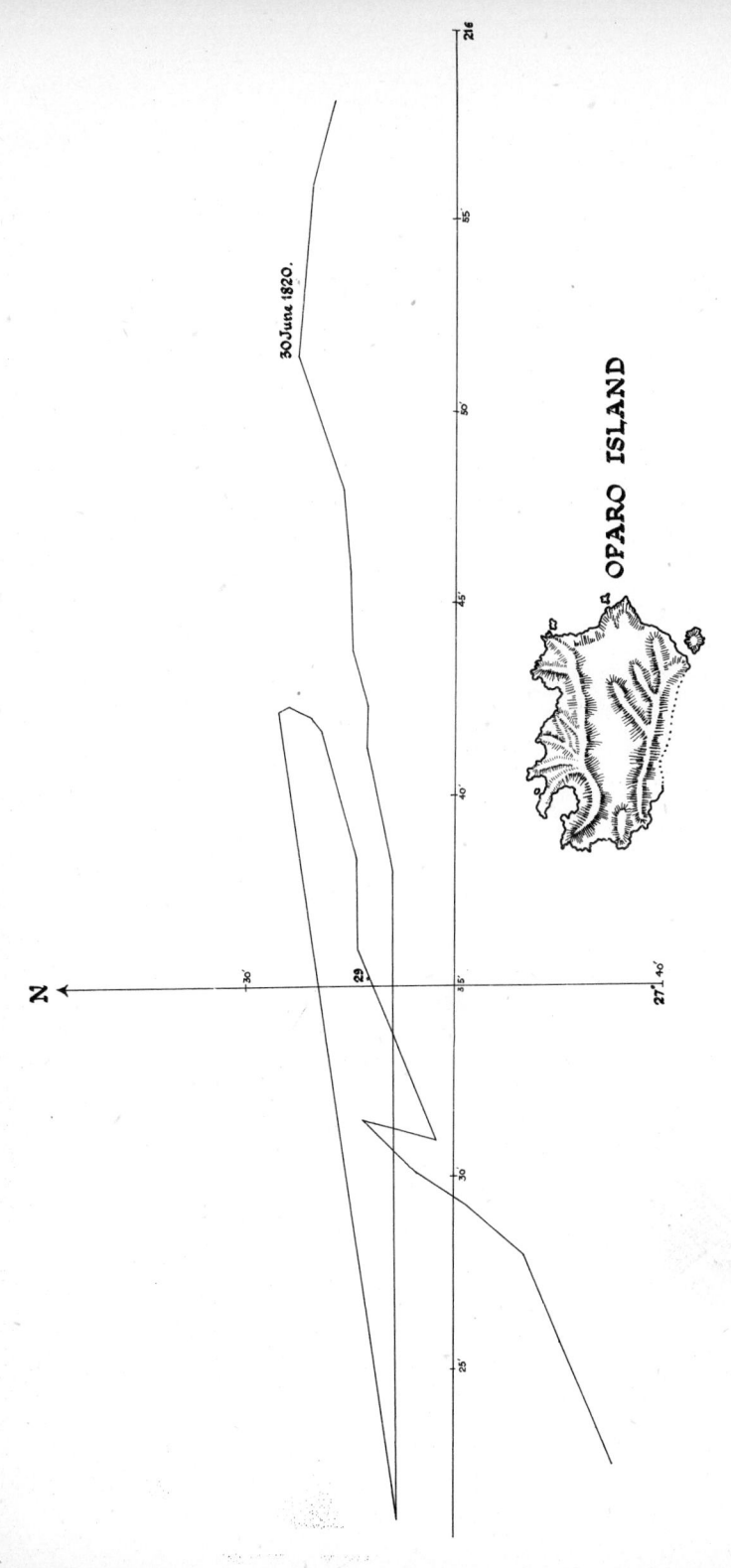

40 miles; but in spite of a good look-out at the top-gallant masthead nothing was seen. The Arrowsmith chart showed the islands of Four Crowns (Las Quatro Coronadas), located by Bass and first surveyed by Quiros, within the visual range of our present track.[1] To judge by this name, one may suppose that the Spanish navigator had sighted Oparo, which presents four summits to a vessel approaching from the westward. But such a conclusion would not agree with the following extract from the *Voyages* of Quiros: "On February 5th of 1606, having proceeded about 25 miles from the land we had surveyed, we sighted in the evening four islands, forming a triangle, each of a size of 5 or 6 miles [whether in diameter or circumference is not stated] which were quite bare, uninhabited and in general resembling the island we had discovered." Torres calls the islands Las Virgenes and Quiros Las Quatro Coronadas. The former islands discovered by him were all almost level with the sea and, consequently, Oparo Island could not be one of them. Moreover it is easy to prove that since Bass locates the islands of Las Quatro Coronadas to be in Lat. 27° 45' S., the other discoveries of Quiros preceding these islands and made on the same voyage must also be farther to the south and La Encarnacion Island, the most southern of all, must lie in Lat. 32° 12' S.; up to the present time no one has found coral islands with lagoons in such high latitudes. They do not extend on the southern hemisphere farther to the south than the southern tropic or latitude 23° and then only in the vicinity of New Holland. All this tends to show that Quiros kept more to the northward than Bass believed and that consequently these islands should not be marked in the latitudes assigned to them on the charts of Arrowsmith and other hydrographers.

1st. As nothing was sighted from the look-out, I proceeded during the night to the southward, inclining a little east. The weather continued beautiful; all on board enjoyed the pleasant tropical evenings; the nights were clear and from time to time meteors passed rapidly across the sky leaving a faint trace of light behind them. The barometer rose to 30·37. On the next day some seaweed floated past us, resembling that which is found in great quantities floating near the Azores and is supposed to come from the Gulf of Mexico. From midday the wind blew from the east-south-east; we saw the first tropical bird.

---

[1] Nevertheless, Bellingshausen was within 30 miles of these islands, now known as the Marotiri Islands. The description of de Quiros is fairly correct, except that they are much smaller. They are bare of vegetation and one of the rocks is 350 feet high.

2nd. The wind shifted and freshened, blowing from the east-south-east in slight gusts. At noon we were in Lat. 24° 10' 13" S., Long. 142° 31' 19" W., and we observed two tropical birds; at 7.0 p.m. we crossed the Tropic of Capricorn for the second time; towards night we shortened sail to reduce speed.

3rd. In the morning we made more sail. At noon a fresh east wind was blowing and we had 90° F. in the shade. At midnight it had been 55° F. and all felt keenly the sudden change from coolness to heat.

4th. Towards night we shortened sail; at about 8.0 a.m. we observed two tropical birds and one frigate bird (*Pelicanus aquilas*). For the first time since passing into warm regions we saw a flying fish. At noon we were in Lat. 20° 25' 50" S., Long. 141° 36' 27" W. The variation of the compass was 5° 31' E. All day we proceeded on a course N. 16° 35' E. and at sunset we were in the latitude of the Prince Henry, the Cumberland and Duke of Gloucester Islands and therefore, towards night, we bore up into the wind and tried to keep our position by making short tacks.

5th. At 6.0 a.m. at daybreak we again set our course N. 16° 35' E. and after about an hour we sighted land towards the north-east from the look-out and I proceeded direct towards it on a course N. 50° E., making more sail. At 9.0 a.m. we found ourselves at a distance of $1\frac{2}{3}$ miles from a small low-lying island in the middle of which there was a lagoon, with a small opening on the south-eastern side. I proceeded northward on a line parallel with the coral island, which is some half a mile in width and in places much less. At 10.0 a.m. we approached the northern extremity. I sent Lieutenant Torson ashore in a boat to a point where there appeared patches of thick low growth. Mr Simanov, Mr Bergh and Mr Demidov accompanied Mr Torson, and Mr Lazarev also sent a boat with his navigating officer. The day was very fine and from observations we fixed our position in Lat. 19° 11' 34" S., Long. 141° 17' 56" W. The centre of the island bore S. 26° E. from us and its position would therefore be Lat. 19° 12' 21" S., Long. 141° 16' W. Mr Simanov, from observations made ashore on the northern extremity, fixed the latitude at 19° 11' 10" S.; if to this is added half the length of the island (which is not more than $3\frac{1}{2}$ miles in length), the latitude of the centre of the island would be 19° 21' 53"; the island is $1\frac{3}{4}$ miles in breadth and 8 miles in circumference.[1]

---

[1] This island is now known as Manuhangi, one of the Tuamotu or Low Archipelago. The Russian ships had sailed past the Gloucester group which are also low.

Although this island resembles externally Prince Henry or Cumberland Island, both of which were discovered by Captain Wallis on June 13th, 1766, the latitude of Prince Henry Island differs from it by $11\frac{1}{2}$ minutes and the longitude by $13\frac{1}{2}$ minutes more to the westward; Cumberland Island lies 5 minutes more to the south and $19\frac{1}{2}$ minutes farther east. For the purposes of this comparison, I placed the position of the islands discovered by Wallis 24 minutes more to the westward, because he fixed Matavai Road at Otahiti Island 24 minutes farther to the westward of the true longitude determined by Captain Cook on his first voyage. This disparity in the position of the above-mentioned islands makes me think that Mr Wallis passed this island in stormy weather and in consequence made a mistake in reckoning the latitude of the island and took it for Prince Henry Island.

Having fixed the geographical position of the island, I signalled with a gun-shot to the boats to return from the shore and at 12.30 p.m. they arrived. Messrs Torson, Simanov, Bergh and Demidov informed me that this narrow strip of land consisted of coral of different colours; the trees were low and poor. They had shot some sea birds and brought back with them some fairly large sea-urchins (*Echinus*) with spikes or prickles about 6 inches in length of a lilac colour like slate pencils. We only found this particular species of all the many known kinds of sea-urchin in the Coral Islands. Mr Mikhailov brought back the fruit of a tree, called by naturalists *Pandanus*. The boat being hoisted, I proceeded on a course to the northward, inclining a little to the eastward. From 25 lunar distances taken by me we fixed the longitude at noon at 141° 22′ 6″ W.: from the same number of distances taken by Navigating Officer Paryadin, the longitude was 141° 19′ 6″ W.

While we were lying off the island, frigate birds and cormorants flew round about us: our best shot, the sailor Gaidukov, brought down a few of them. They were only wounded and lived for some time: they were eventually poisoned and the skins prepared for stuffing. A few of the cormorants belonged to the species called by some naturalists the "biting" (or "snapping") cormorants, because they bite at anyone who comes near and teases them. But all sea birds bite or snap and therefore the attempt to distinguish a species by such an additional adjective seems inadequate.

The frigate birds were seen to dive vertically down into the water from some height and to catch whatever was thrown out from the kitchen at the wake of the vessel. On examining these birds internally we found that the breast bone and the "wish bone" formed together one single bone, which probably enabled them to stand the impact of the water on their breasts when diving from such heights. At 5.0 p.m., when we were 10 miles distant from the island, we lost sight of it. From 9.0 p.m. until midnight we hauled close to the wind on the starboard tack. Mr Lazarev, carrying out the orders for the night signalled to him, followed the *Vostok*.

6th. There was a light wind. Clouds appearing at intervals did not obscure the gleam of the stars throughout the night. At 5.30 a.m., when it was daybreak, small groups of cocoa-nut palms were visible and we steered due east towards them. At 9.0 a.m. we were off the southern point of the island, about 1 mile from the grove of cocoa-nut palms, and we could see with the naked eye men armed with spears. All were copper-coloured and quite naked; they made signals to invite us ashore. I passed along the shore and two islanders ran along the shore parallel with the ships; finally they grew tired, stopped, looked back and returned to their fellows. A canoe was drawn up beside the cluster of cocoa-nut palms and farther in the lagoon two other canoes could be seen which were hastening to that spot. A heavy surf breaking with a loud roar on the coral reef prevented our sending any boat ashore. We could also see the opposite shore of the island at a distance of $1\frac{1}{2}$ miles. On the part of the island nearest the ships we could see some low sandy hummocks. At a few points a little higher up small trees and undergrowth were visible, the low-lying parts near the water were formed by the coral reef; and where the sea communicated through the reef with the lagoon, the cocoa-nut palms, distinguished by their height from the other trees, presented a very beautiful view. The northern and eastern sides of the island were more densely covered with growth, although some parts were bare. We could see a few islanders near the north-western end and the fires lit indicated that the island was fairly well populated.[1]

At noon by observation we were in Lat. 18° 06' 41" S., Long. 141° 03' 44" W. The west headland of the island bore north-east by north from us at a distance of $1\frac{1}{4}$ miles. We only just succeeded in

---

[1] The island of Hao, discovered by Bougainville in 1768 and called by him La Harpe. Cook visited it a year later and called it Bow Island on account of its apparent shape. Modern surveys show, however, that it resembles neither a harp nor a bow.

taking the meridian altitude, for a change in the wind to south by west brought up a mist and obscured the sun and for a short while fine rain fell. We determined the latitude of the northern extremity of the island as 18° 01′ 30″ S., Long. 140° 58′ 04″ W. The southern extremity of it lies in Lat. 18° 22′ 50″ S., Long. 140° 46′ 24″ W. The centre lies in Lat. 18° 12′ 10″ S., Long. 140° 52′ 32″ W. The island extends N. 40° W. for 25 miles. Its greatest width is 7 miles, its circumference being 39 miles. Coral reefs were also visible inside the lagoon, a few showing above the surface of the water lying parallel with the island, and the milky appearance, in patches, of the water indicated shallows. This island was discovered by Captain Cook and called by him Bow Island.

In the afternoon after proceeding 1 mile farther to north-north-east we turned northwards, inclining slightly to the east, with the intention of continuing on that course to latitude 16° and then, proceeding on that parallel westward, to survey the region lying between the "Angry Sea" and the "Dangerous Archipelago".

Although a great number of vessels have passed through the Pacific on their way to Otahiti and other islands, the area along this parallel in the neighbourhood of Otahiti has never been surveyed, apparently solely on account of the threatening names given to this part of the world by the Dutch Captain Schouten* and the French Commander Bougainville.† At 2.30 p.m. we sighted land from the look-out, extending from north-east to east by south, and I therefore kept close to the wind on a course S. 55° E. to the south-eastern extremity of the land as far as the light south-easterly wind would allow. At 3.30 the wind shifted to the east and prevented our approaching nearer, but until nightfall we passed along the western part of it at a distance of 3 miles. We were able to examine the shore well and noted that, like Bow Island, it consisted of narrow low-lying coral reefs with a lagoon in the middle. The portion which lay nearest to us was covered with woods and undergrowth. At various points we could see cocoa-nut palms rising high above the other trees, and we noted two small openings or entrances into the lagoon, across one of which a few

* Schouten and Le Maire, the first to navigate along the parallel of latitude 13°, called this the "Angry Sea" owing to the bad weather, strong winds and dangerous coral reefs encountered there.

† M. Bougainville navigated between the latitudes 18° and 19° and found low-lying coral islands and, on account of the dangers to navigation among them, called this part the "Dangerous Archipelago".

islanders could be seen wading. The western side, on which the surf was breaking, was lower and consisted of a coral reef showing above the water with some undergrowth on it. At 6.0 p.m. owing to thick weather we could not see anything except fires lit in two places on the central headland where the large cocoa-nut palm grove is situated, near which of course the greater proportion of the islanders live.

7th. At night we tried to keep our position under very little sail, but in the morning, at daybreak, we found that the stream had set us away from the shore and, as I intended to stand in close to the island in order to see something of its inhabitants, I beat up towards the island again; but a constantly changing light wind prevented our reaching the northern end of the island before 2.0 p.m. of the 8th.

8th. The eastern shore from the central headland as far as this (northern) end was also covered with wood and some cocoa-nut palms, although with fewer than the part from the centre to the south of the island, along its western shore.

Near the northern end on the western side of the island the lagoon communicates with the sea by a small entrance. The eastern side facing the trade wind is always beaten by a heavy surf and consists mainly of coral ledges.

Lying off the northern end of the island, I went ashore in the boat, taking with me Messrs Mikhailov and Demidov; Mr Lazarev started off in the cutter accompanied by Messrs Galkin, Annenkov and Novosilski. All the officers and men were armed in case of an unfriendly reception on the part of the natives. When we were close to the coral shore, on which a heavy surf was breaking, we found it difficult to get ashore without danger of damaging the boat on the coral bottom. Meanwhile some sixty native men rushed down to the shore and their number was constantly increased by others. A few of them had beards and all had short curly black hair. The islanders were of medium height, the face and body being burned a bronze colour by the strong heat of the sun, as in the case of all the islanders of the Pacific Ocean. They were naked save for a narrow band covering their loins. They were all armed with long spears and a few of them carried in the other hand a wooden club with which they, like the New Zealanders, hit their enemies on the head. The women stood a little farther off along the wood about 50 yards in the rear, also armed with spears and clubs; they wore a sort of matting hanging from the waist to the knee. As we approached to get ashore the islanders, with frightful shouts and brandishing their spears, prevented our landing. We endeavoured by friendly gestures and by throwing presents ashore for them, to reconcile and appease them, but without success. They eagerly picked up the proffered objects but would not consent to allow us to land. We then fired a shot over their heads and they were all terrified; the women and some of the young boys rushed into the wood and all the others sat down. Seeing they had suffered no harm, they took courage, but after each shot they sat down in the water or splashed water over themselves; they then taunted us and laughed at us that we could do them no harm. This clearly proves that they were quite ignorant of the fatal effects of firearms. Seeing the flash of our muskets, they probably thought that we wished to burn them and for that reason they threw water over themselves. When the *Mirnyi* approached and, on a signalled order, fired a cannon ball into the wood over the heads of the islanders, they were all frightened, crouched down, and splashed water over themselves. The women and some of the young boys fled and set fire to the trees along the shore, forming a long unbroken belt of crackling fire which covered their retreat. Of all the presents they seemed to be specially delighted with a bell which we had rung for them. I threw a few more small bells to them, thinking that their pleasant tones would establish friendly relations between us, but as soon as the boats again attempted to approach the shore, the temper of the islanders, with wild shouts, turned from the greatest joy to wildest fury.

Such obstinacy compelled us to turn back. Their obstinacy was of course due to their ignorance of the effects of our firearms and to our inferior numbers. Had we determined to shoot down a few of them I am certain that all the others would have taken to flight and that we should have been able to land without any hindrance. But having got sufficiently near to satisfy our curiosity, I had no particular desire to land on this island, all the less as, although it might offer opportunities for collecting specimens especially of coral, shells and plants, landing would not have been of much use to us since I understand little of natural history and we had no naturalist with us. Not wishing to shoot the natives, I left their closer acquaintanceship with Europeans to the future. When we had got some distance away from the island, the women rushed out of the wood on to the shore and, lifting up their dresses, presented their posterior parts to us, slapped themselves and danced about, probably to show their contempt of our feebleness.

A few of the crew asked for permission to fire at them to teach these natives a lesson, but I refused to permit it.[1]

From observations we found the position of the island to be in Lat. 17° 49′ 30″ S., Long. 140° 40′ W. Its greatest length was 16 miles in a north-easterly direction, the width 7 miles. I called this island "Möller Island" in honour of Vice-Admiral Moller, under whose flag I had commanded the 44-gun frigate *Tikhvinskaya Bogoroditza*. I proceeded on a northerly course from Möller Island, inclining slightly towards the east, to make the parallel of 16°.

9th. It was a moonlit night; the light east wind shifted more to the north-east as we reduced our latitude. At noon we were in Lat. 16° 46′ 21″ S., Long. 141° 01′ 54″ W. The variation was 6° E. The thermometer rose to 77° F. in the shade and at midnight stood as high as 75° F. No case of complaint on the part of any member of my crew of the continual unbearable heat came to my notice while we were navigating among the islands.

10th. From noon until 6.0 a.m. of the following morning the wind continually varied, shifting backwards and forwards two or three points. I concluded, in consequence, that we were navigating to leeward of an undiscovered island. We observed a large whale; we had not encountered any for a long time. At daybreak we heard with delight that land had been sighted to windward from the top and we then indeed saw it lying to the east-north-east; from daybreak we began to beat up towards it. In reply to a request from Mr Lazarev by signal, I gave permission to bring the coast due east of him at noon to fix the exact latitude.

Towards noon, when the vessels were 12 miles distant from the shore, the natives surprised us by their great daring. From the look-out we noted first one canoe and then a second and a third, and finally as many as six on their way out to us. They approached fairly close to the ships and stopped abreast of them. They called out to us but apparently could not make up their minds to come alongside. Finally one canoe did approach the stern of the *Mirnyi*, then came close to the *Vostok*, and the natives in her caught hold of a rope which we let down from the stern.

They were all of medium height, thin rather than stout. Face and

---

[1] This island where the friendly approaches of the Russians were so disgracefully received is now called Amanu. It was discovered in 1774 by Varela, a fact of which Bellingshausen was unaware when he named it Moller Island.

body were swarthy and therein chiefly differed from Europeans. Their hair was tied in a knot on the top of the head, they had small beards and all wore a rope made of grass round their waists, and a strip to cover their privy parts, which constituted the whole of their clothing.

I wished to obtain one of these strips, but not one of the islanders would on any account part with it. This is a proof that exposing the part covered by it is regarded as an act of indecency.

The canoes in which the natives came off to meet us at this distance from the shore were about 20 feet in length and wide enough for two people to sit abreast; they were made of several planks very skilfully put together; the cross-section of these canoes resembles in appearance a low milk-pan; there was an outrigger on one side to steady the boat and the oars were almost the same as those used by all the islanders of the Pacific Ocean. The canoes travelled fairly well and are better suited for the open sea than any of the others hitherto known to me. There were three or four active lithe islanders to a canoe, each with a lasso made of plaited grasses, a spear and a small club. It seemed to us, to judge by these indications, that they had come out to attack us from different sides and if possible to get possession of the ships. It is possible that, having never seen any European vessels, they had taken them at that distance for canoes going from one island to another on business or on a warlike expedition, and thought that they might overpower them. When they approached they were probably astonished at the great size of the ships, out of all proportion to their strength and warlike skill; all the same, hanging on to the rope at the stern, they continually pulled at it in order to cut if off. They treacherously tried to wound one of the officers with a spear who, leaning out of a porthole, endeavoured to assure them of our friendly feelings. Mr Lazarev and I offered them axes, some printed linen, silver and bronze medals, but we were unable to persuade them to come nearer, still less to come on board; at about 4.0 p.m. they started for the shore again.

The wind shifted a little to the north and enabled the ships to reach the shore at the same time as the islanders. We turned on the starboard tack and proceeded along the western shore, at times within a mile of it. The islanders landed within sight of us, pulled the canoes up with the help of their comrades on the shore, lifted them on to their shoulders and carried them to the lagoon inside; then, without delay, they set fire to the trees and undergrowth at several points along the shore against us and made a huge blaze. I believe that the setting alight of these lines of trees is a hostile warning, and is a signal of the approach and attack of the enemy, as had happened to us at our meeting with the inhabitants of Moller Island.[1]

The centre of the island is in Lat. 15° 51′ 05″ S., Long. 140° 49′ 19″ W. Its form is that of a spherical triangle with the acute angle pointing south-south-east. One side, facing north, curves inwards and at this point clumps of cocoa-nut palms are particularly noticeable; all the other sides of the island are low. We were so near that we could quite easily distinguish the red coral from the white; they turn into lime under the action of the sun's rays. The circumference of this island, which I called "Count Arakcheev Island", is about 16 miles. The thermometer stood at 78° F. and at midnight it fell to 76° F. At 6.0 p.m., when the *Vostok* was proceeding along the western side of the island and was already off the north-western extremity, evening fell; we took in a reef in the topsails and I proceeded westward under very little sail, inclining slightly to the southward, to keep near latitude 16°, as I intended to travel westward on this parallel. In order to interest the islanders and impress them with the power of European fire, we sent up some rockets from both ships; some of them scattered variously coloured stars in the air. Such an artistic display of pyrotechnics, fascinating as it still is even to the enlightened European, must have astonished these savage inhabitants of a little island in mid-ocean. They could never have seen anything to resemble it, except falling meteors, and then only on a reduced scale owing to the distance and without the accompaniment of noise and flashing lights.

11*th*. At 1.30 a.m. with clear moonlight we were going at 3 to 4 knots. I signalled to proceed full and by, so as to remain near the spot for the night. There was a light north-east by north wind; the swell from the east was so slight that it also indicated the existence of land to the eastward of Arakcheev Island. At 6.0 a.m., at daybreak, we bore away from the wind, steered a west-south-west course and made more sail. At 11.0 a.m. land was sighted to the north-west from the look-out; I altered course west-north-west and sailed close-hauled under a northerly wind.

---

[1] This was Bellingshausen's first new discovery in the Tuamotu group. It is now known by its native name of Angatau and it is worthy of record that the islanders are still somewhat uncivilized.

From observations at noon our position was Lat. 15° 53' 25" S., Long. 141° 40' 22" W.

We had so light a wind throughout the day that I could not rely on the accuracy of our measured speed, which was our basis for determining the size of the island. During such a light wind the speed of the vessels is affected by the unknown speed and direction of the stream and I therefore hove to for the night near the island. We saw a whale spouting, also a few flying fish. These fish are no larger than a herring and have unusually large and fairly broad side fins. To avoid their enemies, the bonitos, they rise out of the water on the slant and then fly in a straight line not more than 20 feet above the surface when there is no wind. When the lateral fins begin to dry, they slope their flight back towards the water and plunge into it; if the wind happens to strike the fish sideways whilst it is in flight, its flight describes a curve to leeward and according to the increasing force of the wind this curve bends more and more.

As no European vessels had ever visited or sighted this island before, the attention of the natives had been concentrated on the *Vostok* and *Mirnyi* as enemies. When it was dark, I ordered twelve rockets at once to be sent up. These blazing streams of lights must have inspired these people, who could never before have seen anything like it, with unusual fear.

12*th*. At 1.0 a.m. we turned back towards the shore; the very light north-east wind continued until 9.0 a.m., then it shifted to east-north-east and freshened. I turned S.W. by S. ½ W. along the southern shore at a distance of 1 mile until we lay off the southern cape.

This is also a coral island with a lagoon in the middle. The eastern coral shore is very narrow, only about 200 yards in width and almost quite bare; only at rare intervals isolated shrubs could be seen. The northern, western and southern shores were all covered with trees, amongst them some cocoa-nut palms.

Smoke rose from various points amongst the trees, showing that the island was inhabited. From observations, the position of the centre of the island is Lat. 15° 47' 20" S., Long. 142° 11' W. It lies N.N.E. ½ E. and S.S.W. ½ W. and is 12 miles long and 3 miles wide. I called this island which we had discovered "Prince Volkhonski Island".

We soon sighted ahead another island bearing S. 28° W. from the southern extremity of Prince Volkhonski Island and separated from it by a strait 4 miles wide.[1] Proceeding towards it, we lay at noon off the north-eastern side of this island a mile from the shore. From observations we fixed the position of the *Vostok* at Lat. 15° 57′ 52″ S., Long. 142° 12′ 11″ W. From noon until nightfall we proceeded along the narrow eastern coral shore at a distance of from ½ to 2 miles; it is covered with scattered undergrowth and low trees. Surf was breaking heavily on this coral shore. The northern and western sides from which the lagoon was visible were quite covered with trees, and at various points on the north-western shore we could see smoke rising up out of the trees, which showed that the island was inhabited. Mr Lazarev informed me that he could see people and canoes on the shore.

The northern extremity of the island lies in Lat. 15° 55′ 45″ S., Long. 142° 15′ 19″ W. The southern extremity lies in Lat. 16° 13′ 35″ S., Long. 142° 24′ 32″ W.; the centre in Lat. 16° 05′ 35″ S., Long. 142° 19′ 00″ W. The island lies along a N. by E. ½ E. and S. by W. ½ W. direction. I made the length 21 miles, but Mr Lazarev found it to be only 16 miles and 7 miles wide at its greatest width, with a circumference of 44 miles. I called this island "Field-Marshal Prince Barclay de Tolly Island".

The difference between the length of the island as determined by me and that found by Mr Lazarev arose from the fact that Mr Lazarev proceeded along the southern part in the dark and mistook a salient, where the shore changes its direction farther to the westward, for the southern cape, concluding therefore that the island was 5 miles shorter than the length calculated by the *Vostok*. Captain Cook on his first voyage round the world determined the size and position of Bow Island, discovered by him, when proceeding along the southern side of the island. Despite the fact that it was night, he continued observations of position by the sound of the surf breaking on the shore but, since his course carried him gradually away from the direction of the shore and, as this distance increased, the sound made by the surf gradually died away, he decided the size of the island rather prematurely and calculated the length as 13 instead of 35 miles. Such mistakes often happen at sea. At 6.0 p.m., as it was already dark, we took in all extra sail, partly as a precaution for the night and partly to give the *Mirnyi* the opportunity of overtaking us. The speed of the

---

[1] These two islands, Takume and Raroia, were also new discoveries. The native names, both more euphonious and appropriate than the Russian names, now hide the fact that Bellingshausen was the first to report them.

Vostok was thus reduced to 1½ knots and I altered course south-south-west until midnight.

13*th*. At 6.0 a.m. we set a course due west in Lat. 16° 23′ S. The very few clouds did not obscure the moon and stars, which lit up the whole horizon during the night. The *Mirnyi* caught us up and we were able by daybreak to proceed under all sail.

When it was full daylight we sighted from the look-out a low-lying shore to the W.S.W. ¼ W. and I altered course towards it. Very soon we discovered similar land towards the south. I preferred to examine the latter first as it lay on our course to the second, and to do so we turned a little southward. Beautiful weather favoured us; but there was only a very light wind which did not allow us to proceed as quickly as we wished.

At 11.0 a.m. we passed along within half a mile of the north-western cape of the low-lying coral reef, washed by the roaring surf. The whole extent of the island lay open before us. The northern shore was high and covered by a low wood, whilst on the other shores the trees only grew in places. We remarked only three trunks of cocoa-nut palms, and they were without leaves, perhaps uprooted by a gale, or fallen with old age. The surf broke over the high coral reef with a tremendous roar, and flowed across the land into the lagoon inside the island. It lies N. ¼ W. and S. ½ W., is 7 miles along, 2 miles wide and 17 miles in circumference.

Very soon I noted with pleasure a canoe which was coming out towards the *Vostok*. To let it come up to us I hove to, whereupon without any detours the canoe, which contained two men, came on my invitation straight alongside. We were surprised at the unusual audacity of these islanders; one of them at once clambered on to the gangway and proposed to us to barter hooks, made of mussel and ear shells, which they use for catching fish. He then drew a small packet, tied up with cocoa-nut fibre, from his waist cloth, tore off the fibre with his teeth and handed me a few small pearls. In answer to my question if he had any more, he replied, "Nioi, Nioi," i.e. "Many, many," and pointed towards the shore. When we asked him if there were any women ashore he immediately sent his companion, apparently a servant, ashore in his canoe whilst he himself remained on board. We gathered from his talk that he was a chief from the island Anyui and had arrived on the island, off which we were lying, for trading purposes. As it was now dinner-time I invited our guest to sit down at table next to me. He partook of everything, trying to imitate all our actions with the greatest care; but found the proper use of a fork a difficult accomplishment, since he was afraid of pricking himself with it.

Meanwhile Mr Lazarev, with some of the officers from both ships, went off to the shore in two boats but found, on approaching, that there was no possibility of landing owing to the submerged coral reefs and the violent surf, and therefore returned to the ships. On this occasion they also lost an anchor which had got caught so firmly in the coral that they had been unable to raise it. After dinner we dressed our guest up in the red uniform of the Imperial Guard. His inward delight was plainly expressed on his face. Then, amidst three cheers, I hung a silver medal round his neck and, as a sign of friendship, we rubbed noses. In order to enhance the value of the medal each of us went up to him, looked at it closely and admired it. After this the islander would probably take great care of the medal, at least until he met the next Europeans; he would then learn the full value of our gift, since the medal would secure for him new acquaintances and thereby fresh presents as well. The messenger had landed quite easily in his small canoe, which was flat, light and without a keel. He returned very soon, bringing with him a young woman, some dried cuttle-fish and some shelled mussels, dried and strung on to bark fibre. It is probable that this food which he brought from the island represents the object of their trading and their roamings over the inhabited islands. We invited the woman into the cabin, I made her a present of a mirror, ear-rings, a ring and a piece of red cloth, which she wrapped round her body from the waist to the knee; her own fine matting plaited skilfully of grass she left with us, and it is now kept in the Museum of the Imperial Admiralty Department among the rarities. She showed great modesty in exposing herself as little as possible in changing her dress. Our guests were of medium height with curly hair; the Chief was tattooed on the thighs and haunches in a blue-black colour, the marking resembling that on the faces of the islanders on the Marquis de Mendoza Islands and New Zealand. He was naked save for the loin-cloth common to the South Sea Islanders. The woman was not tall but of a full figure. Her hair was black and curly; her pleasant swarthy face was lit up by bright black eyes. Mr Mikhailov made a very careful sketch of our visitors, the Chief standing and the man and woman sitting. His sketch also includes the view of the coral shore and the wood growing on it.

At noon we fixed the position of "Nihera Island", for so our visitors called it, in Lat. 16° 42′ 40″ S., Long. 142° 44′ 50″ W.[1]

The islanders had a large canoe in the lagoon which they use for visiting the other islands: this canoe lay behind the wood from our position so that we could not see it well. Very probably the islanders who came on board to us had friends who did not show themselves. At 4.0 p.m. I took our guests a little farther inshore. They then said good-bye to us, loaded up their little canoe with all the treasures they had received from us, and went ashore.

Having finished my survey of Nihera Island, I turned north-west towards the island which we had first sighted at daybreak from the look-out to west-south-west of us. There was a light south-easterly wind blowing. For safety we remained for the night in one position making short tacks; in the morning we made more sail but we were soon becalmed. The land was visible from the look-out to the northward. At 9.0 a.m., although we made use of the favourable light variable winds, we made slow progress and it was not until 10.0 a.m. that we sighted a low-lying shore from the forecastle. We then set our course N. 50° W. along the southern part of the island; this course brought us up to the south-western part.

At noon our observations put the *Vostok* in Lat. 16° 28′ 38″ S., Long. 143° 07′ 26″ W.; the island extended from N. 68° E. to N. 29° 40′ W.; the nearest headland of coral reef lay at a distance of 3 miles.[2] All along the southern shore we could see the rushing belt of silvery foam of the surf, which broke with a loud roar on this wall of coral, which formed a natural mole. It was possible to see the northern shore across the lagoon and it seemed well wooded. On the southern shore, on the contrary, there were only a few scattered low trees, shrubs and undergrowth. At various points the surf broke across the reef. We observed two canoes in the lagoon, under sail, but except for the triangular sail with one point downwards we could see nothing at that distance. I believe that the natives come here from other islands in search of food and that this island is uninhabited, as we could not see any signs of habitation; there were, besides, no cocoa-nut palms, which could furnish food and sustenance to inha-

[1] Nihiru Island. It is a circular atoll, fairly well wooded, but has never had permanent inhabitants.

[2] Taenga Island, which nowadays has a small but by no means fixed population of about a hundred persons, so that Bellingshausen's suspicions were practically correct.

bitants. The island lies in Lat. 16° 21' 45" S., Long. 143° 05' 36" W. It lies W.N.W. and E.S.E., is 15·5 miles in length, 5·5 miles in width and 34 miles in circumference. I called this island, which we had discovered, "Lieutenant-General Yermolov Island". From midday until 5.0 p.m. we had a light south-west wind; after a brief period of calm it shifted to the south-east quarter. I continued my course parallel with the shore of the island until 5.0 p.m., and then rounded the wooded western part at a distance of $3\frac{1}{2}$ miles. Mr Lazarev now signalled to me that well-wooded land had been sighted to the south-west from the look-out. Having completed my survey of Yermolov Island, I proceeded close-hauled on the starboard tack during the night so as to approach this new wooded island just mentioned. In the evening we saw a fire lit there and soon after 9.0 p.m. we saw the surf breaking right ahead of us. I gave instructions to go about on the port tack and to shorten sail so as to await daylight.

15th. At midnight the temperature was 75° F. in the open air, and below decks, where the crew slept, 80° F.; to Russians, born and bred in a moderate climate, such a heat would seem almost unbearable, nevertheless it did not have any bad effect upon the health of the crew. At 3.30 a.m. I again turned towards the shore and at daybreak the eastern wooded headland lay to windward of us at a distance of 8 miles.[1] I was anxious to approach nearer, but in consequence of the variable winds I was unable to do so and therefore proceeded along the coral shore, which was covered with bushes, at a distance of a mile and a half. Towards the east we could see the narrow entrance into the lagoon. As the wind began to freshen a little, we proceeded along the wooded shore, which extended in a westerly direction. We soon saw a canoe, containing two people, start out from the shore. I hove to and took in the main topsail, but the islanders did not dare to approach the vessel and therefore, without further loss of time, I filled the sails and proceeded along the narrow shore, hidden by undergrowth. This shore forms the northern side of the coral island and is separated from the southern shore, over which the sea was breaking, by a lagoon. The weather changed in the morning and we had clouds with rain; at times the mist increased so much that the shore, which was only a mile away, disappeared from view; towards midday the weather improved.

[1] Makemo Island, which is about 40 miles in length. It has two villages, and the inhabitants, about two hundred in number, are expert divers for pearls.

Natives of the coral island of Nihera

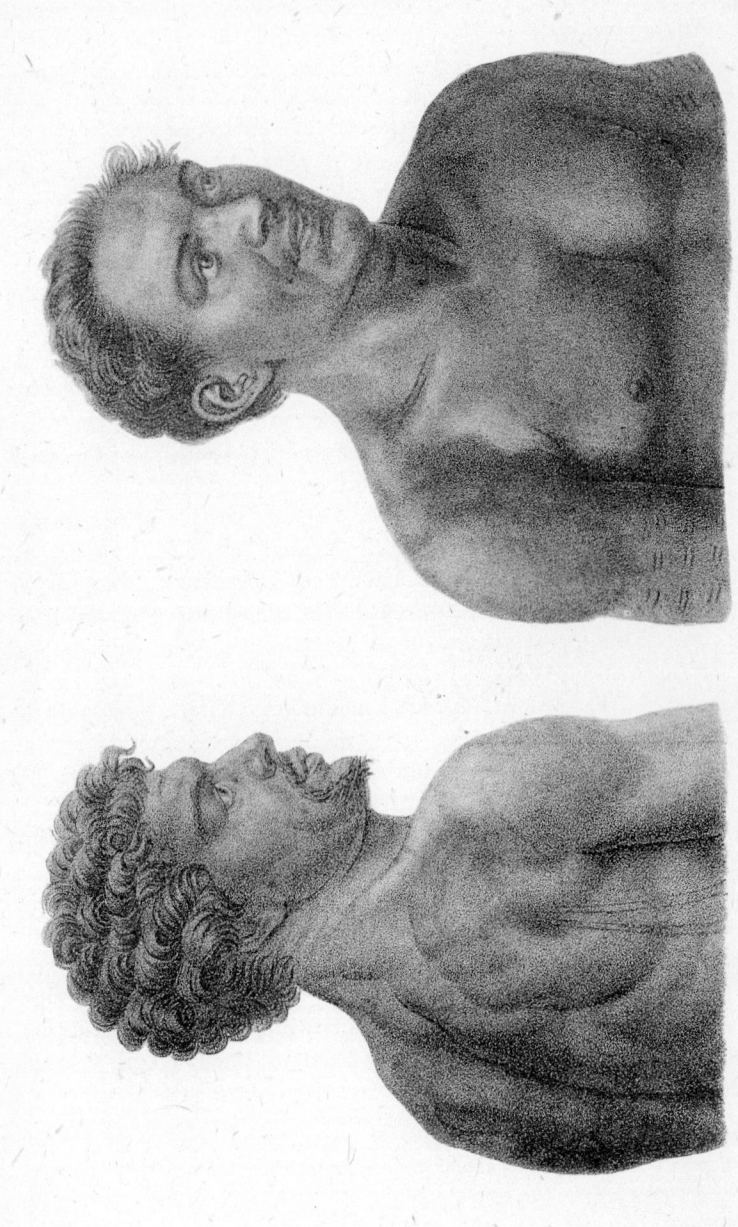

Natives of the Palliser Islands

At noon the *Vostok* from observations was in Lat. 16° 25′ 38″ S., Long. 143° 57′ 57″ W. At this time the western cape of the island lay south-south-west from us 3 miles distant. On the north-western side we perceived a narrow opening into the lagoon within the island.

The north-eastern corner lies in Lat. 16° 36′ 40″ S., Long. 143° 24′ 32″ W.; the western extremity is in Lat. 16° 27′ 35″ S., Long. 143° 56′ W. The island extends W.N.W. ½ W. and E.S.E. ½ E. and is 32 miles in length, 7 miles in width, and 71 miles in circumference. We proceeded along the largest and finest part of the island, but we only saw these two men and neither any sign of fire, nor even a single cocoa-nut palm, which might have provided food for the natives. We therefore concluded that this island too, which I called "Prince Golenitschev-Kutuzov-Smolenski Island", is uninhabited, and that the two men were probably there merely in search of food or raw materials.[1] We had not as yet got clear of the island, when two others were reported from the look-out, the first south-west by south and the second west by south from us.

At 2.45 p.m., when the vessel was in Lat. 16° 32′ 35″ S., Long. 144° 04′ 25″ W., we sighted the well-wooded northern shore of an island lying south of the vessel and about 10 miles distant, judging by the eye. We were unable to approach this island owing to the head wind, and were therefore unable to determine its real dimensions. The northern wooded shore is in Lat. 16° 43′ S., Long. 144° 11′ W. The length of the part we observed is about 11 miles. I named this island "General Raevski Island".[2]

Captain Cook during his second voyage round the world, on his way from New Zealand to Otahiti Island, sighted a low-lying coral island with a lagoon on August 13th, 1773, and called it "Adventure Island". This island, amongst those so far discovered by Europeans, is the nearest to Raevski Island.

Captain Cook does not mention the size and direction of Adventure Island. If it is one of the large islands of this archipelago, then it may well be that the northern shore of Raevski Island is one and the same as Adventure Island and that both form one large island. If, however, Adventure Island is only a medium-sized or small island, Raevski Island must be a new discovery.

---

[1] The island, Makemo, had been discovered, however, in 1803.
[2] The name Raevski has been kept for a group of three islands in this position, the most southern of which, Tepoto, was the one discovered by Bellingshausen.

We had a favourable wind for the survey of the next island, which we sighted to the westward. I shaped a course parallel with the eastern side and then rounded the northern part. Both sides were covered with small trees. On the eastern side we noted two narrow openings into the lagoon within the island, which is in Lat. 16° 28′ 35″ S., Long. 144° 17′ 33″ W., lying N.W. by W. and S.E. by E., 12·5 miles in length, 6·5 miles in width and 30 miles in circumference.[1] We observed no inhabitants. I called this island "General Graf Osten-Saken Island". We proceeded with all speed to carry out our examination of the island before nightfall and consequently we got considerably ahead of the *Mirnyi*. Darkness fell just as we had completed our survey of Graf Osten-Saken Island. Lying off the shore, we took a reef in the topsails and shortened sail for the night. The *Mirnyi* was soon able to come up to us and Mr Lazarev sent us one of his boats with some fresh fish which he had received as a present from the two men in the small canoe, off Golenitschev-Kutuzov Island.

Mr Lazarev told me that these islanders also had their thighs tattooed in a blue-black colour like Eri Tatano, our visitor from Nihera Island, and that they appeared to have seen Europeans before, as they begged for razors, pointing to their beards, and readily ate everything that was put before them without any fear. They were given medals and various European articles.

In the course of the day we saw a whale and a number of flying fish. We had a beautiful bright moonlight night with few clouds. We made short tacks so as to remain near this point.

16*th*. At daybreak low-lying land was again sighted towards the south-west.[2] We shook out the reefs in the topsails, made more sail and proceeded on a south by west course until 9.0 a.m. and, when at a distance of 1 mile from the island, we turned to the west along a narrow wooded shore, at times less than half a mile distant. At 10.0 a.m. we rounded the western extremity of the island; from this point the shore turns at a right angle to the south. The position of this island, which I named "Admiral Chichagov Island",[3] is in Lat. 16° 50′ 05″ S., Long. 144° 52′ 43″ W. It runs in an E. by N. and

---

[1] Tahanea Island, which is only occasionally visited by canoes to gather copra.
[2] Faaite Island, which in spite of an abundant water supply has few really permanent inhabitants.
[3] Chichagov was a Russian admiral who at one stage commanded the Russian fleet in the wars against Gustavus Adolphus of Sweden with considerable success. He lived to fight against Napoleon.

W. by S. direction and is 11 miles long and 3½ miles wide. A large lagoon lies in the middle of the island.

On completing our examination we proceeded farther to the westward towards another island which had been sighted from the look-out as we lay off Chichagov Island. At 10.45 a.m. we approached this new land on a course N. 28° W. and, after rounding the north-eastern cape at a distance of a quarter of a mile, we proceeded along the narrow coral shore.[1]

At noon from observations the position of the *Vostok* proved to be Lat. 16° 41' 57" S., Long. 145° 09' 53" W. The northern shore of the island then lay 1' 10" S. of the ship; we proceeded on a west by north course parallel with the shore. At 1.30 we were already abreast of the western point.

This island is very similar to those in its vicinity and is also of coral formation. The northern side is covered with trees; the other sides form a sort of mole on which the surf breaks with a loud noise; on the eastern side there is a narrow opening into the extensive lagoon within the island. We observed a few cocoa-nut palms on the northern shore at a distance of 2 miles from the western cape. At this point also we saw two men who very probably, like those on Nihera and Kutuzov Islands, had come to gather food and other things. The latitude of this island, which I called "Graf Miloradovich Island",[2] is 16° 47' 20" S., Long. 145° 12' 43" W. and extends W.N.W. ½ W. and E.S.E. ½ E. for 15 miles, its width being 5½ miles and its circumference 39 miles.

When passing the western cape of Miloradovich Island we observed land to the north-west, towards which I proceeded without delay.[3] Soon after 2.0 p.m. we lay off its southern point at a distance of 3 miles, and I sailed on different courses which took us past the south-eastern end at a distance of about half a mile. Both the southern and south-eastern points were covered with woods and joined by a low-

---

[1] Fakarava Island, where Robert Louis Stevenson stayed for a few months in 1888 and described very fully in his book, *In the South Seas*.

[2] This was the Miloradovich who was the central figure in a scene during the evacuation of Moscow before the advancing army of Napoleon. The garrison of the Kremlin was marching out of the city with a band playing. The fiery Miloradovich rebuked the officer commanding, who quoted a rule laid down by Peter the Great that on surrender of a fortress a garrison should go out with music. "But did Peter the Great lay down the rule about the surrender of Moscow? Bid your music cease." Miloradovich was shot in 1825 during the riotous proceedings of the proclamation of Nicholas I, successor to Alexander.

[3] Toau Island, visited now by the inhabitants of Fakarava Island to collect copra.

lying coral shore, on which the surf broke with considerable force in a long line of silvery foam. Having rounded the southern cape, we proceeded along the narrow winding coral shore, with clumps of trees and occasionally a little undergrowth; there were places where nothing was to be seen except the sterile coral which had turned into limestone. At 5.30 p.m., before dusk, we were lying off a point about the middle of the island when we observed some forty people standing on a bare narrow neck of land. A few of them had woven cloaks or mats thrown over the shoulders; they waved to us with mats or stuffs tied to long poles. Near to where the islanders stood large boats were hauled up on the shore, one of which had two masts. I was extremely sorry that the lateness of the hour, the strong wind and the heavy surf on the shore prevented our landing. Both vessels lay off it at a distance of 1 mile. There was a fresh wind with squalls from east by south blowing direct on the shore. We were therefore compelled to haul off and lie well outside the range of possible danger during the night, with the result that at nightfall I was carrying more sail than would ordinarily have been justified by the state of the wind.

17*th*. The night was so dark that it would have been easier to run ashore than to get clear. There were heavy black clouds in the sky with a strong wind, squalls and rain. We hove to for the night under very little sail without getting farther than 15 miles off the land; i.e. a distance at which on the previous evening, at sunset, the land had not been visible from the look-out.

At daybreak we again turned towards the island against a fresh wind which prevented the vessels from reaching the same spot where, on the previous evening, we had observed the people on the shore. At 7.30 a.m., being then below the middle cape at a distance of 5 miles, we bore away on a course N. by W. ½ W. parallel with the narrow strip of shore, partly overgrown with shrubs and trees, but in places quite bare; we observed a few cocoa-nut palms at a distance of about 2 miles from the northern point. After rounding this point at 9.30 a.m. we altered course west-south-west and, having reached a point about 5 miles from the northern end, we found ourselves off a narrow entrance into the lagoon. There was a considerable ripple on the water near the entrance, probably due to the force and set of the tidal streams. The distance between the north and north-western points is 11 miles; the shore is overgrown in places by trees and undergrowth, but the greater part is bare coral. The western shore, apart from the wooded headlands, consists of a coral reef. Owing to its distance we were unable to observe it in detail, but we could see the high silvery line of the surf running down the entire side of the island, which I called "Count Wittgenstein Island".[1] The northern point lies in Lat. 16° 04' 50" S., Long. 145° 33' 55" W. The north-eastern point is in Lat. 16° 09' 20" S., Long. 145° 44' 31" W. The south-eastern point is in Lat. 16° 29' 45" S., Long. 145° 18' W. The southern point is in Lat. 16° 33' 30" S., Long. 145° 23' 18" W. The middle point is in Lat. 16° 20' 40" S., Long. 145° 33' W.

Although, as I have stated above, we had observed some people on the island, I believe that they must have come merely for food or fishing and had collected near their boats drawn up on the beach. Whilst the *Vostok* was lying off the northern cape of Count Wittgenstein Island at a distance of about 1 mile, we had observed from the look-out land to the west-north-west separated from this island by a strait about 9 miles broad. Soon after 10.0 a.m., having completed our survey of Wittgenstein Island, I directed my course towards the southern extremity of this newly observed land.

At noon we were in Lat. 16° 04' 28" S., Long. 145° 49' 04" W. The wooded southern point of the new land lay on a bearing N. 58° W. from us, at a distance of about 3 miles, and the equally wooded south-eastern point north-east 4 miles. The shore between these two headlands consists mainly of bare coral.

After midday we proceeded towards the eastern extremity and then along the northern side of the narrow coral strip of partly wooded shore. In the lagoon within the island were numbers of small wooded islets and coral reefs showing above the water. At 4.45 p.m. we found the northern headland and beyond it observed a narrow entrance into the lagoon. On the western point there were some large rocks which had the appearance of huts when seen from a distance. The southern shore consists for the most part of bare coral with some scattered trees; although we were sometimes only half a mile distant from the island, we did not see any signs of inhabitants. We found its position to be as follows:

The eastern extremity is in Lat. 16° 00' 40" S., Long. 145° 47' 20" W. The western extremity is in Lat. 15° 53' 35" S., Long. 146° 06' 16" W. The centre of the island is in Lat. 15° 55' 40" S., Long. 145° 56' W.

---

[1] Count Wittgenstein was one of the Russian generals who so harassed Napoleon at the crossing of the Beresina.

It extends E.S.E. and W.N.W. and is 19 miles in length, 6 miles in width and 46 miles in circumference.

I admit that this island may be the same as that discovered by Captain Cook on his route from the Marquis de Mendoza Islands to the Society Islands on April 19th, 1773, and named, together with three others, the "Palliser Islands". I shall distinguish them by numbers, as they were discovered one after the other. When Captain Cook passed along Palliser Island I and lay off its southern end (in Lat. 15° 31′ S., Long. 146° 23′ W.), he observed from the masthead land towards the south-east; and if his line of sight was extended in that direction for 24 miles, Captain Cook would see the island now discovered by us. As we were off its northern extremity, we saw towards the north-west by west that same shore off which Captain Cook lay, namely Palliser Island I. The island off which we were lying is Palliser Island II. This island is called Elizabeth Island on the Arrowsmith chart, its position being in the same latitude, but 12 minutes more to the eastward. There can be no doubt that Palliser Island II is the same as the Elizabeth Island on the Arrowsmith chart. When about a mile to the west of the western point of Palliser Island II, we observed land towards the west from the look-out. But it was already growing dark and for the sake of safety during the night, I bore away close-hauled in a south by west direction under very little sail, with a fresh trade wind. The sky was overcast with occasional moonlight.

18th. After midnight the clouds dispersed, the moon shone brightly and the wind became more moderate. Towards 2.0 a.m., thanks to the vigilance of the officer of the watch, Lieutenant C. Torson, breakers were seen with night glasses right ahead of the vessel. We went about at once and at daybreak again turned towards the land. On this course we caught two sharks, from which we prepared a fish soup for the crew, adding cayenne pepper to improve the taste. I was very glad that the men had no prejudices and always ate whatever was prepared for them with complete confidence that they would be given nothing harmful.

When day had broken sufficiently we saw a small island ahead of us; it was higher than any of the coral islands surveyed, a good many of which now lay astern of us.[1]

---

[1] This was the island of Niau and the description is very accurate. It is higher than the nearby islands, being 26 feet above sea level at the highest point. When Bellingshausen visited it the lagoon was a large fresh-water pond, but now, owing to the damage of the hurricane of 1878, it is 25 feet deep and brackish. The Russians landed close to the present village.

At 8.30 a.m. we had approached to within less than half a mile of its eastern edge and then steered westwards along the northern shore. At 9.30 we were abreast of the steep north-western point, consisting of layers of sandstone. The sea was perfectly calm beyond the point and there was very little surf along the shore, so that boats could easily land on the coral reef which formed the beach. I took advantage of this to approach the shore to within half a mile and lowered a boat, in which Messrs Torson and Mikhailov, accompanied by Messrs Simanov, Lyeskov and Bergh, started for the shore. On such occasions I always remembered with regret that the naturalists Kuntze and Mertens, who had promised to accompany us, had altered their minds when it was too late to find anyone to take their places. They had refused on the ground that too little time had been given them to complete preparations for the voyage. Perhaps they were right; but I, as a naval officer, cannot help thinking, that all that a scientist need bring with him is his scientific knowledge; books were to be found at Copenhagen of every kind in quantities, and even if some had been unobtainable all the bookshops in London would have been at their service and they need not have lacked for anything.

Messrs Torson, Mikhailov, and the others, did not remain long ashore, and soon returned on board. They had cut down branches of various kinds of trees, which were all of soft wood, had broken off pieces of coral and collected mussel and shells. They had shot a small kind of parrot, about the size of a sparrow, which had a plumage of a beautiful blue colour, the feet and beak red exactly like morocco leather. They also shot a small turtle-dove[1] of a grey-green colour, and had found a few sponges with small corals on them.

Mr Torson informed us on his return that he had noted traces of human habitation and also places where fires had been lit but had not seen any inhabitants. They had observed various small land birds, small lizards and small turtles which slipped into the water and hid among the corals. An old boat was drawn up on the shore of the lagoon inside; very probably this island, like many others, is only visited by inhabitants of larger islands in search of food and other things.

All on board were glad, on sighting this island, which was higher than any of the other coral islands, thinking that we had now passed

---

Both doves and pigeons are numerous in the South Pacific Islands, especially the latter. The fruit-eating pigeon is doubtless responsible for the distribution of the fruits from which many of the island plants have originated.

out of the Archipelago in which navigation is rather difficult as the earlier navigators too had stated: Roggewein, Schouten, Le Maire, Commander Byron, Wallis, Bougainville and Cook. Although this island was more overgrown than the others, it was possible to see the lagoon through the trees from the look-out. We observed clay boulders[1] on the shore.

At noon, according to observations, the *Vostok* was in Lat. 16° 10′ 04″ S., Long. 146° 19′ 46″ W., about 1 mile due north from the western headland. The centre of the island is in Lat. 16° 11′ 18″ S., Long. 146° 15′ 50″ W., the diameter of the island is $5\frac{1}{2}$ miles; I called this island, discovered by us, after "Vice-Admiral Greig", under whose command I served in the Black Sea.

Soon after midday, when the examination of Greig Island was completed, I directed our course north by west towards the eastern point of the island which we had sighted to the westward on the previous evening from the look-out. There was a fresh easterly wind blowing but no sea, and we were going at a good speed. Land was sighted right ahead from the look-out at a distance of 18 miles.[2]

At 4.17 p.m. we reached the wooded eastern headland of this coral island. The shore ran in a north-westerly direction and curving towards the west disappeared from sight. The southern shore, along which we proceeded on a course south-west by west, consisted of coral reefs. Several coral masses showed as much as 16 feet above water and resembled old leafless oaks of a dark colour. At a distance of half a mile or more we passed along parallel with this formidable reef, on which a tremendous surf was breaking with a loud roar. After clearing the eastern headland and passing along the reef for 8 miles, we again sighted parts of the wooded shore. I concluded from the whitish colour of the water in the lagoon that it was shallow and coral reefs were visible above water inside it; on the north-eastern side of the lagoon the water of the lagoon was blue and consequently indicated no small depth. Soon after, as it began to grow dark, I turned the ship into the wind to the south to make short boards under very little sail, during the night; Mr Lazarev kept astern of us. We shortened sail on the *Vostok* so as not to lose sight of the *Mirnyi* and not to be

---

[1] "Clay boulders" is obscure; they were probably "niggerheads", large masses of coral thrown up on to the reef.

[2] The island of Kaukura, which was so devastated in the hurricane of 1878 that it was hardly visible until it was replanted with trees, especially on the northern side.

separated if bad weather came on. The temperature was 77° F. at midnight on the quarter-deck; below decks, where the crew slept, it was 80° F.

19*th*. During the night a fresh trade wind was blowing from the east. At 5.30 a.m. I altered course north-north-west, but when, from the look-out and the top, they sighted the surf on the coral shore, we inclined our course more to the westward with the object of reaching the western extremity about noon to fix its position.

At 11.0 a.m., on approaching the island, we sighted a wooded headland. The southern side consists for the most part of a coral reef; the northern shore we had not seen on account of distance and approaching darkness. Captain Cook proceeded along that shore from the eastern point and says that the island is exactly like the other low-lying islands, except that the shore is more broken up and consists, as it were, of several small islands. Whilst passing along the island at a distance of half a mile, we observed natives armed with spears, also their huts, canoes and the buildings in which they dry their fish. Approaching the western extremity, we sighted land to the north-north-east. We also saw a few huts on the western shore near the wood and a number of islanders were standing by them; some dogs were running about. Two islanders were sitting in a canoe and were rowing out to the ship. We hove to in order to give them an opportunity of overtaking us. At our invitation they came at once on board; at first they were very timid, but when I had hung medals round their necks, given each of them a strip of printed linen, a knife and some other things, they very quickly took courage and were soon on as free and easy terms with us as if we had been old acquaintances. One of them, who resembled Eri of Nihera Island, drew a little packet out of his loin-cloth containing a few small pearls, handed them to me and, pointing towards the shore, cried, "Nyui! Nyui!"—"More! More!" I gave him a mirror in return. Both islanders were very dark of face and body, probably on account of constant exposure to the sun whilst fishing. In features they did not differ from Europeans; they had curly hair. Mr Mikhailov sketched very good likenesses of them. They themselves noted the resemblance and were as pleased with them as children.

From the noon observations we fixed the following positions:

The eastern extremity of the island is in Lat. 15° 50' 20" S., Long. 146° 25' 55" W. The western extremity is in Lat. 15° 41' 20" S.,

Long. 146° 48′ 30″ W. Captain Cook fixed the eastern end in Lat. 15° 47′, Long. 146° 30′.

The length of the island was determined as follows:

According to the *Vostok* it extended in a W.N.W. and E.S.E. direction $23\frac{1}{2}$ miles. According to the *Mirnyi* it extended in a W.N.W. and E.S.E. direction $26\frac{1}{4}$ miles. According to Captain Cook it extended in a W.N.W. and E.S.E. direction 21 miles.

Such similarity in the observations fixing the position and extent of the island leaves no doubt that this is the Palliser Island II.

This entire chain of coral islands, beginning with Graf Arakcheev Island to Kruzenstern Island, has been described and made known by Russian navigators. Although the four Palliser Islands discovered by Captain Cook are included in this group, since they were described and their actual extent and configuration determined later by Lieutenant Kotzebue and ourselves, I consider it fitting to call this whole chain "The Russian Islands".[1]

If we survey the surface of the inhabited globe, it will be seen everywhere that it appears like waves broken up, as it were, by high mountainous ridges, steep ravines, cavities and plains. The sea bottom is of the same formation, as is shown by the depth of the ocean, in places quite unfathomable; islands which form the summits of high mountains rising from the bed of the sea; often belts of such islands indicate the direction of chains of submerged mountains hidden from our sight by the impenetrable depths. Lastly the shoals and rocky reefs, either hidden entirely under water or running level with the

---

[1] This general name, which seemed reasonable enough at the time, has never been used because the islands only form part of the very extended group known as the Tuamotu (Paumotu) or Low Archipelago. Kotzebue gives a much more graphic description of these islands. Of the island he named Predpriatie, situated close to Graf Arakcheev Island, he writes: "The dazzling whiteness of the coral shore fringed a bright green ground upon which rose a forest of palms; and we distinguished canoes moving upon a large lake in the centre of the island.... A tall, strong, dark-coloured race of naked savages were assembling on the shore, gazing on the ship in great agitation. Some were arriving with long spears and clubs, others kindling piles of wood, probably that the smoke might be a signal to neighbouring islands of their requiring assistance against the unknown sea-monster. From pretty huts of plaited reeds, under the shade of bread-fruit trees, the women, some of them with children in their arms, were flying to conceal themselves in the forest. Such was the commotion our appearance occasioned in this little community...no single canoe, though many lay on the coast, ventured to approach us. Judging from the eye and the good arrangement of their sails, their canoes seemed intended for visits to other and even distant lands. We sailed quite round our discovery without finding any haven by which we could effect a landing...so we were compelled to renounce our desire of becoming more intimately acquainted with the Predpriatians...."

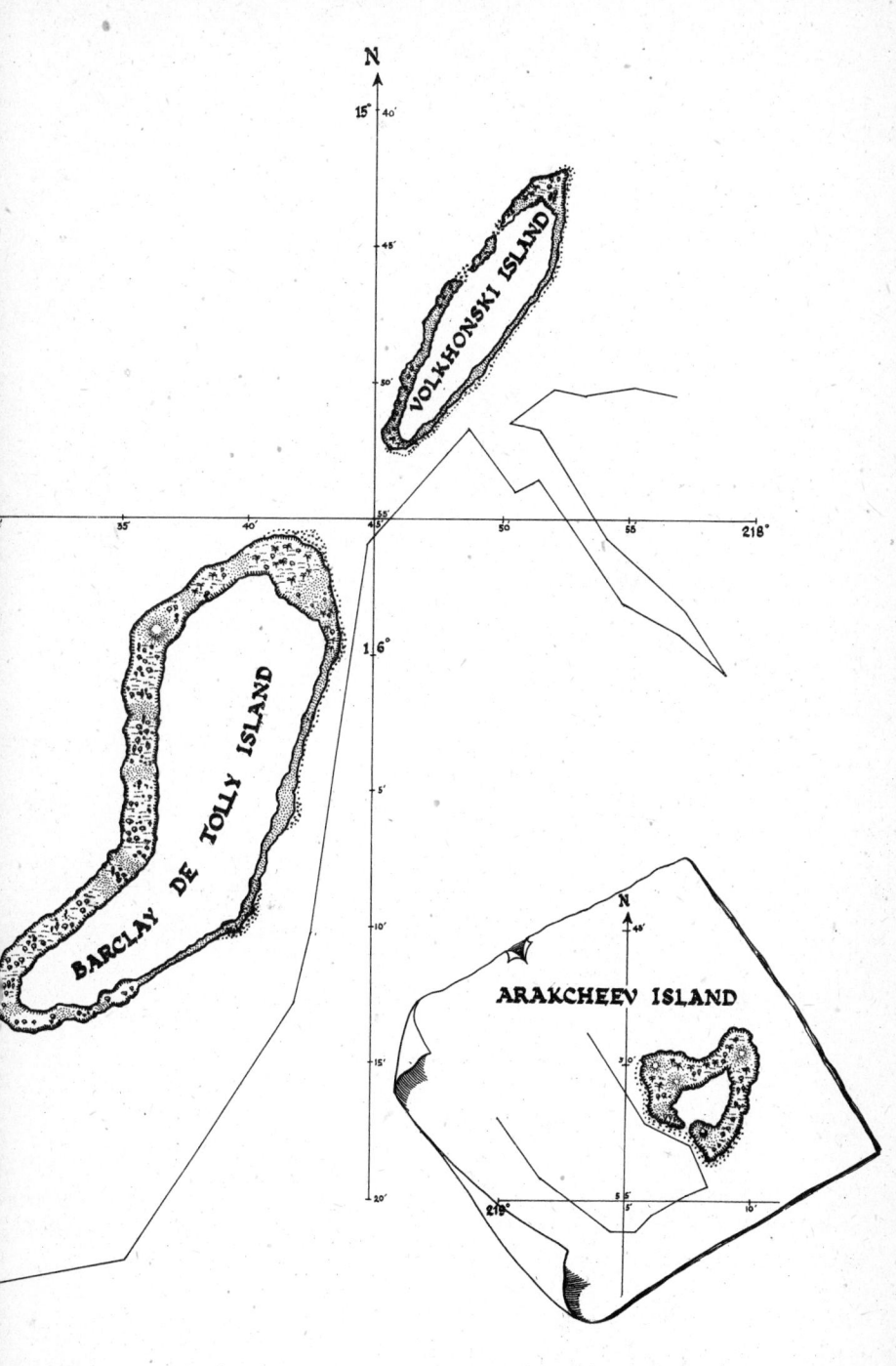

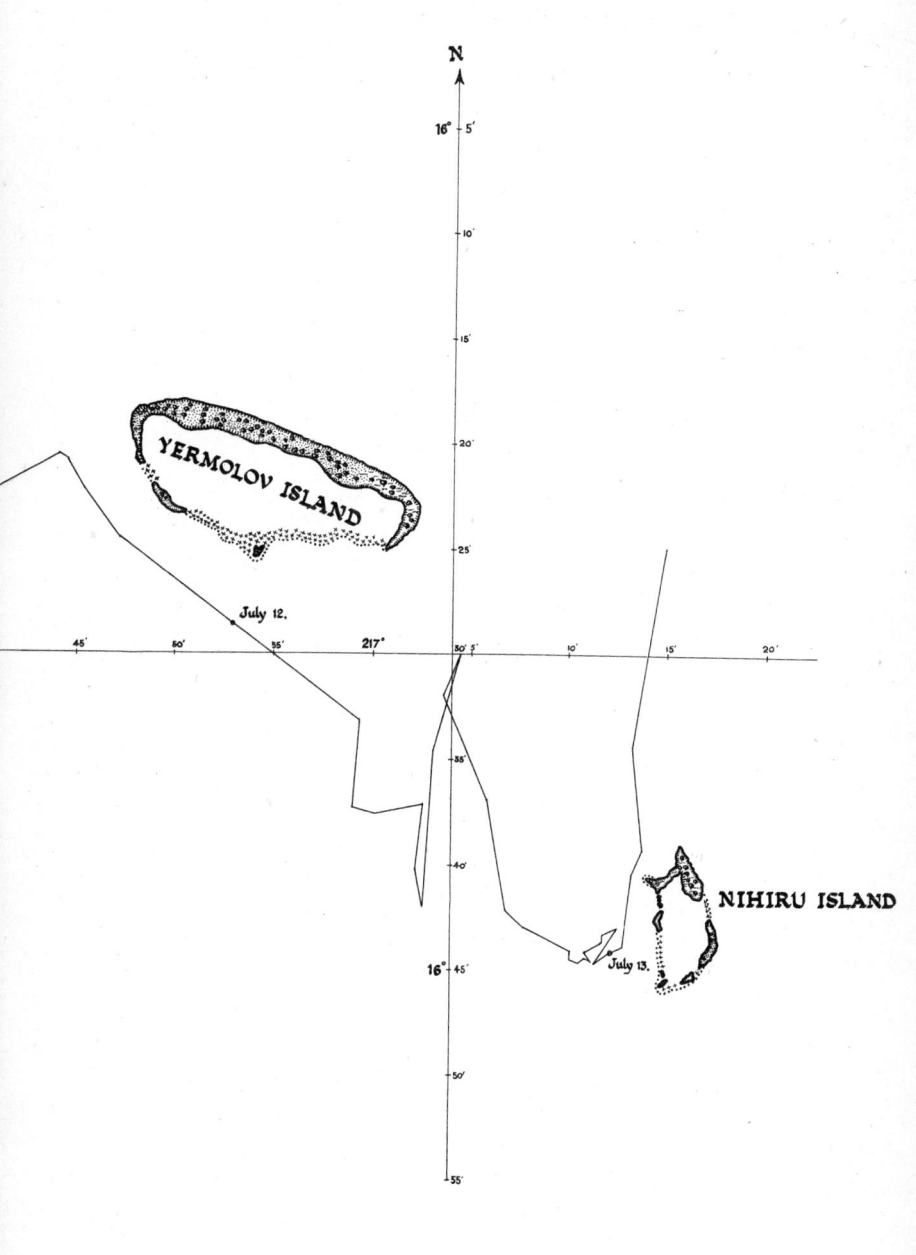

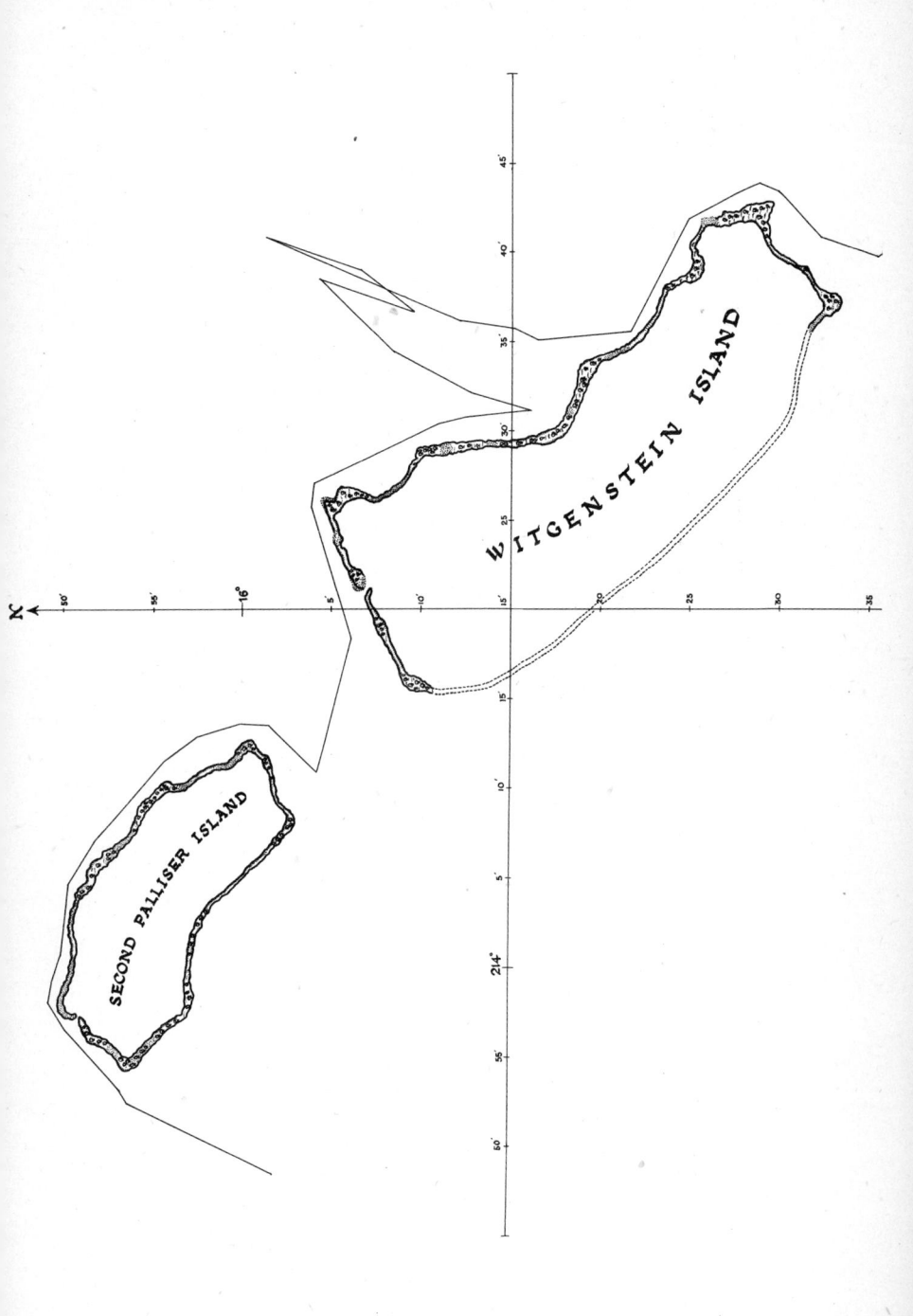

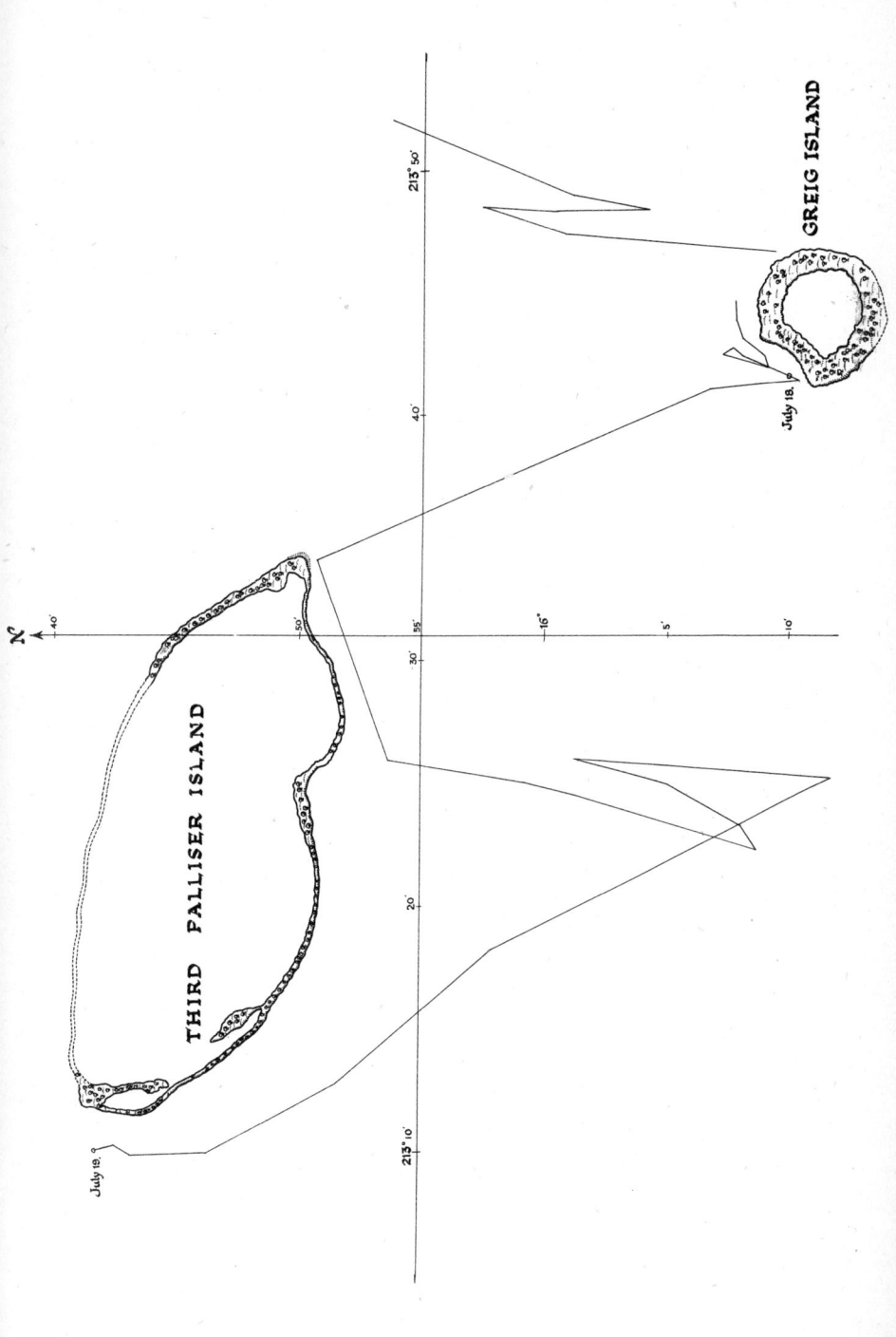

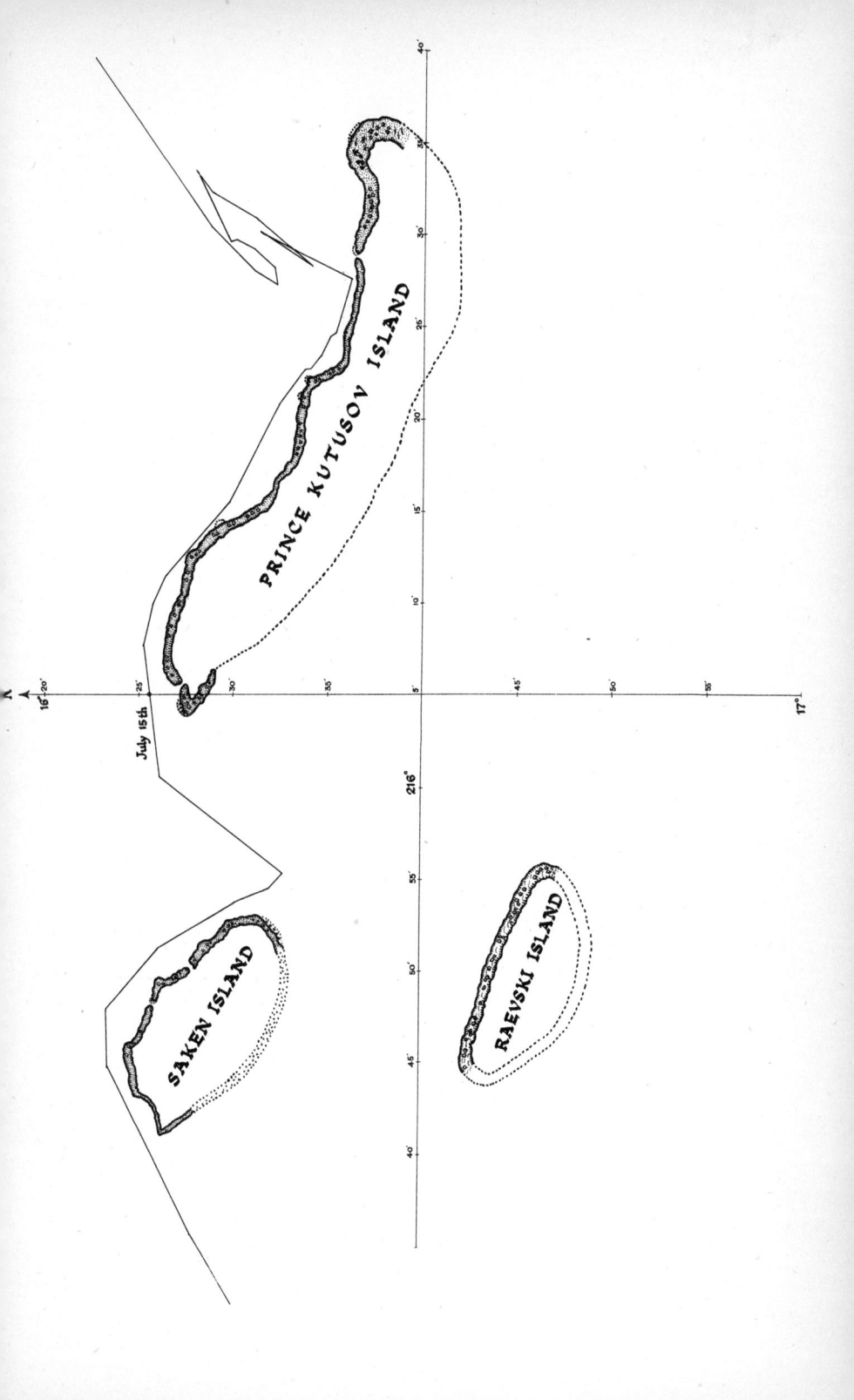

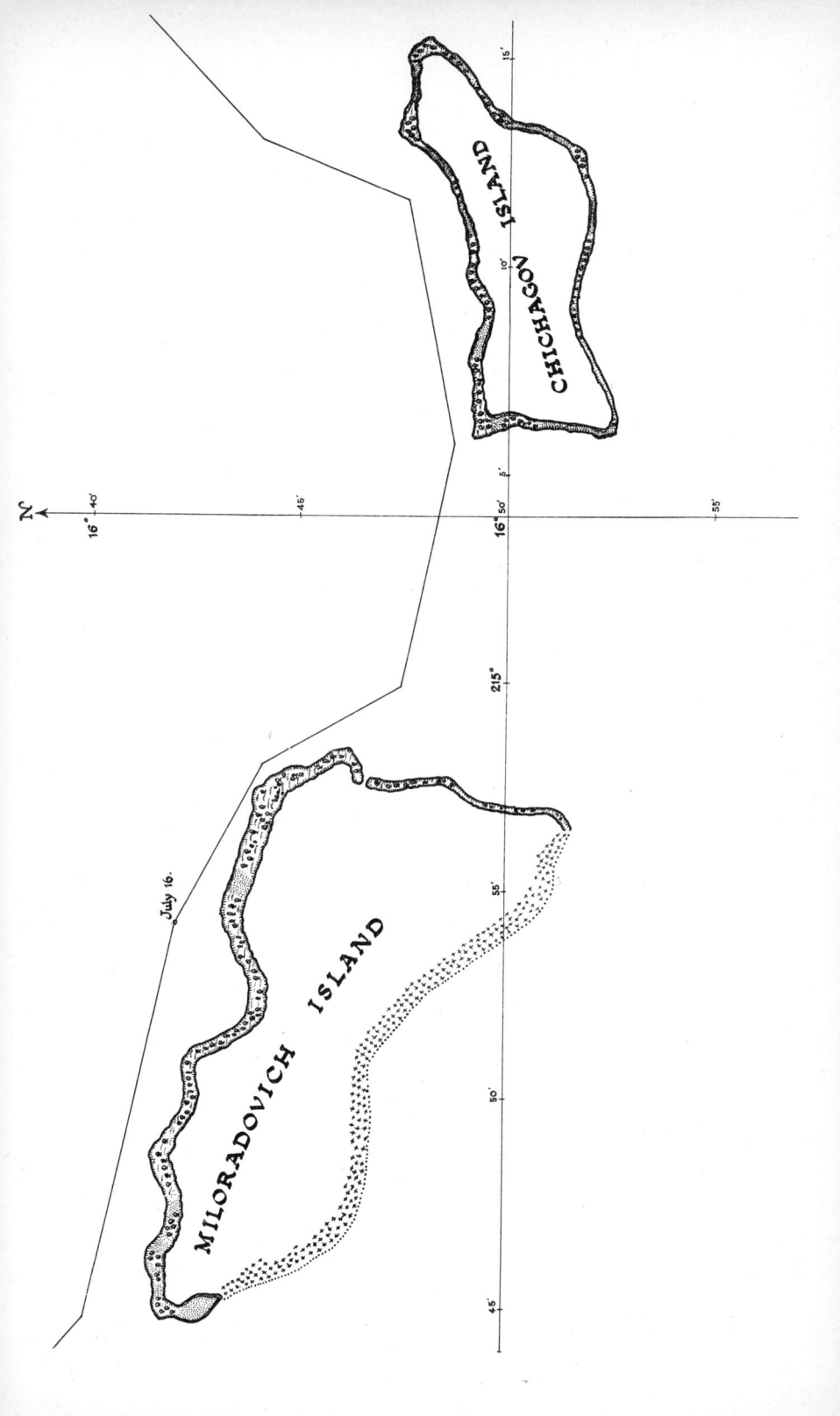

surface, correspond to submerged mountain ridges, as the summits to the islands rising above water. The coral islands and coral reefs, as well as the mountain ridges running parallel to the Cordilleras on the Isthmus of Panama and the main ridges rising out of the sea the summits of which form the Society Islands, the Sandwich Islands, and even the small islands of Pitcairn and Oparo and others, all run in the same direction. The coral islands and reefs have been slowly built up by tiny organisms throughout many centuries. The position of these islands clearly indicates the direction and contours of the submerged ridges which form their foundation. Among the coral islands discovered by me, Greig Island represents a part of the summit of a ridge, rising a little above the surface of the sea, and consisting partly of schist and partly of coral.

The orientation of these coral islands, shown on the chart in the accompanying "Atlas", clearly proves my view.[1] I am convinced that when in future all the coral islands have been correctly charted, it will be possible to count the number of submerged ridges from which they have grown up.[2]

Mr Forster, who accompanied Captain Cook, says: "It would be by no means useless to enquire why, to windward of the Society Islands, low-lying islands should form an extensive and numerous Archipelago, whereas to leeward there are only a few islands." I believe the reason is that, to the east of the Society Islands, there is a corresponding lowering of the upper parts of the submerged mountains, which makes it possible for the sea creatures which construct the coral formations to exist.

The highest summits of the mountains in this region form Otahiti and other islands of the Society Group. To the westward of them a very great depth is suddenly to be found, with the result that the tiny organisms either cannot exist, or the coral formations have not yet reached the surface of the sea.

The coral islands formed by these tiny creatures constitute the greatest constructions on the face of the globe and stagger the human imagination. Their completion is accelerated by the heaping up of different kinds of soil and slimy and other organisms which fill the

---

[1] The drawings by the artist and the charts were published separately from the Russian text in a large "Atlas".

[2] Considering the date at which this was written, this was a rather remarkable generalization on the part of a naval officer, as was also the description below of the process of formation of a coral atoll.

interstices, lodge in the outer edge of the coral and form the beginning of the wall. When these edges get near the surface, the surf breaking over them changes them partly into coral sand; and this process again helps to fill up the spaces between the corals. Now the ledges have risen sufficiently above water and form islands with shores of various heights. Almost all islands possess an entrance into the central lagoon; but we noticed that, as a rule, it lay on the leeward side of the trade winds. The seaweed, rubbish thrown up by the sea, bird droppings, dead birds, all these combined to form the foundation of soil suitable for vegetation; their seeds carried by the sea, washed down by the rains from the higher islands, are the beginning of that vegetation which now protects the inhabitants from the hot rays of the sun on these low-lying islands.

The plant most useful to the islanders is the cocoa-nut palm, which provides them with its refreshing "milk"* to quench their thirst, and the shade of its broad long leaves shelters them from the heat of the sun. Besides, the natives use as food the solid white flesh almost a quarter of an inch thick, lying against the inside of the shell, which is used as a bowl. They cover their sheds and huts with its leaves, the bark is twisted into ropes used for building their boats or as lassoes employed in war. The wood of the cocoa-nut palm itself is apparently of no use except for burning, owing to its softness. It is noteworthy that any island on which we observed many cocoa-nut palms was invariably inhabited.

Another species of tree, growing in great quantities on these coral islands, is called "Faro" by the natives. It is spongy in texture and is not as high as a cocoa-nut palm; its large oblong leaves with sharp thorns grow in all directions from the ends of the branches. The natives cover the roofs of their huts with them. The fruit grows in the midst of the leaves, is about the size of a man's head, turns yellow when ripe and resembles in appearance a pine-apple. The islanders cut the fruit into pieces and suck out the inner part.[1]

---

* In places where the cocoa-nut palms receive a great deal of moisture, pure water, a little sweet in taste and covered with foam when poured into a glass, is found in the shell. When the nuts are taken a long distance by sea, this water begins to resemble whey after a time, and it is this which we in Russia call the milk of the cocoa-nut.

---

[1] One of the *pandanus* or screw-pine palms. The fruit is really an assembly of nuts. The stem is spongy inside but the external part is so hard that it is used for spear points.

We also saw another fruit-bearing tree not known to us; the islands are covered by a great quantity of undergrowth, the fallen leaves from which form a loam and raise the level of the island. Double canoes, either drawn up on the shore or lying in the lagoon, showed that it is possible to obtain trees of the necessary thickness for the construction of such boats in these islands.

To European eyes this archipelago of coral islands, with its abundant vegetation, presents a pleasant and at the same time strange picture. At the water's edge there is the reddish-coloured coral; a little higher up it is whiter and above that again there is the coral sand. Pieces of coral and empty shells are transformed into absolutely white lime by the sun's action, and above this there is the green grass, the undergrowth and finally the uncommon, picturesque trees found in the tropics.

In this part of the Pacific Ocean the longitude of Venus Point was fixed with great exactitude by the astronomers Green and Baillie, who accompanied Captain Cook on his first and second voyages round the world. I therefore chose Otahiti as a port of call, in preference to the other Society Islands, to check our chronometers by the longitude of Venus Point and to determine more accurately the longitudes calculated from the last observations, as well as those of the coral islands discovered by us, and their positions with regard to the Society Islands. I decided to make a stay at Otahiti also to fill up with fresh water and to allow the crew to rest themselves and to recuperate with the fresh air of the island, and the fresh food and fruit which abound in Otahiti.

I arranged our route in such a way as to make it of all possible service to geography. On the 19th we proceeded westward from midday until evening, with a light trade wind from east by south, an overcast sky and a slight swell from the south-west. The last of the Palliser Islands disappeared from view astern to the eastward at a distance of 18 miles. At that time the variation was $6° 48'$ E. At 6.0 p.m. we were 26 miles to the westward of Palliser Island, and before nightfall we still had a visual range of 15 miles ahead, but saw no island. Towards night we shortened sail and altered our course to the southward, going at a very low speed.

During the night the few clouds did not obscure the light of the moon and stars. The temperature was $76°$ F. in the open air; below decks, where the crew slept, it was $79°$ F. At 6.30 a.m., when it was daylight, there were no signs of land on the horizon from the look-out.

We were then on the parallel of Makatea Island which is, according to the Arrowsmith chart, in Lat. 15° 53′ S., Long. 147° 28′ W.[1] I steered to the west under all sail in order to verify its position on the way. As I did not sight it at daybreak, I hoped to find it more to the westward. On the following morning, Mr Lazarev signalled to us that he was of opinion that the land which we had seen the previous evening and three days before had been that sighted by Lieutenant Kotzebue.* This conclusion seemed to me well founded and I agreed with him. Captain Cook had passed this island† on the northern side. We were travelling very well, but it was not until 9.30 a.m. that we saw Makatea Island, which lay 20 miles to the westward of us. At noon the *Vostok* was in Lat. 15° 53′ 28″ S., Long. 148° 02′ 24″ W. The centre of the island lay N. 82° W. from us, distant 10·5 miles. The island resembled a wedge in form, being cut away sharply at the northern side and sloping to the south to the water's edge; in the middle were slight eminences. At 1.0 p.m., having approached the eastern end of the island, we passed along the northern shore, at times only a mile distant from it. All this side consists of a steep cliff, on the top of which there were clumps of cocoa-nut palms and other trees. When we were abreast of the north-eastern point of the island we observed four people on the shore. Three of them waved to us with green branches and the fourth had a piece of matting attached to a stick. The weather was favourable; there was no heavy sea or surf near the island and I therefore made for the headland, hoisted the ship's ensign, and then hove to whilst a boat was lowered and Lieutenant Ignatiev, Mikhailov, Father Rezanov and Midshipman Adams went ashore. Mr Lazarev also sent a boat. The weather was hotter than usual; the thermometer stood at 80° F. until nightfall, when it dropped two degrees. It was at this time that, to everybody's great delight, Commander Zavodovski was able to get up for the first time, after an eight weeks' illness; indeed one might say that he had been snatched from the jaws of death, and even his recovery had been very doubtful as the available medicines had lost much of their efficacy

---

* Lieutenant Kotzebue, whilst lying off the southern side of Ryurik Island, sighted land from the look-out towards the south-south-west. See Kotzebue, *Voyage Round the World*, Part I.
† The third of the Palliser Islands discovered and so named by Captain Cook.

---

[1] The correct position of Makatea is Lat. 15° 50′ S., Long. 148° 10′ W.

owing to the many changes of climate. At 3.0 p.m. the party returned on board with an unexpected acquisition in the shape of two boys. One of them was about seventeen and the other about nine years of age; two others had been taken on board the *Mirnyi*. Mr Ignatiev told me that they had not seen anyone except these four boys and that there was plenty of fresh water on shore. The breadfruit and cocoa-nuts gathered by the boys show that there is enough food on the island to support a few people. The sole possessions of these lads consisted of a fish-hook made of a kind of slate and a few cups made from the cocoa-nut shells, which also served them as vessels. There is not the slightest doubt that these islanders, like the Scotsman, Alexander Selkirk, whose adventures provided the occasion for the writing of the celebrated novel *Robinson Crusoe*, had to invent ways of obtaining the necessaries of life, but fortunately succeeded and suffered no privations. Had Providence miraculously saved a few girls together with these four boys, the history of the settlement on Makatea Island would have begun from that time.[1] It is indeed probable that the colonization of other islands in the Pacific Ocean has had a similar beginning.

The western shore of Makatea Island is also well wooded and is more convenient for landing as the shore is not so steep. We fixed the latitude of the island at 15° 52′ 35″ S., Long. 148° 13′ 04″ W.; it extends N.W. by W. ½ W. and S.E. by E. ½ E. and is 4·5 miles in length, 2 miles in width and 12 miles in circumference. The latitude of the place, as we fixed it, agrees with that of Makatea Island on the Arrowsmith chart but its longitude is 51′ 40″ more to the westward.

Mr Turnbull, in the course of his voyage from 1800 to 1804, visited Makatea Island and writes of it as follows: "We found it was governed by a deputy sent by Pomarre from Otahiti, being the most distant spot under his authority.

"In this island lay a very large double canoe which had left Otahiti six months before to collect tribute. The natives brought off to us abundance of breadfruit and cocoa-nuts as articles for traffic, taking in return looking-glasses, nails, etc., etc. No hogs were produced for sale as the island furnishes very few, the principal food of the in-

---

[1] Makatea Island is a good example of an atoll which has been raised above the level of the sea. It now supports a population of over 1000 people most of whom are connected with the phosphate industry there.

habitants being derived from the sea. In manners and appearance the inhabitants of this little island bore a strong resemblance to those of Otahiti, but were less civilized and our arrival excited amongst them a much greater degree of curiosity than had been shown by the natives of the other islands we had just visited. The gorget, made of the pearl oyster-shell, was very generally worn, but their cloth, of which they produced some specimens, seemed to be much inferior to that of Otahiti. Many of the natives were dressed in a teboota, made of long knotted grass carelessly thrown over their shoulders and descending to the knees. Their canoes, on the other hand, were superior in point of execution to those of Otahiti, being ornamented with a profusion of carved work."

We did not see any inhabitants on this island and I therefore concluded that the islanders whom Turnbull saw only came from time to time from other coral islands lying to the south-east in connection with fishing or some other purpose.

When the boats were hoisted we made more sail and proceeded on a course S. by W. ½ W. with a fresh trade wind from south-east by east. I kept on boldly during the night as I knew that there were no islands to be found on the route to Otahiti. At midnight the temperature was 78° F. in the open air, and below decks, where the crew slept, it was 82° F.

21*st*. In the morning we learned from the eldest of these boys, with considerable difficulty, that they came from Anaa Island, from which they had been carried away to Makatea Island by a gale and that some inhabitants from another island had also been wrecked on the island.[1] These islanders were continually at war with each other and the party to which these boys had belonged had all been massacred and eaten by their enemies; they had hidden in the undergrowth of the interior until finally, when their enemies had gone away, they remained alone on the island.

I gave orders to have them washed and their hair cut, to dress them in shirts and to make short jackets and breeches for them out of striped tick. This attire interested them and pleased them very much, but they soon discarded the shoes which were given to them and went barefoot.

I questioned the eldest boy repeatedly, in which direction lay Anaa

---

[1] Anaa Island is about 200 miles to the south-east of Makatea Island and was formerly the most populous island in the Archipelago.

Island, but he always replied by asking "Where is Taich?"* and when I showed him where Otahiti lay, he pointed with his hand towards the south-east against the trade wind. When I told him that he was not indicating the position of his island and that it lay to the northward† of us, the boy always dissented and persisted in his opinion, always pointing in the direction of Chains Island.‡

At 9.0 a.m. we sighted from the look-out the island of Otahiti showing blue as two peaks on the south-western horizon. The high ridge of Great Otahiti lay S. 12° 30′ W. from us, the lower one, situated on Little Otahiti,[1] lay S. 2° 20′ W. from us. We continued on a south by west course with a light trade wind from south-east by east. The weather was beautiful. We were all eager to reach the island as quickly as possible. The wind also cheered us, as it blew fresher after noon, so that towards 7.0 p.m. we were only 4 miles from the north-eastern point of the island. Although it grew dark by then, the fires lit ashore indicated the position of the houses of the natives whom Captain Cook and his fellow-travellers, Banks and Forster, had praised so highly.

The night was dark; dense black clouds hung over the summits of the mountains. On the shores of the barely visible island, fires were twinkling. Frequently the little waves stood out on the dark waters in phosphorescent belts extending at moments into the distance in different directions, and the faintly glowing streaks of passing fish died slowly away. We passed the whole night in the presence of this wonderful spectacle, making short boards under shortened sail, to keep near the shore.

22nd. In the morning we proceeded along the shore to Venus Point.[2] We were all on deck admiring the beautiful view of the shore.

---

* This is the name they give to Otahiti.
† According to the Arrowsmith chart, Anaa Island lay northward of us.
‡ Discovered and so named by Captain Cook on his first voyage round the world.

---

[1] Little Otahiti is really a peninsula of the main island, joined to it by a low neck of land, and is now known as the Taiarapu Peninsula.
[2] Kotzebue writes of Venus Point, as he approached it in March 1824: "It was not till the 14th that we reached the Cape, called by Cook, Cape Venus, because he twice observed the transit of this planet over the sun, and from its beauty it deserves to be named after the charming goddess herself. It is a low narrow tongue of land, thickly shadowed by cocoanut trees and forming, by its curve, the harbour of Matavai, not a very secure one but generally preferred by sailors on account of the celebrity bestowed upon it by Cook."

The high mountains covered with forests, the deep valleys, the steep ravines, the broad, level, green plain at the foot of the mountain covered with cocoa-nut palms, banana and breadfruit trees that sheltered the neat little dwellings of the inhabitants, the yellow beach, the rivulets flowing down the mountain sides, the islanders bustling about, moving about in their little rowing or sailing canoes with outriggers; all this inspired us with the most delightful feelings. Such varied indications of well-being, enhanced by a perfect climate, arouse a peculiar feeling of confidence in the inhabitants of this beautiful country.[1]

A European boat, which had arrived from the island, interrupted our contemplation. The men at the oars were islanders; the man who occupied the seat of honour we thought—though we afterwards discovered our mistake—must be one of the missionaries who were resident in Otahiti since the time when Captain Wilson visited the island in 1797. I hove to so as to make it possible for the boat to make fast alongside. A man of great height, thick-set, with a swarthy complexion, hair cut short in front and hanging in one curl at the back like a woman's, came on board. He wore a cotton shirt; the lower part of the body was wrapped in a cotton garment which fell to his heels. I invited him into the cabin; he went below immediately and sat down. When I asked him, in English, what he wished to say to me, he drew a letter out of his belt, handed it to me and said a few words in broken English which I could not understand. The letter ran as follows:

Tuesday Morning.

Sir,
    I have sent off a Pilot to conduct you in to Matavai Bay, and shall be glad to see you safe at anchor.

I am Sir,
Yours, etc.
POMARE.

Finding it very difficult to understand the bad English of this Otahitian, I asked Mr Lazarev to come, but he too was not able to understand one word; he nevertheless gathered that he was a pilot and that there was another pilot in the boat. I asked Mr Lazarev to

---

[1] The view of Tahiti from the sea is justly famous and other early navigators expressed themselves in similar terms.

take him on board with him and told him we should anchor in Matavai Harbour beyond the Cape.[1]

Having braced up, I proceeded on a course towards Venus Point and we soon passed a coral reef outside, which protects the cape from the heavy seas and enables the natives to navigate inside it without risk. Bringing the vessels to leeward I proceeded into the road by the narrow channel, between the above-mentioned coral reef and the shoal to westward of it. The depth over this shoal is only 2 fathoms. At 10.0 a.m. on arriving in Matavai Bay, I anchored in 8 fathoms, bottom mud and sand, on the exact spot where Captain Wallis had a fight with the natives on June 14th, 1767, and where, on April 13th, 1769, Captain Cook and the renowned patron of science, Sir Joseph Banks, were received with such friendliness by the very same people. Soon afterwards the *Mirnyi* rounded the shoal and lay at anchor near the *Vostok*.

[1] Kotzebue thus describes his arrival in Matavai Bay: "Our frigate, as it entered the Bay, attracted to the beach a crowd of curious gazers who greeted our arrival with a shout of joy. Numerous boats laden with all kinds of fruits, provisions and other articles of merchandise, immediately put off from the shore and we were soon surrounded by gay and noisy Tahitians. As soon as the sails were taken in, I gave them permission to come on board, of which they eagerly availed themselves. With their wares on their backs, they climbed merrily up the sides of the ship and the deck was soon transformed into a busy market place, where all was frolic and fun; the goods were offered with a jest and the bargains concluded with laughter.... Our clothing appeared to be prized by the Tahitians above everything we could offer them and the possession of any article of this kind set them leaping, as if out of their wits, for joy. On this day we saw no females; and when we were afterwards occasionally visited by the women, they always behaved with the greatest propriety. When the sun declined our new acquaintances left us to return to their homes, satisfied with their bargains and delighted with the presents they had received, and without having stolen anything, although above a hundred of them had been on board at once."

End of PART I